Externalism and Self-Knowledge

CSLI LECTURE NOTES
NUMBER 85

Externalism and Self-Knowledge

edited by
Peter Ludlow &
Norah Martin

CSLI Publications
Center for the Study of
Language and Information
Stanford, California

Copyright © 1998
CSLI Publications
Center for the Study of Language and Information
Leland Stanford Junior University
02 01 00   5 4 3 2

Library of Congress Cataloging-in-Publication Data

Externalism and self-knowledge / edited by Peter Ludlow & Norah Martin.
p.   cm.–(CSLI lecture notes ; no. 85)
Includes bibliographical references and index.
ISBN 1-57586-107-0 (hardcover : alk. paper).—ISBN 1-57586-106-2
(pbk. : alk. paper)
1. Externalism (Philosophy of mind) 2. Self-knowledge, Theory of.
I. Ludlow, Peter, 1957–   . II.   Martin, Norah, 1962–   . III. Series.
BD418.3.E87   1998
128' . 2–dc21   98-14147
CIP

"Individualism and the Mental" © The University of Minnesota Press
"The Brown–McKinsey Charge of Inconsistency" © Mind Association
"Social Externalism and Memory: A Problem?" © Peter Ludlow

The painting on the cover of the paperback edition of this book, Edward Hopper's
People in the Sun, appears courtesy of the National Museum of American Art,
Smithsonian Institution. Gift of S.C. Johnson & Son, Inc.

Contents

v

Acknowledgments

Paul Boghossian, "Content and Self-Knowledge" was originally published in *Philosophical Topics* 17 (1989), pp. 5–26 and is reprinted with the permission of *Philosophical Topics* and Paul Boghossian.

Jessica Brown, "The Incompatibility of Anti-Individualism and Privileged Access" originally appeared in *Analysis* 55 (1995), pp. 149–56 and is reprinted with the permission of Jessica Brown.

Anthony Brueckner, "Externalism and Memory" originally appeared in *Pacific Philosophical Quarterly* vol. 78, no. 1 (1997) pp. 1–12 and is reprinted with the permission of Anthony Brueckner.

Anthony Brueckner, "What an Anti-Individualist Knows A Priori" originally appeared in *Analysis* 52 (1992), pp. 111–18 and is reprinted with the permission of Anthony Brueckner.

Tyler Burge, "Individualism and the Mental" was originally published in *Midwest Studies in Philosophy* 4 (1979), pp. 73–122 and is reprinted with permission of Tyler Burge and University of Minnesota Press.

Tyler Burge, "Individualism and Self-Knowledge" was originally published in *The Journal of Philosophy* LXXXV, 11 (November 1988), pp. 649–63 and is reprinted with the permission of *The Journal of Philosophy* and Tyler Burge.

Tyler Burge, "Our Entitlement to Self-Knowledge" originally appeared in *Proceedings of the Aristotelian Society* XCVI (1996), pp. 91–116 and is reprinted by courtesy of the Editor of the Aristotelian society: © 1996.

Donald Davidson, "Knowing One's Own Mind" was originally published in *Proceedings of the American Philosophical Association* (1987) and is reprinted with the permission of the American Philosophical Association and Donald Davidson.

John Heil, "Privileged Access" was originally published in *Mind* 97 (1988), pp. 238–251 and is reprinted by permission of Oxford University Press.

Peter Ludlow, "On the Relevance of Slow Switching" initially appeared in *Analysis* 57 (1997), pp. 285–86.

Peter Ludlow, "Externalism and Memory: A Problem?" was originally published in *Acta Analytica* 14, 1996 and is reprinted with the permission of *Acta Analytica*.

Peter Ludlow, "Externalism, Self-Knowledge, and the Prevalence of Slow-Switching" was originally published in *Analysis* 55 (1995), pp. 45–9.

Peter Ludlow, "Social Externalism, Self-Knowledge, and Memory" was originally published in *Analysis* 55(1995), pp. 157–59.

Michael McKinsey, "Anti-Individualism and Privileged Access" originally appeared in *Analysis* 51 (1991), pp. 9–16 and is reprinted with the permission of Michael McKinsey.

Brian McLaughlin and Michael Tye, "The Brown-McKinsey Charge of Inconsistency" is reprinted from McDonald, Smith and Wright, eds. *Knowing Our Own Minds: Essays in Self-Knowledge*, Oxford University Press, 1998 by permission of Oxford University Press.

Christopher Peacocke, "Entitlement, Self-Knowledge and Conceptual Redeployment" initially appeared in *Proceedings of the Aristotelian Society* XCVI (1996), pp. 117–58 and is reprinted with the permission of Christopher Peacocke.

Ted A. Warfield, "Privileged Self-Knowledge and Externalism are Compatible" originally appeared in *Analysis* 52 (1992) pp. 232–37 and is reprinted here with the permission of Ted A. Warfield.

Ted A. Warfield, "Externalism, Self-Knowledge and the Irrelevance of Slow-Switching" initially appeared in *Analysis* 57 (1997) and is reprinted with the permission of Ted A. Warfield.

Introduction

One of the most provocative projects in recent analytic philosophy has been the development of the doctrine of externalism, or, as it is often called, anti-individualism. The main thesis of this position is that the content of our mental states depends at least in part on relations between ourselves and the environment. Externalism is, in other words, a denial of the traditional Cartesian view that holds that the contents of our thoughts are what they are independently of the surrounding world.

Although much ink continues to be spilt on the question of whether externalism is true or not, a number of recent investigations have begun to explore the question of what follows *if* it is true. So, for example, philosophers have begun exploring (and defending) the consequences of externalism for psychology, perception, mental causation and skepticism.

Among the most interesting threads of these investigations has been the question of whether externalism has consequences for the doctrine that we have a priori knowledge of our mental states. At least since Descartes, it has been held that we stand in a privileged relation to the contents of our own thoughts – that we can know them by introspection, and that such knowledge is infallible, or at least highly reliable. On this traditional picture, thoughts are private, so however we individuate them, it must be in such a way as to preserve that privacy. On the Cartesian view we could tell one thought from another even if there were no external world at all. Yet, if we are externalists, it appears that we cannot know the contents of our mental states simply by introspection, for those contents are determined by our environment. Thus, it appears that to know the contents of our mental states we shall have to investigate our environment. Thus we must give up a priori self-knowledge. Many of the defenders of

We are indebted to Anthony Brueckner, Tyler Burge, and Ted Warfield for comments on an earlier draft of this introduction.

1

externalism, however, are not at all happy with this conclusion and have taken a number of different approaches to showing that this apparent problem is chimeral and that in fact externalism and authoritative self-knowledge are compatible.

The papers in this volume are meant to be representative of this debate, but certainly not exhaustive. The collection has been organized into six sections, beginning (in section I) with pieces that describe the idea of authoritative self-knowledge and the basic tenets of externalism. The three pieces in Section II attempt to argue that there is no tension between authoritative self-knowledge and externalism. Section III includes three pieces that take the incompatibilist line. Section IV offers rebuttals by compatibilists. The discussion of the compatibility of externalism and self-knowledge has led to a number of interesting subsidiary investigations which apparently need to be settled before the issue of compatibility can be resolved. Two of these are epistemic warrant, which is discussed in section V, and the consequences of externalism for memory, to which the papers in section VI are devoted.

Authoritative Self-Knowledge: The Problem

We begin with passages by Descartes which illustrate the relevant view about the authority of our first person knowledge of our mental states. For Descartes, such knowledge is a priori in character. We need not investigate our environment to obtain it. Indeed, we need merely reflect on our own mental activities.

Descartes' view stands in marked contrast with the doctrine of externalism as developed in Putnam (1975) and Burge's "Individualism and the Mental" (chapter 2 in this volume). Burge develops externalism using a number of thought experiments, including the case of an agent, call her Arabella, who thinks (incorrectly) that one can have arthritis in the thigh. Burge contrasts her with a molecular duplicate, Twin Arabella, who lives in a twin world that differs from ours only in the way that the medical community applies the term 'arthritis' – in the twin world 'arthritis' applies to rheumatoid ailments of the thighs as well as the joints. Although the internal mental episodes of these agents are identical, their thoughts are quite different. According to Burge, Arabella's thought are about arthritis, but Twin Arabella's are not (they are about tharthritis). These cases can be pumped even further. As Burge notes,

> The argument [for external content] has an extremely wide application. It does not depend, for example, on the kind of word 'arthritis' is. We

could have used an artifact term, an ordinary natural kind word, a color adjective, a social role term, a term for historical style, an abstract noun, an action verb, a physical movement verb, or any of various other sorts of words (p. 29).

In other words, the social character of content pervades virtually every expression of our language, and virtually every aspect of our thoughts.

Consider how this view differs from Descartes' views on the nature of the mind. Descartes had distinguished between clear and distinct ideas and obscure and confused ones. For an idea to be distinct, it must be distinct from all other ideas, as in, for example, the way I can distinguish the idea of the mind from the idea of the body. Similarly, arthritis is a rheumatoid ailment afflicting only the joints. In some twin community an ailment called 'arthritis' is a rheumatoid ailment afflicting the thigh as well as the joints (tharthritis). Thus they are two wholly distinct concepts and if we have authoritative self-knowledge we should be able to distinguish the concept of arthritis not only from our many unrelated concepts (like those of dog and cat) but also from concepts that might seem similar, like tharthritis, without having to do any sort of empirical investigation. Yet it appears that for the externalist, investigation would be necessary. Arabella would have to know which community she was in before she could know whether she was having arthritis thoughts or tharthritis thoughts.

Externalism and Self-Knowledge Are Compatible

Davidson nicely frames the apparent conflict between externalism and self-knowledge in "Knowing One's Own Mind" (ch. 3), suggesting that the alleged difficulty stems from two unquestioned assumptions:

(i) If a thought is identified by a relation to something outside the head, it isn't wholly in the head (It ain't in the head).

(ii) If a thought isn't wholly in the head, it can't be 'grasped' by the mind in the way required by first person authority.

He challenges both of these assumptions, arguing that (i) is no more true than the notion that because a sunburn presupposes the existence of the sun, that my sunburn isn't a condition of my skin. As Davidson notes, "Individual states and events don't conceptually presuppose anything in themselves; some of their descriptions may, however." This appears to allow that I may well have authoritative self-knowledge of my mental states, though not necessarily under all possible descriptions of those states.

Against assumption (ii) Davidson challenges the very idea that beliefs, desires, etc. are objects to be "grasped" or "entertained" or are objects that we can "be acquainted with." According to Davidson, the problem does not stem from externalism per se, but rather from the mistaken metaphor of thoughts as objects before the mind.

> ...if to have a thought is to have an object 'before the mind', and the identity of the object determines what the thought is, then it must always be possible to be mistaken about what one is thinking. For unless one knows everything about the object, there will always be senses in which one does not know what the object is...The only object that would satisfy the twin requirements of being 'before the mind' and also such that it determines what the content of a thought must, like Hume's ideas and impressions, 'be what it seems and seem what it is'. There are no such objects, public or private, abstract or concrete. (p. 108)

Davidson thinks we are better off sweeping away this metaphor, and replacing it with the understanding that "what a person's words mean depends in the most basic cases on the kinds of objects and events that have caused the person to hold the words to be applicable; similarly for what the person's thoughts are about." But what of self-attribution? "The agent herself is not in a position to wonder whether she is generally using her own words to apply to the right objects and events, since whatever she regularly does apply them to gives her words the meaning they have and her thoughts the contents they have." We thus get a kind of transcendental argument for the authority of such self-knowledge. In short, as Davidson puts it, "unless there is a presumption that the speaker knows what she means ... there would be nothing for the interpreter to interpret."

In "Individualism and Self-Knowledge" (ch. 4), Burge independently pursues the line of attack suggested in Davidson's challenge to assumption (ii) above. Burge draws a helpful analogy to the theory of direct perception. For example, one can authoritatively say that one sees a table in the room, and this judgment may well be justified[1] by facts about the human perceptual system, but one needn't know these facts (one may be completely ignorant of the theory of perception) to know that one sees

---

[1] Rather than 'justified' it is perhaps more accurate to say that the facts in question are, in Burge's terminology, the "enabling conditions" for perceptual knowledge of this form.

the table. Likewise, one may know one has a belief about water, and yet be ignorant of the conditions which make such knowledge possible. "Knowing one's thoughts no more requires separate investigation of the conditions that make the judgment possible than knowing what one perceives." Burge claims that,

> Basic self-knowledge is self-referential in a way that insures that the object of reference just is the thought being thought. If background conditions are different enough so that there is another object of reference in one's self-referential thinking, they are also different enough so that there is another thought. (pp. 121–122)

To illustrate this last point, Burge encourages us to consider a thought experiment in which a speaker undergoes a series of slow switches between Earth and Twin Earth. When the background conditions change, the thoughts of the speaker change accordingly. So, for example, on Earth the agent entertains thoughts about water, on Twin Earth the agent entertains thoughts about twin water (assuming adequate time spent in the new location). What of the second order thoughts, such as "I think that water is wet"? For Burge, the content of those second order thoughts must likewise change as the agent shifts between worlds; "The fact that the person does not know that a switch has occurred is irrelevant to the truth and justified character of these judgments."

John Heil (ch. 5) offers additional considerations to illustrate how a conflict between externalism and self-knowledge need not arise. According to Heil, the standard externalist position is one in which a mental representation M, has an external content p, by virtue of standing in a certain state of affairs A, which includes the environment. The nature of A will depend on the particular flavor of externalism. It could be a causal relation, a more complex social relation, etc. But now consider the second order mental state M'. M' is intuitively a belief about M, so how plausible is it that M' could also have p as part of its content?

According to Heil, the solution is to see that just as M had the content p by virtue of the state of affairs A, M' will also have p as part of its content by virtue of another state of affairs, call it A', possibly including the state of affairs A. As Heil states the solution:

> The content of both thoughts is generated externally. The content of second-order thoughts – introspections – would be determined, I have suggested, by a complex condition that included, perhaps, the condition responsible for the content of corresponding first-order states. (p. 139)

The Incompatibilist Challenge

Paul Boghossian (ch. 6) grants the externalist assumptions, but, against Davidson, Burge and Heil, argues that these assumptions appear to pose difficulties for authoritative self-knowledge. According to Boghossian, the claim that we do not need to know the conditions underwriting the content of our beliefs amounts to the claim that our beliefs are "based on nothing – at any rate, on nothing empirical." The problem with this, according to Boghossian, is that this implies that our thoughts are cognitively insubstantial, when crucially, interesting cases of self-knowledge will involve some form of cognitive achievement.

Boghossian also draws incompatibilist consequences from the slow switching thought experiment introduced by Burge. It appears that it is possible for an agent to know his thoughts at time t, forget nothing, yet at some time later than t (having been informed that switches were taking place) be unable to say what the contents of his thoughts were at t. Boghossian concludes:

> The only explanation, I venture to suggest, for why S will not know tomorrow what he is said to know today, is not that he has forgotten but that he never knew. Burge's self-verifying judgments do not constitute genuine knowledge. What other reason is there for why our slowly transported thinker will not know tomorrow what he is said to know directly and authoritatively today? (p. 172)

Michael McKinsey (ch. 7) opens a second front against the compatibilists. First, according to McKinsey, the solution articulated by Davidson will not do. If thoughts are "inner episodes which exist independently of our means of describing them" then we can certainly have privileged access to them, but it is not clear what that would amount to. "What would one have privileged access too, in such a case?" Would we have access to anything more than Davidson's swampman does, for example? If not, then it is not even clear that we are even in a position to know that these episodes are thoughts!

McKinsey then turns to Burge's compatibility thesis, arguing that it amounts to the claim that the following three propositions are consistent.

(1) Oscar knows a priori that he is thinking that water is wet.

(2) The proposition that Oscar is thinking that water is wet necessarily depends on E.

(3) The proposition E cannot be known a priori, but only by empirical investigation.

According to McKinsey, the consistency of these three propositions depends on how we are to take the notion of necessary dependency in (2). If we take it to be a notion of metaphysical entailment, then no contradiction arises, but the notion of necessary dependency will be far too broad; for example, Oscar's thinking that water is wet would metaphysically entail that Oscar had the mother that he did. But this is not intuitively part of Oscar's wide psychological state in this case.

Alternatively, if we take necessary dependence to be a notion of conceptual entailment, for example if the proposition that Oscar is thinking that water is wet conceptually entails E, then it is in principle possible for Oscar to deduce E by a priori reasoning. But this would contradict (3). This way of understanding necessary dependence would lead to an inconsistency. In short, "if knowing a priori that you are in a given mental state conceptually or logically implies the existence of external objects, then you could know a priori that the external word exists." But, at least according to McKinsey, you can't know that a priori. Other reformulations of (2) are possible, but the implication is that those formulations which are not too broad and which don't lead to contradiction, may well be subject to the kind of criticism that McKinsey initially leveled against Davidson.

A third front is opened up by Jessica Brown (ch. 8), who offers additional support for the McKinsey incompatibilism thesis. Drawing on remarks about non-natural kind concepts in Burge's (1982) "Other Bodies", Brown argues that Burge is committed to the conjunction of two theses, Q and R,

(Q) Necessarily, if x has a thought involving the concept of a natural kind k and x is agnostic about the application conditions of the concept k, then either x is in an environment which contains k, or x is part of a community with the concept k.

(R) Necessarily, if x has a thought involving a non-natural kind concept, c, and x is agnostic about the application conditions of c, then x is part of a community which has the concept c.

which in turn commits him to (S).

(S)   Necessarily, if x has a thought involving a concept c, and x is agnostic about the application conditions of c, then either x is in an environment which contains instances of c and c is a natural kind concept, or x is part of a community which has the concept x, whether or not c is a natural kind concept.

The problem is that by the privileged access thesis it is knowable a priori that one is having a concept c and that one is agnostic about the application conditions of c, so it should follow from (S) and privileged access that one can know a priori that one is in an environment which either contains instances of c, a natural kind concept, or is part of a community which has the concept c. But by hypothesis we can't have a priori knowledge of that character.

The Compatibilist Response

Anthony Brueckner (ch. 9), takes aim at the argument offered by McKinsey, arguing that McKinsey has incorrectly characterized Burge's position. The alleged error becomes clear when we consider a plausible candidate for E in premises (2) and (3) above. If for example, E is the following,

(E1) Oscar inhabits an environment containing H_2O and not XYZ.

then by McKinsey's argument it would follow that Oscar could know a priori that he is in an environment containing H_2O rather than XYZ. The problem, according to Brueckner, is that Burge explicitly denies the possibility of knowing something like E1 a priori. One must be careful to distinguish between the following:

(A)   Oscar would not have been thinking water is wet had he been in an environment containing XYZ rather than H_2O

(B)   Every world in which Oscar thinks water is wet is a world containing H_2O

For Burge, (A) is presumably true, while (B) is not. (B) is not true, since there are worlds which lack water, yet in which water might be postulated by chemical theory, for example. One might think it possible to recast the McKinsey argument, suggesting a version of (2) along the following lines.

(2c)   If Oscar's environment had been sufficiently different from the way it in fact is (for example, if it had contained XYZ instead of H_2O), then, even holding fixed Oscar's phenomenology, functional structure, behavior etc., Oscar would not have been thinking water is wet.

But Brueckner argues that something has been smuggled into (2c). To see this, we need to break down (2c) into the following two claims.

(2c1) If Oscar's environment had been sufficiently different from the way it in fact is, then, even holding fixed Oscar's phenomenology, functional structure, behavior etc., Oscar would not have been thinking water is wet.

(2c2) Oscar's environment in fact contains H_2O instead of XYZ.

The first of these claims is knowable a priori, but the latter is not. The moral is that McKinsey has attempted to saddle Burge with a commitment to a priori knowledge of a character Burge would dismiss.

There is, however, something that is knowable a priori on Brueckner's view. Specifically, the following:

(P)   It is necessary that if Oscar is thinking water is wet, then there exist some physical entities distinct from Oscar.

But, Brueckner asks, is it so implausible to suppose that we have knowledge of this a priori?

In Chapter 10 Brian McLaughlin and Michael Tye take aim at Brown's formulation of the incompatibilist thesis. They argue that her (R)

(R)   Necessarily, if x has a thought involving a non-natural kind concept, c, and x is agnostic about the application conditions of c, then x is part of a community which has the concept c.

is in no way a thesis that Burge is committed to, hence the argument collapses. They draw on one of Brown's own examples to show that (following Burge's assumptions) it is possible for an agent to have a non-natural kind concept, despite being be agnostic about the application conditions of the concept and despite not be part of a linguistic community.

Ted Warfield (Ch. 11) turns his attention to Boghossian's incompatibilist argument. Warfield begins by formalizing Boghossian's argument as follows.

(P1)   To know that P by introspection, S must be able to introspectively discriminate P from all relevant alternatives of P.

(P2)   S cannot introspectively discriminate water thoughts from twater thoughts.

(P3) If the Switching Case is actual, then twater thoughts are relevant alternatives of water thoughts.

(C1) So, S doesn't know that P by introspection.

But, Warfield points out, this argument is invalid, since all that follows is the much weaker (C1')

(C1') If the Switching case is actual, then S doesn't know that P by introspection.

As Warfield argues, this is simply not enough to undermine the authority of our self-knowledge. Indeed, he suggests that the mere possibility of a switching case no more undermines our self-knowledge than the possibility of our possessing a counterfeit coin undermines the authority of our knowledge of how much money we have in our pockets. Switching cases, even if they exist are never relevant alternatives, and hence do not undermine our self-knowledge.

The Nature of Epistemic Warrant

The Warfield paper discussed above did more than attempt to advance the cause of the compatibilist – it also introduced a new issue into the debate: the nature of our epistemic warrant. According to Warfield our self-knowledge was not undermined by switching cases because switching cases, though possible, are nonexistent, or at least rare. In "Externalism, Self-Knowledge, and the Prevalence of Slow-Switching," (ch. 12) Peter Ludlow argues that switching cases may not be so rare after all – indeed, they may be entirely commonplace. For a social externalist, switching cases may well occur every time we fail to detect that we have slid between social groups with differing individuating conditions for certain key terms. We may defer to a different group of individuals for the meaning of terms like 'cool' or 'bore', unaware that this new group individuates the term differently. Ludlow concludes that if switching cases are commonplace, then Boghossian's incompatibilist argument does not break down here.

For his part, Warfield (ch. 13) suggests that the move proposed by Ludlow is not enough to undermine the general compatibility of externalism and self-knowledge. At best it shows that in the actual world we can't have the co-occurance of externalism and authoritative self-knowledge. It would take much more to show that this is a case of genuine incompatibility. Ludlow replies (ch. 14) by arguing that incompatibility in *any* nearby world is enough to show that either the authority of self-knowledge or externalism would have to be surrendered.

In chapters 15 and 16 Tyler Burge and Christopher Peacocke come at the issue of epistemic warrant from a rather different direction than Ludlow and Warfield. Burge, for example, argues that for an anti-individualist, the epistemic entitlement to self-knowledge is not grounded in the reliability of a causal perceptual relation between our self-knowledge and its object. Rather, the entitlement is grounded (in part) in the role that our self-knowledge plays in critical reasoning – reasoning that involves "an ability to recognize and effectively employ reasonable criticism or support for reasons and reasoning," an ability which in turn requires a second order ability to think about thought contents (for checking steps in proofs, etc.). Even stronger, Burge argues that critical reasoning requires that one knows one's thoughts. Since we are all critical reasoners, (indeed even skeptics must recognize a place for critical reasoning) we are all entitled to self-knowledge.

Christopher Peacocke, takes issue with several key points of Burge's proposal. For example, he suggests that while certain forms of self-knowledge may not be underwritten by some causal perceptual relation, certain other forms clearly are (indeed three such kinds are examined). More importantly, Peacocke suggests that our ability to engage in critical reasoning cannot be the source of our entitlement, but to the contrary is posterior to such entitlement. Critical reasoning is "the result of the combination of the capacity for second tier thought with the capacity to self-ascribe attitudes," where the entitlement to such self-ascriptions must be independently motivated.

Externalism and the Nature of Memory

Paul Boghossian's incompatibilist paper helped launch the discussion of epistemic warrant, but it also, perhaps unintentionally, opened a second line of investigation into the nature of externalism and memory. In "Social Externalism, Self-Knowledge, and Memory" (ch. 17) Peter Ludlow reconstructs Boghossian's argument as follows,

(1) If S forgets nothing, then what S knows at t1, S knows at t2

(2) S forgot nothing

(3) S does not know that P at t2

(4) therefore, S did not know that P at t1

and claims that the argument turns on an individualistic assumption about the nature of memory – specifically in premise (1). Ludlow argues that this is a premise that the careful social externalist would not accept.

The reasoning here is that if (following Burge) the contents of our mental states are determined by our social environment, it is natural to suppose that the contents of our memories will depend upon our social environment. As we move from one environmental condition to another (perhaps without even noticing the environmental change), the contents of our memories will shift accordingly. Applying this line of reasoning to Boghossian's paper, Ludlow argues as follows.

> ...let's say that at time t1 I know that I am thinking that chickory is bitter. Suppose that at time t2 later than t1, I recall that initial thought about chickory, but, due to undetected changes in my linguistic community, the content of my thoughts about chickory have shifted.[2] Boghossian is arguably correct in asserting that I do not know at t2 what I knew at t1, but he is incorrect in supposing that "the only explanation" for this is that I "never knew" my thoughts in the first place. It is entirely consistent with the social externalist view of memory that I forgot nothing, but that the contents of my memories have nonetheless shifted. Indeed, this is not only *possible* according to social externalism, but given the prevalence of slow switching it should be a rather common state of affairs. (pp. 309–310)

Despite the intuitive appeal of this move, it is not without its apparent unwelcome consequences. One such consequence is that memories do not preserve the contents of our initial episodes of thought. So, for example, at some time t0 I might have a chickory thought, which would be followed at t1 by the "memory" of a tchickory thought. Isn't this just to say that memory has failed us?

In "Externalism and Memory: A Problem?" (ch.18), Ludlow suggests that this is simply a mistaken way for an externalist to think about the role of memory.

> ...is there any reason to suppose that it is the job of memory to "record the contents" of past mental episodes? On the face of it, this assumption begs the central question at issue. According to the externalist

---

[2] As Anthony Brueckner has noted (ch. 19), this formulation is sloppy. It's not at all clear that I can "recall that initial thought about chickory," since the event of my recollection is actually about tchickory (the twin substance).

conception of memory ..., it is not the job of memory to record contents, but rather to provide information about past episodes relative to current environmental conditions. Even if there were a mechanism which could, as it were, freeze the contents of an initial mental episode and carry it in memory indefinitely, I'm not sure that it would have any utility. Indeed, it would be a way of preserving the content of a thought which we could no longer have (if, as the externalist supposes, the contents of our current thoughts are determined by our new environment). (p. 316)

Anthony Brueckner (ch. 19) raises a related consideration about externalism and memory which may undermine some of the conclusions drawn by Ludlow. According to Brueckner's reasoning, memories will have to be individuated on the basis of their contents, so it is simply incorrect to say that the contents of our memories have shifted. It is more accurate to say that we have false or apparent memories. The issue is not whether it is the job of memory to record contents. The issue is rather one of how memories are to be individuated, and it appears that they are individuated by their contents. Ludlow is simply mistaken to reject premise (1) of Boghossian's argument.

This does not mean that Boghossian's argument is rescued, however. To the contrary it now follows that premise (2) of the argument will fall.

(2) S forgot nothing

Boghossian tried to help himself to an assumption that is out of reach. On Brueckner's view if the content of S's t0 mental state is no longer available to S at t1, then that is a clear case of forgetting, and Boghossian's argument crumbles.

Sven Bernecker's contribution (ch. 20) is primarily about epistemic warrant, but a key point turns on the Ludlow/Brueckner claims about memory. In particular, he balks at Brueckner's views about the identity of memories and the nature of forgetting. While we might identify certain memories on the basis of their (external) contents, he holds that there is no reason to suppose that memory is sensitive to twin earth scenarios. Why not suppose that forgetting consists principally in the degradation of the narrow, phenomenological aspect of memory? Shifts in external content need not count as forgetting.

While Bernecker is in Ludlow's camp on the individuation of memories, he notes that this view of memory undermines the Ludlow (ch. 12) claim that switching cases are commonplace and are epistemically relevant alternatives. To the contrary, once the switch has taken place, there is no access to the old contents – not even through memory. Thus, not only are there no *relevant* alternatives for the switcher, there are no alternatives at all!

Bernecker adds that the other considerations raised by Boghossian (ch. 6) evaporate once one gets clear on the nature of epistemic warrant. For example, there is no real difficulty that arises with respect to the issue of cognitive achievement. Indeed, we have many warranted beliefs that do not involve "cognitive achievement" in the sense discussed by Boghossian.

The papers on memory by Ludlow, Brueckner, and Bernecker take the view that in switching cases the old contents are annihilated after enough time has passed. But not all externalists are persuaded by such reasoning. Tyler Burge, for example, argues in "Self-Knowledge and Memory" (ch. 21) that memory is not so environmentally sensitive – indeed it serves to link us to our past thought contents in a manner akin to the role that anaphora plays in linking the contents of pronouns to the contents of noun phrases which appear earlier in the discourse. Burge does agree, however, that the weak link in Boghossian's argument is the discussion of memory. The difference is that Burge challenges Boghossian on premise (3) above, reasoning that there is no reason why the agent cannot know that P at time t2, since the agent can be linked to the content P via memory.

Conclusion

Clearly, externalist assumptions have rich and intricate consequences for the philosophical analysis of self-knowledge, and these consequences give rise in turn to a number of important philosophical questions – questions about the nature of epistemic warrant, and questions about the nature of memory. Nor do the questions stop there. Once one begins pursuing the philosophical consequences of any of these assumptions, new issues begin to emerge immediately. Indeed, there are philosophers today using these consequences to explore questions surrounding personal identity, the nature of the self and epistemic power relations, amongst other things. By beginning with a particular assumption about the nature of thought contents, we find that an entire domain of philosophical investigation has opened up before us. Perhaps some of the consequences that emerge in this domain will convince us that the initial externalist assumptions were all wrong. Or perhaps the ensuing investigation will lead us to rethink our most cherished assumptions about the nature of knowledge, the self, and memory. Whatever the outcome, there is plenty of room for lively philosophical discussion, and the best part is that it's not too late to join the discussion. It's just getting started. Welcome to the party!

REFERENCES

Burge, T. 1982. Other Bodies. Pp. 649–663 in *Thought and Object: Essays on Intentionality*, ed. A. Woodfield. Oxford: Oxford University Press.

Putnam, H. 1975. The Meaning of 'Meaning'. Pp. 131–193 in *Minnesota Studies in the Philosophy of Science*, volume VII, ed. K. Gunderson. Minneapolis: University of Minnesota Press.

Part I: Externalism and Self-Knowledge – Preliminaries

1

Descartes on Self-Knowledge

René Descartes

Principles of Philosophy, part 1

From Section 8:

[T]he notion that we have of our soul, or of our thought, precedes the notion we have of our body, and it is more certain in view of the fact that we still doubt the existence of things in the external world while we know with certainty that we think.

From Section 9:

By the term "to think" I mean everything that occurs in us such that we are immediately aware of it. This is why not only to understand, to will and to imagine, but also to sense, is the same as to think.

From Section 10:

… and when I say that this proposition, *I think, I am* is the first and most certain that presents itself to s/he who thinks in an orderly way, I do not for this reason deny that it must be known before thought, certainty and existence, or that in order to think it is necessary to exist and other such things. But, because these notions are so simple that of themselves they do not give us knowledge of anything that exists, I find that they do not need to be listed here.

Section 11:

Now in order to know how the knowledge that we have of our thoughts precedes the knowledge we have of our bodies and that it is incomparably more evident, we should notice that it is manifest by the natural light in our souls that nothingness has no properties or qualities and that where we see some qualities or properties, we necessarily find a thing or substance on which they are dependent. By this same light we also see that the more properties a thing or substance has the better we know it. Now it is certain that we find many more in our thoughts than in any other things that might exist in that there is nothing that we know which does not lead us to know our own thoughts more certainly. For example, if I persuade myself that the earth exists because I touch it or I see it, this also gives me an even stronger reason to be persuaded that my thought is or exists because it may be the case that I think I touch the earth, yet the earth does not exist. But it is not possible for me, that is my soul, not to exist while I am thinking this thought. The same is true with regard to all the other things which have come to us in thought, that is, that we know that we who think of them exist, even though they may be false or may have no existence.

From *Rules for the Direction of the Mind* #8:

Nothing can be known before the mind, because knowledge of all other things depends upon the mind and not the other way around.

2

Individualism and the Mental

Tyler Burge

Since Hegel's *Phenomenology of Spirit*, a broad, inarticulate division of emphasis between the individual and his social environment has marked philosophical discussions of mind. On one hand, there is the traditional concern with the individual subject of mental states and events. In the elderly Cartesian tradition, the spotlight is on what exists or transpires "in" the individual – his secret cogitations, his innate cognitive structures, his private perceptions and introspections, his grasping of ideas, concepts, or forms. More evidentially oriented movements, such as behaviorism and its liberalized progeny, have highlighted the individuals' publicly observable behavior – his input-output relations and the dispositions, states, or events that mediate them. But both Cartesian and behaviorist viewpoints tend to feature the individual subject. On the other hand, there is the Hegelian preoccupation with the role of social institutions in shaping the individual and the content of his thought. This tradition has dominated the continent since Hegel. But it has found echoes in English-speaking philosophy during this century in the form of a concentration on language. Much philosophical work on language and mind has been in the interests of Cartesian or behaviorist viewpoints that I shall term "individualistic." But many of Wittgenstein's remarks about mental representation point up a social orientation that is discernible from his flirtations with behaviorism. And more recent work on the theory of reference has provided glimpses of the role of social cooperation in determining what an individual thinks.

In many respects, of course, these emphases within philosophy – individualistic and social – are compatible. To an extent, they may be regarded simply as different currents in the turbulent stream of ideas that has washed the intellectual landscape during the last hundred and some odd years. But the role of the social environment has received considerably less clear-headed philosophical attention (though perhaps not less philosophical attention) than the role of the states, occurrences, or acts in, on, or by the individual. Philosophical discussions of social factors have tended to be obscure, evocative, metaphorical, or platitudinous, or to be bent on establishing some large thesis about the course of history and the destiny of man. There remains much room for sharp delineation. I shall offer some considerations that stress social factors in descriptions of an individual's mental phenomena. These considerations call into question individualistic presuppositions of several traditional and modern treatments of mind. I shall conclude with some remarks about mental models.

I. Terminological Matters

Our ordinary mentalistic discourse divides broadly into two sorts of idiom. One typically makes reference to mental states or events in terms of sentential expressions. The other does not. A clear case of the first kind of idiom is 'Alfred thinks that his friends' sofa is ugly.' A clear case of the second sort is 'Alfred is in pain.' Thoughts, beliefs, intentions, and so forth are typically specified in terms of subordinate sentential clauses, that-clauses, which may be judged as true or false. Pains, feels, tickles, and so forth have no special semantical relation to sentences or to truth or falsity. There are intentional idioms that fall in the second category on this characterization, but that share important semantical features with expressions in the first – idioms like 'Al worships Buicks.' But I shall not sort these out here. I shall discuss only the former kind of mentalistic idiom. The extension of the discussion to other intentional idioms will not be difficult.

In an ordinary sense, the noun phrases that embed sentential expressions in mentalistic idioms provide the *content* of the mental state or event. We shall call that-clauses and their grammatical variants "*content clauses.*" Thus the expression 'that sofas are more comfortable than pews' provides the content of Alfred's belief that sofas are more comfortable than pews. My phrase 'provides the content' represents an attempt at remaining neutral, at least for present purposes, among various semantical and metaphysical accounts of precisely how that-clauses function and precisely what, if anything, contents are.

Although the notion of content is, for present purposes, ontologically neutral, I do think of it as holding a place in a systematic *theory* of mentalistic language. The question of when to count contents different, and when the same, is answerable to theoretical restrictions. It is often remarked that in a given context we may ascribe to a person two that-clauses that are only loosely equivalent and count them as attributions of the "same attitude." We may say that Al's intention to climb Mt. McKinley and his intention to climb the highest mountain in the United States are the "same intention." (I intend the terms for the mountain to occur obliquely here. See later discussion.) This sort of point extends even to content clauses with extensionally non-equivalent counterpart notions. For contextually relevant purposes, we might count a thought that the glass contains some water as "the same thought" as a thought that the glass contains some thirst-quenching liquid, particularly if we have no reason to attribute either content as opposed to the other, and distinctions between them are contextually irrelevant. Nevertheless, in both these examples, every systematic theory I know of would want to represent the semantical contribution of the content-clauses in distinguishable ways – as "providing different contents."

One reason for doing so is that the person himself is capable of having different attitudes described by the different content-clauses, even if these differences are irrelevant in a particular context. (Al might have developed the intention to climb the highest mountain before developing the intention to climb Mt. McKinley – regardless of whether he, in fact, did so.) A second reason is that the counterpart components of the that-clauses allude to distinguishable elements in people's cognitive lives. 'Mt. McKinley' and 'the highest mountain in the U.S.' serve, or might serve, to indicate cognitively different notions. This is a vague, informal way of generalizing Frege's point: the thought that Mt. McKinley is the highest mountain in the U.S. is potentially interesting or informative. The thought that Mt. McKinley is Mt. McKinley is not. Thus when we say in a given context that attribution of different contents is attribution of the "same attitude," we use 'same attitude' in a way similar to the way we use 'same car' when we say that people who drive Fords (or green 1970 Ford Mavericks) drive the "same car." For contextual purposes different cars are counted as "amounting to the same."

Although this use of 'content' is theoretical, it is not I think theoretically controversial. In cases where we shall be counting contents different, the cases will be uncontentious: On any systematic theory, differences in the *extension* – the actual denotation, referent, or application – of counterpart expressions in that-clauses will be semantically represented, and will, in our terms, make for differences in content. I shall be avoiding the more controversial, but interesting, questions about the general conditions under which sentences in that-clauses can be expected to provide the same content.

I should also warn of some subsidiary terms. I shall be (and have been) using the term '*notion*' to apply to components or elements of contents. Just as whole that-clauses provide the content of a person's attitude, semantically relevant components of that-clauses will be taken to indicate notions that enter into the attitude (or the attitude's content). This term is supposed to be just as ontologically neutral as its fellow. When I talk of understanding or mastering the notion of contract, I am not relying on any special epistemic or ontological theory, except insofar as the earlier-mentioned theoretical restrictions on the notion of content are inherited by the notion of notion. The expression, '*understanding (mastering) a notion*' is to be construed more or less intuitively. Understanding the notion of contract comes roughly to knowing what a contract is. One can master the notion of contract without mastering the term 'contract' – at the very least if one speaks some language other than English that has a term roughly synonymous with 'contract'. (An analogous point holds for my use of 'mastering a content.') Talk of notions is roughly similar to talk of concepts in an informal sense. 'Notion' has the advantage of being easier to separate from traditional theoretical commitments.

I speak of *attributing* an attitude, content, or notion, and of *ascribing* a that-clause or other piece of language. Ascriptions are the linguistic analogs of attributions. This use of 'ascribe' is nonstandard, but convenient and easily assimilated.

There are semantical complexities involving the behavior of expressions in content clauses, most of which we can skirt. But some must be touched on. Basic to the subject is the observation that expressions in content clauses are often not intersubstitutable with extensionally equivalent expressions in such a way as to maintain the truth value of the containing sentence. Thus from the facts that water is H_2O and that Bertrand thought that water is not fit to drink, it does not follow that Bertrand thought that H_2O is not fit to drink. When an expression like 'water' functions in a content clause so that it is not freely exchangeable with all extensionally equivalent expressions, we shall say that it has *oblique occurrence*. Roughly speaking, the reason why 'water' and 'H_2O' are not interchangeable in our report of Bertrand's thought is that 'water' plays a role in characterizing a different mental act or state from that which 'H_2O' would play a role in characterizing. In this context at least, thinking that water is not fit to drink is different from thinking that H_2O is not fit to drink.

By contrast, there are non-oblique occurrences of expressions in content clauses. One might say that some water – say, the water in the glass over there – is thought by Bertrand to be impure; or that Bertrand thought that *that* water is impure. And one might intend to make no distinction that would be lost by replacing 'water' with 'H_2O' – or 'that water' with 'that H_2O' or 'that common liquid,' or any other expression extensionally equivalent with 'that water.' We might allow these exchanges even though Bertrand had never heard of, say, H_2O. In such purely non-oblique occurrences, 'water' plays *no role* in providing the *content* of Bertrand's thought, *on our use of 'content,'* or (in any narrow sense) in characterizing Bertrand or his mental state. Nor is the water part of Bertrand's thought content. We speak of Bertrand *thinking his content of* the water. At its nonoblique occurrence, the term 'that water' simply isolates, in one of many equally good ways, a portion of wet stuff to which Bertrand or his thought is related or applied. In certain cases, it may also mark a context in which Bertrand's thought is applied. But it is expressions at oblique occurrences within content clauses that primarily do the job of providing the content of mental states or events, and in characterizing the person.

Mentalistic discourse containing obliquely occurring expressions has traditionally been called *intentional discourse*. The historical reasons for this nomenclature are complex and partly confused. But roughly speaking, grammatical contexts involving oblique occurrences have been fixed upon as specially relevant to the representational character (sometimes called "intentionality") of mental states and events. Clearly oblique occurrences in mentalistic discourse have something to do with characterizing a person's epistemic perspective – how things seem to him, or in an informal sense, how they are represented to him. So without endorsing all the commitments of this tradition, I shall take over its terminology.

The crucial point in the preceding discussion is the assumption that obliquely occurring expressions in content clauses are a primary means of identifying a person's intentional mental states or events. A further point is worth remarking here. It is normal to suppose that those content clauses correctly ascribable to a person that are not in general intersubstitutable *salva veritate* – and certainly those that involve extensionally non-equivalent counterpart expressions – identify different mental states or events.

I have cited contextual exceptions to this normal supposition, at least in a manner of speaking. We sometimes count distinctions in content irrelevant for purposes of a given attribution, particularly where our evidence for the precise content of a person or animal's attitude is skimpy. Different contents may contextually identify (what amount to) the "same attitude." I have indicated that even in these contexts, I think it best, strictly speaking, to construe distinct contents as describing different mental states or events that are merely equivalent for the purposes at hand. I believe that this view is widely accepted. But nothing I say will depend on it. For any distinct contents, there will be imaginable contexts of attribution in which, even in the loosest, most informal ways of speaking, those contents would be said to describe different mental states or events. This is virtually a consequence of the theoretical role of contents, discussed earlier. Since our discussion will have an "in principle" character, I shall take these contexts to be the relevant ones. Most of the cases we discuss will involve *extensional* differences between obliquely occurring counterpart expressions in that-clauses. In such cases, it is particularly natural and normal to take different contents as identifying different mental states or events.

II. A Thought Experiment
IIa. First Case
We now turn to a three-step thought experiment. Suppose first that:

A given person has a large number of attitudes commonly attributed with content clauses containing 'arthritis' in oblique occurrence. For example, he thinks (correctly) that he has had arthritis for years, that his arthritis in his wrists and fingers is more painful than his arthritis in his ankles, that it is better to have arthritis than cancer of the liver, that stiffening joints is a symptom of arthritis, that certain sorts of aches are characteristic of arthritis, that there are various kinds of arthritis, and so forth. In short, he has a wide range of such attitudes. In addition to these unsurprising attitudes, he thinks falsely that he has developed arthritis in the thigh.

Generally competent in English, rational and intelligent, the patient reports to his doctor his fear that his arthritis has now lodged in his thigh. The doctor replies by telling him that this cannot be so, since arthritis is specifically an inflammation of joints. Any dictionary could have told him the same. The patient is surprised, but relinquishes his view and goes on to ask what might be wrong with his thigh.

The second step of the thought experiment consists of a counterfactual supposition. We are to conceive of a situation in which the patient proceeds from birth through the same course of physical events that he actually does, right to and including the time at which he first reports his fear to his doctor. Precisely the same things (non-intentionally described) happen to him. He has the same physiological history, the same diseases, the same internal physical occurrences. He goes through the same motions, engages in the same behavior, has the same sensory intake (physiologically described). His dispositions to respond to stimuli are explained in physical theory as the effects of the same proximate causes. All of this extends to his interaction with linguistic expressions. He says and hears the same words (word forms) at the same times he actually does. He develops the disposition to assent to 'Arthritis can occur in the thigh' and 'I have arthritis in the thigh' as a result of the same physically described proximate causes. Such dispositions might have arisen in a number of ways. But we can suppose that in both actual and counterfactual situations, he acquires the word 'arthritis' from casual conversation or reading, and never hearing anything to prejudice him for or against applying it in the way that he does, he applies the word to an ailment in his thigh (or to ailments in the limbs of others) which seems to produce pains or other symptoms roughly similar to the disease in his hands and ankles. In both actual and counterfactual cases, the disposition is never reinforced or extinguished up until the time when he expresses himself to his doctor. We further imagine that the patient's non-intentional, phenomenal experience is the same. He has the same pains, visual fields, images, and internal verbal rehearsals. The *counterfactuality* in the supposition touches on the patient's social environment. In actual fact, 'arthritis,' as used in his community, does not apply to ailments outside joints. Indeed, it fails to do so by a standard, non-technical dictionary definition. But in our imagined case, physicians, lexicographers, and informed laymen apply 'arthritis' not only to arthritis but to various other rheumatoid ailments. The standard use of the term is to be conceived to encompass the patient's actual misuse. We could imagine either that arthritis had not been singled out as a family of diseases, or that some other term besides 'arthritis' were applied, though not commonly by laymen, specifically to arthritis. We may also suppose that this difference and those necessarily associated with it are the only differences between the counterfactual situation and the actual one. (Other people besides the patient will, of course, behave differently.) To summarize the second step:

The person might have had the same physical history and non-intentional mental phenomena while the word 'arthritis' was conventionally applied, and defined to apply, to various rheumatoid ailments, including the one in the person's thigh, as well as to arthritis.

The final step is an interpretation of the counterfactual case, or an addition to it as so far described. It is reasonable to suppose that:

In the counterfactual situation, the patient lacks some – probably *all* – of the attitudes commonly attributed with content clauses containing 'arthritis' in oblique occurrence. He lacks the occurrent thoughts or beliefs that he has arthritis in the thigh, that he has had arthritis for years, that stiffening joints and various sorts of aches are symptoms of arthritis, that his father had arthritis, and so on.

We suppose that in the counterfactual case we cannot correctly ascribe any content clause containing an oblique occurrence of the term 'arthritis.' It is hard to see how the patient could have picked up the notion of arthritis. The word 'arthritis' in the counterfactual community does not mean *arthritis*. It does not apply only to inflammations of joints. We suppose that no other word in the patient's repertoire means *arthritis*. 'Arthritis,' in the counterfactual situation, differs both in dictionary definition and in extension from 'arthritis' as we use it. Our ascriptions of content clauses to the patient (and ascriptions within his community) would not constitute attributions of the same contents we actually attribute. For counterpart expressions in the content clauses that are actually and counterfactually ascribable are not even extensionally equivalent. However we describe the patient's attitudes in the counterfactual situation, it will not be with a term or phrase extensionally equivalent with 'arthritis.' So the patient's counterfactual attitude contents differ from his actual ones.

The upshot of these reflections is that the patient's mental contents differ while his entire physical and non-intentional mental histories, considered in isolation from their social context, remain the same. (We could have supposed that he dropped dead at the time he first expressed his fear to the doctor.) The differences seem to stem from differences "outside" the patient considered as an isolated physical organism, causal mechanism, or seat of consciousness. The difference in his mental contents is attributable to differences in his social environment. In sum, the patient's internal qualitative experiences, his physiological states and events, his behaviorally described stimuli and responses, his dispositions to behave, and whatever sequences of states (non-intentionally described) mediated his input and output – all these remain constant, while his attitude contents differ, even in the extensions of counterpart notions. As we observed at the outset, such differences are ordinarily taken to spell differences in mental states and events.

IIb. Further Exemplification

The argument has an extremely wide application. It does not depend, for example, on the kind of word 'arthritis' is. We could have used an artifact term, an ordinary natural kind word, a color adjective, a social role term, a term for a historical style, an abstract noun, an action verb, a physical movement verb, or any of various other sorts of words. I prefer to leave open precisely how far one can generalize the argument. But I think it has a very wide scope. The argument can get under way in any case where it is intuitively possible to attribute a mental state or event whose content involves a notion that the subject incompletely understands. As will become clear, this possibility is the key to the thought experiment. I want to give a more concrete sense of the possibility before going further.

It is useful to reflect on the number and variety of intuitively clear cases in which it is normal to attribute a content that the subject incompletely understands. One need only thumb through a dictionary for an hour or so to develop a sense of the extent to which one's beliefs are infected by incomplete understanding.[1] The phenomenon is rampant in our pluralistic age.

a. Most cases of incomplete understanding that support the thought experiment will be fairly idiosyncratic. There is a reason for this. Common linguistic errors, if entrenched, tend to become common usage. But a generally competent speaker is bound to have numerous words in his repertoire, possibly even common words, that he somewhat misconstrues. Many of these misconstruals will not be such as to deflect ordinary ascriptions of that-clauses involving the incompletely mastered term in oblique occurrence. For example, one can imagine a generally compe-

---

[1] Our examples suggest points about learning that need exploration. It would seem naive to think that we first attain a mastery of expressions or notions we use and then tackle the subject matters we speak and think about in using those expressions or notions. In most cases, the processes overlap. But while the subject's understanding is still partial, we sometimes attribute mental contents in the very terms the subject has yet to master. Traditional views take mastering a word to consist in matching it with an already mastered (or innate) concept. But it would seem, rather, that many concepts (or mental content components) are like words in that they may be employed before they are mastered. In both cases, employment appears to be an integral part of the process of mastery.

tent, rational adult having a large number of attitudes involving the notion of sofa – including beliefs that *those* (some sofas) are sofas, that some sofas are beige, that his neighbors have a new sofa, that he would rather sit in a sofa for an hour than on a church pew. In addition, he might think that sufficiently broad (but single-seat) overstuffed arm-chairs are sofas. With care, one can develop a thought experiment parallel to the one in section IIa, in which at least some of the person's attitude contents (particularly, in this case, contents of occurrent mental events) differ, while his physical history, dispositions to behavior, and phenomenal experience – non-intentionally and asocially described – remain the same.

b. Although most relevant misconstruals are fairly idiosyncratic, there do seem to be certain types of error which are relatively common – but not so common and uniform as to suggest that the relevant terms take on new sense. Much of our vocabulary is taken over from others who, being specialists, understand our terms better than we do.[2] The use of scientific terms by laymen is a rich source of cases. As the arthritis example illus-

---

[2] A development of a similar theme may be found in Hilary Putnam's notion of a division of linguistic labour. Cf. Putnam (1975 pp. 227 ff.). Putnam's imaginative work is in other ways congenial with points I have developed. Some of his examples can be adapted in fairly obvious ways so as to give an argument with different premises, but a conclusion complementary to the one I arrive at in Section IIa:

Consider Alfred's belief contents involving the notion of water. Without changing Alfred's (or his fellows') non-intentional phenomenal experiences, internal physical occurrences, or dispositions to respond to stimuli on sensory surfaces, we can imagine that not water (H_2O), but a different liquid with different structure but similar macro-properties (and identical phenomenal properties) played the role in his environment that water does in ours. In such a case, we could ascribe no content clauses to Alfred with 'water' in oblique position. His belief contents would differ. The conclusion (with which I am in sympathy) is that mental contents are affected not only by the physical and qualitatively mental way the person is, but by the nature of his *physical environment*.

Putnam himself does not give quite this argument. He nowhere states the first and third steps, though he gives analogs of them for the meaning of 'water'. This is partly just a result of his concentration on meaning instead of propositional attitudes. But some of what he says even seems to oppose the argument's conclusion. He remarks in effect that the subject's *thoughts* remain constant between his actual and counterfactual cases (p. 224). In his own argument he explicates the difference between actual and counterfactual cases in terms of a difference in the extension of terms, not a difference in those aspects of their meaning that play a role in the cognitive life of the subject. And he tries to explicate his examples in terms of indexicality – a mistake, I think, and one that tends to divert attention from major implications of the examples he gives. (Cf. Section IId.) In my view, the examples do illustrate the fact that all attitudes involving natural kind notions, including *de dicto* attitudes, presuppose *de re* attitudes. But the examples do not show that natural kind linguistic expressions are in any ordinary sense indexical. Nor do they show that beliefs in-

trates, the thought experiment does not depend on specially technical terms. I shall leave it to the imagination of the reader to spin out further examples of this sort.

c. One need not look to the laymen's acquisitions from science for examples. People used to buying beef brisket in stores or ordering it in restaurants (and conversant with it in a general way) probably often develop mistaken beliefs (or uncertainties) about just what brisket is. For example, one might think that brisket is a cut from the flank or rump, or that it includes not only the lower part of the chest but also the upper part, or that it is specifically a cut of beef and not of, say, pork. No one hesitates to ascribe to such people content-clauses with 'brisket' in oblique occurrence. For example, a person may believe that he is eating brisket under these circumstances (where 'brisket' occurs in oblique position); or he may think that brisket tends to be tougher than loin. Some of these attitudes may be false; many will be true. We can imagine a counterfactual case in which the person's physical history, his dispositions, and his non-intentional mental life, are all the same, but in which 'brisket' is commonly applied in a different way – perhaps in precisely the way the person thinks it applies. For example, it might apply only to beef and to the

---

volving natural kind notions are always *de re*. Even if they did, the change from actual to counterfactual cases would affect oblique occurrences of natural kind terms in that-clauses – occurrences that are the key to attributions of cognitive content. (Cf. above and footnote 3). In the cited paper and earlier ones, much of what Putnam says about psychological states (and implies about mental states) has a distinctly individualistic ring. Below in Section IV, I criticize viewpoints about mental phenomena influenced by and at least strongly suggested in his earlier work on functionalism. (Cf. note 9).

On the other hand, Putnam's articulation of social and environmental aspects of the meaning of natural kind terms complements and supplements our viewpoint. For me, it has been a rich rewarder of reflection. More recent work of his seems to involve shifts in his viewpoint on psychological states. It may have somewhat more in common with our approach than the earlier work, but there is much that I do not understand about it.

The argument regarding the notion of water that I extracted from Putnam's paper is narrower in scope than our argument. The Putnam-derived argument seems to work only for natural kind terms and close relatives. And it may seem not to provide as direct a threat to certain versions of functionalism that I discuss in Section IV: At least a few philosophers would claim that one could accommodate the Putnamian argument in terms of *non*-intentional formulations of input-output relations (formulations that make reference to the specific nature of the physical environment). Our argument does not submit to this maneuver. In our thought experiment, the physical environment (sofas, arthritis, and so forth in our examples) and the subject's causal relations with it (at least as these are usually conceived) were held constant. The Putnamian argument, however, has fascinatingly different implications from our argument. I have not developed these comparisons and contrasts here because doing justice to Putnam's viewpoint would demand a distracting amount of space, as the ample girth of this footnote may suggest.

upper and lower parts of the chest. In such a case, as in the sofa and arthritis cases, it would seem that the person would (or might) lack some or all of the propositional attitudes that are actually attributed with content clauses involving 'brisket' in oblique position.

d. Someone only generally versed in music history, or superficially acquainted with a few drawings of musical instruments, might naturally but mistakenly come to think that clavichords included harpsichords without legs. He may have many other beliefs involving the notion of clavichord, and many of these may be true. Again, with some care, a relevant thought experiment can be generated.

e. A fairly common mistake among lawyers' clients is to think that one cannot have a contract with someone unless there has been a written agreement. The client might be clear in intending 'contract' (in the relevant sense) to apply to agreements, not to pieces of paper. Yet he may take it as part of the meaning of the word, or the essence of law, that a piece of formal writing is a necessary condition for establishing a contract. His only experiences with contracts might have involved formal documents, and he undergeneralizes. It is not terribly important here whether one says that the client misunderstands the term's meaning, or alternatively that the client makes a mistake about the essence of contracts. In either case, he misconceives what a contract is; yet ascriptions involving the term in oblique position are made anyway.

It is worth emphasizing here that I intend the misconception to involve the subject's attaching counterfactual consequences to his mistaken belief about contracts. Let me elaborate this a bit. A common dictionary definition of 'contract' is 'legally binding agreement.' As I am imagining the case, the client does not explicitly define 'contract' to himself in this way (though he might use this phrase in explicating the term). And he is not merely making a mistake about what the law happens to enforce. If asked why unwritten agreements are not contracts, he is likely to say something like, 'They just aren't' or 'It is part of the nature of the law and legal practice that they have no force.' He is not disposed without prodding to answer, 'It would be possible but impractical to give unwritten agreements legal force.' He might concede this. But he would add that such agreements would not be contracts. He regards a document as inseparable from contractual obligation, regardless of whether he takes this to be a matter of meaning or a metaphysical essentialist truth about contracts.

Needless to say, these niceties are philosopher's distinctions. They are not something an ordinary man is likely to have strong opinions about. My point is that the thought experiment is independent of these distinctions. It does not depend on misunderstandings of dictionary meaning. One might say that the client understood the term's dictionary meaning, but misunderstood its essential application in the law – misconceived the nature of contracts. The thought experiment still flies. In a counterfactual case in which the law enforces both written and unwritten agreements and in which the subject's behavior and so forth are the same, but in which 'contract' *means* 'legally binding agreement based on written document,' we would not attribute to him a mistaken belief that a contract requires written agreement, although the lawyer might have to point out that there are other legally binding agreements that do not require documents. Similarly, the client's other propositional attitudes would no longer involve the notion of contract, but another more restricted notion.

f. People sometimes make mistakes about color ranges. They may correctly apply a color term to a certain color, but also mistakenly apply it to shades of a neighboring color. When asked to explain the color term, they cite the standard cases (for 'red,' the color of blood, fire engines, and so forth). But they apply the term somewhat beyond its conventionally established range – beyond the reach of its vague borders. They think that fire engines, including *that* one, are red. They observe that red roses are covering the trellis. But they also think that *those* things are a shade of red (whereas they are not). Second looks do not change their opinion. But they give in when other speakers confidently correct them in unison.

This case extends the point of the contract example. The error is linguistic or conceptual in something like the way that the shopper's mistake involving the notion of brisket is. It is not an ordinary empirical error. But one may reasonably doubt that the subjects misunderstand the dictionary meaning of the color term. Holding their non-intentional phenomenal experience, physical history, and behavioral dispositions constant, we can imagine that 'red' were applied as they mistakenly apply it. In such cases, we would no longer ascribe content-clauses involving the term 'red' in oblique position. The attribution of the correct beliefs about fire engines and roses would be no less affected than the attribution of the beliefs that, in the actual case, display the misapplication. Cases bearing out the latter point are common in anthropological reports on communities whose color terms do not match ours. Attributions of content typically allow for the differences in conventionally established color ranges.

Here is not the place to refine our rough distinctions among the various kinds of misconceptions that serve the thought experiment. Our philosophical purposes do not depend on how these distinctions are drawn. Still, it is important to see what an array of conceptual errors is common among us. And it is important to note that such errors do not always or automatically prevent attribution of mental content provided by the very terms that are incompletely understood or misapplied. The thought experiment is nourished by this aspect of common practice.

IIc. Expansion and Delineation of the Thought Experiment

As I have tried to suggest in the preceding examples, the relevant attributions in the first step of the thought experiment need not display the subject's error. They may be attributions of a true content. We can begin with a propositional attitude that involved the misconceived notion, but in a true, unproblematic application of it: for example, the patient's belief that he, like his father, developed arthritis in the ankles and wrists at age 58 (where 'arthritis' occurs obliquely).

One need not even rely on an underlying *mis*conception in the thought experiment. One may pick a case in which the subject only partially understands an expression. He may apply it firmly and correctly in a range of cases, but be unclear or agnostic about certain of its applications or implications which, in fact, are fully established in common practice. Most of the examples we gave previously can be reinterpreted in this way. To take a new one, imagine that our protagonist is unsure whether his father has mortgages on the car and house, or just one on the house. He is a little uncertain about exactly how the loan and collateral must be arranged in order for there to be a mortgage, and he is not clear about whether one may have mortgages on anything other than houses. He is unsure, however, that Uncle Harry paid off his mortgage. Imagine our man constant in the ways previously indicated and that 'mortgage' commonly applied only to mortgages on houses. But imagine banking practices themselves to be the same. Then the subject's uncertainty would plausibly not involve the notion of mortgage. Nor would his other propositional attitudes be correctly attributed with the term 'mortgage' in oblique position. Partial understanding is as good as misunderstanding for our purposes.

On the other hand, the thought experiment does appear to depend on the possibility of someone's having a propositional attitude despite an incomplete mastery of some notion in its content. To see why this appears to be so, let us try to run through a thought experiment, attempting to avoid any imputation of incomplete understanding. Suppose the subject thinks falsely that all swans are white. One can certainly hold the features of swans and the subject's non-intentional phenomenal experience, physical history, and non-intentional dispositions constant, and imagine that 'swan' meant 'white swan' (and perhaps some other term, unfamiliar to the subject, meant what 'swan' means). Could one reasonably interpret the subject as having different attitude contents without at some point invoking a misconception? The questions to be asked here are about the subject's dispositions. For example, in the actual case, if he were shown a black swan and told that he was wrong, would he fairly naturally concede his mistake? Or would he respond, "I'm doubtful that's a swan," until we brought in dictionaries, encyclopedias, and other native speakers to correct his usage? In the latter case, his understanding of 'swan' would be deviant. Suppose then that in the actual situation he would respond normally to the counterexample. Then there is reason to say that he understands the notion of swan correctly; and his error is not conceptual or linguistic, but empirical in an ordinary and narrow sense. (Of course, the line we are drawing here is pretty fuzzy.) When one comes to the counterfactual stage of the thought experiment, the subject has the same dispositions to respond pliably to the presentation of a black specimen. But such a response would suggest a misunderstanding of the term 'swan' as counterfactually used. For in the counterfactual community, what they call "swans" could not fail to be white. The mere presentation of a black swan would be irrelevant to the definitional truth 'All swans are white.' I have not set this case up as an example of the thought experiment's going through, Rather I have used it to support the conjecture that *if* the thought experiment is to work, one must at some stage find the subject believing (or having some attitude characterized by) a content, despite an incomplete understanding or misapplication. An ordinary empirical error appears not to be sufficient.

It would be a mistake, however, to think that incomplete understanding, in the sense that the argument requires, is in general an unusual or even deviant phenomenon. *What I have called "partial understanding" is common or even normal in the case of a large number of expressions in our vocabularies.* 'Arthritis' is a case in point. Even if by the grace circumstance a person does not fall into views that run counter to the term's meaning or application, it would not be in the least deviant or "socially unacceptable" to have no clear attitude that would block such views. 'Brisket,' 'contract,' 'recession,' 'sonata,' 'deer,' 'elm' (to borrow a well-known example), 'pre-amplifier,' 'carburetor,' 'gothic,' 'fermentation,' probably provide analogous cases. Continuing the list is largely a matter of patience. The sort of "incomplete understanding" required by the thought experiment includes quite ordinary, nondeviant phenomena.

It is worth remarking that the thought experiment as originally presented might be run in reverse. The idea would be to start with an ordinary belief or thought involving no incomplete understanding. Then we find the incomplete understanding in the second step. For example, properly understanding 'arthritis,' a patient may think (correctly) that he has arthritis. He happens to have heard of arthritis only occurring in joints, and he correctly believes that that is where arthritis always occurs. Holding his physical history, dispositions, and pain constant, we imagine that 'arthritis' commonly applies to rheumatoid ailments of all sorts. Arthritis has not been singled out for special mention. If the patient were told by a doctor 'You also have arthritis in the thigh', the patient would be disposed (as he is in the actual case) to respond, 'Really? I didn't know that one could have arthritis except in joints.' The doctor would answer, 'No, arthritis occurs in muscles, tendons, bursas, and elsewhere.' The patient would stand corrected. The notion that the doctor and patient would be operating with in such a case would not be that of arthritis.

My reasons for not having originally set out the thought experiment in this way are largely heuristic. As will be seen, discussion of the thought experiment will tend to center on the step involving incomplete understanding. And I wanted to encourage you, dear reader, to imagine actual cases of incomplete understanding in your own linguistic community. Ordinary intuitions in the domestic case are perhaps less subject to premature warping in the interests of theory. Cases involving not only mental content attribution, but also translation of a foreign tongue are more vulnerable to intrusion of side issues.

A secondary reason for not beginning with this "reversed" version of the thought experiment is that I find it doubtful whether the thought experiment always works in symmetric fashion. There may be special intuitive problems in certain cases – perhaps, for example, cases involving perceptual natural kinds. We may give special interpretations to individuals' misconceptions in imagined foreign communities, when those misconceptions seem to match our conceptions. In other words, there may be some systematic intuitive bias in favor of at least certain of our notions for purposes of interpreting the misconceptions of imagined foreigners. I do not want to explore the point here. I think that any such bias is not always crucial, and that the thought experiment frequently works "symmetrically." We have to take account of a person's community in interpreting his words and describing his attitudes – and this holds in the foreign case as well as in the domestic case.

The reversal of the thought experiment brings home the important point *even those propositional attitudes not infected by incomplete understanding* depend for their content on social factors that are independent of the individual, asocially and non-intentionally described. For if the social environment had been appropriately different, the contents of those attitudes would have been different.

Even *apart* from reversals of the thought experiment, it is plausible (in the light of its original versions) that our well-understood propositional attitudes depend partly for their content on social factors independent of the individual, asocially and non-intentionally construed. For each of us can reason as follows. Take a set of attitudes that involve a given notion and whose contents are well-understood by me. It is only contingent that I understand that notion as well as I do. Now holding my community's practices constant, imagine that I understand the given notion incompletely, but that the deficient understanding is such that it does not prevent my having attitude contents involving that notion. In fact, imagine that I am in the situation envisaged in the first step of one of the original thought experiments. In such a case, a proper subset of the original set of my actual attitude contents would, or might, remain the same – intuitively, at least those of my actual attitudes whose justification or point is untouched by my imagined deficient understanding. (In the arthritis case, an example would be a true belief that many old people have arthritis.) These attitude contents remain constant despite the fact that my understanding, inference patterns, behavior, dispositions, and so on would in important ways be different and partly inappropriate to applications of the given notion. What is it that enables these unaffected contents to remain applications of the relevant notion? It is not *just* that my understanding, inference patterns, behavior, and so forth are enough like my actual understanding, inference patterns, behavior, and so forth are enough like my actual understanding, inference patterns, behavior, and so forth. For if communal practice had *also* varied so as to apply the relevant notion as I am imagining I misapply it, then my attitude contents would not involve the relevant notion at all. This argument suggests that communal practice is a factor (in addition to my understanding, inference patterns, and perhaps behavior, physical activity, and other features) in fixing the contents of my attitudes, even in cases where I fully understand the content.

IId. Independence from Factive-Verb and Indexical-Reference Paradigms

The thought experiment does not play on psychological "success" verbs or "factive" verbs – verbs like 'know,' 'regret,' 'realize,' 'remember,' 'foresee,' 'perceive.' This point is important for our purposes because such verbs suggest an easy and clearcut distinction between the contribution of the individual subject and the objective, "veridical" contribution of the environment to making the verbs applicable. (Actually the matter becomes more complicated on reflection, but we shall stay with the simplest cases.) When a person knows that snow is common in Greenland, his knowledge obviously depends on more than the way the person is. It depends on there actually being a lot of snow in Greenland. His mental state (belief that snow is common in Greenland) must be successful in a certain way (true). By changing the environment, one could change the truth value of the content, so that the subject could no longer be said to know the content. It is part of the burden of our argument that even intentional mental states of the individual like beliefs, which carry no implication of veridicality or success, cannot be understood by focusing purely on the individual's acts, dispositions, and "inner" goings on.

The thought experiment also does not rest on the phenomenon of indexicality, or on *de re* attitudes, in any direct way. When Alfred refers to an apple, saying to himself "That is wholesome," what he refers to depends not just on the content of what he says or thinks, but on what apple is before him. Without altering the meaning of Alfred's utterance, the nature of his perceptual experiences, or his physical acts or dispositions, we could conceive an exchange of the actual apple for another one that is indistinguishable to Alfred. We would thereby conceive him as referring to something different and even as saying something with a different truth value.

This rather obvious point about indexicality has come to be seen as providing a model for understanding a certain range of mental states or events – *de re* attitudes. The precise characterization of this range is no simple philosophical task. But the clearest cases involve non-obliquely occurring terms in content clauses. When we say that Bertrand thinks of some water that it would not slake his thirst (where 'water' occurs in purely non-oblique position), we attribute a *de re* belief to Bertrand. We assume that Bertrand has something like an indexical relation to the water. The fact that Bertrand believes something of some water, rather than of a portion of some other liquid that is indistinguishable to him, depends partly on the fact that it is water to which Bertrand is contextually, "indexically" related. For intuitively we could have exchanged the liquids without changing Bertrand and thereby changed what Bertrand believed his belief content *of* – and even whether his belief was true of it.[3] It is easy to interpret such cases by holding that the subject's mental states and contents (with allowances for brute differences in the contexts in which he applies those contents) remain the same. The differences in the situations do not pertain in any fundamental way to the subject's mind or the nature of his mental content, but to how his mind or content is related to the world.

I think this interpretation of standard indexical and *de re* cases is broadly correct, although it involves oversimplifications and demands refinements. But what I want to emphasize here is that it is inapplicable to the cases our thought experiment fixes upon.

It seems to me clear that the thought experiment need not rely on *de re* attitudes at all. The subject need not have entered into special *en rapport* or quasi-indexical relations with objects that the misunderstood term applies to in order for the argument to work. We can appeal to attitudes that would usually be regarded as paradigmatic cases of *de dicto* non-indexical, *non-de re*, mental attitudes or events. The primary mistake in the contract example is one such, but we could choose others to suit the reader's taste. To insist that such attitudes must all be indexically infected or *de re* would, I think, be to trivialize and emasculate these notions, making nearly all attitudes *de re*. All *de dicto* attitudes presuppose *de re* attitudes. But it does not follow that indexical or *de re* elements survive in every attitude. (Cf. footnotes 2 and 3).

I shall not, however, argue this point here. The claim that is crucial is not that our argument does not fix on *de re* attitudes. It is, rather, that the social differences between the actual and counterfactual situations affect the *content* of the subject's attitudes. That is, the difference affects standard cases of obliquely occurring, cognitive-content-conveying expressions in content clauses. For example, still with his misunderstanding, the

---

[3] I have discussed *de re* mental phenomena in (Burge 1977: 338–62). There I argue that all attitudes with content presuppose *de re* attitudes. Our discussion here may be seen as bearing on the details of this presupposition. But for reasons I merely sketch in the next paragraph, I think it would be a superficial viewpoint that tried to utilize our present argument to support the view that nearly all intentional mental phenomena are covertly indexical or *de re*.

subject might think that this (referring to his disease in his hands) is arthritis. Or he might think *de re* of the disease in his ankle (or of the disease in his thigh) that his arthritis is painful. It does not really matter whether the relevant attitude is *de re* or purely *de dicto*. What is crucial to our argument is that the occurrence of 'arthritis' is oblique and contributes to a characterization of the subject's mental content. One might even hold, implausibly I think, that all the subject's attitudes involving the notion of arthritis are *de re*, that 'arthritis' in that-clauses *indexically* picks out the property of being arthritis, or something like that. The fact remains that the term occurs obliquely in the relevant cases and serves in characterizing the *dicta* or contents of the subject's attitudes. The thought experiment exploits this fact.

Approaches to the mental that I shall later criticize as excessively individualistic tend to assimilate environmental aspects of mental phenomena to either the factive-verb or indexical-reference paradigm. (Cf. footnote 2.) This sort of assimilation suggests that one might maintain a relatively clearcut distinction between extramental and mental aspects of mentalistic attributions. And it may encourage the idea that the distinctively mental aspects can be understood fundamentally in terms of the individual's abilities, dispositions, states, and so forth, considered in isolation from his social surroundings. Our argument undermines this latter suggestion. Social context infects even the distinctively mental features of mentalistic attributions. No man's intentional mental phenomena are insular. Every man is a piece of the social continent, a part of the social main.

III. Reinterpretations

I find that most people unspoiled by conventional philosophical training regard the three steps of the thought experiment as painfully obvious. Such folk tend to chafe over my filling in details or elaborating on strategy. I think this naivete appropriate. But for sophisticates the three steps require defense.

Before launching a defense, I want to make a few remarks about its methodology. My objective is to better understand our common mentalistic notions. Although such notions are subject to revision and refinement, I take it as evident that there is philosophical interest in theorizing about them as they now are. I assume that a primary way of achieving theoretical understanding is to concentrate on our *discourse* about mentalistic notions. Now it is, of course, never obvious at the outset how much idealization, regimentation, or special interpretation is necessary in order to adequately understand ordinary discourse. Phenomena such as ambiguity, ellipsis, indexicality, idioms, and a host of others certainly demand some regimentation or special interpretation for purposes of linguistic theory. Moreover, more global considerations – such simplicity in accounting for structural relations – often have effects on the cast of one's theory. For all that, there is a methodological bias in favor of taking natural discourse literally, other things being equal. For example, unless there are clear reasons for construing discourse as ambiguous, elliptical or involving special idioms, we should not so construe it. Literal interpretation is *ceteris paribus* preferred. My defense of the thought experiment, as I have interpreted it, partly rests on this principle.

This relatively non-theoretical interpretation of the thought experiment should be extended to the gloss on it that I provided in Section IIc. The notions of misconception, incomplete understanding, conceptual or linguistic error, and ordinary empirical error are to be taken as carrying little theoretical weight. I assume that these notions mark defensible, common-sense distinctions. But I need not take a position on available philosophical interpretations of these distinctions. In fact, I do not believe that understanding, in our examples, can be explicated as independent of empirical knowledge, or that the conceptual errors of our subjects are best seen as "purely" mistakes about concepts and as involving no "admixture" of error about "the world." With Quine, I find such talk about purity and mixture devoid of illumination or explanatory power. But my views on this matter neither entail nor are entailed by the premises of the arguments I give (cf. e.g., IIId). Those arguments seem to me to remain plausible under any of the relevant philosophical interpretations of the conceptual-ordinary-empirical distinction.

I have presented the experiment as appealing to ordinary intuition. I believe that common practice in the attribution of propositional attitudes is fairly represented by the various steps. This point is not really open to dispute. Usage may be divided in a few of the cases in which I have seen it as united. But broadly speaking, it seems to me undeniable that the individual steps of the thought experiment are acceptable to ordinary speakers in a wide variety of examples. The issue open to possible dispute is whether the steps should be taken in the literal way in which I have taken them, and thus whether the conclusion I have drawn from those steps is justified. In the remainder of Section III, I shall try to vindicate the literal interpretation of our examples. I do this by criticizing, in order of increasing generality or abstractness, a series of attempts to reinterpret the thought experiment's first step. Ultimately, I suggest (IIId and IV) that these attempts derive from characteristically philosophical models that have little or no independent justification. A thoroughgoing review of these models would be out of bounds, but the present paper is intended to show that they are deficient as accounts of our actual practice of mentalistic attribution.

I shall have little further to say in defense of the second and third steps of the thought experiment. Both rest on their intuitive plausibility, not on some particular theory. The third step, for example, certainly does not depend on a view that contents are merely sentences the subject is disposed to utter, interpreted as his community interprets them. It is compatible with several philosophical accounts of mental contents, including those that appeal to more abstract entities such as Fregean thoughts or Russelian propositions, and those that seek to deny that content-clauses indicate any *thing* that might be called a content. I also do not claim that the fact that our subject lacks the relevant beliefs in the third step follows from the facts I have described. The point is that it is plausible, and certainly possible, that he would lack those beliefs.

The exact interpretation of the second step is relevant to a number of causal or functional theories of mental phenomena that I shall discuss in Section IV. The intuitive idea of the step is that none of the different physical, non-intentionally described causal chains set going by the differences in communal practice need affect our subjects in any way that would be relevant to an account of their mental contents. Differences in the behavior or other members of the community will, to be sure, affect the gravitational forces exerted on the subject. But I assume that these differences are irrelevant to macro-explanations of our subjects' physical movements and inner processes. They do not relevantly affect ordinary non-intentional physical explanations of how the subject acquires or is disposed to use the symbols in his repertoire. Of course, the social origins of a person's symbols do differ between actual and counterfactual cases. I shall return to this point in Sections IV and V. The remainder of Section III will be devoted to the first step of the thought experiment.

IIIb. Incomplete Understanding and Standard Cases of Reinterpretation

The first step, as I have interpreted it, is the most likely to encounter opposition. In fact, there is a line or resistance that is second nature to linguistically oriented philosophers. According to this line, we should deny that, say, the patient really believed or thought that arthritis can occur outside of joints because he misunderstood the word 'arthritis.' More generally, we should deny that a subject could have any attitudes whose contents he incompletely understands.

What a person understands is indeed one of the chief factors that bear on what thought he can express in using words. If there were not deep and important connections between propositional attitudes and understanding, one could hardly expect one's attributions of mental content to facilitate reliable predictions of what a person will do, say, or think. But our examples provide reason to believe that these connections are not simple entailments to the effect that having a propositional attitude strictly implies full understanding of its content.

There are, of course, numerous situations in which we normally reinterpret or discount a person's words in deciding what he thinks. Philosophers often invoke such cases to bolster their animus against such attributions as the ones we made to our subjects: "If a foreigner were to mouth the words 'arthritis may occur in the thigh' or 'my father had arthritis,' not understanding what he uttered in the slightest, we would not say that he believed that arthritis may occur in the thigh, or that his father had arthritis. So why should we impute the belief to the patient?" Why, indeed? Or rather, why do we?

The question is a good one. We do want a general account of these cases. But the implied argument against our attribution is anemic. We tacitly and routinely distinguish between the cases I described and those in which a foreigner (or anyone) utters something without any comprehension. The best way to understand mentalistic notions is to recognize such differences in standard practice and try to account for them. One can hardly justify the assumption that full understanding of a content is in general a necessary condition for believing the content by appealing to some cases that tend to support the assumption in order to reject others that conflict with it.

It is a good method of discovery, I think, to note the sorts of cases philosophers tend to gravitate toward when they defend the view that the first step in the thought experiment should receive special interpretation. By reflecting on the differences between these cases and the cases we have cited, one should learn something about principles controlling mentalistic attribution.

I have already mentioned foreigners without command of the language. A child's imitation of our words and early attempts to use them provide similar examples. In these cases, mastery of the language and responsibility to its precepts have not been developed; and mental content attribution based on the meaning of words uttered tends to be precluded.

There are cases involving regional dialects. A person's deviance or ignorance judged by the standards of the larger community may count as normality or full mastery when evaluated from the regional perspective. Clearly, the regional standards tend to be the relevant ones for attributing content when the speaker' training or intentions are regionally oriented. The conditions for such orientation are complex, and I shall touch on them again in Section V. But there is no warrant in actual practice for treating each persons idiolect as always analogous to dialects whose words we automatically reinterpret – for purposes of mental content attribution – when usage is different. People are frequently held and hold themselves, to the standards of their community when misuse or misunderstanding are at issue. One should distinguish these cases, which seem to depend on a certain *responsibility* to communal practice, from cases of automatic reinterpretation.

Tongue slips and Spoonerisms form another class of example where reinterpretation of a person's words is common and appropriate in arriving at an attribution of mental content. In these cases, we tend to exempt the speaker even from commitment to a homophonically formulated assertion content, as well as to the relevant mental content. The speaker's own behavior usually follows this line, often correcting himself when what he uttered is repeated back to him.

Malapropisms form a more complex class of examples. I shall not try to map it in detail. But in a fairly broad range of cases, we reinterpret a person's words at least in attributing mental content. If Archie says, 'Lead the way and we will precede,' we routinely reinterpret the words in describing his expectations. Many of these cases seem to depend on the presumption that there are simple, superficial (for example, phonological) interference or exchange mechanisms that account for the linguistic deviance.

There are also examples of quite radical misunderstandings that sometimes generate reinterpretation. If a generally competent and reasonable speaker thinks that 'orangutan' applies to a fruit drink, we would be reluctant, and it would unquestionably be misleading, to take his words as revealing that he thinks he has been drinking orangutans for breakfast for the last few weeks. Such total misunderstanding often *seems* to block literalistic mental content attribution, at least in cases where we are not directly characterizing his mistake. (Contrary to philosophical lore, I am not convinced that such a man cannot correctly and literally be attributed a belief that an orangutan is a kind of fruit drink. But I shall not deal with the point here.)

There are also some cases that do not seem generally to prevent mental content attribution on the basis of literal interpretation of the subject's words in quite the same way as the others, but which deserve some mention. For almost any content except for those that directly display the subject's incomplete understanding, there will be many contexts in which it would be misleading to attribute that content to the subject without further comment. Suppose I am advising you about your legal liabilities in a situation where you have entered into what may be an unwritten contract. You ask me what Al would think. It would be misleading for me to reply that Al would think that you do not have a contract (or even do not have any legal problems), if I know that Al thinks a contract must be based on a formal document. Your evaluation of Al's thought would be crucially affected by his inadequate understanding. In such cases, it is incumbent on us to cite the subject's eccentricity: "(He would think that you do not have a contract, but then) he thinks that there is no such thing as a verbally based contract."

Incidentally, the same sort of example can be constructed using attitudes that are abnormal, but that do not hinge on misunderstanding of any one notion. If Al had thought that only traffic laws and laws against violent crimes are ever prosecuted, it would be misleading for me to tell you that Al would think that you have no legal problems.

Both sorts of cases illustrate that in reporting a single attitude content, we typically suggest (implicate, perhaps) that the subject has a range of other attitudes that are normally associated with it. Some of these may provide reasons for it. In both sorts of cases, it is usually important to keep track of, and often to make explicit, the nature and extent of the subject's deviance. Otherwise, predictions and evaluations of his thought and action, based on normal background assumptions, will go awry. When the deviance is huge, attributions demand reinterpretation of the subject's words. Radical misunderstanding and mental instability are cases in point. But frequently, common practice seems to allow us to cancel the misleading suggestions by making explicit the subject's deviance, retaining literal interpretation of his words in our mentalistic attributions all the while.

All of the foregoing phenomena are relevant to accounting for standard practice. But they are no more salient than cases of straightforward belief attribution where the subject incompletely understands some notion in the attributed belief content. I think any impulse to say that common practice is *simply* inconsistent should be resisted (indeed, scorned). We cannot expect such practice to follow general principles rigorously. But even our brief discussion of the matter should have suggested the beginnings of generalizations about differences between cases where reinterpretation is standard and cases where it is not. A person's overall linguistic competence, his allegiance and responsibility to communal standards, the degree source, and type of misunderstanding, the purposes of the report – all affect the issue. From a theoretical point of view, it would be a mistake to try to assimilate the cases in one direction or another. We do not want to credit a two-year-old who memorizes 'e=mc^2' with belief in relativity theory. But the patient's attitudes involving the notion of arthritis should not be assimilated to the foreigner's uncomprehending pronunciations.

For purposes of defending the thought experiment and the arguments I draw from it, I can afford to be flexible about exactly how to generalize about these various phenomena. The thought experiment depends only on there being some cases in which a person's incomplete understanding does not force reinterpretation of his expressions in describing his mental contents. Such cases appear to be legion.

IIIc. Four Methods of Reinterpreting the Thought Experiment

I now want to criticize attempts to argue that even in cases where we ordinarily do ascribe content clauses despite the subject's incomplete understanding of expressions in those clauses, such ascriptions should not be taken literally. In order to overturn our interpretation of the thought experiment's first step, one must argue that none of the cases I have cited is appropriately taken in the literal manner. One must handle (apparent) attributions of unproblematically true contents involving incompletely mastered notions, as well as attributions of contents that display the misconceptions or partial understandings. I do not doubt that one can erect logically coherent and metaphysically traditional reinterpretations of all these cases. What I doubt is that such reinterpretations taken *in toto* can present a plausible view, and that taken individually they have any claim to superiority over the literal interpretations – either as accounts of the language of ordinary mentalistic ascription, or as accounts of the evidence on which mental attributions are commonly based.

Four types of reinterpretation have some currency. I shall be rather short with the first two, the first of which I have already warned against in Section IId. Sometimes relevant mentalistic ascriptions are reinterpreted as attributions of *de re* attitudes *of* entities not denoted by the misconstrued expressions. For example, the subject's belief that he has arthritis in the thigh might be interpreted as a belief *of* the non-arthritic rheumatoid ailment that is in the thigh. The subject will probably have such a belief in this case. But it hardly accounts for the relevant attributions. In particular, it ignores the oblique occurrence of 'arthritis' in the original ascription. Such occurrences bear on a characterization of the subject's viewpoint. The subject thinks of the disease in his thigh (and or his arthritis) in a certain way. He thinks of each disease that it is arthritis. Other terms for arthritis (or for the actual trouble in his thigh) may not enable us to describe his attitude content nearly as well. The appeal to *de re* attitudes in this way is not adequate to the task of reinterpreting these ascriptions so as to explain away the difference between actual and counterfactual situations. It simply overlooks what needs explication.

A second method of reinterpretation, which Descartes proposed (cf. Section IV) and which crops up occasionally, is to claim that in cases of incomplete understanding, the subject's attitude or content is indefinite. It is surely true that that in cases where a person is extremely confused, we are sometimes at a loss in describing his attitudes. Perhaps in such cases, the subject's mental content *is* indefinite. But in the cases I have cited, common practice lends virtually no support to the contention that the subject's mental contents are indefinite. The subject and his fellows typically know and agree on precisely *how to confirm or infirm* his beliefs – both in the cases where they are unproblematically true (or just empirically false) and in the cases where they display the misconception. Ordinary attributions typically specify the mental content without qualifications or hesitations.

In cases of partial understanding – say, in the mortgage example – it may indeed be unclear, short of extensive questioning, just how much mastery the subject has. But even this sort of unclarity does not appear to prevent, under ordinary circumstances, straightforward attributions utilizing 'mortgage' in oblique position. The subject is uncertain whether his father has two mortgages; he knows that his uncle has paid off the mortgage on his house. The contents are unhesitatingly attributed and admit of unproblematic testing for truth value, despite the subject's partial understanding. There is thus little *prima facie* ground for the appeal to indefiniteness. The appeal appears to derive from a prior assumption that attribution of a content entails attributions of full understanding. Lacking an easy means of attributing something other than the misunderstood content, one is tempted to say that there *is* no definite content. But this is unnecessarily mysterious. It reflects on the prior assumption, which so far has no independent support.

The other two methods of reinterpretation are often invoked in tandem. One is to attribute a notion that just captures the misconception, thus replacing contents that are apparently false on account of the misconception, by true contents. For example, the subject's belief (true or false) that that is a sofa would be replaced by, or reinterpreted as, a (true) belief that that is a *chofa*, where 'chofa' is introduced to apply not only to sofas, but also to the armchairs the subject thinks are sofas. The other method is to count the error of the subject as purely metalinguistic. Thus the patient's apparent belief that he had arthritis in the thigh would be reinterpreted as a belief that 'arthritis' applied to something (or some disease) in his thigh. The two methods can be applied simultaneously, attempting to account for an ordinary content attribution in terms of a reinterpreted object-level content together with a metalinguistic error. It is important to remember that in order to overturn the thought experiment, these methods must not only establish that the subject held the particular attitudes that they advocate attributing; they must also justify a *denial* of the ordinary attributions literally interpreted.

The method of invoking object-level notions that precisely capture (and that replace) the subject's apparent misconception has little to be said for it as a natural and generally applicable account of the language of mentalistic ascriptions. We do not ordinarily seek out true object-level attitude contents to attribute to victims of errors based on incomplete understanding. For example, when we find that a person has been involved in a misconception in examples like ours, we do not regularly reinterpret those ascriptions that involved the misunderstood term, but were untuitively unaffected by the error. An attribution to someone of a true belief that he is eating brisket, or that he has just signed a contract, or that Uncle Harry has paid off his mortgage, is not typically reformulated when it is learned that the subject has not fully understood what brisket (or a contract, or a mortgage) is. A similar point applies when we know about the error at the time of the attribution – at least if we avoid misleading the audience in cases where the error is crucial to the issue at hand. Moreover, we shall frequently see the subject as sharing beliefs with others who understand the relevant notions better. In counting beliefs as shared, we do not require, in every case, that the subjects "fully understand" the notions in those belief contents, or understand them in just the same way. Differences in understanding are frequently located as differences over other belief contents.

We agree that you have signed a contract, but disagree over whether some-one else could have made a contract by means of a verbal agreement.

There are reasons why ordinary practice does not follow the method of object-level reinterpretation. In many cases, particularly those involving partial understanding, finding a reinterpretation in accord with the method would be entirely nontrivial. It is not even clear that we have agreed upon means of pursuing such inquiries in all cases. Consider the arthritic patient. Suppose we are to reinterpret the attribution of his erro-neous belief that he has arthritis in the thigh. We make up a term 'tharthri-tis' that covers arthritis and whatever it is he has in his thigh. The appropriate restrictions on the application of this term and of the patient's supposed notion are unclear. Is just any problem in the thigh that the patient wants to call 'arthritis' to count as tharthritis? Are other ailments covered? What would decide? The problem is that there are no recognized standards governing the application of the new term. In such cases, the method is patently *ad hoc*.

The method's willingness to invoke new terminology whenever con-ceptual error or partial understanding occurs is *ad hoc* in another sense. It proliferates terminology without evident theoretical reward. We do not engender better understanding of the patient by inventing a new word and saying that he thought (correctly) that tharthritis can occur outside joints. It is simpler and equally informative to construe him as thinking that arthritis may occur outside joints. When we are making other attributions that do not directly display the error, we must simply bear the deviant belief in mind, so as not to assume that all of the patient's inferences involving the notion would be normal.

The method of object-level reinterpretation often fails to give a plausi-ble account of the evidence on which we base mental attributions. When caught in the sorts of errors we have been discussing, the subject does not normally respond by saying that his views had been misunderstood. The patient does not say (or think) that he had thought he had some-category-of-disease-like-arthritis-and-including-arthritis-but-also-capable-of-occurring-outside-of-joints in the thigh *instead* of the error commonly attributed. This sort of response would be disingenuous. Whatever other beliefs he had, the subject thought that he had arthritis in the thigh. In such cases, the subject will ordinarily give no evidence of having main-tained a true object-level belief. In examples like ours, he typically admits his mistake, changes his views, and leaves it at that. Thus the subject's own behavioral dispositions and inferences often fail to support the method.

The method may be seen to be implausible as an account of the relevant evidence in another way. The patient knows that he has had arthritis in the ankle and wrists for some time. Now with his new pains in the thigh, he fears and believes that he has got arthritis in the thigh, that his arthritis is spreading. Suppose we reinterpret all of these attitude attributions in accord with the method. We use our recently coined term 'tharthritis' to cover (somehow) arthritis and whatever it is he has in the thigh. On this new interpretation, the patient is right in thinking that he has tharthritis in the ankle and wrists. His belief that it has lodged in the thigh is true. His fear is realized. But these attributions are out of keeping with the way we do and should view his actual beliefs and fears. His belief is not true, and his fear is not realized. His relief is bound up with a network of assumptions that he makes about his arthritis: that it is a kind of disease, that there are debilitating consequences of its occurring in multiple locations, and so on. When told that arthritis cannot occur in the thigh, the patient does not decide that his fears were realized, but that perhaps he should not have had those fears. he does not think: Well, my tharthritis *has* lodged in the thigh; but judging from the fact that what the doctor called "arthritis" cannot occur in thigh, tharthritis may not be a single kind of disease; and I suppose I need not worry about the effects of its occurring in various locations, since evidently the tharthritis in my thigh is physiologically unrelated to the tharthritis in my joints. There will rarely if ever be an empirical basis for such a description of the subject's inferences. The patient's behavior (including his reports, or thinkings-out-loud) in this sort of case will normally not indicate any such pattern of inferences at all. But this is the description that the object-level reinterpretation method appears to recommend.

On the standard attributions, the patient retains his assumptions about the relation between arthritis, kinds of disease, spreading, and so on. And he concludes that his arthritis is not appearing in new locations – at any rate, not in his thigh. These attributions will typically be supported by the subject's behavior. The object-level reinterpretation method postulates inferences that are more complicated and different in focus from the inferences that the evidence supports. The method's presentation in such a case would seem to be an *ad hoc* fiction, not a description with objective validity.

None of the foregoing is meant to deny that frequently when a person incompletely understands an attitude content he has some other attitude content that more or less captures his understanding. For example, in the contract example, the client will probably have the belief that if one breaks *a legally binding agreement based on formal documents,* then one may get into trouble. There are also cases in which it is reasonable to say that, at least in a sense, a person has a notion that is expressed by his dispositions to classify things in a certain way – even if there is no conventional term in the person's repertoire that neatly corresponds to that "way." The sofa case may be one such. Certain animals as well as people may have nonverbal notions of this sort. On the other hand, the fact that such attributions are justifiable *per se* yields no reason to deny that the subject (also) has object-level attitudes whose contents involve the relevant incompletely understood notion.

Whereas the third method purports to account for the subject's thinking at the object level, the fourth aims at accounting for his error. The error is construed as purely a metalinguistic mistake. The relevant false content is seen to involve notions that denote or apply to linguistic expressions. In examples relevant to our thought experiment, we ordinarily attribute a metalinguistic as well as an object-level attitude to the subject, at least in the case of non-occurrent propositional attitudes. For example, the patient probably believes that 'arthritis' applies in English to the ailment in his thigh. He believes that his father had a disease called "arthritis." And so on. Accepting these metalinguistic attributions, of course, does nothing *per se* toward making plausible a denial that the subjects in our examples have the counterpart object-level attitudes.

Like the third method, the metalinguistic reinterpretation method has no *prima facie* support as an account of the language of mentalistic ascriptions. When we encounter the subject's incomplete understanding in examples like ours, we do not decide that all the mental contents which we had been attributing to him with the misunderstood notion must have been purely metalingustic in form. We also count people who incompletely understanding terms in ascribed content clauses as sharing true and unproblematic object-level attitudes with others who understand the relevant terms better. For example, the lawyer and his client may share a wish that the client had not signed for the contract to buy the house without reading the small print. A claim that these people share *only* attitudes with metalinguistic contents would have no support in linguistic practice.

The point about shared attitudes goes further. If the metalinguistic reinterpretation account is to be believed, we cannot say that a relevant English speaker shares a view (for example) that many old people have arthritis, with *anyone* who does not use the English word 'arthritis'. For the foreigner does not have the word 'arthritis' to hold beliefs about, though he does have attitudes involving the notion arthritis. And the attribution to the English speaker is to be interpreted metalinguistically, making reference to the word, so as not to involve attribution of the notion arthritis. This result is highly implausible. Ascriptions of such that-clauses as the above, regardless of the subject's language, serve to provide single descriptions and explanations of similar patterns of behavior, inference, and communication. To hold that we cannot accurately ascribe single content-clauses to English speakers and foreigners in such cases would not only accord badly with linguistic practice. It would substantially weaken the descriptive and explanatory power of our common attributions. In countless cases, unifying accounts of linguistically disparate but cognitive and behaviorally similar phenomena would be sacrificed.

The method is implausible in other cases as an account of standard evidence on which mental attributions are based. Take the patient who fears that his arthritis is spreading. According to the metalinguistic reinterpretation method, the patient's reasoning should be described as follows. He thinks that the word 'arthritis' applies to a single disease in him, that the disease in him called "arthritis" is debilitating if it spreads, that 'arthritis' applies to the disease in his wrists and ankles. He fears that the disease called "arthritis" has lodged in his thigh, and so on. Of course, it is often difficult to find evidential grounds for attributing an object-level attitude *as opposed* to its metalinguistic counterpart. As I noted, when a person holds one attitude, he often holds the other. But there are types of evidence, in certain contexts, for making such discriminations, particularly contexts in which *occurrent* mental events are at issue. The subject may maintain that his reasoning did not fix upon words. He may be brought up short by a metalinguistic formulation of his just-completed ruminations, and may insist that he was not interested in labels. In such cases, especially if the reasoning is not concerned with linguistic issues in any informal or antecedently plausible sense, attribution of an object-level thought content is supported by the relevant evidence, and metalinguistic attribution is not. To insist that the occurrent mental event really involved a metalinguistic content would be a piece of *ad hoc* special pleading, undermined by the evidence we actually use for deciding whether a thought was metalinguistic.

In fact, there appears to be a general presumption that a person is reasoning at the object level, other things being equal. The basis for this presumption is that metalinguistic reasoning requires a certain self-consciousness about one's words and social institutions. This sort of sophistication emerged rather late in human history. (Cf. any history of linguistics.) Semantical notions were a product of this sophistication.

Occurrent propositional attitudes prevent the overall reinterpretation strategy from providing a plausible total account which would block our thought experiment. For such occurrent mental events as the patient's thought that his arthritis is especially painful in the knee this morning are, or can be imagined to be, clear cases of object-level attitudes. And such thoughts may enter into or connect up with pieces of reasoning – say the reasoning leading to relief that the arthritis had not lodged in the thigh – which cannot be plausibly accounted for in terms of object-level reinterpretation. The other reinterpretation methods (those that appeal to *de re* contents and to indefiniteness) are non-starters. In such examples, the literally interpreted ascriptions appear to be straightforwardly superior accounts of the evidence that is normally construed to be relevant. Here one need not appeal to the principle that literal interpretation is, other things equal, preferable to reinterpretation. Other things are not equal.

At this point, certain philosophers may be disposed to point out that what a person says and how he behaves do not infallibly determine what his attitude contents are. Despite the apparent evidence, the subject's attitude contents may in all cases I cited be metalinguistic, and may fail to involve the incompletely understood notion. It is certainly true that how a person acts and what he says, even sincerely, do not determine his mental contents. I myself have mentioned a number of cases that support the point. (Cf. IIIb.) But the point is often used in a sloppy and irresponsible manner. It is incumbent on someone making it (and applying it to cases like ours) to indicate considerations that override the linguistic and behavioral evidence. In Section IIId, I shall consider intuitive or *a priori* philosophical arguments to this end. But first I wish to complete our evaluation of the metalinguistic reinterpretation method as an account of the language of mentalistic ascription in our examples.

In this century philosophers have developed the habit of insisting on metalinguistic reinterpretation for any content attribution that directly *displays* the subject's incomplete understanding. These cases constitute but a small number of the attributions that serve the thought experiment. One could grant these reinterpretations and still maintain our overall viewpoint. But even as applied to these cases, the method seems dubious. I doubt that any evidentially supported account of the language of these attributions will show them in general to be attributions of metalinguistic contents – contents that involve denotative reference to linguistic expressions.

The ascription 'He believes that broad overstuffed armchairs are sofas,' as ordinarily used, does not in general *mean* "He believes that broad, overstuffed armchairs are covered by the expression 'sofas'" (or something like that). There are clear grammatical and semantical differences between

(i) broad, overstuffed armchairs are covered by the expression 'sofas'

and

(ii) broad, overstuffed armchairs are sofas.

When the two are embedded in belief contexts, they produce grammatically and semantically distinct sentences.

As noted, ordinary usage approves ascriptions like

(iii) He believes that broad, overstuffed armchairs are sofas.

It would be wildly *ad hoc* and incredible from the point of view of linguistic theory to claim that there is *no* reading of (iii) that embeds (ii). But there is no evidence from speaker behavior that *true* ascriptions of (iii) always (or perhaps even *ever*) derive from embedding (i) rather than (ii). In fact, I know of no clear evidence that (iii) is ambiguous between embedding (i) and (ii), or that (ii) is ambiguous, with one reading identical to that of (i). People do not in general seem to regard ascriptions like (iii) as elliptical. More important, in most cases no amount of nonphilosophical badgering will lead them to withdraw (iii), under some interpretation, *in favor of* an ascription that clearly embeds (i). At least in the cases of *non-occurrent* propositional attitudes, they will tend to agree to a clearly metalinguistic ascription – a belief sentence explicitly embedding something like (i) – in cases where they make an ascription like (iii). But this is evidence that they regard ascriptions that embed (i) and (ii) as both true. It hardly tells against counting belief ascriptions that embed (ii) as true, or against taking (iii) in the obvious, literal manner. In sum, there appears to be no ordinary empirical pressure on a theory of natural language to represent true ascriptions like (iii) as *not* embedding sentences like (ii). And other things being equal, literal readings are correct readings. Thus it is strongly plausible to assume that ordinary usage routinely accepts as true and justified even ascriptions like (iii), literally interpreted as embedding sentences like (ii).

There are various contexts in which we may be indifferent over whether to attribute a metalinguistic attitude or the corresponding object-level attitude. I have emphasized that frequently, though not always, we may attribute both. Or we might count the different contents as describing what contextually "amount to the same attitude." (Cf. Section I.) Even this latter locution remains compatible with the thought experiment, as long as both contents are *equally attributable* in describing "the attitude." In the counterfactual step of the thought experiment, the metalinguistic content (say, that broad, overstuffed armchairs are called "sofas") will still be attributable. But in these circumstances it contextually "amounts to the same attitude" as an object-level attitude whose content is in no sense equivalent to, or "the same as," the original object-level content. For they have different truth values. Thus, assuming that the object-level and metalinguistic contents are equally attributable, it remains informally plausible that the person's attitudes are different between actual and counterfactual steps in the thought experiment. This contextual conflation of object-level and metalinguistic contents is not, however, generally acceptable even in describing non-occurrent attitudes, much less occurrent ones. There are contexts in which the subject himself may give evidence of making the distinction.

IIId. Philosophical Arguments for Reinterpretation

I have so far argued that the reinterpretation strategies that I have cited do not provide a plausible account of evidence relevant to a theory of the language of mentalistic ascriptions or to descriptions of mental phenomena themselves. I now want to consider characteristically philosophical arguments for revising ordinary discourse or for giving it a nonliteral reading, arguments that rely purely on intuitive or *a priori* considerations. I have encountered three such arguments, or argument sketches.[4]

---

[4] Cf. Burge (1978, pp. 119–38), Section III, where I concentrate on attribution of belief contents containing "one criterion" terms like 'vixen' or 'fortnight' which the subject misunderstands. The next several pages interweave some of the points in that paper. I think that a parallel thought experiment involving even these words is constructible, at least for a narrowly restricted set of beliefs. We can imagine that the subject believes that some female foxes – say, those that are virgins – are not vixens. Or he could believe that a fortnight is a period of ten days. (I believed this for many years.) Holding his physical history, qualitative experience, and dispositions constant, we can conceive of his linguistic community defining these terms as he actually misunderstands them. In such a case, his belief contents would differ from his actual ones.

One holds that the content clauses we ascribed must be reinterpreted so as to make reference to words because they clearly concern linguistic matters – or are about language. Even if this argument were sound, it would not affect the though experiment decisively. For most of the mental contents that vary between actual and counterfactual situations are not in any intuitive sense "linguistic." The belief that certain armchairs are sofas is intuitively linguistic. But beliefs that some sofas are beige, that Kirkpatrick is playing a clavichord, and that Milton has severe arthritis in his hands are not.

But the argument is unpersuasive even as applied to the contents that, in an intuitive sense, do concern linguistic matters. A belief that broad, overstuffed armchairs are sofas is linguistic (or "about" language) in the same senses as an "analytically" true belief that no armchairs are sofas. But the linguistic nature of the latter belief does not make its logical form metalinguistic. So citing the linguistic nature of the formal belief does not suffice to show it metalinguistic. No semantically relevant component of either content applies to or denotes linguistic expressions.

Both the "analytically" true and the "analytically" false attitudes are linguistic in the sense that they are tested by consulting a dictionary or native linguistic intuitions, rather than by ordinary empirical investigation. We do not scrutinize pieces of furniture to test these beliefs. The pragmatic focus of expressions of these attitudes will be on usage, concepts, or meaning. But it is simply a mistake to think that these facts entail, or even suggest, that the relevant contents are metalinguistic in form. Many contents with object-level logical forms have primarily linguistic or conceptual implications.

A second argument holds that charitable interpretation requires that we not attribute to rational people beliefs like the belief that one may have arthritis in the thigh. Here again, the argument obviously does not touch most of the attitudes that may launch the thought experiment; for many are straightforwardly true, or false on ordinary empirical grounds. Even so, it is not a good argument. There is nothing irrational or stupid about the linguistic or conceptual errors we attribute to our subjects. The errors are perfectly understandable as results of linguistic misinformation.

In fact, the argument makes sense only against the background of the very assumption that I have been questioning. A belief that arthritis may occur in the thigh appears to be inexplicable or uncharitably attributed only if it is assumed that the subject must fully understand the notions in his attitude contents.

A third intuitive or *a priori* argument is perhaps the most interesting. Sometimes it is insisted that we should not attribute contents involving incompletely understood notions because *the individual must mean something different by the misunderstood word than what we non-deviant speakers mean by it.* Note again that it would not be enough to use this argument from deviant speaker meaning to show that the subject has notions that are not properly expressed in the way he thinks they are. In some sense of 'expressed', this is surely often the case. To be relevant, the argument must arrive at a negative conclusion: that the subject cannot have the attitudes that seem commonly to be attributed.

The expression 'the individual meant something different by his words' can be interpreted in more than one way. On one group of interpretations, the expression says little more than that the speaker incompletely understood his words: The patient thought 'arthritis' meant something that included diseases that occur outside of joints. The client would have misexplained the meaning, use, or application of 'contract.' The subject applied 'sofa' to things that, unknown to him, are not sofas. A second group of interpretations emphasizes that not only does the speaker misconstrue or misapply his words, but he had *in mind* something that the words do not denote or express. The subject sometimes had in mind certain armchairs when he used 'sofa.' The client regarded the notion of legal agreement based on written documents as approximately interchangeable with what is expressed by 'contract,' and thus had such a notion in mind when he used 'contract.' A person with a problem about the range of red might sometimes have in mind a mental image of a non-red color when he used 'red.'

The italicized premise of the argument is, of course, always true in our examples under the first group of interpretations, and often true under the second. But interpreted in these ways, the argument is a *non sequitir.* It does not follow from the assumption that the subject thought that a word means something that it does not (or misapplies the word, or is disposed to misexplain its meaning) that the word cannot be used in literally describing his mental contents. It does not follow from the assumption that a person has in mind something that a word does not denote or express that the word cannot occur obliquely (and be interpreted literally) in that-clauses that provide some of his mental contents. As I have pointed out in Section IIIb, there is a range of cases in which we commonly reinterpret a person's incompletely understood words for purposes of mental-content attribution. But the present argument needs to show that deviant speaker-meaning always forces such reinterpretation.

In many of our examples, the idea that the subject has some deviant notion *in mind* has no intuitively clear application. (Consider the arthritis and mortgage examples.) But even where this expression does seem to apply, the argument does not support the relevant conclusion. At best it shows that a notion deviantly associated with a word plays a role in the subject's attitudes. For example, someone who has in mind the notion of an agreement based on written documents when he says, "I have just entered into a contract," may be correctly said to believe that he has just entered into an agreement based on written documents. It does not follow from this that he *lacks* a belief or thought that he has just entered into a contract. In fact, in our view, the client's having the deviant notion in mind is a *likely consequence* of the fact that he believes that contracts are impossible without a written document.

Of course, given the first, more liberal set of interpretations of 'means something different,' the fact that in our examples the subject means something different by his words (or at least applies them differently) is *implied* by certain of his beliefs. It is implied by a belief that he has arthritis in the thigh. A qualified version of the converse implication also holds. Given appropriate background assumptions, the fact that the subject has certain deviant (object-level) beliefs is implied by his meaning something different by his words. So far, no argument has shown that we cannot accept these implications and retain the literal interpretation of common mentalistic ascriptions.

The argument from deviant speaker-meaning downplays an intuitive feature that can be expected to be present in many of our examples. The subject's willingness to submit his statement and belief to the arbitration of an authority suggests a willingness to have his words taken in the normal way – regardless of mistaken associations with the word. Typically, the subject will regard recourse to a dictionary, and to the rest of us, as at once a check on his usage and his belief. When the verdict goes against him, he will not usually plead that we have simply misunderstood his views. This sort of behavior suggests that (given the sorts of background assumptions that common practice uses to distinguish our examples from those of foreigners, radical misunderstandings, and so forth) we can say that in a sense our man meant by 'arthritis' *arthritis* – where '*arthritis*' occurs, of course, obliquely. We can say this despite the fact that his incomplete understanding leads us, in one of the senses explicated earlier, to say that he meant something different by 'arthritis.'

If one tries to turn the argument from deviant speaker-meaning into a valid argument, one arrives at an assumption that seems to guide all three of the philosophical arguments I have discussed. The assumption is that what a person thinks his words mean, how he takes them, fully determines what attitudes he can express in using them: the contents of his mental states and events are strictly limited to notions, however idiosyncratic, that he understands; a person cannot think with notions he incompletely understands. But supplemented with this assumption, the argument begs the question at issue.

The least controversial justification of the assumption would be an appeal to standard practice in mentalistic attributions. But standard practice is what brought the assumption into question in the first place. Of course, usage is not sacred if good reasons for revising it can be given. But none have been.

The assumption is loosely derived, I think, from the old model according to which a person must be directly acquainted with, or must immediately apprehend, the contents of his thoughts. None of the objections explicitly invoke this model – and many of their proponents would reject it. But I think that all the objections derive some of their appeal from philosophical habits that have been molded by it. I shall discuss this model further in Section IV.

One may, of course, quite self-consciously neglect certain aspects of common mentalistic notions in the interests of a revised or idealized version of them. One such idealization could limit itself to just those attitudes involving "full understanding" (for some suitably specified notion of understanding). This limitation is less clearcut than one might suppose, since the notion of understanding itself tends to be used according to misleading stereotypes. Still, oversimplified models, idealizations, of mentalistic notions are defensible, as long as the character and purpose of the oversimplifications are clear. In my opinion, limiting oneself to "fully understood" attitudes provides no significant advantage in finding elegant and illuminating formal semantical theories of natural language. Such a strategy has perhaps a better claim in psychology, though even there its propriety is controversial. (Cf. Section IV.) More to the point, I think that models that neglect the relevant social factors in mentalistic attributions are not likely to provide long-run philosophical illumination of our actual mentalistic notions. But this view hardly admits of detailed support here and now.

Our argument in the preceding pages may, at a minimum, be seen as inveighing against a long-standing philosophical habit of denying that it *is* an oversimplification to make "full understanding" of a content a necessary condition for having a propositional attitude with that content. The oversimplification does not constitute neglect of some quirk of ordinary usage. Misunderstanding and partial understanding are pervasive and inevitable phenomena, and attributions of content despite them are an integral part of common practice.

I shall not here elaborate a philosophical theory of the social aspects of mentalistic phenomena, though in Section V I shall suggest lines such a theory might take. One of the most surprising and exciting aspects of the thought experiment is that its most literal interpretation provides a perspective on the mental that has received little serious development in the philosophical tradition. The perspective surely invites exploration.

IV. Applications

I want to turn now to a discussion of how our argument bears on philosophical approaches to the mental that may be termed *individualistic*. I mean this term to be somewhat vague. But roughly, I intend to apply it to philosophical treatments that seek to see a person's intentional mental phenomena ultimately and purely in terms of what happens to the person, what occurs within him, and how he responds to his physical environment, without any essential reference to the social context in which he or the interpreter of his mental phenomena are situated. How I apply the term 'individualistic' will perhaps become clearer by reference to the particular cases that I shall discuss.

a. As I have already intimated, the argument of the preceding sections affects the traditional intro- (or extro-) spectionist treatments of the mind, those of Plato, Descartes, Russell, and numerous others. These treatments are based on a model that likens the relation between a person and the contents of his thought to seeing, where seeing is taken to be a kind of direct, immediate experience. On the most radical and unqualified versions of the model, a person's inspection of the contents of his thought is infallible: the notion of incompletely understanding them has no application at all.

The model tends to encourage individualistic treatments of the mental. For it suggests that what a person thinks depends on what occurs or "appears" within his mind. Demythologized, what a person thinks depends on the power and extent of his comprehension and on his internal dispositions toward the comprehended contents. The model is expressed in perhaps its crudest and least qualified form in a well-known passage by Russell:

> Whenever a relation of supposing or judging occurs, the terms to which the supposing or judging mind is related by the relation of supposing or judging must be terms with which the mind in question is acquainted.... It seems to me that the truth of this principle is evident as soon as the principle is understood.[5]

Acquaintance is (for Russell) direct, infallible, non-propositional, non-perspectival knowledge. "Terms" like concepts, ideas, attributes, forms, meanings, or senses are entities that occur in judgments more or less immediately before the mind on a close analogy to the way sensations are supposed to.

The model is more qualified and complicated in the writings of Descartes. In particular, he emphasizes the possibility that one might perceive the contents of one's mind unclearly or indistinctly. He is even high-handed enough to write, "Some people throughout their lives perceive nothing so correctly as to be capable of judging it properly."[6] This sort of remark appears to be a concession to the points made in Sections I and II about the possibility of a subject's badly understanding his mental contents. But the concession is distorted by the underlying introspection model. On Descartes' view, the person's faculty of understanding, properly so-called, makes no errors. Failure to grasp one's mental contents results from either blind prejudice or interference by "mere" bodily sensations and corporeal imagery. The implication is that with sufficiently careful reflection on the part of the individual subject, these obstacles to perfect understanding can be cleared. That is, one need only be careful or properly guided in one's introspections to achieve full understanding of

---

[5] Cf. Russell (1959, p. 221). Although Russell's statement is unusually unqualified, its kinship to Descartes' and Plato's model is unmistakable. Cf. Plato, *Phaedrus*, 249b–c, *Phaedo*, 47b6–c4; Descartes (1955), *Rules for the Direction of the Mind*, section XII, Vol. I, pp. 41–42, 45; *Principles of Philosophy*, Part I, XXXII–XXXV. Vol. I, pp. 232–33; *Replies*, Vol. II, 52; Hume, *A Treatise of Human Nature*, 1,3, 5; II, 2,6; Kant, *A Critique of Pure Reason*, A7–B11; Frege, *The Foundations of Arithmetic*, section 105; G.E. Moore, *Principia Ethica*, 86.

[6] Descartes, *Principles of Philosophy*, XLV–XLI.

the content of one's intentional mental phenomena. Much that Descartes says suggests that where the subject fails to achieve such understanding, no definite content can be attributed to him. In such cases, his "thinking" consists of unspecifiable or indeterminate imagery; attribution of definite conceptual content is precluded. These implications are reinforced in Descartes' appeal to self-evident, indubitable truths:

> There are some so evident and at the same time so simple that we cannot think of them without believing them to be true.... For we cannot doubt them unless we think of them; and we cannot think of them without at the same time believing them to be true, i.e. we can never doubt them.[7]

The self-evidence derives from the mere understanding of the truths, and fully understanding them is a precondition for thinking them at all. It is this last requirement that we have been questioning.

In the Empiricist tradition Descartes' qualifications on the direct experience model – particularly those involving the interfering effects of sensations and imagery – tend to fall away. What one thinks comes to be taken as a sort of impression (whether more imagistic or more intellectual) on or directly grasped by the individual's mind. The tendency to make full comprehension on the part of the subject a necessary condition for attributing a mental content to him appears both in philosophers who take the content to be a Platonic abstraction and in those who place it, in some sense, inside the individual's mind. This is certainly the direction in which the model pulls, with its picture of immediate accessibility to the individual. Thus Descartes' original concessions to cases of incomplete understanding became lost as his model became entrenched. What Wölfflin said of painters is true of philosophers: they learn more from studying each other than from reflecting on anything else.

The history of the model makes an intricate subject. My remarks are meant merely to provide a suggestive caricature of it. It should be clear, however, that in broad outline the model mixes poorly with the thought experiment of Section II, particularly its first step. The thought experiment indicates that certain "linguistic truths" that have often been held to be indubitable can be thought yet doubted. And it shows that a person's thought *content* is not fixed by what goes on in him, or by what is accessible to him simply by careful reflection. The reason for this last point about

---

[7] Descartes, *Philosophical Works*, Vol. II., *Replies*, p. 42.

"accessibility" need not be that the content lies too deep in the uncon-scious recesses of the subject's psyche. Contents are sometimes "inaccessi-ble" to introspection simply because much mentalistic attribution does not presuppose that the subject has fully mastered the content of his thought.

In a certain sense, the metaphysical model has fixed on some features of our use of mentalistic notions to the exclusion of others. For example, the model fastens on the facts that we are pretty good at identifying our own beliefs and thoughts, and we have at least a *prima facie* authority in reporting a wide range of them. It also underlines the point that for cer-tain contents we tend to count understanding as a sufficient condition for acknowledging their truth. (It is debatable, of course, how well it explains or illumines these observations.) The model also highlights the truism that a certain measure of understanding is required of a subject if we are to attribute intentional phenomena on the basis of what he utters. As we have noted, chance or purely rote utterances provide no ground for men-tal content attributions; certain verbal pathologies are discounted. The model extrapolates from these observations to the claim that a person can never fail to understand the content of his beliefs or thoughts, or that the remedy for such failure lies within his own resources of reflection (whether autonomous and conscious, or unconscious and guided). It is this extrapolation that requires one to pass over the equally patent practice of attributing attitudes where the subject incompletely understands expressions that provide the content of those attitudes. Insistence on met-alinguistic reinterpretation and talk about the indefiniteness of attitude contents in cases of incomplete understanding seem to be rearguard defenses of a vastly overextended model.

The Cartesian-Russellian model has few strict adherents among promi-nent linguistic philosophers. But although it has been widely rejected or politely talked around, claims that it bore and nurtured are commonplace, even among its opponents. As we have seen in the objections to the first step of the argument of Section II, these claims purport to restrict the contents we can attribute to a person on the basis of his use of language. The restrictions simply mimic those of Descartes. Freed of the picturesque but vulnerable model that formed them, the claims have assumed the power of dogma. Their strictures, however, misrepresent ordinary men-talistic notions.

b. This century's most conspicuous attempt to replace the traditional Cartesian model has been the behaviorist movement and its heirs. I take it as obvious that the argument of Section II provides yet another reason to reject the most radical version of behaviorism – "philosophical," "logical" or "analytical" behaviorism. This is the view that mentalistic attributions can be "analytically" defined, or given strict meaning equivalences, purely in non-mental, behavioral terms. No analysis resting purely on the individual's dispositions to behavior can give an "analytic" definition of a mental content attribution because we can conceive of the behavioral definiens applying while the mentalistic definiendum does not. But a new argument for this conclusion is hardly needed since "philosophical" behaviorists are, in effect, extinct.

There is, however, an heir of behaviorism that I want to discuss at somewhat greater length. The approach sometimes goes by the name "functionalism," although that term is applied to numerous slogans and projects, often vaguely formulated. Even views that seem to me to be affected by our argument are frequently stated so sketchily that one may be in considerable doubt about what is being proposed. So my remarks should be taken less as an attempt to refute the theses of particular authors than as an attack on a way of thinking that seems to inform a cluster of viewpoints. The quotations I give in footnotes are meant to be suggestive, if not always definitive, of the way of thinking the argument tells against.[8]

The views affected by the argument in Section II attempts to give something like a philosophical "account" of the mental. The details and strategy – even the notion of "account" – vary from author to author. But a recurrent theme is that mental notions are to be seen ultimately in terms of the individual subject's input, output, and inner dispositions and states, where these latter are characterized purely in terms of how they lead to or from output, input, or other inner states similarly characterized. Mental notions are to be explicated or identified in functional, non-mentalistic,

---

[8] Certain movements sometimes called "functionalist" are definitely not my present concern. Nothing I say is meant to oppose the claim that hypotheses in psychology do and should make reference to "sub-personal" states and processes in explaining human action and ordinary mental states and processes. My remarks may bear on precisely how such hypotheses are construed philosophically. But the hypotheses themselves must be judged primarily by their fruits. Similarly, I am not concerned with the claim that computers provide an illuminating perspective for viewing the mind. Again, our view may bear on the interpretation of the computer analogy, but I have no intention of questioning its general fruitfulness. On the other hand, insofar as functionalism is merely a slogan to the effect that "once you see how computers might be made to work, you realize such and such about the mind," I am inclined to let the cloud condense a little before weighing its contents.

non-intentional terminology. Proponents of this sort of idea are rarely very specific about what terms may be used in describing input and output, or even what sorts of terms count as "functional" expressions. But the impression usually given is that input and output are to be specified in terms (acceptable to a behaviorist) of irritations of the subject's surfaces and movements of his body. On some versions, neurophysiological terms are allowed. More recently, there have been liberalized appeals to causal input and output relations with particular, specified physical objects, stuffs, or magnitudes. Functional terms include terms like 'causes,' 'leads,' to with probability n,' and the like. For our purposes, the details do not matter much, as long as an approach allows no mentalistic or other intentional terms (such as 'means' or that-clauses) into its vocabulary, and as long as it applies to individuals taken one by one.

A difference between this approach and that of philosophical behaviorism is that a whole array of dispositional or functional states – causally or probabilistically interrelated – may enter into the "account" of a single mental attribution. The array must be ultimately secured to input and output, but the internal states need not be so secured one by one. The view is thus not immediately vulnerable to claims against simplistic behaviorisms, that a *given* stimulus-response pattern may have different contents in different social contexts. Such claims, which hardly need a defender, have been tranquilly accepted on this view. The view's hope is that differences in content depend on functional differences in the individual's larger functional structure. From this viewpoint, analytical behaviorism erred primarily in its failure to recognize the interlocking or wholistic character of mental attributions and in its oversimplification of theoretical explanation.

As I said, the notion of an account of the mental varies from author to author. Some authors take over the old-fashioned ideal of an "analysis" from philosophical behaviorism and aim at a definition of the meaning of mentalistic vocabulary, or a definitional elimination of it. Others see their account as indicating a series of scientific hypotheses that identify mental states with causal or functional states, or roles, in the individual. These authors reject behaviorism's goal of providing meaning equivalences, as well as its restrictive methods. The hypotheses are supposed to be type or property identities and are nowadays often thought to hold necessarily, even if they do not give meaning relations. Moreover, these hypotheses are offered not merely as speculation about the future of psychology, but as providing a philosophically illuminating account of our ordinary notion of the mental. Thus if the view systematically failed to make plausible type identities between functional states and mental states, ordinarily construed, then by its own lights it would have failed to give a philosophical "account" of the mental. I have crudely over-schematized the methodological differences among the authors in this tradition. But the differences fall roughly within the polar notions of *account* that I have described. I think our discussion will survive the oversimplification.[9]

Any attempt to give an account of specific beliefs and thoughts along the lines I have indicated will come up short. For we may fix the input, output, and total array of dispositional or functional states of our subject, as long as these are non-intentionally described and are limited to what is

---

[9] A representative of the more nearly "analytical" form of functionalism is David Lewis, (1972, pp. 249–58): "Applied to common-sense psychology–folk science rather than professional science, but a theory nonetheless – we get the hypothesis ... that a mental state M ... is definable as the occupant of a certain causal role R – that is, as the state, of whatever sort, that is causally connected in specified ways to sensory stimuli, motor responses, and other mental states" (249–50). Actually, it should be noted that the argument of Section I applies to Lewis's position less directly than one might suppose. For reasons unconnected with matters at hand, Lewis intends his *definition* to apply to relational mentalistic predicates like 'thinks' but not to complex predicates that identify actual mental states or events, like 'thinks that snow is white'. Cf. *Ibid.*, p. 256, n13. This seems to me a puzzling halfway house for some of Lewis's philosophical purposes. But our argument appears to apply anyway, since Lewis is explicit in holding that physical facts about a person taken in isolation from his fellows "determine" all his specific intentional events and states. Cf. (Lewis, 1974 p. 331 ff.) I cite Lewis's definitional approach because it has been the most influential recent piece of its genre, and many of those influenced by it have not excluded its application to specific intentional mental states and events. Other representatives of the definitional approach are J.J.C. Smart (1972, pp. 149–62); D. M. Armstrong (1968, pp. 90–91) and *passim*; Sidney Shoemaker (1975, pp. 306–7). A representative of the more frequently held "hypothesis" version of functionalism is Hilary Putnam (1975b), and (1975c, p. 437): "... if the program of finding psychological laws that are not species specific ... ever succeeds, then it will bring it its wake a delineation of the kind of functional organization that is necessary and sufficient for a given psychological state, as well as a precise definition of the notion 'psychological state'." In more recent work, Putnam's views on the relation between functional organization and psychological (and also mental) states and events have become more complicated. I make no claims about how the argument of Section II bears on them. Other representatives of the "hypothesis" approach are Gilbert Harman (1968) and (1969, p. 21); and (1973, pp. 43–46, 56–65), for example, p. 45: "... mental states and processes are to be functionally defined (by a psychological theory). They are constituted by their function or role in the relevant program"; Jerry Fodor (1975) Chapter I; Armstrong (1968, p. 84). An attempt to articulate the common core of the different types of functionalist "account" occurs in Ned Block and Jerry Fodor (1972, p. 173): "... functionalism in the broad sense of that doctrine which holds that type identity conditions for psychological states refer only to their relations to inputs, outputs and one another."

relevant to accounting for his activity taken in isolation from that of his fellows. But we can still conceive of his mental contents as varying. Functionally equivalent people – on any plausible notion of functional equivalence that has been sketched – may have non-equivalent mental-state and event contents, indicated by obliquely non-equivalent content clauses. Our argument indicates a systematic inadequacy in attempts of the sort I described.

Proponents of functionalist accounts have seen them as revealing the true nature of characteristic marks of the mental and as resolving traditional philosophical issues about such marks. In the case of beliefs, desires, and thoughts, the most salient mark is intentionality – the ill-specified information-bearing, representational feature that seems to invest these mental states and events.[10] In our terminology, accounting for intentionality largely amounts to accounting for the content of mental states and events. (There is also, of course, the application of content in *de re* cases. But we put this aside here.) Such content is clearly part of what the functional roles of our subjects' states fail to determine.

It is worth re-emphasizing here that the problem is unaffected by suggestion that we specify input and output in terms of causal relations to particular objects or stuffs in the subject's physical environment. Such specifications may be thought to help with some examples based on indexicality or psychological success verbs, and perhaps in certain arguments concerning natural kind terms (though even in these cases I think that one will be forced to appeal to intentional language). (Cf. note 2.) But this sort of suggestion has no easy application to our argument. For the relevant causal relations between the subject and the physical environment to which his terms apply – where such relations are non-intention-

---

[10] Often functionalists give mental contents only cursory discussion, if any at all. But claims that a functional account explains intentionality by accounting for all specific intentional states and events in non-intentional, functional language occur in the following: Daniel Dennett (1969), Chapter II and *passim*; Harman (1973, for example, p. 60): "To specify the meaning of a sentence used in communication is partly to specify the belief or other mental state expressed; and the representative character of that state is determined by its functional role"; Fodor (1975, Chapters I and II, for example, p. 75): "The way that information is stored, computed ... or otherwise processed by the organism explains its cognitive states and in particular, its propositional attitudes"; Smart, (1972); Hartry Field (1978). I shall confine discussion to the issue of intentionality. But it seems to me that the individualistic cast of functionalist accounts renders them inadequate in their handling of another major traditional issue about intentional mental states and events – first-person authority.

ally specified – were among the elements held constant while the subject's beliefs and thoughts varied.

The functionalist approaches I have cited seem to provide yet another case in which mental contents are not plausibly accounted for in non-intentional terms. They are certainly not explicable in terms of causally or functionally specified states and events of the *individual* subject. The intentional or semantical role of mental states and events is not a function merely of their functionally specified roles in the individual. The failure of these accounts of intentional mental states and events derives from an underestimation of socially dependent features of cognitive phenomena.

Before extending the application of our argument, I want to briefly canvass some ways of being influenced by it, ways that might appeal to someone fixed on the functionalist ideal. One response might be to draw a strict distinction between mental states, ordinarily so-called, and psychological states. One could then claim that the latter are the true subject matter of the science of psychology and may be identified with functional states functionally specified, after all. Thus one might claim that the subject was in the same psychological (functional) states in both the actual and the imagined situations, although he had different beliefs and thoughts ordinarily so-called.

There are two observations that need to be entered about this position. The first is that it frankly jettisons much of the philosophical interest of functionalist accounts. The failure to cope with mental contents is a case in point. The second observation is that it is far from clear that such a distinction between the psychological and the mental is or will be sanctioned by psychology itself. Functionalist accounts arose as philosophical interpretations of developments in psychology influenced by computer theory. The interpretations have been guided by philosophical interests, such as throwing light on the mind-body problem and accounting for mentalistic features in non-mentalistic terms. But the theories of cognitive psychologists, including those who place great weight on the computer analogy, are not ordinarily purified of mentalistic or intentional terminology. Indeed, intentional terminology plays a central role in much contemporary theorizing. (This is also true of theories that appeal to "sub-personal" states or processes. The "sub-personal" states themselves are often characterized intentionally.) Purifying a theory of mentalistic and intentional features in favor of functional or causal features is more clearly demanded by the goals of philosophers than by the needs of psychology. Thus it is at least an open question whether functional approaches of the sort we have discussed give a satisfactory account of *psychological* states and events. It is not evident that psychology will ever be methodologically "pure" (or theoretically purifiable by some definitional device) in the way these approaches demand. *This* goal of functionalists may be simply a meta-psychological mistake.

To put the point another way, it is not clear that functional states, characterized purely in functional, non-intentional terms (and non-intentional descriptions of input and output) are the natural subject matter of psychology. Psychology would, I think, be an unusual theory if it restricted itself (or could be definitionally restricted) to specifying abstract causal or functional structures in purely causal or functional terms, together with vocabulary from other disciplines. Of course, it *may* be that functional states, functionally specified, form a psychological natural kind. And it is certainly not to be assumed that psychology will respect ordinary terminology in its individuation of types of psychological states and events. Psychology must run its own course. But the assumption that psychological terminology will be ultimately non-intentional and purely functional seems without strong support. More important from our viewpoint, if psychology did take the individualistic route suggested by the approaches we have cited, then its power to illumine the everyday phenomena alluded to in mentalistic discourse would be correspondingly limited.

These remarks suggest a second sort of functionalist response to the argument of Section II, one that attempts to take the community rather than the individual as the object of functional analysis. One might, for example, seek to explain an individual's responsibility to communal standards in terms of his having the right kind of interaction with other individuals who collectively had functional structures appropriate to those standards. Spelling out the relevant notions of interaction and appropriateness is, of course, anything but trivial. (Cf. Section V.) Doing so in purely functional, non-intentional terms would be yet a further step. Until such a treatment is developed and illustrated in some detail, there is little point in discussing it. I shall only conjecture that, if it is to remain non-intentional, such a treatment is likely to be so abstract – at least in our present state of psychological and sociological ignorance – that it will be unilluminating from a philosophical point of view. Some of the approaches we have been discussing already more than flirt with this difficulty.

c. Individualistic assumptions about the mental have infected theorizing about the relation between mind and meaning. An example is the Gricean project of accounting for conventional or linguistic meaning in terms of certain complex intentions and beliefs of individuals.[11] The Gricean program analyzes conventional meaning in terms of subtle "mutual knowledge," or beliefs and intentions about each others' beliefs and intentions, on the part of most or all members of a community. Seen as a quasi-definitional enterprise, the program presupposes that the notion of an individual's believing or intending something is always "conceptually" independent of the conventional meaning of symbols used to express that something. Insofar as 'conceptually' has any intuitive content, this seems not to be the case. Our subject's belief or intention contents can be conceived to vary simply by varying conventions in the community around him. The content of individuals' beliefs seems sometimes to depend partly on social conventions in their environment. It is true that our subjects are actually rather abnormal members of their community, at least with respect to their use and understanding of a given word. But normality here is judged against the standards set by communal conventions. So stipulating that the individuals whose mental states are used in defining conventional meaning be relevantly normal will not avoid the circularity that I have indicated. I see no way to do so. This charge of circularity has frequently been raised on intuitive grounds. Our argument gives the intuitions substance. Explicating convention in terms of belief and intention may provide various sorts of insight. But it is not defining a communal notion in terms of individualistic notions. Nor is it reducing, in any deep sense, the semantical, or the intentional generally, to the psychological.

d. Individualistic assumptions have also set the tone for much discussion of the ontology of the mental. This subject is too large to receive detailed consideration here. It is complicated by a variety of crosscur-

---

[11] H.P. Grice (1957); (1968); Stephen Schiffer (1972), cf. especially pp. 13, 50, 63ff; Jonathan Bennett (1974). Another example of an individualistic theory of meaning is the claim to explicate all kinds of meaning ultimately in psychological terms, and these latter in functionalistic terms. See, for example Harman, (1968) note 9. This project seems to rest on the functionalist approaches just criticized.

rents among different projects, methodologies, and theses. I shall only explore how our argument affects a certain line of thinking closely allied to the functionalist approaches already discussed. These approaches have frequently been seen as resuscitating an old argument for the materialist identity theory. The argument is three-staged. First, one gives a philosophical "account" of each mentalistic locution, an account that is *prima facie* neutral as regards ontology. For example, a belief or a thought that sofas are comfortable is supposed to be accounted for as one functionally specified state or event within an array of others – all of which are secured to input and output. Second, the relevant functionally specified states or events are expected to be empirically correlated or correlatable with physiological states or events in a person (states or events that have those functions). The empirical basis for believing in these correlations is claimed to be provided by present or future physical science. The nature of the supposed correlations is differently described in different theories. But the most prevalent views expect only that the correlations will hold for each organism and person (perhaps at a given time) taken one by one. For example, the functionally specified event type that is identified with a thought that sofas are comfortable may be realized in one person by an instance (or "token") of one physiological event type, and in another person by an instance of another physiological event type. Third, the ("token") mental state or event in the person is held to be identical with the relevant ("token") physiological state or event, on general grounds of explanatory simplicity and scientific method. Sometimes, this third state is submerged by building uniqueness of occupancy of functional role into the first stage.[12]

I am skeptical about this sort of argument at every stage. But I shall doubt only the first stage here. The argument we gave in Section II directly undermines the attempt to carry out the first stage by recourse to the sort of functionalist approaches that we discussed earlier. Sameness of functional role, individualistically specified, is compatible with difference of content. I know of no better non-intentional account of mentalistic locutions. If a materialistic argument of this genre is to arrive, it will require a longer first step.

---

[12] Perhaps the first reasonably clear modern statement of the strategy occurs in J. J. C. Smart (1959). This article treats qualitative experiences; but Smart is explicit in applying it to specific intentional states and events in (1972). Cf. also David Lewis (1966, pp. 17–25); (1972); Armstrong (1968); Harman (1973, pp. 42–43); Fodor (1975), Introduction.

I shall not try to say whether there is a philosophically interesting sense in which intentional mental phenomena are physical or material. But I do want to note some considerations against materialistic *identity* theories.

State-like phenomena (say, beliefs) raise different problems from event-like phenomena (say, occurrent thoughts). Even among identity theorists, it is sometimes questioned whether an identity theory is the appropriate goal for materialism in the case of states. Since I shall confine myself to identify theories, I shall concentrate event-like phenomena. But our considerations will also bear on views that hope to establish some sort of token identity theory for mental states like beliefs.

One other preliminary. I want to remain neutral about how best to describe the relation between the apparent event-like feature of occurrent thoughts and the apparent relational feature (their relation to a content). One might think of there being an event, the token thought event, that is in a certain relation to a content (indicated by the that-clauses). One might think of the event as consisting – as not being anything "over and above" – the relevant relation's holding at a certain time between a person and a content. Or one might prefer some other account. From the viewpoint of an identity theory, the first way of seeing the matter is most advantageous. So I shall fit my exposition to the point of view.

Our ordinary method of identifying occurrent thought events and differentiating between them is to make reference to the person or organism to whom the thought occurs, the time of its occurrence, and the content of the thought. If person, time, and content are the same, we would normally count the thought event the same. If any one of these parameters differs in descriptions of thought events (subject to qualifications about duration), then the events or occurrences described are different. Of course, we can differentiate between events using descriptions that do not home in on these particular parameters. But these parameters are dominant. (It is worth nothing that differentiations in terms of causes and effects usually tend to rely on the content of mental events or states at some point, since mental states or events are often among the causes or effects of a given mental event, and these causes or effects will usually be identified partly in terms of their content.) The important point for our purposes is that in ordinary practice, sameness of thought content (or at least some sort of strong equivalence of content) is taken as a necessary condition for sameness of thought occurrence.

Now one might codify and generalize this point by holding that no occurrence of a thought (that is, no token thought event) could have a different (or extensionally non-equivalent) content and be the very same token event. If this premise is accepted, then our argument of Section II can be deployed to show that a person's thought event is not *identical* with any event in him that is described by physiology, biology, chemistry, or physics. For let *b* be any given event described in terms of one of the physical sciences that occurs in the subject while he thinks the relevant thought. Let '*b*' be such that it denotes the same physical event occurring in the subject in our counterfactual situation. (If you want, let '*b*' be rigid in Kripke's sense, though so strong a stipulation is not needed.) The second step of our argument in Section II makes it plausible that *b* not be affected by counterfactual differences in the communal use of the word 'arthritis'. Actually, the subject thinks that his ankles are stiff from arthritis, while *b* occurs. But we can conceive of the subject's *lacking* a thought event that his ankles are stiff from arthritis, while *b* occurs. Thus in view of our initial premise, *b* is not identical with the subject's occurrent thought.[13]

Identity theorists will want to reject the first premise – the premise that no event with a different content could be identical with a given thought event. On such a view, the given thought event that his ankles are stiff from arthritis might well have been a thought that his ankles are stiff from thar-thritis, yet be precisely the same token thought event. Such a view is intuitively very implausible. I know of only one reasonably spelled-out basis of support for this view. Such a basis would be provided by showing that mentalistic phenomena are causal or functional states, in one of the strong senses discussed earlier, and that mental events are physical tokens or realizations of those states. If 'that thought that his ankles are stiff from arthritis' could be accounted for in terms like 'that event with such and such a causal or functional role' (where 'such and such' does not itself involve

---

[13] The argument is basically Cartesian in style, (cf. *Meditations* II), though the criticism of functionalism, which is essential to its success, is not in any obvious sense Cartesian. (Cf. note 14.) Also the conclusion gives no special support to Cartesian ontology. The terminology of rigidity is derived from Saul Kripke (1972), though as mentioned above, a notion of rigidity is not essential for the argument. Kripke has done much to clarify the force of the Cartesian sort of argument. He gives such an argument aimed at showing the non-identity of sensations with brain processes. The argument as presented seems to suffer from a failure to criticize materialistic accounts of sensation language and from not indicating clearly how token physical events and token sensation events that are *prima facie* candidates for identification could have occurred independently. For criticism of Kripke's argument, see Fred Feldman (1974); William G. Lycan (1974); Richard Boyd (1980); Colin McGinn (1977). It seems to me, however, that these issues are not closed.

intentional terminology), and if independently identified physical events systematically filled these roles (or realized these states), we could perhaps see a given thought event as having a different role – and hence content – in different possible situations. Given such a view, the functional specification could perhaps be seen as revealing the contingency of the intentional specification as applied to mental event tokens. Just as we can imagine a given physiological event that actually plays the role of causing the little finger to move two inches, as playing the role of causing the little finger to move three inches (assuming compensatory differences in its physiological environment), so we could perhaps imagine a given thought as having a different functional role from its actual one – and hence, assuming the functionalist account, as having a different content. But the relevant sort of functionalist account of intentional phenomena has not been made good.[14]

The recent prosperity of materialist-functionalist ways of thinking has been so great that it is often taken for granted that a given thought event might have been a thought with a different, obliquely non-equivalent content. Any old event, on this view, could have a different content, a different significance, if its surrounding context were changed. But in the case of occurrent thoughts – and intentional mental events generally – it is hardly

---

[14] It is important to note that our argument against functionalist specifications of mentalistic phenomena did not depend on the assumption that no occurrent thought could have a different content from the one it has and be the very same occurrence or event. If it did, the subsequent argument against the identity theory would, in effect, beg the question. The strategy of the latter argument is rather to presuppose an independent argument that undermines non-intentional functionalist specifications of what it is to be *a* thought that (say) sofas are comfortable; then to take as plausible and undefeated the assumption that no occurrent thought could have a different (obliquely non-equivalent) content and be the same occurrence or event; and, finally, to use this assumption with the modal considerations appealed to earlier, to arrive at the non-identity of an occurrent thought event with any event specified by physical theory (the natural sciences) that occurs within the individual.

Perhaps it is worth saying that the metaphorical claim that mental events are identified by their *role* in some "inference-action language game" (to use a phrase of Sellars's) does not provide a plausible ground for rejecting the initial premise of the argument against the identity theory. For even if one did not reject the "role-game" idea as unsupported metaphor, one could agree with the claim on the understanding that the roles are largely the intentional contents themselves and the same event in *this* sort of "game" could not have a different role. A possible view in the philosophy of mathematics is that numbers are identified by their role in a progression and such roles are essential to their identity. The point of this comparison is just that appeal to the role metaphor, even if accepted, does not settle the question of whether an intentional mental event or state could have had a different content.

obvious, or even initially plausible, that anything is more essential to the identity of the event than the content itself. Materialist identity theories have schooled the imagination to picture the content of a mental event as varying while the event remains fixed. But whether such imaginings are possible fact or just philosophical fancy is a separate question.[15]

At any rate, functionalist accounts have not provided adequate specification of what it is to be a thought that ____, for particular fillings of the blank. So a specification of a given thought event in functionalist terms does not reveal the contingency of the usual, undisputed intentional specifications.

Well, *is* it possible for a thought event to have had a different content from the one it has and be the very same event? It seems to me natural and certainly traditional to assume that this is not possible. Rarely, however, have materialists seen the identity theory as natural or intuitive. Material-

---

[15] There are *prima facie* viable philosophical accounts that take sentences (whether tokens or types) as truth bearers. One might hope to extend such accounts to mental contents. On such treatments, contents are not things over and above sentences. They simple *are* sentences interpreted in a certain context, treated in a certain way. Given a different context of linguistic interpretation, the content of the same sentence might be different. One could imagine mental events to be analogous to the sentences on this account. Indeed, some philosophers have thought of intentional mental events as being inner, physical sentence (or symbol) tokens – a sort of brain writing. Here again, there is a picture according to which the same thought event might have had a different content. But here again the question is whether there is any reason to think it is a true picture. There is the prior question of whether sentences can reasonably be treated as contents. (I think sentence types probably can be; but the view has hardly been established, and defending it against sophisticated objections is treacherous.) Even if this question is answered affirmatively, it is far from obvious that the analogy between sentences and contents, on the one hand, and thought events and contents, on the other, is a good one. Sentences (types or tokens) are commonly identified independently of their associated contents (as evidenced by inter- and intra-linguistic ambiguity). It is *relatively* uncontroversial that sentences can be identified by syntactical, morphemic, or perceptual criteria that are in principle specifiable independently of what particular content the sentence has. The philosophical question about sentences and contents is whether discourse about contents can be reasonably interpreted as having an ontology of nothing more than sentences (and intentional agents). The philosophical question about mental events and contents is "What is the nature of the events?" "Regardless of what contents are, could the very same thought event have a different content?" The analogous question for sentences – instead of thought events – has an uncontroversial affirmative answer. Of course, we know that when and where non-intentionally identifiable physical events have contents, the same physical event could have had a different content. But it can hardly be *assumed* for purposes of arguing a position on the mind-body problem that mental events are non-intentionally identifiable physical events.

ists are generally revisionist about intuitions. What is clear is that we currently do identify and distinguish thought events primarily in terms of the person who has them, the rough times of their occurrence, and their contents. And we do assume that a thought event with a different content is a different thought event (insofar as we distinguish at all between the thinking event and the person's being related to a thought content at a time). I think these facts give the premise *prima facie* support and the argument against the identity theory some interest. I do not claim that we have "*a priori*" certainty that no account of intentional phenomena will reveal intentional language to be only contingently applicable to belief states or thought events. I am only dubious.

One might nurture faith or hope that some more socially oriented functionalist specification could be found. But no such specification is ready to hand. And I see no good reason to think that one must be found. Even if such a specification were found, it is far from clear that it would deflect the argument against the identity theory just considered. The "functional" states envisaged would depend not merely on what the individual does and what inner causal states lead to his activity – non-intentionally specified – but also on what his fellows do. The analogy between functional states and physiological states in causing the individual's internal and external activity was the chief support for the view that a given token mental event might have been a token of a different content. But the envisaged socially defined "functional states" bear no intuitive analogy to physiological states or other physical causal states within the individual's body. Their function is not simply that of responding to environmental influences and causing the individual's activity. It is therefore not clear (short of *assuming* an identity theory) that any event that is a token of one of the envisaged socially defined "functional states" could have been a token of a different one. The event might be essentially identified in terms of its social role. There is as yet no reason to identify it in terms of physically described events in the individual's body. Thus it is not clear that such a socially oriented functional account of thought contents would yield grounds to believe that the usual intentional specifications of mental events are merely contingent. It is, I think, even less clear that an appropriate socially oriented functional account is viable.

Identity theories, of course, do not exhaust the resources of materialism. To take one example, our argument does not speak directly to a materialism based on composition rather than identity. On such a view, the same physical material might compose different thoughts in different circumstances. I shall say nothing evaluative about this sort of view. I have also been silent about other arguments for a token identity theory – such as those based on philosophical accounts of the notions of causality or explanation. Indeed, my primary interest has not been ontology at all. It has been to identify and question individualistic assumptions in materialist as well as Cartesian approaches to the mental.

V. Models of the Mental

Traditional philosophical accounts of mind have offered metaphors that produce doctrine and carry conviction where argument and unaided intuition flag. Of course, any such broad reconstructions can be accused of missing the pied beauties of the natural article. But the problem with traditional philosophy of mind is more serious. The two overwhelmingly dominant metaphors of the mental – the infallible eye and the automatic mechanism – have encouraged systematic neglect of prominent features of a wide range of mental phenomena, broadly speaking, social features. Each metaphor has its attractions. Either can be elaborated or doctored to fit the facts that I have emphasized. But neither illuminates those facts. And both have played some part in inducing philosophers to ignore them.

I think it optimistic indeed to hope that any one picture, comparable to the traditional ones, will provide insight into all major aspects of mental phenomena. Even so, a function of philosophy is to sketch such pictures. The question arises whether one can make good the social debts of earlier accounts while retaining at least some of their conceptual integrity and pictorial charm. This is no place to start sketching. But some summary remarks may convey a sense of the direction in which our discussion has been tending.

The key feature of the examples of Section II was the fact that we attribute beliefs and thoughts to people even where they incompletely understand contents of those very beliefs and thoughts. This point about intentional mental phenomena is not everywhere applicable: non-linguistic animals do not seem to be candidates for misunderstanding the contents of their beliefs. But the point is certainly salient and must be encompassed in any picture of intentional mental phenomena. Crudely put, wherever the subject has attained a certain competence in large relevant parts of his language and has (implicitly) assumed a certain general commitment or responsibility to the communal conventions governing the language's symbols, the expressions the subject uses take on a certain inertia in determining attributions of mental content to him. In particular, the expressions the subject uses sometimes provide the content of his mental states or events even thought he only partially understands, or even misunderstands, some of them. Global coherence and responsibility seem sometimes to override localized incompetence.

The detailed conditions under which this "inertial force" is exerted are complicated and doubtless more than a little vague. Clearly, the subject must maintain a minimal internal linguistic and rational coherence and a broad similarity to others' use of the language. But meeting this condition is hardly sufficient to establish the relevant responsibility. For the condition is met in the case of a person who speaks a regional dialect (where the same words are sometimes given different applications). The person's aberrations relative to the larger community may be normalities relative to the regional one. In such cases, of course, the regional conventions are dominant in determining what contents should be attributed. At this point, it is natural to appeal to etiological considerations. The speaker of the dialect developed his linguistic habits from interaction with others who were a party to distinctively regional conventions. The person is committed to using the words according to the conventions maintained by those from whom he learned the words. But the situation is more complicated than this observation suggests. A person born and bred in the parent community might simply decide (unilaterally) to follow the usage of the regional dialect or even to fashion his own usage with regard to particular words, self-consciously opting out of the parent community's conventions in these particulars. In such a case, members of the parent community would not, and should not, attribute mental contents to him on the basis of homophonic construal of his words. Here the individual's intentions or attitudes toward communal conventions and communal conceptions seem more important than the causal antecedents of his transactions with a word – unless those intentions are simply included in the etiological story.

I shall not pursue these issues here. The problem of specifying the conditions under which a person has the relevant general competence in a language and a responsibility to its conventions is obviously complicated. The mixture of "causal" and intentional considerations relevant to dealing with it has obvious near analogs in other philosophical domains (etiological accounts of perception, knowledge, reference). I have no confidence that all of the details of the story would be philosophically interesting. What I want to stress is that to a fair degree, mentalistic attribution rests not on the subject's having mastered the contents of the attribution, and not on his having behavioral dispositions peculiarly relevant to those contents, but on his having a certain responsibility to communal conventions governing, and conceptions associated with, symbols that he is disposed to use. It is this feature that must be incorporated into an improved model of the mental.

I think it profitable to see the language of content attribution as constituting a complex *standard* by reference to which the subject's mental states and events are estimated, or an abstract grid on which they are plotted. Different people may vary widely in the degree to which they master the elements and relations within the standard, even as it applies to them all. This metaphor may be developed in several directions and with different models: applied geometry, measurement of magnitudes, evaluation by a monetary standard, and so forth. A model I shall illustrate briefly here borrows from musical analysis.

Given that a composer has fulfilled certain general conditions for establishing a musical key, his chordal structures are plotted by reference to the harmonic system of relations appropriate to the tonic key. There is vast scope for variation and novelty within the harmonic framework. The chords may depart widely from traditional "rules" or practices governing what count as interesting or "reasonable" chordal structures and progressions. And the composer may or may not grasp the harmonic implications and departures present in his composition. The composer may sometimes exhibit harmonic incompetence (and occasionally harmonic genius) by radically departing from those traditional rules. But the harmonic system of relations applies to the composition in any case. Once established, the tonic key and its associated framework are applied unless the composer takes pains to set up another tonic key or some atonal arrangement (thereby intentionally opting out of the original tonal framework), or writes down notes by something like a slip of the pen (suffering mechanical interference in his compositional intentions), or unintentionally breaks the harmonic rules in a massive and unprincipled manner (thereby indicating chaos or complete incompetence). The tonic key provides a standard for describing the composition. The application of the standard depends on the composer's maintaining a certain overall coherence and minimal competence in conforming to the standard's conventions. And there are conditions under which the standard would be replaced by another. But once applied, the harmonic framework – its formal interrelations, its applicability even to deviant, pointless progressions – is partly independent of the composer's degree of harmonic mastery.

One attractive aspect of the metaphor is that it has some application to the case of animals. In making sounds, animals do sometimes behave in such a way that a harmonic standard can be roughly applied to them, even though the standard, at least in any detail, is no part of what they have mastered. Since they do not master the standard (though they may master some of its elements), they are not candidates for partial understanding or misunderstanding. (Of course, this may be said of many people as regards the musical standard.) The standard applies to both animals and people. But the condition for its application are sensitive in various ways to whether the subject himself has mastered it. Where the subject does use the standard (whether the language, or a system of key relationships), his uses take on special weight in applications of the standard to him.

One of the metaphor's chief virtues is that it encourages one to seek social explications for this special weight. The key to our attribution of mental contents in the face of incomplete mastery or misunderstanding lies largely in social functions associated with maintaining and applying the standard. In broad outline, the social advantages of the "special weight" are apparent. Symbolic expressions are the overwhelmingly dominant source of detailed information about what people think, intend, and so forth. Such detail is essential not only to much explanation and prediction, but also to fulfilling many of our cooperative enterprises and to relying on one another for second-hand information. Words interpreted in conventionally established ways are familiar, palpable, and public. They are common coin, a relatively stable currency. These features are crucial to achieving the ends of mentalistic attribution just cited. They are also critical in maximizing interpersonal compatibility. And they yield a bias toward taking others at their word and avoiding *ad hoc* reinterpretation, once overall agreement in usage and commitment to communal standards can be assumed.

This bias issues in the practice of expressing even many differences in understanding without reinterpreting the subject's words. Rather than reinterpret the subject's word 'arthritis' and give him a trivially true object-level belief and merely a false metalinguistic belief about how 'arthritis' is used by others, it is common practice, and correct, simply to take him at his word.

I hardly need re-emphasize that the situation is vastly more complicated that I have suggested in the foregoing paragraphs. Insincerity, tongue slips, certain malapropisms, subconscious blocks, mental instability all make the picture more complex. There are differences in our handling of different sorts of expressions, depending, for example, on how clear and fixed social conventions regarding the expressions are. There are differences in our practices with different subject matters. There are differences in our handling of different degrees of linguistic error. There are differences in the way meaning-, assertion-, and mental-contents are attributed (Cf. note 4.) I do not propose ignoring these points. They are all parameters affecting the inertial force of "face value" construal. But I want to keep steadily in mind the philosophically neglected fact about social practice: Our attributions do not require that the subject always correctly or fully understand the content of his attitudes.

The point suggests fundamental misorientations in the two traditional pictures of the mental. The authority of a person's reports about his thoughts and beliefs (*modulo* sincerity, lack of subconscious interference, and so forth) does not issue from a special intellectual vision of the contents of those thoughts and beliefs. It extends even to some cases in which the subject incompletely understands those contents. And it depends partly on the social advantages of maintaining communally established standards of communication and mentalistic attribution. Likewise the descriptive and explanatory role of mental discourse is not adequately modeled by complex non-intentional mechanisms or programs for the production of an individual's physical movement and behavior. Attributing intentional mentalistic phenomena to individuals serves not only to explain their behavior viewed in isolation but also to chart their activity (intentional, verbal, behavioral, physical) by complex comparison to others – and against socially established standards.[16] Both traditional metaphors make the mistake, among others, of treating intentional mental phenomena individualistically. New approaches must do better. The sense

---

[16] In emphasizing social and pragmatic features in mentalistic attributions, I do not intend to suggest that mental attributions are any the less objective, descriptive, or on the ontological up and up. There are substantial arguments in the literature that might lead one to make such inferences. But my present remarks are free of such implications. Someone might want to insist that from a "purely objective viewpoint" one can described "the phenomena" equally well in accord with common practice, literally interpreted, or in accord with various reinterpretation strategies. Then our arguments would, perhaps, show only that it is "objectively indeterminate" whether functionalism and the identity theory are true. I would be inclined to question the application of the expressions that are scare-quoted.

in which man is a social animal runs deeper than much mainstream philosophy of mind has acknowledged.[17]

REFERENCES

Armstrong, D. M. 1968. *A Materialist Theory of Mind.* London: Routledge and Kegan Paul.

Bennett, J. 1974. The Meaning-Nominalist Strategy. *Foundations of Language* 10: 141–68.

Block, N. and J. Fodor. 1972. What Psychological States are Not. *Philosophical Review* 81: 159–81.

Boyd, R. 1980. Materialism Without Reductionism: What Physicalism Does not Entail. Pp. 67–106 in *Readings in the Philosophy of Psychology,* ed. N. Block.

Burge, T. 1977. Belief *De Re. The Journal of Philosophy* 74: 338–62.

———. 1978. Belief and Synonymy. *The Journal of Philosophy* 75: 119–38.

Dennett, D. 1969. *Content and Consciousness.* London: Routledge and Kegan Paul.

Descartes, R. 1955. *Philosophical Works,* eds. Haldane and Ross 2 vols. New York: Dover Publications.

Feldman, F. 1974. Kripke on the Identity Theory. *The Journal of Philosophy* 71: 665–76.

Field, H. 1978. Mental Representation. *Erkenntnis* 13: 9–61.

Fodor, J. 1975. *The Language of Thought.* New York: Crowell.

Grice, H. P. 1957. Meaning. *Philosophical Review* 66: 377–88.

———. 1968. Utterer's Meaning, Sentence-Meaning, and Word-Meaning. *Foundations of Languge* 4: 225–42.

Harman, G. 1968. Three Levels of Meaning. *The Journal of Philosophy* 65: 590–601.

———. 1969. An Introduction to 'Translation and Meaning'. In *Words and Objections,* eds. Davidson, D. and J. Hintikka. Dordrecht: Reidel.

———. 1973. *Thought.* Princeton: Princeton University Press.

---

[17]I am grateful to participants at a pair of talks given at the University of London in the spring of 1978, and to Richard Rorty for discussions earlier. I am also indebted to Robert Adams and Rogers Albritton whose criticisms forced numerous improvements. I appreciatively acknowledge support of the John Simon Guggenheim Foundation.

Kripke, S. 1972. Naming and Necessity. *Semantics of Natural Language*, eds. Davidson and G. Harman. Dordrecht: Reidel.

Lewis, D. 1972. Psychophysical and Theoretical Identifications. *Australasian Journal of Philosophy* 50: 249–58.

———. 1974. Radical Interpretation. *Synthese* 27: 331–44.

———. An Argument for the Identity Theory. *The Journal of Philosophy* 63: 17–25.

Lycan, W. G. 1974. Kripke and the Materialists. *The Journal of Philosophy* 71: 677–89.

McGinn, C. 1977. Anomalous Monism and Kripke's Cartesian Intuitions. *Analysis* 37: 78–80.

Putnam, H. 1975a. The Meaning of 'Meaning'. Pp. 215–71 in *Philosophical Papers* 2. Cambridge, UK: Cambridge University Press.

———. 1975b. The Mental Life of Some Machines. Pp. 408–28 in *Philosophical Papers* 2. Cambridge, UK: Cambridge University Press.

———. 1975c. The Nature of Mental States. Pp. 429–40 in *Philosophical Papers* 2. Cambridge, UK: Cambridge University Press.

Russell, B. 1959. *Mysticism and Logic.* London: G. Allen and Unwin.

Schiffer, S. 1972. *Meaning.* Oxford: Oxford University Press.

Shoemaker, S. 1975. Functionalism and Qualia. *Philosophical Studies* 27: 291–315.

Smart, J. J. C. 1972. Further Thoughts on the Identity Theory. *Monist* 56: 149–62.

———. 1959. Sensations and Brain Processes. *Philosophical Review* 68: 141–56.

Part II: Externalism and Authoritative Self-Knowledge are Compatible

3

Knowing One's Own Mind

Donald Davidson

There is no secret about the nature of the evidence we use to decide what other people think: we observe their acts, read their letters, study their expressions, listen to their words, learn their histories, and note their relations to society. How we are able to assemble such material into a convincing picture of a mind is another matter; we know how to do it without necessarily knowing how we do it. Sometimes I learn what I believe in much the same way someone else does, by noticing what I say and do. There may be times when this is my only access to my own thoughts. According to Graham Wallas,

> The little girl had the making of a poet in her who, being told to be sure of her meaning before she spoke, said, 'How can I know what I think till I see what I say?'[1]

A similar thought was expressed by Robert Motherwell: 'I would say that most good painters don't know what they think until they paint it.'

Gilbert Ryle was with the poet and the painter all the way in this matter; he stoutly maintained that we know our own minds in exactly the same way we know the minds of others, by observing what we say, do, and paint. Ryle was wrong. It is seldom the case that I need or appeal to evidence or observation in order to find out what I believe; normally I know what I think before I speak or act. Even when I have evidence, I seldom make use of it. I can be wrong about my own thoughts, and so the appeal to what

---

Presidential Address delivered before the Sixtieth Annual Pacific Division Meeting of the American Philosophical Association in Los Angeles, California, March 28, 1986.

[1] Graham Wallas, *The Art of Thought.*

can be publicly determined is not irrelevant. But the possibility that one may be mistaken about one's own thoughts cannot defeat the overriding presumption that a person knows what he or she believes; in general, the belief that one has a thought is enough to justify that belief. But though this is true, and even obvious to most of us, the fact has, so far as I can see, no easy explanation. While it is clear enough, at least in outline, what we have to go on in trying to fathom the thoughts of others, it is obscure why, in our own case, we can so often know what we think without appeal to evidence or recourse to observation.

Because we usually know what we believe (and desire and doubt and intend) without needing or using evidence (even when it is available), our sincere avowals concerning our present states of mind are not subject to the failings of conclusions based on evidence. Thus sincere first person present-tense claims about thoughts, while neither infallible nor incorrigible, have an authority no second or third person claim, or first person other-tense claim, can have. To recognize this fact is not, however to explain it.

Since Wittgenstein it has become routine to try to relieve worries about 'our knowledge of other minds' by remarking that it is an essential aspect of our use of certain mental predicates that we apply them to others on the basis of behavioral evidence but to ourselves without benefit of such aid. The remark is true, and when properly elaborated, it ought to answer someone who wonders how we can know the minds of others. But as a response to the skeptic, Wittgenstein's insight (if it is Wittgenstein's) should give little satisfaction. For, first, it is a strange idea that claims made without evidential or observational support should be favored over claims with such support. Of course, if evidence is not cited in support of a claim, the claim cannot be impugned by questioning the truth or relevance of the evidence. But these points hardly suffice to suggest that in general claims without evidential support are more trustworthy than those with. The second, and chief, difficulty is this. One would normally say that what counts as evidence for the application of a concept helps define the concept, or at least places constraints on its identification. If two concepts regularly depend for their application on different criteria or ranges of evidential support, they must be different concepts. So if what is apparently the same expression is sometimes correctly employed on the basis of a certain range of evidential support and sometimes on the basis of another range of evidential support (or none), the obvious conclusion would seem to be that the expression is ambiguous. Why then should we suppose that a predicate like '*x* believes that Ras Dashan is the highest mountain in Ethiopia,' which is applied sometimes on the basis of behavioral evidence and sometimes not, is unambiguous? If it is ambiguous, then there is no reason to suppose it has the same meaning when applied to oneself that it has when applied to another. If we grant (as we should) that the necessarily public and interpersonal character of language guarantees that we often correctly apply these predicats to others, and that therefore we often do know what *other* think, then the question must be raised what grounds each of us has for thinking he knows what (in the same sense) *he* thinks. The Wittgensteinian style of answer may solve the problem of other minds, but it creates a corresponding problem about knowledge of one's own mind. The correspondence is not quite complete, however. The original problem of other minds invited the question how one knows others have minds at all. The problem we now face must be put this way: I know what to look for in attributing thoughts to others. Using quite different criteria (or none), I apply the same predicates to myself; so the skeptical question arises why I should think it is *thoughts* I am attributing to myself. But since the evidence I use in the case of others is open to the public, there is no reason why I shouldn't attribute thoughts to myself in the same way I do to others, in the mode of Graham Wallace, Robert Motherwell, and Gilbert Ryle. In other words, I don't, but I could, treat my own mental states in the same way I do those of others. No such strategy is available to someone who seeks the same sort of authority with respect to the thoughts of others as he apparently has in dealing with his own thoughts. So the asymmetry between the cases remains a problem, and it is first person authority that creates the problem.

I have suggested an answer to this problem in another paper (Davidson 1984). In that paper I argued that attention to how we attribute thoughts and meanings to others would explain first person authority without inviting skeptical doubts. In recent years, however, some of the very facts about the attribution of attitudes on which I relied to defend first person authority have been employed to attack that authority: It has been argued, on what are thought to be new grounds, that while the methods of the third person interpreter determine what we usually deem to be the contents of an agent's mind, the contents so determined may be unknown to the agent. In the present paper I consider some of these arguments, and urge that they do not constitute a genuine threat to first person authority. The explanation I offered in my earlier paper of the asymmetry between first and other-person attributions of attitudes seems to me if anything to be strengthened by the new considerations, or those of them that seem valid.

It should be stressed again that the problem I am concerned with does not require that our beliefs about our own contemporary states of mind be infallible or incorrigible. We can and do make mistakes about what we believe, desire, approve, and intend; there is also the possibility of self-deceit. But such cases, though not infrequent, are not and could not be standard; I do not argue for this now, but take it as one of the facts to be explained.

Setting aside, then, self-deception and other anomalous or borderline phenomena, the question is whether we can, without irrationality, inconsistency, or confusion, simply and straightforwardly think we have a belief we do not have, or think we do not have a belief we do have. A number of philosophers and philosophically-minded psychologists have recently entertained views that entail or suggest that this could easily happen – indeed, that it must happen all the time.

The threat was there in Russell's idea of propositions that could be known to be true even though they contained 'ingredients' with which the mind of the knower was not acquainted; and as the study of the *de re* attitudes evolved the peril grew more acute.

But it was Hilary Putnam who pulled the plug. Consider Putnam's 1975 argument to show that meanings, as he put it, 'just ain't in the head' (Putnam 1975). Putnam argues persuasively that what words mean depends on more that 'what is in the head'. He tells a number of stories the moral of which is that aspects of the natural history of how someone learned the use of a word necessarily make a difference to what the word means. It seems to follow that two people might be in physically identical states, and yet mean different things by the same words.

The consequences are far-reaching. For if people can (usually) express their thoughts correctly in words, then their thoughts – their beliefs, desires, intentions, hopes, expectations – also must in part be identified by events and objects outside the person. If meanings ain't in the head, then neither, it would seem, are beliefs and desires and the rest.

Since some of you may be a little weary of Putnam's doppelganger on Twin Earth, let me tell my own science fiction story – if that is what it is. My story avoids some irrelevant difficulties in Putnam's story, though it introduces some new problems of its own.[2] (I'll come back to Earth, and Twin Earth, a little later.) Suppose lightning strikes a dead tree in a swamp; I am standing nearby. My body is reduced to its elements, while entirely by coincidence (and out of different molecules) the tree is turned into my physical replica. My replica, The Swampman, moves exactly as I did; according to its nature it departs the swamp, encounters and seems to recognize my friends, and appears to return their greetings in English. It moves into my house and seems to write articles on radical interpretation. No one can tell the difference.

But there *is* a difference. My replica can't recognize my friends; it can't *re*cognize anything, since it never cognized anything in the first place. It can't know my friends' names (though of course it seems to), it can't remember my house. It can't mean what I do by the word 'house', for example, since the sound 'house' it makes was not learned in a context that would give it the right meaning – or any meaning at all. Indeed, I don't see how my replica can be said to mean anything by the sounds it makes, nor to have any thoughts.

Putnam might not go along with this last claim, for he says that if two people (or objects) are relevantly similar physical states, it is 'absurd' to think their psychological states are 'one bit different' (Putnam 1975, p. 144). It would be a mistake to be sure that Putnam and I disagree on this point, however, since it is not yet clear how the phrase 'psychological state' is being used.

Putnam holds that many philosophers have wrongly assumed that psychological states like belief and knowing the meaning of a word are both (I) 'inner' in the sense that they do not presuppose the existence of any individual other than the subject to whom the state is ascribed, and (II) that these are the very states which we normally identify and individuate as we do beliefs and the other propositional attitudes. Since we normally identify and individuate mental states and meanings in terms partly of

---

[2] I make no claim for originality here; Steven Stich has used a very similar example in Stich (1978, p. 573 ff). I should emphasize that I am not suggesting that an object accidentally or artificially created could not think; The Swampman simply needs time in which to acquire a causal history that would make sense of the claim that he is speaking of, remembering, identifying, or thinking of items in the world. (I return to this point later.)

relations to objects and events other than the subject, Putnam believes (I) and (II) come apart: In his opinion, no states can satisfy both conditions.

Putnam calls psychological states satisfying condition (I) 'narrow'. He thinks of such states as solipsistic, and associates them with Descartes' view of the mental. Putnam may consider these states to be the only 'true' psychological states; in much of his paper he omits the qualifer 'narrow', despite the fact that narrow psychological states (so called) do not correspond to the propositional attitudes as normally identified. Not everyone has been persuaded that there is an intelligible distinction to be drawn between narrow (or inner, or Cartesian, or individualistic – all these terms are current) psychological states and psychological states identified (if any are) in terms of external facts (social or otherwise). Thus John Searle has claimed that our ordinary propositional attitudes satisfy condition (I), and so there is no need of states satisfying condition (II), while Tyler Burge has denied that there are, in any interesting sense, propositional attitudes that satisfy condition (I).[3] But there seems to be universal agreement that no states satisfy both conditions.

The thesis of this paper is that there is no reason to suppose that ordinary mental states do not satisfy both conditions (I) and (II): I think such states are 'inner', in the sense of being identical with states of the body, and so identifiable without reference to objects or events outside the body; they are at the same time 'nonindividualistic' in the sense that they can be, and usually are, identified in part by their causal relations to events and objects outside the subject whose states they are. A corollary of this thesis will turn out to be that contrary to what is often assumed, first person authority can without contradiction apply to states that are regularly identified by their relations to events and objects outside the person.

I begin with the corollary. Why is it natural to assume that states that satisfy condition (II) may not be known to the person who is in those states?

Now I must talk about Putnam's Twin Earth. He asks us to imagine two people exactly alike physically and (therefore) alike with respect to all 'narrow' psychological states. One of the two people, an inhabitant of Earth, has learned to use the word 'water' by being shown water, reading and hearing about it, etc. The other, an inhabitant of Twin Earth, has learned to use the word 'water' under conditions not observably different, but the substance to which she has been exposed is not water but a looka-

---

[3] See John Searle (1983) and Tyler Burge (1986).

like substance we may call 'twater'. Under the circumstances, Putnam claims, the first speaker refers to water when she uses the word 'water'; her twin refers to twater when *she* uses the word 'water'. So we seem to have a case where 'narrow' psychological states are identical, and yet the speakers mean different things by the same word.

How about the thoughts of these two speakers? The first says to herself, when facing a glass of water, 'Here's a glass of water'; the second mutters exactly the same sounds to herself when facing a glass of twater. Each speaks the truth, since their words mean different things. And since each is sincere, it is natural to suppose they believe different things, the first believing there is a glass of water in front of her, the second believing there is a glass of twater in front of *her*. But do they know what they believe? If the meanings of their words, and thus the beliefs expressed by using those words, are partly determined by external factors about which the agents are ignorant, their beliefs and meanings are not narrow in Putnam's sense. There is therefore nothing on the basis of which either speaker can tell which state she is in, for there is no internal or external clue to the difference available. We ought, it seems, to conclude that neither speaker knows what she means or thinks. The conclusion has been drawn explicity by a number of philosophers, among them Putnam. Putnam declares that he '...totally abandons the idea that if there is a difference in meaning ... then there *must* be some difference in our concepts (or in our psychological state)' What determines meaning and extension '...is not, in general, fully known to the speaker.' (Putnam 1975, pp. 164–5). Here 'psychological state' means *narrow* psychological state, and it is assumed that only such states are 'fully known'. Jerry Fodor believes that ordinary propositional attitudes are (pretty nearly) 'in the head', but he agrees with Putnam that *if* propositional attitudes were partly identified by factors outside the agent, they would not be in the head, and would not necessarily be known to the agent (Fodor 1982, p. 103; Fodor 1980). John Searle also, though his reasons are not Fodor's, holds that meanings are in the head ('there is nowhere else for them to be'), but seems to accept the inference that if this were not the case, first person authority would be lost (Searle 1986, chapter 8). Perhaps the plainest statement of the position appears in Andrew Woodfield's introduction to a book of essays on the objects of thought. Referring to the claim that the contents of the mind are often determined by facts external to and perhaps unknown to the person whose mind it is, he says:

Because the external relation is not determined subjectively, the subject is not authoritative about that. A third person might well be in a better position than the subject to know which object the subject is thinking about, hence be better placed to know which thought it was. (Woodfield 1982, p. viii).

Those who accept the thesis that the contents of propositional attitudes are partly identified in terms of external factors seem to have a problem similar to the problem of the skeptic who finds we may be altogether mistaken about the 'outside' world. In the present case, ordinary skepticism of the senses is avoided by supposing the world itself more or less correctly determines the contents of thoughts about the world. (The speaker who thinks it is water is probably right, for he learned the use of the word 'water' in a watery environment; the speaker who thinks twater is probably right, for he learned the word 'water' in a twatery environment.) But skepticism is not defeated; it is only displaced onto knowledge of our own minds. Our ordinary beliefs about the external world are (on this view) directed onto the world, but we don't know what we believe.

There is, of course, a difference between water and twater, and it can be discovered by normal means, whether it is discovered or not. So a person might find out what he believes by discovering the difference between water and twater, and finding out enough about his own relations to both to determine which one his talk and beliefs are about. The skeptical conclusion we seem to have reached concerns the extent of first person authority: It is far more limited than we supposed. Our beliefs about the world are mostly true, but we may easily be wrong about what we think. It is a transposed image of Cartesian skepticism.

Those who hold that contents of our thoughts and the meanings of our words are often fixed by factors of which we are ignorant have not been much concerned with the apparent consequence of their views which I have been emphasizing. They have, of course, realized that if they were right, the Cartesian idea that the one things we can be certain of is the contents of our own minds, and the Fregean notion of meanings fully 'grasped', must be wrong. But they have not made much of an attempt, so far as I know, to resolve the seeming conflict between their views and the strong intuition that first person authority exists.

One reason for the lack of concern may be that some seem to see the problem as confined to a fairly limited range of cases, cases where concepts or words latch on to objects that are picked out or referred to using proper names, indexicals, and words for natural kinds. Others, though, argue that the ties between language and thought on the one hand and external affairs on the other are so pervasive that no aspect of thought as usually conceived is untouched. In this vein Daniel Dennett remarks that '…one must be richly informed about, intimately connected with, the world at large, its occupants and properties, in order to be said with any propriety to have beliefs' (Dennett 1982, p. 76). He goes on to claim that the identification of *all* beliefs is infected by the outside, non-subjective factors that are recognized to operate in the sort of case we have been discussing. Burge also emphasizes the extent to which our beliefs are affected by external factors, though for reasons he does not explain, he apparently does not view this as a threat to first person authority (Burge 1979, 1982a, 1982b, 1986).

The subject has taken a disquieting turn. At one time behaviorism was invoked to show how it was possible for one person to know what was in another's mind; behaviorism was then rejected in part because it could not explain one of the most obvious aspects of mental states: the fact that they are in general known to the person who has them without appeal to behavioristic evidence. The recent fashion, though not strictly behavioristic, once more identifies mental states partly in terms of social and other external factors, thus making them to that extent publicly discoverable. But at the same time it reinstates the problem of accounting for first person authority.

Those who are convinced of the external dimension of the contents of thoughts as ordinarily identified and individuated have reacted in different ways. One response has been to make a distinction between the contents of the mind as subjectively and internally determined, on the one hand, and ordinary beliefs, desires, and intentions, as we normally attribute them on the basis of social and other outward connections, on the other. This is clearly the trend of Putnam's argument (although the word 'water' has different meanings, and is used to express different beliefs when it is used to refer to water and to twater, people using the word for these different purposes may be in 'the same psychological state'). Jerry Fodor accepts the distinction for certain purposes, but argues that psychology should adopt the stance of 'methodological solipsism' (Putnam's phrase) – that is, it should deal exclusively with inner states, the truly subjective psychological states which owe nothing to their relations to the outside world (Fodor 1980).

Steven Stich makes essentially the same distinction, but draws a sterner moral: where Fodor thinks we merely need to tinker a bit with propositional attitudes as usually conceived to separate out the purely subjective element, Stich holds that psychological states as we now think of them belong to a crude and confused 'folk psychology' which must be replaced by a yet to be invented 'cognitive science'. The subtitle of his recent book is 'The Case Against Belief' (Stich 1983).

Clearly those who draw such a distinction have insured that the problem of first person authority, at least as I have posed it, cannot be solved. For the problem I have set is how to explain the asymmetry between the way in which a person knows about his contemporary mental states and the way in which others know about them. The mental states in question are beliefs, desires, intentions, and so on, as ordinarily conceived. Those who accept something like Putnam's distinction do not even try to explain first person authority with respect to these states; if there is first person authority at all it attaches to quite different states. (In Stich's case, it is not obvious that it can attach to anything.)

I think Putnam, Burge, Dennet, Fodor, Stich, and others are right in calling attention to the fact that ordinary mental states, at least the propositional attitudes, are partly identified by relations to society and the rest of the environment, relations which may in some respects not be known to the person in those states. They are also right, in my opinion, in holding that for this reason (if for no other), the concepts of 'folk psychology' cannot be incorporated into a coherent and comprehensive system of laws of the sort for which physics strives. These concepts are part of a common-sense theory for describing, interpreting, and explaining human behavior which is a bit freestyle, but (so I think) indispensable. I can imagine a science concerned with people and purged of 'folk psychology', but I cannot think in what its interest would consist. This is not, however, the topic of this paper.

I am here concerned with the puzzling discovery that we apparently do not know what we think – at least in the way we think we do. This is a real puzzle if, like me, you believe it is true that external factors partly determine the contents of thoughts, and also believe that in general we do know, and in a way others do not, what we think. The problem arises because admitting the identifying and individuating role of external factors seems to lead to the conclusion that our thoughts may not be known to us.

But does this conclusion follow? The answer depends, I believe, on the way in which one thinks the identification of mental contents depends on external factors.

The conclusion does follow, for example, for any theory which holds that propositional attitudes are identified by objects (such as propositions, tokens of propositions, or representations) which are in or 'before' the mind, and which contain or incorporate (as 'ingredients') objects or events outside the agent; for it is obvious that everyone is ignorant of endless features of every external object. That the conclusion follows from these assumptions is generally conceded (Evans 1982, pp. 45, 199, 201). However, for reasons I shall mention below, I reject the assumptions on which the conclusion is in this case based.

Tyler Burge has suggested that there is another way in which external factors enter into the determination of the contents of speech and thought. One of his 'thought experiments' happens pretty well to fit me. Until recently, I believed arthritis was an inflammation of the joints caused by calcium deposits; I did not know that any inflammation of the joints, for example gout, also counted as arthritis. So when a doctor told me (falsely as it turned out) that I had gout, I believed I had gout but I did not believe that I had arthritis. At this point Burge asks us to imagine a world in which I was physically the same but in which the word 'arthritis' happened actually to apply only to inflammation of the joints caused by calcium deposits. Then the sentence 'Gout is not a form of arthritis' would have been true, not false, and the belief that I expressed by this sentence would not have been the false belief that gout is not a form of arthritis but a true belief about some disease other than arthritis. Yet in the imagined world all my physical states, my 'internal qualitative experiences', my behavior and dispositions to behave, are the same as they are in this world. My *belief* would have changed, but I would have no reason to suppose that it had, and so could not be said to know what I had believed.

Burge stresses the fact that his argument depends on

> ...the possibility of someone's having a propositional attitude despite an incomplete mastery of some notion in its content ... *if* the thought experiment is to work, one must at some state find the subject believing (or having some attitude characterized by) a content, despite an incomplete understanding or misapplication (Burge 1979, p. 83).

It seems to follow that if Burge is right, whenever a person is wrong, confused, or partially misinformed about the meaning of a word, he is wrong, confused, or partially misinformed about any of his beliefs that is (or would be?) expressed by using that word. Since such 'partial understanding' is 'common or even normal in the case of a large number of expressions in our vocabularies' according to Burge, it must be equally common or normal for us to be wrong about what we believe (and, of course, fear, hope for, wish were the case, doubt, and so on).

Burge apparently accepts this conclusion; at least so I interpret his denial that '...full understanding of a content is in general a necessary condition for believing the content'. He explicity rejects '...the old model according to which a person must be directly acquainted with, or must immediately apprehend, the contents of his thoughts ... a person's thought *content* is not fixed by what goes on in him, or by what is accessible to him simply by careful reflection' (Burge 1979, pp. 90, 102, 104).

I am uncertain how to understand these claims, since I am uncertain how seriously to take the talk of 'direct acquaintance' with, and of 'immediately apprehending', a content. But in any case I am convinced that if what we mean and think is determined by the linguistic habits of those around us in the way Burge believes they are, then first person authority is very seriously compromised. Since the degree and character of the compromise seem to me incompatible with what we know about the kind of knowledge we have of our own minds, I must reject some premise of Burge's. I agree that what I mean and think is not 'fixed' (exclusively) by what goes on in me, so what I must reject is Burge's account of how social and other external factors control the contents of a person's mind.

For a number of reasons, I am inclined to discount the importance of the features of our attributions of attitudes to which Burge points. Suppose that I, who think the word 'arthritis' applies to inflammation of the joints only if caused by calcium deposits, and my friend Arthur, who knows better, both sincerely utter to Smith the words 'Carl has arthritis'. According to Burge, if other things are more or less equal (Arthur and I are both generally competent speakers of English, both have often applied the word 'arthritis' to genuine cases of arthritis, etc.) then our words on this occasion mean the same thing, Arthur and I mean the same thing by our words, and we express the same belief. My error about the dictionary meaning of the word (or about what arthritis is) makes no difference to what I meant or thought on this occasion. Burge's evidence for this claim seems to rest on his conviction that this is what anyone (unspoiled by philosophy) would report about Arthur and me. I doubt that Burge is right about this, but even if he is, I don't think it proves his claim. Ordinary attributions of meanings and attitudes rest on vast and vague assumptions about what is and is not shared (linguistically and otherwise) by the attributer, the person to whom the attribution is made, and the attributer's intended audience. When some of these assumptions prove false, we may alter the words we use to make the report, often in substantial ways. When nothing much hinges on it, we tend to choose the lazy way: We take someone at his word, even if this does not quite reflect some aspect of the speaker's thought or meaning. But this is not because we are bound (outside of a law court, anyway) to be legalistic about it. And often we aren't. If Smith (unspoiled by philosophy) reports to still another party (perhaps a distant doctor attempting a diagnosis on the basis of a telephone report) that Arthur and I both have said, and believe, that Carl has arthritis, he may actively mislead *his* hearer. If this danger were to arise, Smith, alert to the facts, would not simply say 'Arthur and Davidson both believe Carl has arthritis'; he would add something like, 'But Davidson thinks arthritis must be caused by calcium deposits'. The need to make this addition I take to show that the simple attribution was not quite right; there was a relevant difference in the thoughts Arthur and I expressed when we said 'Carl has arthritis'. Burge does not have to be budged by this argument, of course, since he can insist that the report is literally correct, but could, like any report, be misleading. I think, on the other hand, that this reply would overlook the extent to which the contents of one belief necessarily depend on the contents of others. Thoughts are not independent atoms, and so there can be no simple, rigid, rule for the correct attribution of a single thought.[4]

---

[4] Burge suggests that the reason we normally take a person to mean by his words what others in his linguistic community mean, whether or not the speaker knows what others mean, is that 'People are frequently held, and hold themselves, to the standards of the community when misuse or misunderstanding are at issue.' He also says such cases '...depend on a certain responsibility to communal practice' (Burge 1979, p. 90). I don't doubt the phenomenon, but its bearing on what it is supposed to show. (a) It is often reasonable to hold people responsible for knowing what their words mean; in such cases we may treat them as committed to positions they did not know or believe they were committed to. This has nothing (directly) to do with what they meant by their words, nor what they believed. (b) As good citizens and parents we want to encourage practices that enhance the chances for communication; using words as we think others do may enhance communication. This thought (whether or not justified) may help explain why some people tend to attribute meanings and beliefs in a legalistic way; they hope to encourage conformtiy. (c) A speaker who wishes to be understood must intend his words to be interpreted (and hence interpretable) along certain lines; this intention may be served by using words as others do (though often this is not the case). Similarly, a hearer who wishes to understand a speaker must intend to interpret the speaker's words as the speaker intended (whether or not the interpretation is 'standard'). These reciprocal intentions become morally important in endless situations which have no necessary connection with the determination of what someone has in mind.

Though I reject Burge's insistence that we are bound to give a person's words the meaning they have in his linguistic community, and to interpret his propositional attitudes on the same basis, I think there is a somewhat different, but very important, sense in which social factors do control what a speaker can mean by his words. If a speaker wishes to be understod, he must intend his words to be interpreted in a certain way, and so must intend to provide his audience with the clues they need to arrive at the intended interpretation. This holds whether the hearer is sophisticated in the use of a language the speaker knows or is the learner of a first language. It is the requirement of learnability, interpretability, that provides the irreducible social factor, and that shows why someone can't mean something by his words that can't be correctly deciphered by another. ((Burge 1982b, p. 289) seems to make this point himself in a later paper.)

Now I would like to return to Putnam's Twin Earth example, which does not depend on the idea that social linguistic usage dictates (under more or less standard conditions) what speakers mean by their words, nor, of course, what their (narrow) psychological states are. I am, as I said, persuaded that Putnam is right; what our words mean is fixed in part by the circumstances in which we learned, and used, the words. Putnam's single example (water) is not enough, perhaps, to nail down this point, since it is possible to insist that 'water' doesn't apply just to stuff with the same molecular structure as water but also to stuff enough like water in structure to be odorless, potable, to support swimming and sailing, etc. (I realize that this remark, like many others in this piece, may show that I don't know a rigid designator when I see one. (don't.) The issue does not depend on such special cases nor on how we do or should resolve them. The issue depends simply on how the basic connection between words and things, or thoughts and things, is established. I hold, along with Burge and Putnam if I understand them, that it is established by causal interactions between people and parts and aspects of the world. The dispositions to react differentially to objects and events thus set up are central to the correct interpretation of a person's thoughts and speech. If this were not the case, we would have no way of discovering what others think, or what they mean by their words. The principle is as simple and obvious as this: a sentence someone is inspired (caused) to hold true by and only by sightings of the moon is apt to mean something like 'There's the moon'; the thought expressed is apt to be that the moon is there; the thought insred by and only by sightings of the moon is apt to be the thought that the moon is there. Apt to be, allowing for intelligible error, second hand reports, and so on. Not that all words and sentences are this directly conditioned to what they are about; we can perfectly well learn to use the word 'moon' without ever seeing it. The claim is that all thought and language must have a foundation in such direct historical connections, and these connections constrain the interpretation of thoughts and speech. Perhaps I should stress that the arguments for this claim do not rest on intuitions concerning what we would say if certain counterfactuals were true. No science fiction or thought experiments are required.[5]

I agree with Putnam and Burge, then, that

> ...the intentional content of ordinary propositional attitudes ... cannot be accounted for in terms of physical, phenomenal, causal-functional, computational, or syntactical states or processes that are specified non-intentionally and are defined purely on the individual in isolation from his physical and social environment (Burge 1982b, p. 288).

The question remains whether this fact is a threat to first person authority, as Burge seems to think, and Putnam and others certainly think. I have rejected one of Burge's arguments which, if it were right, would pose such a threat. But there is the position described in the previous paragraph, and which I hold whether or not others do, since I think this much 'externalism' is required to explain how language can be learned, and how words and attitudes can be identified by an interpreter.

Why does Putnam think that if the reference of a word is (sometimes) fixed by the natural history of how the word was acquired, a user of the word may lose first person authority? Putnam claimes (correctly, in my view) that two people can be in all relevant physical (chemical, psychological, etc.) respects the same and yet mean different things by their words and have different propositional attitudes (as these are normally identified). The differences are due to environmental differences about which the two agents may, in some respects, be ignorant. Why, under these circumstances, should we suppose these agents may not know what they

---

[5] Burge (1986, p. 5) has described 'thought experiments' which do not involve language at all; one of these experiments prompts him to claim that someone brought up in an environment without aluminum could not have 'aluminum thoughts'. Burge does not say why he thinks this, but it is by no means obvious that counterfactual assumptions are needed to make the point. In any case, the new thought experiments seem to rest on intuitions quite different from the intuitions invoked in "Individualism and the Mental"; it is not clear how social norms feature in the new experiments, and the linguistic habits of the community are apparently irrelevant. At this point it may be that Burge's position is close to mine.

mean and think? Talking with them will not easily show this. As we have noted, each, when faced with a glass of water or twater says honestly, 'Here's a glass of water'. If they are in their home environments, each is right; if they have switched earths, each is wrong. If we ask each one what he means by the word 'water', he gives the right answer, using the same words, of course. If we ask each one what he believes, he gives the right answer. These answers are right because though verbally identical, they must be interpreted differently. And what is it that they do not know (in the usual authoritative way) about their own states? As we have seen, Putnam distinguishes the states we have just been discussing from 'narrow' psychological states which do not presuppose the existence of any individual other than the subject in that state. We may now start to wonder why Putnam is interested in narrow psychological states. Part of the answer is, of course, that it is these states that he thinks have the 'Cartesian' property of being known in a special way by the person who is in them. (The other part of the answer has to do with constructing a 'scientific psychology'; this does not concern us here.)

The reasoning depends, I think, on two largely unquestioned assumptions. These are:

(1) If a thought is identified by a relation to something outside the head, it isn't wholly in the head. (It ain't in the head.)

(2) If a thought isn't wholly in the head, it can't be 'grasped' by the mind in the way required by the first person authority.

That this is Putnam's reasoning is suggested by his claim that if two heads are the same, narrow psychological states must be the same. Thus if we suppose two people are 'molecule for molecule' the same ('in the sense in which two neckties can be "identical"'; you may add, if you wish, that each of the two people 'thinks the same verbalized thoughts..., has the same sense data, the same dispositins, etc.'), then 'it is absurd to think [one] psychological state is one bit different from' the other. These are, of course, narrow psychological states, not the ones we normally attribute, which ain't in the head (Putnam 1975, p. 227).

It is not easy to say in exactly what way the verbalized thoughts, sense data, and dispositions can be identical without reverting to the necties, so let us revert. Then the idea is this: the narrow psychological states of two people are identical when their physical states cannot be distinguished. There would be no point in disputing this, since narrow psychological states are Putnam's to define; what I wish to question is assumption (1) above which led to the conclusion that ordinary propositional attitudes aren't in the head, and that therefore first person authority doesn't apply to them.

It should be clear that it doesn't follow, simply from the fact that meanings are identified in party by relations to objects outside the head, that meanings aren't in the head. To suppose this would be as bad as to argue that because my being sunburned presupposes the existence of the sun, my sunburn isn't a condition of my skin. My sunburned skin may be indistinguishable from someone else's skin that achieved its burn by other means (our skins may be identical in 'the necktie sense'); yet one of us is really sunburned and the other not. This is enough to show that an appreciation of the external factors that enter into our common ways of identifying mental states does not discredit an identity theory of the mental and the physical. Andrew Woodfield seems to think it does. He writes:

No *de re* state about an object that is external to the person's brain can possibly be identical with a state of that brain, since no brain state presupposes the existence of an external object. (1982, p. viii.)

Individual states and events don't *conceptually* presuppose anything in themselves; some of their *descriptions* may, however. My paternal grandfather didn't presuppose me, but if someone can be described as my paternal grandfather, several people besides my grandfather, including me, must exist.

Burge may make a similar mistake in the following passage:

...no occurrence of a thought...could have a different content and be the very same token event... [T]hen...a person's thought event is not *identical* with any event in him that is described by physiology, biology, chemistry, or physics. For let *b* be any given event described in terms of one of the physical sciences that occurs in the subject while he thinks the relevant thought. Let '*b*' be such that it denotes the same physical event occurring in the subject in our counterfactual situation...*b* need not be affected by counterfactual differences [that do not change the contents of the thought event]. Thus...*b* [the physical event] is not identical with the subject's occurrent thought. (Burge 1979, p. 111).

Burge does not claim to have established the premise of this argument, and so not its conclusion. But he holds that the denial of the premise is 'intuitively very implausible'. He goes on, '...materialist identity theories have schooled the imagination to picture the content of a mental event as varying while the event remains fixed. But whether such imaginings are possible fact or just philosophical fancy is a separate question'. It is because he thinks the denial of the premise to be very improbable that he holds that 'materialist identity theories' are themselves 'rendered implausible by the non-individualistic thought experiments. (Burge 1986, p. 15, note 7; 1979, p. 111).

I accept Burge's premise; I think its denial not merely implausible but absurd. If two mental events have different contents they are surely different events. What I take Burge's and Putnam's imagined cases to show (and what I think The Swampman example shows more directly) is that people who are in all relevant physical respects similar (or 'identical' in the necktie sense) can differ in what they mean or think, just as they can differ in being grandfathers or being sunburned. But of course there is *something* different about them, even in the physical world; their causal histories are different.

I conclude that the mere fact that ordinary mental states and events are individuated in terms of relations to the outside world has no tendency to discredit mental–physical identity theories as such. In conjunction with a number of further (plausible) assumptions, the 'externalism' of certain mental states and events can be used, I think, to discredit type–type identity theories; but if anything it supports token–token identity theories. (I see no good reason for calling all identity theories 'materialist'; if some mental events are physical events, this makes them no more physical than mental. Identity is a symmetrical relation.)

Putnam and Woodfield are wrong, then, in claiming that it is 'absurd' to think two people could be physically identical (in the 'necktie' sense) and yet differ in their ordinary psychological states. Burge, unless he is willing to make far stronger play than he has with essentialist assumptions, is wrong in thinking he has shown all identity theories implausible. We are therefore free to hold that people can be in all relevant physical respects identical while differing psychologically: this is in fact the position of 'anomalous monism' for which I have argued elsewhere. (Davidson 1982).

One obstacle to nonevidential knowledge of our own ordinary propositional attitudes has now been removed. For if ordinary beliefs and the other attitudes can be 'in the head' even though they are identified as the attitudes they are partly in terms of what is not in the head, then the threat to first person authority cannot come simply from the fact that external factors are relevant to the identification of the attitudes.

But an apparent difficulty remains. True, my sunburn, though describable as such only in relation to the sun, is identical with a condition of my skin which can (I assume) be described without reference to such 'external' factors. Still, if, as a scientist skilled in all the physical sciences, I have access only to my skin, and am denied knowledge of the history of its condition, then by hypothesis there is no way for me to tell that I am sunburned. Perhaps, then, someone has first person authority with respect to the contents of his mind only as those contents can be described or discovered without reference to external factors. In so far as the contents are identified in terms of external factors, first person authority necessarily lapses. I can tell by examining my skin what my private or 'narrow' condition is, but nothing I can learn in this restricted realm will tell me that I am sunburned. The difference between referring to and thinking of water and referring to and thinking of twater is like the difference between being sunburned and one's skin being in exactly the same condition through another cause. The semantic difference lies in the outside world, beyond the reach of subjective or sublunar knowledge. So the argument might run.

This analogy, between the limited view of the skin doctor and the tunnel vision of the mind's eye, is fundamentally flawed. It depends for its appeal on a faulty picture of the mind, a picture which those who have been attacking the subjective character of ordinary psychological states share with those they attack. If we can bring ourselves to give up this picture, first person authority will no longer be seen as a problem; indeed, it will turn out that first person authority is dependent on, and explained by, the social and public factors that were supposed to undermine that authority.

There is a picture of the mind which has become so ingrained in our philosophical tradition that it is almost impossible to escape its influence even when its worst faults are recognized and repudiated. In one crude, but familiar, version, it goes like this: the mind is a theater in which the conscious self watches a passing show (the shadows on the wall). The show consists of 'appearances', sense data, qualia, what is given in experience. What appear on the stage are not the ordinary objects of the world that the outer eye registers and the heart loves, but their purported representatives. Whatever we know about the world outside depends on what we can glean from the inner clues.

The difficulty that has been apparent from the start with this description of the mental is to see how it is possible to beat a tract from the inside to the outside. Another conspicuous, though perhaps less appreciated, difficulty is to locate the self in the picture. For the self seems on the one hand to include theater, stage, actors, and audience; on the other hand, what is known and registered pertains to the audience alone. This second problem could be as well stated as the problem of the location of the objects of the mind: are they *in* the mind, or simply viewed *by* it?

I am not now concerned with such (now largely disavowed) objects of the mind as sense-data, but with their judgmental cousins, the supposed objects of the propositional attitudes, whether thought of as propositions, tokens of propositions, representations, or fragments or 'mentalese'. The central idea I wish to attack is that these are entities that the mind can 'entertain', 'grasp', 'have before it', or be 'acquainted' with. (These metaphors are probably instructive: voyeurs merely want to have representations before the mind's eye, while the more aggressive grasp them; the English may be merely acquainted with the contents of the mind, while more friendly types will actually entertain them.)

It is easy to see how the discovery that external facts enter into the individuation of states of mind disturbs the picture of the mind I have been describing. For if to be in a state of mind is for the mind to be in some relation like grasping to an object, then whatever helps determine what object it is must equally be grasped if the mind is to know what state it is in. This is particularly evident if an external object is an 'ingredient' in the object before the mind. But in either case, the person who is in the state of mind may not know what state of mind he is in.

It is at this point that the concept of the subjective – of a state of mind – seems to come apart. On the one hand, there are the true inner states, with respect to which the mind retains its authority; on the other hand there are the ordinary states of belief, desire, intention, and meaning, which are polluted by their necessary connections with the social and public world.

In analogy, there is the problem of the sunburn expert who cannot tell by inspecting the skin whether it is a case of sunburn or merely an identical condition with another cause. We can solve the sunburn problem by distinguishing between sunburn and sunnishburn; sunnishburn is just like sunburn except that the sun need not be involved. The expert can spot a case of sunnishburn just by looking, but not a case of sunburn. This solution works because skin conditions, unlike objects of the mind, are not required to be such that there be a special someone who can tell, just by looking, whether or not the condition obtains.

The solution in the case of mental states is different, and simpler; it is to get rid of the metaphor of objects before the mind. Most of us long ago gave up the idea of perceptions, sense data, the flow of experience, as things 'given' to the mind; we should treat propositional objects in the same way. Of course people have beliefs, wishes, doubts, and so forth; but to allow this is not to suggest that beliefs, wishes and doubts are *entities* in or before the mind, or that being in such states requires there to be corresponding mental objects.

This has been said before, in various tones of voice, but for different reasons. Ontological scruples, for example, are no part of my interest. We will always need an infinite supply of objects to help describe and identify attitudes like belief; I am not suggesting for a moment that belief sentences, and sentences that attribute the other attitudes, are not relational in nature. What I am suggesting is that the objects to which we relate people in order to describe their attitudes need not in any sense be *psychological* objects, objects to be grasped, known, or entertained by the person whose attitudes are described.

This point, too, is familiar; Quine makes it when he suggests that we may use our own sentences to keep track of the thoughts of people who do not know our language. Quine's interest is semantical, and he says nothing in this context about the epistemological and psychological aspects of the attitudes. We need to bring these various concerns together. Sentences about the attitudes are relational; for *semantical* reasons there must therefore be objects to which to relate those who have attitudes. But having an attitude is not having an entity before the mind; for compelling *psychological* and *epistemological* reasons we should deny that there are objects of the mind.

The source of the trouble is the dogma that to have a thought is to have an object before the mind. Putnam and Fodor (and many others) have distinguished two sorts of objects, those that are truly inner and thus 'before the mind' or 'grasped' by it, and those that identify the thought in the usual way. I agree that no objects can serve these two purposes. Putnam (and some of the other philosophers I have mentioned) think the difficulty springs from the fact that an object partly identified in terms of external relations cannot be counted on to coincide with an object before the mind because the mind may be ignorant of the external relation. Perhaps this is so. But it does not follow that we can find *other* objects which will insure the desired coincidence. For if the object *isn't* connected with the world, we can never learn about the world by having that object before the mind; and for reciprocal reasons, it would be impossible to detect such a thought in another. So it seems that what is before the mind cannot include its outside connections – its semantics. On the other hand, if the object *is* connected with the world, then it cannot be fully 'before the mind' in the relevant sense. Yet unless a *semantic* object can be before the mind *in its semantic aspect*, thought, conceived in terms of such objects, cannot escape the fate of sense data.

The basic difficulty is simple: if to have a thought is to have an object 'before the mind', and the identity of the object determines what the thought is, then it must always be possible to be mistaken about what one is thinking. For unless one knows *everything* about the object, there will always be senses in which one does not know what object it is. Many attempts have been made to find a relation between a person and an object which will in all contexts hold if and only if the person can intuitively be said to know what object it is. But none of these attempts has succeeded, and I think the reason is clear. The only object that would satisfy the twin requirements of being 'before the mind' and also such that it determines what the content of a thought must, like Hume's ideas and impressions, 'be what it seems and seem what it is'. There are no such objects, public or private, abstract or concrete.

The arguments of Burge, Putnam, Dennett, Fodor, Stich, Kaplan, Evans and many others to show that propositions can't *both* determine the contents of our thoughts *and* be subjectively assured are, in my opinion, so many variants on the simple and general argument I have just sketched. It is not just propositions that can't do the job; no objects could.

When we have freed ourselves from the assumption that thoughts must have mysterious objects, we can see how the fact that mental states as we commonly conceive them are identified in part by their natural history not only fails to touch the internal character of such states or to threaten first person authority; it also opens the way to an explanation of first person authority. The explanation comes with the realization that what a person's words mean depends in the most basic cases on the kinds of objects and events that have caused the person to hold the words to be applicable; similarly for what the person's thoughts are about. An interpreter of another's words and thoughts must depend on scattered information, fortunate training, and imaginative surmise in coming to understand the other. The agent herself, however, is not in a position to wonder whether she is generally using her own words to apply to the right objects and events, since whatever she regularly does apply them to gives her words the meaning they have and her thoughts the contents they have. Of course, in any particular case, she may be wrong in what she believes about the world; what is impossible is that she should be wrong most of the time. The reason is apparent: unless there is a presumption that the speaker knows what she means, i.e., is getting her own language right, there would be nothing for an interpreter to interpret. To put the matter another way, nothing could count as someone regularly misapplying her own words. First person authority, the social character of language, and the external determinants of thought and meaning go naturally together, once we give up the myth of the subjective, the idea that thoughts require mental objects.

REFERENCES

Burge, T. 1979. Individualism and the Mental. *Midwest Studies in Philosophy, Volume 4,* eds. P. French, T. Uehling, H. Wettstein. University of Minnesota Press. Chapter 2 in this volume.

———. 1982a. Other Bodies. *Thought and Object,* ed. A. Woodfield. Oxford: Clarendon Press.

———. 1982b. Two Thought Experiments Reviewed. *Notre Dame Journal of Formal Logic* 23: 284–93.

———. 1986. Individualism and Psychology. *The Philosophical Review* 95.

Davidson, D. 1984. First Person Authority. *Dialectica,* 38: 101–111.

———. 1982. Mental Events. In *Essays on Actions and Events.* Oxford: Oxford University Press.

Dennett, D. 1982. Beyond Belief. *Thought and Object,* ed. A. Woodfield. Oxford: Clarendon Press.

Evans, G. 1982. *The Varieties of Reference.* Oxford: Oxford University Press.

Fodor, J. 1982. Cognitive Science and the Twin Earth Problem. *Notre Dame Journal of Formal Logic* 23.

———. 1980. Methodological Solipsism Considered as a Research Strategy in Cognitive Psychology. *The Behavioral and Brain Sciences* 3.

Putnam, H. 1975. The Meaning of 'Meaning'. Reprinted in *Philosophical Papers, Vol II.–Mind, Language, and Reality.* Cambridge, UK: Cambridge University Press.

Searle, J. 1983. *Intentionality.* Cambridge, UK: Cambridge University Press.

Stich, S. 1978. Autonomous Psychology and the Belief-Desire Thesis. *The Monist* 61: 573–591.

————. 1983. *From Folk Psychology to Cognitive Science*. Cambridge, MA: MIT Press.

Woodfield, A. 1982. *Thought and Object*. Oxford: Clarendon Press.

Note: I am greatly indebted to Akeel Bilgrami and Ernie LePore for criticism and advice. Tyler Burge generously tried to correct my understanding of his work.

4

Individualism and Self-Knowledge

Tyler Burge

The problem I want to discuss derives from the juxtaposition of a restricted Cartesian conception of knowledge of one's own thoughts and a nonindividualistic conception of the individuation of thoughts. Both conceptions are complex and controversial. But I shall not explain them in detail, much less defend them. I shall explicate them just enough to make the shape of the problem vivid. Then I shall say something about solving the problem.

Descartes held that we know some of our propositional mental events in a direct, authoritative, and not merely empirical manner. I believe that this view is correct. Of course, much of our self-knowledge is similar to the knowledge of others' mental events. It depends on observation of our own behavior and reliance on others' perceptions of us. And there is much that we do not know, or even misconstrue, about our own minds. Descartes tended to underrate these points. He tended to overrate the power of authoritative self-knowledge and its potential for yielding metaphysical conclusions. Characterizing the phenomenon that interested Descartes is a substantial task. I shall not take on this task here. I think, however, that Descartes was right to be impressed with the directness and certainty of some of our self-knowledge. This is the point I shall rely on.

Descartes's paradigm for this sort of knowledge was the cogito. The paradigm includes not only this famous thought, but fuller versions of it – not merely 'I am now thinking', but 'I think (with this very thought) that

Presented in an APA symposium on Individuation and Self-Knowledge, December 30, 1988. Donald Davidson commented; see *The Journal of Philosophy*, LXXXV, 11 (November, 1988), 664/5. Substantially this paper was the Nelson Lecture, University of Michigan, February 1986. I benefited from the occasion.

writing requires concentration' and 'I judge (or doubt) that water is more common than mercury'. This paradigm goes further toward illuminating knowledge of our propositional attitudes than has generally been thought. But I note it here only to emphasize that Descartes's views about the specialness of some self-knowledge are not merely abstract philosophical doctrine. It is certainly plausible that these sorts of judgments or thoughts constitute knowledge, that they are not products of ordinary empirical investigation, and that they are peculiarly direct and authoritative. Indeed, these sorts of judgments are self-verifying in an obvious way: making these judgments itself makes them true. For mnemonic purposes, I shall call such judgments *basic self-knowledge*.

Let us turn from knowledge of one's thoughts to individuation of one's thoughts. My view on this matter is that many thoughts are individuated nonindividualistically: individuating many of a person or animal's mental kinds – certainly including thoughts about physical objects and properties – is necessarily dependent on relations that the person bears to the physical, or in some cases social, environment. This view is founded on a series of thought experiments, which I shall assume are familiar.[1] Their common strategy is to hold constant the history of the person's bodily motion, surface stimulations, and internal chemistry. Then, by varying the environment with which the person interacts while still holding constant the molecular effects on the person's body, one can show that some of the person's thoughts vary. The details of the thought experiments make it clear that the variation of thoughts is indicative of underlying principles for individuating mental kinds. The upshot is that which thoughts one has – indeed, which thoughts one can have – is dependent on relations one bears to one's environment.

Our problem is that of understanding how we can know some of our mental events in a direct, nonempirical manner, when those events depend for their identities on our relations to the environment. A person need not investigate the environment to know what his thoughts are. A person does have to investigate the environment to know what the environment is like.

---

[1] Cf. Burge (1979); (1982); (1986a); (1986b); (1986).

Does this not indicate that the mental events are what they are independently of the environment?

By laying aside certain contrary elements in Descartes's views, one can reconstruct a tempting inference to an affirmative answer from his conception of self-knowledge.

In reflecting on the demon thought experiment, one might think that, since we can know our thoughts authoritatively, while doubting whether there is any physical world at all, the natures of our thoughts – our thought kinds – must be independent of any relation to a physical world. A parallel inference is presupposed in Descartes's discussion of the real distinction between mind and body. In *Meditations* vi, he argues that the mind can exist independently of any physical entity. He does so by claiming that he has a "clear and distinct idea" of himself as only a thinking and unextended thing, and a "clear and distinct idea" of body as only an extended and unthinking thing. He claims that it follows that the mind that makes him what he is can exist independently of any physical body. The argument also occurs in *Principles* I, LX:

> ... because each one of us is conscious [through clear and distinct ideas] that he thinks, and that in thinking he can shut off from himself all other substance, either thinking or extended, we may conclude that each of us ... is really distinct from every other thinking substance and from every corporeal substance.[2]

Descartes also believed that he had "clear and distinct ideas" of his thoughts. One might argue by analogy that, since one can "shut off" these thoughts from all corporeal substance, they are independent for their natures from physical bodies in the environment, and presumably from other thinkers. This line of argument implies that knowledge of one's own thoughts guarantees the truth of individualism.'[3]

The root mistake here has been familiar since Arnauld's reply. It is that there is no reason to think that Descartes's intuitions or self-knowledge give him sufficient clarity about the nature of mental events to justify him in claiming that their natures are independent of relations to physical objects. Usually, this point has been made against Descartes's claim to have shown that mental events are independent of a person's body. But it applies equally to the view that mental kinds are independent of the physi-

---

[2] Haldane and Ross (1955, pp. 243–4.)

[3] Cf. Haldane and Ross (1955, p. 190.)

cal environment. One can know what one's mental events are and yet not know relevant general facts about the conditions for individuating those events. It is simply not true that the cogito gives us knowledge of the individuation conditions of our thoughts which enables us to "shut off" their individuation conditions from the physical environment. Our thought experiments, which have directly to do with conditions for individuation, refute the independence claim.[4]

It is one thing to point out gaps in inferences from self-knowledge to individualism. It is another to rid oneself of the feeling that there is a puzzle here. Why is our having nonempirical knowledge of our thoughts not impugned by the fact that such thoughts are individuated through relations to an environment that we know only empirically?

Let us assume that our thoughts about the environment are what they are because of the nature of entities to which those thoughts are causally linked. According to our thought experiments, a person with the same individualistic physical history could have different thoughts if the environment were appropriately different. One senses that such a person could not, by introspection, tell the difference between the actual situation (having one set of thoughts) and the counterfactual situation (having another).

This intuition must be articulated carefully. What do we mean by 'introspection'? In each situation, the person knows what his thoughts are; and in each situation the thoughts are different. If 'introspection' were explicated in terms of self-knowledge, there would be an introspectible difference.

Certainly, if one were stealthily shifted back and forth between actual situations that modeled the counterfactual situations, one would not notice some feature in the world or in one's consciousness which would tell one whether one was in the "home" or the "foreign" situation. But this remark does not capture the idea that the two lives would feel the same. The thoughts would not switch as one is switched from one actual situation to another twin actual situation. The thoughts would switch only if one remained long enough in the other situation to establish environmental relations necessary for new thoughts. So quick switching

---

[4] I have discussed this and other features of the inference in Burge (1986c). See also Burge (1988). I now think that Descartes's views have more anti-individualistic elements than I realized in writing those articles. I hope to discuss these matters elsewhere.

would not be a case in which thoughts switched but the introspection remained the same.

But slow switching could be such a case. Suppose that one underwent a series of switches between actual earth and actual twin earth so that one remained in each situation long enough to acquire concepts and perceptions appropriate to that situation. Suppose occasions where one is definitely thinking one thought, and other occasions where one is definitely thinking its twin.[5] Suppose also that the switches are carried out so that one is not aware that a switch is occurring. The continuity of one's life is not obviously disrupted. So, for example, one goes to sleep one night at home and wakes up in twin home in twin bed – and so on. (Your standard California fantasy.) Now suppose that, after decades of such switches, one is told about them and asked to identify when the switches take place. The idea is that one could not, by making comparisons, pick out the twin periods from the "home" periods.

I grant these ideas. The person would have no signs of the differences in his thoughts, no difference in the way things "feel." The root idea is that at least some aspects of one's mental life are fixed by the chemical composition of one's body. One might call these aspects *pure phenomenological feels*. If one were uncomfortable with this notion, one could explicate or replace it in terms of an abstraction from the person's inability to discriminate between different mental events under the stated switching situations.

The upshot of all this is that the person would have different thoughts under the switches, but the person would not be able to compare the situations and note when and where the differences occurred. This point easily, though I think mistakenly, suggests the further point that such a person could not know what thoughts he had unless he undertook an empirical investigation of the environment which would bring out the environmental differences. But this is absurd. It is absurd to think that, to know which thoughts we think, we must investigate the empirical envi-

---

[5] Of course, there can arise difficult questions about whether one is still employing thoughts from the departed situation or taking over the thoughts appropriate to the new situation. I think that general principles govern such transitions, but such principles need not sharply settle all borderline cases. Insofar as one finds problems associated with actual switches distracting, one could carry out the objection I am articulating in terms of counterfactual situations.

ronment in such a way as to distinguish our actual environment from various twin environments.

In basic self-knowledge, a person does individuate his thoughts in the sense that he knows the thought tokens as the thought tokens, and types, that they are. We know which thoughts we think. When I currently and consciously think that water is a liquid, I typically know that I think that water is a liquid. So much is clear.

How can one individuate one's thoughts when one has not, by empirical methods, discriminated the empirical conditions that determine those thoughts from empirical conditions that would determine other thoughts?

It is uncontroversial that the conditions for thinking a certain thought must be presupposed in the thinking. Among the conditions that determine the contents of first-order empirical thoughts are some that can be known only by empirical means. To think of something as water, for example, one must be in some causal relation to water – or at least in some causal relation to other particular substances that enable one to theorize accurately about water. In the normal cases, one sees and touches water. Such relations illustrate the sort of conditions that make possible thinking of something as water. To know that such conditions obtain, one must rely on empirical methods. To know that water exists, or that what one is touching is water, one cannot circumvent empirical procedures. But to *think* that water is a liquid, one need not *know* the complex conditions that must obtain if one is to think that thought. Such conditions need only be presupposed.

Now let us turn to knowledge of one's thoughts. Knowing what one is thinking when one has thoughts about physical entities presupposes some of the same conditions that determine the contents of the empirical thoughts one knows one is thinking. This is a result of the second-order character of the thoughts. A knowledgeable judgment that one is thinking that water is a liquid must be grounded in an ability to think that water is a liquid.

When one knows that one is thinking that p, one is not taking one's thought (or thinking) that p merely as an object. One is thinking that p in the very event of thinking knowledgeably that one is thinking it. It is thought and thought about in the same mental act. So any conditions that are necessary to thinking that p will be equally necessary to the relevant knowledge that one is thinking that p. Here again, to think the thought, one need not know the enabling conditions. It is enough that they actually be satisfied.

Both empirical thoughts and thinking that one is thinking such thoughts presuppose conditions that determine their contents. In both cases, some of these conditions can be known to be satisfied only by empirical means. Why do these points not entail that one cannot know that one is thinking that such and such unless one makes an empirical investigation that shows that the conditions for thinking such and such are satisfied? The answer is complex, but it can be seen as a series of variations on the point that one must start somewhere.

It is helpful in understanding self-knowledge to consider parallel issues regarding perceptual knowledge. It is a fundamental mistake to think that perceptual knowledge of physical entities requires, as a precondition, knowledge of the conditions that make such knowledge possible. Our epistemic right to our perceptual judgments does not rest on some prior justified belief that certain enabling conditions are satisfied. In saying that a person knows, by looking, that there is food there, we are not required to assume that the person knows the causal conditions that make his perception possible. We certainly do not, in general, require that the person has first checked that the light coming from the food is not bent through mirrors, or that there is no counterfeit food in the vicinity. We also do not require that the person be able to recognize the difference between food and every imaginable counterfeit that could have been substituted.

In fact, it is part of our common conception of the objectivity of perception that there is no general guarantee that the perceiver's beliefs, dispositions, and perceptions could in every context suffice to discriminate the perceived object from every possible counterfeit. The possibility of unforeseeable misperceptions and illusions is fundamental to objectivity. So the very nature of objective perception insures that the perceiver need not have a perfect, prior mastery over the conditions for his perceptual success.

This point is obvious as applied to common practice. But it is the business of philosophy and the pleasure of skepticism to question common practice. My discussion of knowledge and individualism has proceeded on the unargued assumption that skepticism is mistaken. Granted this assumption, the point that perceptual knowledge does not require knowledge of its enabling conditions is obvious.

I shall not overburden this essay with an attempt to disarm skepticism. But it is worth noting that nearly all currently defended responses to skepticism, other than transcendental ones, agree in denying that perceptual knowledge must be justified by separately insuring that the enabling conditions hold and the skeptic's defeating conditions do not hold.[6] And since transcendental responses provide at most general guarantees against skepticism, the only tenable responses, which I know of, that attempt to justify particular perceptual knowledge claims in the face of skepticism take this route. I think that it is the right route.

I have maintained that perceptual knowledge of physical objects does not presuppose that one has first checked to insure that the background enabling conditions are fulfilled. The same point applies to knowledge of one's own mental events, particularly knowledge of the sort that interested Descartes. Such knowledge consists in a reflexive judgment which involves thinking a first-order thought that the judgment itself is about. The reflexive judgment simply inherits the content of the first-order thought.

Consider the thought, 'I hereby judge that water is a liquid'. What one needs in order to think this thought knowledgeably is to be able to think the first-order, empirical thought (that water is a liquid) and to ascribe it to oneself, simultaneously. Knowing one's thoughts no more requires separate investigation of the conditions that make the judgment possible than knowing what one perceives.

One knows one's thought to be what it is simply by thinking it while exercising second-order, self-ascriptive powers. One has no "criterion,"

---

[6] This remark applies to reliabilist theories, Moorean theories that insist on the directness of perception, Quinean theories that attempt to show that the skeptic's doubt is covertly a bad empirical doubt, and Carnapian theories that attempt to show that the skeptic's question is somehow irrelevant to actual empirical claims. The words 'first' and 'separately' are crucial in my formulations. As against some reliabilist views that try to block skepticism by denying closure principles, I think that we can know that no demon is fooling us. But we know this by inferring it from our perceptual knowledge.

Several philosophers have thought that anti-individualism, combined with the view that we are authoritative about what thoughts we think, provides a "transcendental" response to skepticism. Cf. Putnam (1981). Putnam's argument is criticized by Anthony L. Brueckner (1986). I agree with Brueckner that Putnam's arguments do not do much to undermine skepticism. But Brueckner seems to hold that, if anti-individualism and the authority of self-knowledge are accepted, one would have an antiskeptical argument. He suggests that the assumption of anti-individualism undercuts the assumption of authoritative self-knowledge. I do not accept this suggestion. I believe, however, that there is no easy argument against skepticism from anti-individualism and authoritative self-knowledge. This is a complicated matter best reserved for other occasions.

or test, or procedure for identifying the thought, and one need not exercise comparisons between it and other thoughts in order to know it as the thought one is thinking. Getting the "right" one is simply a matter of thinking the thought in the relevant reflexive way. The fact that we cannot use phenomenological signs or empirical investigation to discriminate our thoughts from other thoughts that we might have been thinking if we had been in a different environment in no way undermines our ability to know what our thoughts are. We "individuate" our thoughts, or discriminate them from others, by thinking those and not the others, self-ascriptively. Crudely put, our knowledge of our own thoughts is immediate, not discursive. Our epistemic right rests on this immediacy, as does our epistemic right to perceptual beliefs. For its justification, basic self-knowledge in no way needs supplementation from discursive investigations or comparisons.[7]

So far I have stressed analogies between basic self-knowledge and perceptual belief. But there are fundamental differences. A requirement that, to know what thoughts we are thinking, we must be able first to discriminate our thoughts from twin thoughts is, in my view, even less plausible than the analogous position with regard to perceptual knowledge.

Why? In developing an answer to this question, I want to dwell on some fundamental ways in which perceptual knowledge of physical entities differs from the sort of self-knowledge that we have been featuring. We commonly regard perceptual knowledge as *objective*. For our purposes, there are two relevant notions of objectivity. One has to do with the relation between our perceptions and the physical entities that are their objects. We commonly think that there is no necessary relation between any one person's abilities, actions, thoughts, and perceptions up to and including the time of a particular perception, on one hand, and the natures of those entities which that person perceptually interacts with at that time, on the other. On any given occasion, our perceptions could have been misperceptions. The individual physical item that one perceptually interacts with at any given time is fundamentally independent from any one person's perceptions – and conceptions. The nature of the physical entity could have been different even while one's perceptual states, and other mental states, remained the same.

---

[7] I shall not develop the issue of one's epistemic right to one's authoritative self-ascriptions here. It is an extremely complex issue, which deserves separate attention.

This fact underlies a normative point about perception. We are subject to certain sorts of possible errors about empirical objects – misperceptions and hallucinations that are "brute." Brute errors do not result from any sort of carelessness, malfunction, or irrationality on our part. A person can be perceptually wrong without there being anything wrong with him. Brute errors depend on the independence of physical objects' natures from how we conceive or perceive them, and on the contingency of our causal relations to them. The possibility of such errors follows from the fact that no matter what one's cognitive state is like (so, no matter how rational or well-functioning one is) one's perceptual states could in individual instances fail to be veridical – if physical circumstances were sufficiently unfortunate.

There is a second sense in which perceptual knowledge is objective. This sense bears on the relation between one person's perceptions of an object and other persons' perceptions of the same object. The idea is that perceptual knowledge, like all other empirical knowledge, is impersonal. Any observer could have been equally well placed to make an observation. Others could have made an observation with the same type of presentation of the scene, if they had been in the same position at the relevant time. And this possible observation could have had the same justificatory status as the original observation. Even though empirical commitments must be made by persons, nothing relevant to the justification of any empirical commitment regarding the physical world has anything essentially to do with any particular person's making the commitment.

The paradigmatic cases of self-knowledge differ from perceptual knowledge in both of these respects. To take the first: in the case of cogito-like judgments, the object, or subject matter, of one's thoughts is not contingently related to the thoughts one thinks about it. The thoughts are self-referential and self-verifying. An error based on a gap between one's thoughts and the subject matter is simply not possible in these cases. When I judge: I am thinking that writing requires concentration, the cognitive content that I am making a judgment about is self-referentially fixed by the judgment itself; and the judgment is self-verifying. There is a range of cases of self-knowledge which extend out from this paradigm. I think that, in all cases of authoritative knowledge, brute mistakes are impossible. All errors in matters where people have special authority about themselves are errors which indicate something wrong with the thinker. Dealing with the whole range requires subtlety. But the point as applied to what I take to be the basic cases is straightforward. No errors at all are possible in strict cogito judgments; they are self-verifying.[8]

The paradigmatic cases of self-knowledge also differ from perceptual knowledge in that they are essentially personal. The special epistemic status of these cases depends on the judgments' being made simultaneously from and about one's first-person point of view. The point of view and time of the judgment must be the same as that of the thought being judged to occur. When I judge: I am thinking that writing requires concentration, the time of the judgment and that of the thought being judged about are the same; and the identity of the first-person pronouns signals an identity of point of view between the judge and the thought being judged about. In all cases of authoritative self-knowledge, even in those cases which are not "basic" in our sense, it is clear that their first-person character is fundamental to their epistemic status.

These differences between perceptual knowledge and authoritative self-knowledge ground my claim that it is even less plausible than it is in the case of perceptual knowledge to think that basic self-knowledge requires, as a precondition, knowledge of the conditions that make such knowledge possible.

Let us think about the difference as regards objectivity in the relation to an object. In the case of perceptual knowledge, one's perception can be mistaken because some counterfeit has been substituted. It is this possibility which tempts one into the (mistaken) view that, to have perceptual knowledge, one must first know something that rules out the possibility of a counterfeit. But in the cases of the cogito-like self-verifying judgments there is no possibility of counterfeits. No abnormal background condition could substitute some other object in such a way as to create a gap between what we think and what we think about. Basic self-knowledge is self-referential in a way that insures that the object of reference just is the thought being thought. If background conditions are different enough so that there is another object of reference in one's self-referential thinking, they

---

[8] Mistakes about the *res* in *de re* judgments are not counterexamples to the claim that basic cogito-like judgments are self-verifying (hence infallible). Suppose I judge: I am thinking that my aunt is charming; and suppose that the person that I am judging to be charming is not my aunt (I have some particular person in mind). It is true that I am making a mistake about the identity of the person thought about; I have no particular authority about that, or even about her existence. But I am not making a mistake about what I am thinking about that person; there is no mistake about the intentional act and intentional content of the act. Authority concerns those aspects of the thought which have intentional (about-ness) properties. For me, those are the only aspects of the content of a thought.

are also different enough so that there is another thought. The person would remain in the same reflexive position with respect to this thought, and would again know, in the authoritative way, what he is thinking.

For example, imagine a case of slow switching between actual home and actual twin-home situations. In the former situation, the person may think "I am thinking that water is a liquid." In the latter situation, the person may think "I am thinking that twater is a liquid." In both cases, the person is right and as fully justified as ever. The fact that the person does not know that a switch has occurred is irrelevant to the truth and justified character of these judgments. Of course, the person may learn about the switches and ask "Was I thinking yesterday about water or twater?" – and not know the answer. Here knowing the answer may sometimes indeed depend on knowing empirical background conditions. But such sophisticated questions about memory require a more complex story. If a person, aware of the fact that switching has occurred, were to ask "Am I now thinking about water or twater?", the answer is obviously "both." Both concepts are used. Given that the thought is fixed and that the person is thinking it self-consciously, no new knowledge about the thought could undermine the self-ascription – or therefore its justification or authority.

In basic self-knowledge, one simultaneously thinks through a first-order thought (that water is a liquid) and thinks about it as one's own. The content of the first-order (contained) thought is fixed by non-individualistic background conditions. And by its reflexive, self-referential character, the content of the second-order judgment is logically locked (self-referentially) onto the first-order content which it both contains and takes as its subject matter. Since counterfeit contents logically cannot undermine such self-knowledge, there should be no temptation to think that, in order to have such knowledge, one needs to master its enabling conditions.

The view I constructed on Descartes runs contrary. On that view, since basic self-knowledge is more certain than perceptual knowledge, it is more imperative that one be master of all its enabling conditions. One temptation toward this sort of reasoning may derive from construing self-knowledge as a perfected perceptual knowledge. If one thinks of one's relation to the subject matter of basic self-knowledge on an analogy to one's relation to objects of empirical investigation, then the view that one's thoughts (the subject matter) are dependent for their natures on relations to the environment will make it appear that one's knowledge of one's thoughts cannot be any more direct or certain than one's knowledge of the environment. If one begins by thinking of one's thoughts as objects like physical objects, except that one cannot misperceive or have illusions about them, then to explicate authoritative self-knowledge, one makes one of two moves. Either one adds further capacities for ruling out the possible sources of misperception or illusion in empirical perception, or one postulates objects of knowledge whose very nature is such that they cannot be misconstrued or misconceived. In the first instance, one grants oneself an omniscient faculty for discerning background conditions whose independence from us, in the case of perceptual knowledge, is the source of error. In the second instance, one imagines objects of thought (propositions that can be thought only if they are completely understood, or ideas whose *esse* is their *percipi*) whose natures are such that one cannot make any mistakes about them – objects of thought which one can "see" from all sides at once. In either case, one takes oneself to have ultimate insight into the natures of one's thoughts.

This line of reasoning is deeply misconceived. One need only make it explicit to sense its implausibility. The source of our strong epistemic right, our justification, in our basic self-knowledge is not that we know a lot about each thought we know we have. It is not that we can explicate its nature and its enabling conditions. It is that we are in the position of thinking those thoughts in the second-order, self-verifying way. Justification lies not in the having of supplemental background knowledge, but in the character and function of the self-evaluating judgments.

Let us turn to the point that self-knowledge is personal. The view that anti-individualism is incompatible with authoritative self-knowledge is easily engendered by forgetting the essentially first-person character of self-knowledge. We switch back and forth between thinking our thoughts and thinking about ourselves from the point of view of another person who knows more about our environment than we do. This is a key to Descartes's skeptical thought experiments. And it would not be surprising if he tended to think about self-knowledge in such a way as to give it a sort of omniscience from the third-person point of view – in order to protect the first-person point of view from the fallibilities to which impersonal or third-person judgments (especially empirical judgments) are prone. Since we are not omniscient about empirical matters, it is natural to reduce the scope of the relevant third-person perspective so that the character of one's thoughts is independent of an environment about which we cannot be omniscient. Individualism ensues.

To illustrate the train of thought in a more concrete way: we think that we are thinking that water is a liquid. But then, switching to a third-person perspective, we imagine a situation in which the world is not as we currently think it is – a situation, say, in which there is no water for us to interact with. We take up a perspective on ourselves from the outside. Having done this, we are easily but illegitimately seduced into the worry that our original first-person judgment is poorly justified unless it can somehow encompass the third-person perspective, or unless the third-person perspective on empirical matters is irrelevant to the character of the first-person judgment. In this fallen state, we are left with little else but a distorted conception of self-knowledge and a return to individualism.[9]

As one thinks a thought reflexively, it is an object of reference and knowledge, but simultaneously a constituent of one's point of view. The essential role that the first-person singular plays in the epistemic status of authoritative self-knowledge differentiates this knowledge not only from empirical knowledge, but also from most a priori knowledge, the justification of which does not depend on the first-person point of view in the same way.

The tendency to blur distinctions between a priori knowledge (or equally, knowledge involved in explication of one's concepts) and author-

---

[9] My knowledge that I am thinking that mercury is an element depends on an ability to think – not explicate – the thought that mercury is an element. Compare my knowledge that my words 'mercury is an element' are true if and only if mercury is an element. This knowledge depends on understanding the words 'mercury is an element' well enough to say with them, or think with them, that mercury is an element. It is this ability which distinguishes this knowledge from mere knowledge that the disquotation principle as applied to 'mercury is an element' is true (mere knowledge that the sentence "'mercury is an element' is true if and only if mercury is an element" is true). I know that my word 'mercury' applies to mercury (if to anything), not by being able to provide an explication that distinguishes mercury from every conceivable twin mercury, but by being a competent user of the word, whose meaning and reference are grounded in this environment rather than in some environment where the meaning of the word form would be different. The fact that one may not be able to explicate the difference between mercury and every possible twin mercury should not lead one to assimilate one's use of 'mercury' to knowledge of purely formal relationships (e.g., knowledge that all instances of the disquotation principle are true).

One other comparison: I know that I am here (compare: on earth) rather than somewhere else (compare: twin earth). My knowledge amounts to more than knowing I am wherever I am. I have normal ability to perceive and think about my surroundings. I have this knowledge because I perceive my surroundings and not other conceivable surroundings, and I have it even though other places that I could not distinguish by perception or description from here are conceivable. For a variety of reasons, one should not assimilate terms like 'water' to indexicals like 'here'. Cf. Burge (1982). But these analogies may be helpful here.

itative self-knowledge is, I think, an instance of Descartes's central mistake: exaggerating the implications of authoritative self-knowledge for impersonal knowledge of necessary truths. One clearly does not have first-person authority about whether one of one's thoughts is to be explicated or individuated in such and such a way. Nor is there any apparent reason to assume that, in general, one must be able to explicate one's thoughts correctly in order to know that one is thinking them.

Thus, I can know that I have arthritis, and know I think I have arthritis, even though I do not have a proper criterion for what arthritis is. It is a truism that to think one's thoughts, and thus to think cogito-like thoughts, one must understand what one is thinking well enough to think it. But it does not follow that such understanding carries with it an ability to explicate correctly one's thoughts or concepts via other thoughts and concepts; nor does it carry an immunity to failures of explication. So one can know what one's thoughts are even while one understands one's thoughts only partially, in the sense that one gives incomplete or mistaken explications of one's thoughts or concepts. One should not assimilate 'knowing what one's thoughts are' in the sense of basic self-knowledge to 'knowing what one I s thoughts are' in the sense of being able to explicate them correctly – being able to delineate their constitutive relations to other thoughts.[10]

For its justification, basic self-knowledge requires only that one think one's thoughts in the self-referential, self-ascriptive manner. It neither requires nor by itself yields a general account of the mental kinds that it specifies. Conceptual explication – knowledge of how one's thought kinds relate to other thought kinds – typically requires more objectification: reasoning from empirical observation or reflection on general principles. It requires a conceptual mastery of the conditions underlying one's thoughts and a conceptual mastery of the rules one is following. These masteries are clearly beyond anything required to think thoughts in the

---

[10] Davidson's views about self-knowledge have some crucial points in common with mine. But he may be making this mistake when he writes that, if one concedes the possibility of partial understanding as I do, one must concede that anti-individualism undermines the authority of self-knowledge. Cf. Davidson (1987, p. 448). Cf. also Davidson (1984). It is unclear to me why Davidson says this. I have discussed the distinction between the sort of understanding necessary to think and the sort of understanding necessary to explicate one's thoughts, in Burge (1979); (1986c); "Frege on Sense and Linguistic Meaning," forthcoming in *The Analytic Tradition*, David Bell and Neil Cooper, eds. (New York: Blackwell); and "Wherein is Language Social?" forthcoming in a volume edited by Alexander George (New York: Blackwell).

second-order, self-ascriptive way. Explicative knowledge is neither self-verifying nor so closely tied to particular mental events or particular persons' points of view.[11]

Despite, or better because of, its directness and certainty, basic self-knowledge is limited in its metaphysical implications. It is nonetheless epistemically self-reliant. By itself it yields little of metaphysical interest; but its epistemic credentials do not rest on knowledge of general principles, or on investigation of the world.

REFERENCES

Brueckner, A. L. 1986. Brains in a Vat. *The Journal of Philosophy*, LXXXIII, 3 (March): 148–167.

Burge, T. 1979. Individualism and the Mental. *Midwest Studies in Philosophy*, IV: 73–121. Chapter 2 in this volume.

———. 1982. Other Bodies. *Thought and Object*, ed. Woodfield, A. New York: Oxford University Press.

———. 1986a. Individualism and Psychology. *The Philosophical Review* XCV, 1: 3–45.

———. 1986b. Cartesian Error and the Objectivity of Perception. *Subject, Thought, and Context*, eds. Pettit, P. and J. McDowell. New York: Oxford University Press.

———. 1986c. Intellectual Norms and Foundations of Mind. *The Journal of Philosophy*, LXXXIII, 12 (December): 697–720.

———. 1988. Perceptual Individualism and Authoritative Self-Knowledge. In *Contents of Thought*, Grimm, R. and D. Merrill, eds. Tucson: Arizona University Press.

Davidson, D. 1987. Knowing One's Own Mind. Pp. 441–58 in *Proceedings and Addresses of the American Philosophical Association*, LX. Chapter 3 in this volume.

---

[11] As I indicated earlier, basic self-knowledge is at most an illuminating paradigm for understanding a significant range of phenomena that count as self-knowledge. Thus, the whole discussion has been carried out under a major simplifying assumption. A full discussion of authoritative self-knowledge must explicate our special authority, or epistemic right, even in numerous cases where our judgments are not self-verifying or immune to error. I think, however, that reflection on the way that errors can occur in such cases gives not the slightest encouragement to the view that anti-individualism (as regards either the physical or social environments) is a threat to the authority of our knowledge of the contents of our thoughts.

————. 1984. First Person Authority. *Dialectica*, XXXVILL, 2–3: 101–11.

Haldane, E. S. and G. R. T. Ross. Trans. 1955. *The Philosophical Works of Descartes*, vol. i. New York: Dover.

Putnam, H. 1981. *Reason, Truth, and History*. New York: Cambridge University Press.

5

Privileged Access

John Heil

Epistemic Privilege

Philosophical tradition has it that one's own mental life enjoys a privileged epistemic standing. I know my own states of mind immediately and with confidence. You may discover what I am thinking, of course, but you are liable to err in your assessment of my thoughts in ways that I cannot. Asymmetry of access evidently lies close to the centre of our conception of mentality. A theory of intentionality that failed to square with this aspect of the mental must be regarded with suspicion. What, however, are we to make of the notion of epistemic privilege?[1]

Descartes promoted the view that access to one's own mental states is infallible and incorrigible. In the third *Meditation*, for instance, he remarks that '...for certainly, if I considered the ideas only as certain modes of my thought, without intending them to refer to some other exterior object, they could hardly offer me a chance of making a mistake'. Conveniently, *ideas* – that is, generic mental contents considered just in themselves, and not as representatives of outer things – have all and only the properties we take them to have.

For most of us, however, there are times when we are uncertain what we really want or believe. We are prone to myriad forms and degrees of self-deception. Infallibility with respect to mental requires that whenever we exemplify a given mental property we know that we do so. But the ease with which we engage in talk of repression and the unconscious, together

---

Work on this paper was supported by the National Endowment for Humanities.

[1] The concept of privileged access is discussed usefully and at length in Alston (1971).

with our willingness to admit that we can fail to know our deepest prefer-
ences and opinions, suggest that infallibility is not part of the ordinary
conception of mentality. Similar considerations tell against incorrigibility,
the doctrine that beliefs we harbour concerning our own states of mind
cannot fail to be true. If our aim is to capture some plausible conception of
privileged access, then, it seems likely that both infallibility and incorrigibility are best left behind.

Direct Knowledge

One aspect of epistemic privilege is manifested in our conviction that we
possess a capacity to *know directly* the contents of our own minds. Direct
knowledge, I shall suppose, is knowledge not based on evidence. This
cannot be all there is to privileged access, however. It is unlikely either that
the scope of direct knowledge is limited to one's mental states, or that
one's mental states are knowable only directly. In general, whatever can be
known directly could be known as well on the basis of evidence. I know,
perhaps, at least some of my own mental states directly. Your knowledge
of them is indirect, mediated by your observation of what I say and do.
Like you, however, I may know nothing of certain of my states of mind.
And to the extent that I know my unconscious thoughts, I know them
exclusively on the basis of evidence, evidence perhaps supplied by others –
most especially by those who are acute observers of my behaviour.

It is important to be clear on what is and is not required for something
to be directly known. The directness in question is, of course, epistemological, not causal. Direct knowledge is not to be confused with Russellian
knowledge by acquaintance. What I know by acquaintance I know directly.
But what, if anything, I can know directly is a contingent matter. My
knowledge that a certain shrub is a Toyon may be based evidence concerning the shape of its leaves, the character of its bark, and the colour of
the blossoms it produces. If you are a botanist, your knowledge may, in
contrast, be direct. I can know directly what a blind person knows only by
inference. If mute creatures can be said to possess knowledge, then some
of these – pigeons, for instance, or honeybees – can know directly things I
know exclusively on the basis of evidence.

Although, in general, claims to direct knowledge can be supplemented
by appeals to evidence, this seems not to be so when the object of knowledge are one's own mental states. I may know directly that I harbour some
thought, or I may know this only indirectly, perhaps by means of some
elaborate process of self-analysis. When my knowledge is direct, however,

it is unlikely that, when prompted, I could produce relevant supporting evidence. Compare this with the case of a botanist who can tell at a glance that the shrub I am looking at is a Toyon. If I express doubts, the botanist can appeal to evidence of the sort I should need were I to make the identification.[2]

The asymmetry exhibited by such cases is undoubtedly important. It is difficult, however, to know what to make of it. I know directly – without evidence – that the vegetables I am eating are green and that my legs are crossed as I sit at my desk. If you insist that I produce evidence, I should not know what to do beyond indicating the items in question. It will not do, then, to imagine that privileged access can be explicated simply by an appeal to what can be known directly. The relation is not nearly so straightforward.

Is it, then, merely a contingent fact about my own mental states that I can know them directly? Although it is contingently true that on a given occasion I know myself to be in a certain mental state, it is plausible to suppose that such states are *essentially* such that they are directly knowable by agents to whom they belong. This may seem too weak to be helpful. After all, things other than states of mind can be known directly.[3] It is nevertheless, not obviously an essential property of such things that they are directly knowable.

This, however, even if correct, is scarcely illuminating. We have noted already that my enjoying privileged access cannot be a matter of my knowing *all* of my thoughts directly. Nor can it be that, for every thought I *do* know myself to possess, my knowledge of it is direct. Once we embrace a modest view of epistemic privilege, however, we encounter immodest prospects. If, for instance, it is possible that I fail to know *some* of my thoughts directly, then might not I fail to know most (or *all*) of them directly – or, indeed, fail to know them *at all*, directly or otherwise? The possibility seems ridiculous. Once it is admitted that I might fail to know some of my thoughts, however, what entitles me to suppose that I am, in general, in a better position than others to assess their character? The supposition apparently requires that I be aware of two classes of thought –

---

[2] Evidence thus produced would bear on the character of the botanist's knowledge *claim*. It need not, however, figure in his *knowing*.

[3] I mean by this that if they are known, they can be so known. The claim is not that we in fact possess knowledge, only that, if there is knowledge, some of it is direct. For stylistic reasons I shall omit the qualification in what follows.

those I do and those I do not know about – and that I recognize the latter class to be much smaller than the former. But of course I cannot compare two classes, one of which is known to me and the other of which I am ignorant.

Consider now my knowledge of *your* thoughts. This is not, in typical cases, direct. Nevertheless it is at least conceivable that I could come to know your states of mind directly, without, that is, inferring them in the usual ways. I might, for instance, be wired to you in such a way that I share your nervous system. Science fiction aside, most of us learn to read the thoughts of colleagues and loved-ones just as a botanist learns to read the flora of the surrounding countryside. Given a measure of ignorance about my own thoughts, then, it is conceivable that I could know your mind better than my own.[4]

A characterization of privileged access based exclusively on what is directly known is anaemic, hence unsatisfactory: I know some of my thoughts directly (but know some of them only by inference); I know some of your thoughts by inference (although there is nothing to prevent me from knowing some of them directly). Asymmetry survives only quantitatively: the proportion of my thoughts that I know directly appears invariably to be greater than the proportion of yours I know directly. One may, however, wonder why there could not be cases in which the proportion is reversed. Something has gone wrong surely. A conception of privileged access that takes us along our present path must somewhere have taken the wrong turning. We should do well, then, to backtrack and look more carefully at the terrain.

Direct Knowability and Intentional Content

Intentional states, by and large, exhibit two components, a particular content and an attitude or disposition of some sort toward that content. In the case of beliefs, desires, and other propositional attitudes, content is specifiable sententially and attitudes are characterizable as acceptings, withholdings, wants, and the like. Contents and attitudes can vary independently. This suggests that knowledge of intentional states incorporates a pair of distinguishable aspects, one pertaining to the content of the state, the other to its place in an agent's psychological economy. It suggests, as well, that in so far as we can be wrong about such things, we can be wrong

---

[4] Thus breathing new life into the old joke about two behaviourists meeting on the street. One says to the other: 'You're fine, how am I?'

in different ways – as when we fail to get the attitude right while being clear about the content, or grasp the attitude but misapprehend its object. And if we can be mistaken about each, it must be possible as well to be in the dark about both at once.

Until recently, doubts about infallible and incorrigible access to mental items have mostly been focused on considerations of the attitudes involved. A climber may wonder whether he really *believes* that his rope is safe or merely *hopes* that it is. He is, however, unlikely to be similarly puzzled about the content of the thought that concerns him. One may wonder whether such puzzlement is intelligible. Perhaps it is. A physicist reflecting on his belief that elections carry observers with them into superposition may do so without having any very satisfactory conception of what this comes to.[5]

Psychological theorizing in this century has provided ammunition for sceptics about attitudes. Recent work in the philosophy of mind may abet another sort of sceptic, one who doubts that we ever know for certain the *contents* of our own states of mind. For reasons I shall take up presently, the most promising accounts of mental content lend themselves to this form of radical scepticism. Before attempting to plumb those depths, however, we should be clear about what is included in the ordinary conception of privileged access.

Two points bear emphasizing. First, direct knowability of mental states holds, if at all, only for 'occurrent' states, those entertained at the time they are considered, and not, say, for those once, but no longer, possessed. My access to repressed states of mind or to those present only at some earlier time may be highly indirect. Second, beliefs we have about mental states and processes are neither infallible nor incorrigible. I may fail to know, directly or otherwise, what thoughts I harbour. And I may err in various ways in assessing their character. A plausible conception of direct knowability requires only that my mental states and processes be essentially such that they are directly knowable by me, not that they are in every case directly known.

Some such conception of direct knowability is required by our ordinary notion on mentality. We can accept this, I think while remaining agnostic about its realization, whatever it may be in virtue of which it obtains when and if it does obtain. Direct knowability constrains accounts of intention-

---

[5] Tyler Burge has argued that such cases are common. See, e.g., Burge (1986).

ality weakly but non-trivially. The point may be illustrated by reflecting on externalist theories of mental content.

Scepticism About Content

To focus the discussion, let us consider one important class of cognitive system, a class incorporating the capacity for something like *self-aware-ness*.[6] I have in mind systems capable of second- as well as first-order inten-tionality. Systems of this sort might, for instance, entertain beliefs about their own beliefs, desires, and intentions. More generally, such systems are capable of harbouring intentional states that include in their content the content of other intentional states. Self-awareness, when it is veridical, affords direct knowledge of mental contents.

Ordinary human beings count as self-aware systems in this sense. Whether other, non-human, creatures might achieve self-awareness is controversial. Differing intuitions concerning the reasonableness of ascribing intentional properties to mute creatures, or to computing machines, or thermostats, hinge partly on differences in one's willingness to regard systems lacking in self-awareness as properly intentional at all. The notion that a system possesses first-order intentional states only if it recognizes (or is capable of recognizing) its possession of these states is interesting and worth exploring in detail.[7] I shall be concerned here, how-ever, only with the *phenomenon* of self-awareness. My immediate aim is to show that one may consistently accept a relational or externalist explica-tion of intentional content and retain the conviction that access to one's own states of mind is epistemically privileged.

---

[6] I shall use the express 'self-awareness' in what is perhaps a non-standard way. I am con-cerned here only with the capacity to 'introspect' on mental states and goings-on, not any-thing more elaborate. I shall not address, for instance, the ability sometimes ascribed to human beings to focus inwardly on an ego, self, or other mental substrate.

[7] It meshes, certainly, in obvious ways with the notion that mental goings-on are essentially directly knowable. See, e.g., Searle (1985); and Davidson (1984). Searle and Davidson dif-fer importantly, however. Searle emphasizes the role of *consciousness*; Davidson focuses on the capacity for entertaining thoughts in which beliefs figure, thoughts about thoughts. The latter capacity is neither necessary nor sufficient for the possession of consciousness as it is ordinarily understood. Conscious thoughts are not – or not typically – thoughts about thoughts; and if first-order thoughts can be unconscious, there is nothing to prevent thoughts about thoughts from being similarly unconscious.

The matter is important, I think, because the conviction that intentional content must depend on environmental circumstances of agents whose states possess that content appears to eliminate entirely the possibility of privileged access. We are faced with a dilemma. On the one hand, when we consider introspection, it seems patent that we have something like a direct Cartesian entrée to the contents of our own thoughts. We have seen that this need not be taken to imply that we are infallible or incorrigible concerning the mental. It requires only that to the extent that we do comprehend our own thoughts, we typically do so directly – that is, without relying on inference or evidence. On the other hand, if we suppose that the content of a given state of one's mind is determined in part by complicated features of one's circumstances, features of which one is mostly unaware, it would seem that, in order to grasp the content of that state, one would first have to get at those external circumstances.

The prospect is doubly unsettling. First, it seems to oblige me to base beliefs about the contents of my own thoughts on evidence. This flies in the face of the ordinary conviction that our knowledge of such things is, on the whole, epistemologically direct, not founded on evidence. Second, if beliefs I entertain about my own states of mind depend on evidential backing, then I might, with fair frequency, *make mistakes* about those states. I might have evidence, for instance, that a particular belief I harbour is the belief that *p*, the belief, say, that snow is white. But I could be wrong. My belief *might*, for all I know, be a belief about something altogether different – that the sky is blue or even that snow is *not* white. My getting its content right apparently requires that I get the determinants of that content right, and, so long as these are epistemically mediated, I may easily fail to do so. Worse, I seem open to sceptical worries about whether I am *ever* right about the content of my own thoughts.

Reflections on such things produce a variety of responses. Thus, one may be inclined to reject out of hand any conception of mentality that leads in this direction. If there are any intentional states with content, these must be, typically anyway, self-intimating, our access to them direct and unproblematic. In contrast, one may regard these consequences not as counter-examples to the theory in question, but as interesting, though perhaps startling, *discoveries* about the epistemic status of states of mind. They force us to abandon discredited superstitions about access to our own thoughts.[8] Alternatively, we may follow Putnam and embrace anti-realism hoping thereby to salvage self-awareness and disarm the sceptic.[9]

It is possible, however, to reconcile direct access to mental content with both externalism and common-sense realism. At least this is what I shall contend. An ulterior motive stems from a conviction that it is important to make a place for intentional contents as legitimate psychological *phenomena*, *data*, items about which one might reasonably expect theories of intelligent behaviour to have something to say.

Externalist Accounts of Content

Let us begin by pretending that the contents of one's mental states are determined, not by intrinsic features of those states, but by their *circumstances*, by goings-on external to them. We may suppose, further, that the circumstances in question include a good deal that is outside the agent to whom the states belong. Let us call theories that explicate intentionality this way *externalist* theories.

Imagine, then, that some particular mental state of mine, M, has the content that p in virtue of the obtaining of some state of affairs, A, that includes states or events outside M, occurrences in my environment. On a very simple externalist theory M might have the content that *this is a tree* in virtue of being caused in me by a tree. Here the state of affairs, A, M's being caused by a tree, has, as it were, one foot inside me, in M, and another anchored in the outside world. Of course different versions of externalism will provide different accounts of A, whatever it is in virtue of which states of mind have their particular content. In some instances A will be a causal relation of a certain sort. In others it might be something else entirely.

Suppose now that I pause to consider the content of M, I *introspect* on my own state of mind. Let us dub this introspective state M', and let us call the external state of affairs in virtue of which M' has whatever content it has, A'. What can be said about the content of M'? Is it plausible to suppose that its content *includes* that of M, my first-order mental state? And, even if this is so, is there any reason to think *either* that M's content, whatever it is, could be accurately preserved in my introspective thought, M',

---

[8] See, e.g., Ruth Garrett Millikan, *Language, Thought and Other Biological Categories*, Cambridge, Bradford Books/M.I.T. Press, 1984.

[9] See, e.g., Hilary Putnam, *Reason, Truth and History*, Cambridge, Cambridge, University Press, 1981, ch. 1. See also J. Heil (1988).

or that my access to the content of *M* could be in any sense epistemically *direct*?

It might seem at first blush that access to the contents of first-order states like *M* would necessitate my somehow coming to recognize the obtaining of states of affairs like *A*, those responsible for first-order content. In our simplified example this would mean that for me to come to know that *M* was a state with the content that *this is a tree*, I should first have to discover that *M* was *caused by* a tree. This is not something I could discover simply by getting at *M*. I should need, it seems, *evidence* about the circumstances in which *M* was produced, evidence that could easily fall short of conclusiveness. Thus, even if I happened to be right about what caused *M*, hence about *M*'s intentional content, my access to that content would hardly be direct or privileged. It would be based on clues I assembled, and inferences I drew from these. In general, my beliefs about the content of my own thoughts might depend on the results of delicate tests and experiments.

It goes without saying that, under these circumstances, I might err in identifying the cause of *M*, hence err in my assessment of *M*'s content. And in cases where I did not take the trouble to investigate the aetiology of my thoughts, my beliefs about their contents would be scarcely more than shots in the dark. After all, if externalism were true, one could not discover a state's intentional properties merely by inspecting that state. A particular mental item, just in itself, might have any content whatever, or none at all.

Externalism without Scepticism

The emerging picture belies the ordinary conception of self-awareness. More seriously, we have seen that it portends an especially pernicious form of scepticism. A traditional sceptic seeks reasons for supposing that the world is as we think it is. We appear now to be faced with the prospect of a nastier sceptic, one who questions the presumption that we think what we think we think.[10]

---

[10] Similar concerns have been voiced by Donald Davidson whole position on this matter is discussed below. See, e.g., Davidson (1987). Difficulties one encounters in attempting to formulate a coherent version of scepticism about the contents of one's thoughts suggest, in any case, underlying incoherencies in theories of content inspiring such scepticism.

This altogether bleak outlook is, however, founded on a fundamental mischaracterization of externalism. Consider again my second-order introspective state M'. We are supposing that externalism is correct, hence that the content of M' is determined by some state of affairs, A', that is at least partly distinct from M'. What, now, is to prevent A' from determining an intentional content for M' that *includes* the content of M? What, for instance, keeps our simplified theory from allowing that a causal relation of a certain sort endows my introspective thought with a content encompassing the content of the thought on which I am introspecting? The envisaged causal relation might plausibly be taken to include as a component the causal relation required to establish the content of the state on which I am introspecting, and it might include much more as well.

To see the point, it is important to keep in mind that externalist theories of the sort under discussion require only that certain conditions *obtain* in order for a given state to have a particular intentional content. They do not, or anyhow need not, require in addition that one know or believe these states to obtain.[11] Thus the content of M, that p, was determined by its being the case that A, not by my knowing or believing that A obtains. In our simplified externalist theory, my thought concerns a tree because it was prompted by a tree, not because I know or believe it was so prompted. The same must be true for second-order states of mind. When I introspect, the content of my introspection will be determined by its being caused in an appropriate way, not by my discovering that it was caused in that way.

One may be suspicious of the last move. It might be granted that my introspective thought could be about my thought that p, without thereby granting that the content of my introspection includes the *content* of the introspected thought. Just as a thought of George Herman Ruth need not include the Sultan of Swat in its content, even though George Herman Ruth *is* the Sultan of Swat, so it seems perfectly possible for me to introspect my thought that p without comprehending it as the thought *that p*. If externalism were true, my introspections would seem *typically* to have

---

[11] An externalist theory that did so would incorporate an epistemic component. I doubt that anything is to be gained by such as emendation, but even if an epistemic condition is added the point at issue here remains unaffected provided we also allow the epistemic condition itself to be externally satisfiable, that is, provided we allow that I might know, for instance, that p just in virtue of certain, possibly external, conditions obtaining. The matter is discussed in more detail in 'The Epistemic Route to Anti-Realism'. See also Wittgenstein's remark in the *Tractatus*, § 4.002.

this character. This, at any rate, appears to follow from the view that the determinants of the content of an intentional state are external to that state.

It is possible, certainly, for me to entertain a second-order thought about the thought that *p*, without *that p* occurring as part of the content of the second-order thought. I may think, for instance, of a complicated idea I had yesterday, without having a very clear notion of what that idea included. Similarly, I may apprehend an expression of the thought that *p* (in Urdu, say) without recognizing it to express the thought that *p*. The case we are considering, however, is the familiar one in which I introspect my own occurrent thought.

The contents of ordinary intentional goings-on, according to externalism, are determined by the obtaining of states of affairs that include components distinct from those goings-on. Contents, so determined, need not, and almost certainly will not, reflect important aspects of those external components. Similarly, the contents of introspective states need not, and almost certainly will not, reflect features of the external determinants of either those states themselves or the introspected states. My second-order introspective awareness of a particular intentional state can incorporate the latter's content without having to include (as part of *its* content) the conditions ultimately responsible for fixing the sense of the introspected thought. The content of *both* thoughts is generated externally. The content of second-order thoughts – introspections – would be determined, I have suggested, by a complex condition that included, perhaps, the condition responsible for the content of corresponding first-order states.

Privileged Access and the Mind's Eye

I have been discussing externalist theories of content as though only these could motivate doubts about the possibility of privileged access. We worry that, if the determinants of content are not, or not exclusively, 'in the head', our access to content will be a chancy thing. But why should *proximity* be thought to matter? If the contents of one's thoughts were determined entirely by the state of one's brain, why should this fact alone make our access to them any less indirect or difficult? Nor is it clear that a Cartesian is in any better position to account for epistemic privilege. A thought's occurring in a non-physical substance does not, by itself, afford a reason for supposing that one's apprehension of it is unproblematic. Considerations of this sort suggest that worries about access to mental contents associated with externalism are misplaced. Precisely the same worries can be generated for non-externalist, even Cartesian, theories. Difficulties arise, if at all, not from the external or relational character of whatever fixes content, but from some other source.

The culprit, according to Donald Davidson, is not externalism but a certain 'picture of the mind' in which beliefs about the contents of one's mental states are taken to be based on inward glimpses of those states or on the grasping of particular entities (*contents*, perhaps, or *propositions*, or *sentences in mentalese*). He recommends that we abandon the notion that knowledge of mental contents requires our inwardly perceiving in this way. Once we do so, we remove at least one of the reasons for supposing that externalism undermines privileged access.

Although our discussion has focused on propositional attitudes, it will be useful to reflect briefly on a distinct class of mental occurrence, the entertaining of visual images. I say to you: 'Form an image of your grandmother', and you comply. Suppose I now ask: 'How do you know that the image is of your *grandmother* – and not, say someone *just like* her?' The question is ill-conceived. It is not that you cannot be wrong about what it is you imagine. If the person whom you had been raised to regard as your grandmother were an imposter, then you would be wrong in supposing that the image you now form is of your grandmother. It is an image of an imposter. This however, seems not to be a mistake you make about the image. You mislabel that image because you are mistaken about your grandmother.

Imagining, at least in this respect, resembles drawing – as distinct from observing – a picture. In the course of a lecture on the battle of Borodino, you make *X*s on the blackboard to mark the location of Napoleon's forces and *O*s to mark the disposition of Kutuzov's army. I enquire: 'How do you know the *X*s stand for Napoleon's troops and not Kutuzov's?' The question misfires no less that the corresponding question about an image you form of your grandmother. You may be wrong in many ways about Borodino, of course, in which case you will be wrong in supposing that your diagram depicts things as they were on the day of the battle. But the diagram is yours, and there cannot be any question of its failing to mean what you intend it to mean. As an observer, my situation is different. I could well be wrong or confused about your *X*s and *O*s. The asymmetry here is instructive. You and I are differently related to what you have drawn. I am an observer and, like an observer, may err in understanding or describing what I see. You, however, are not, at any rate, not essentially an observer. I must take your word concerning what you have drawn, not because you have a better, more proximate view of it, but because the drawing is yours.

The privileged status we enjoy with respect to the contents of our own minds is analogous. That is, in introspecting and describing our thoughts, we are not reporting episodes that appear before our mind's eye. Were that so, we should be at a loss to account for the privileged status such reports are routinely accorded. The access I enjoy to my own mental contents would be superior to what is available to you, perhaps, but only accidentally so. Its superiority would be like that I enjoy with respect to the contents of my trouser pockets.

Consider the following description of visual imagining:

> ...[V]isual images might be like displays produced on a cathode ray tube (CRT) by a computer program operating on stored data. That is, ... images are temporary spatial displays in active memory that are generated from more abstract representations in long-term memory. Interpretive mechanisms (the 'mind's eye') work over ('look at') these internal displays and classify them in terms of semantic categories (as would be involved in realizing that a particular spatial configuration corresponds to a dog's ear, for example).[12]

An account of this sort, whatever its empirical credentials, exudes an aura of implausibility at least in part because it promotes a conception of mental access that threatens to undermine epistemic privilege. If the conception were apt, then whatever asymmetry we find in the beliefs you and I have about your states of mind is purely fortuitous. If I could look over your mind's shoulder, then my epistemological position would be no different from yours as you gazed inwardly. Indeed I might see clearly what you apprehend only darkly.

Davidson holds that we are bound to misconstrue privileged access – what he calls first-person authority – so long as we persist in depicting the mind in this way.

> There is a picture of the mind which has become so ingrained in our philosophical tradition that it is almost impossible to escape its influence even when its worst faults are recognized and repudiated. In one crude, but familiar, version, it goes like this: the mind is a theatre in

---

[12] Kosslyn et al. (1979). A discussion of the liabilities of this conception of imagery may be found in Heil (1982).

which the conscious self watches a passing show ... The show consists of 'appearances', sense data, qualia, what is given in experience. What appear on the stage are not the ordinary objects of the world that the outer eye registers and the heart loves, but their purported representatives. Whatever we know about the world outside depends on what we can glean from the inner clues.[13]

Although Davidson's point is intended to apply, not to mental images, but to propositional attitudes, the moral is the same.

Most of us long ago gave up the idea of perceptions, sense data, the flow of experience, as things 'given' to the mind; we should treat propositional objects in the same way. Of course people have beliefs, wishes, doubts, and so forth; but to allow this is not to suggest that beliefs, wishes, and doubts are *entities* in or before the mind, or that being in such states requires there to be corresponding mental objects. ...Sentences about the attitudes are relational; for *semantic* reasons there must therefore be objects to which to relate those who have attitudes. But having an attitude is not having an entity before the mind; for compelling *psychological* and *epistemological* reasons we should deny that there are objects of the mind.[14]

Davidson is convinced that worries about privileged access can be dispelled provided we abandon the notion that our awareness of mental contents is best regarded as the apprehension of content-bearing entities or episodes. In the case of mental images, this requires that we let go of the traditional conception of images as pictures or picture-like copies of external things gazed at inwardly. In the case of beliefs, desires, and other propositional attitudes, we are to turn away from the notion that, in introspecting, we encounter propositions, mental sentences, senses, or contents.

If this were so, and I am inclined to believe it is so, then we should have a way of defusing worries about privileged access that might other-wise to be thought to arise from externalist or naturalistic accounts of mental contents. We should be able to see how something like a Cartesian entrée to the contents of one's own mind does not depend on the Cartesian conception of mental substance. Indeed the picture of introspection encour-

---

[13] Davidson (1987, p 453).

[14] Davidson (1987, pp. 454–5).

aged by that conception is precisely the source of the difficulties we have been considering.

Concluding Remarks

Davidson's suggestion requires that we jettison the notion that content-bearing states of mind are usefully regarded as entities – Cartesian ideas, sentences in mentalese, neural inscriptions, pictures on an interior television screen. Such entities might exist. Indeed we may be obliged to mention them in ascriptions and descriptions of thoughts, images, and the like. The point, then, is not one issuing from considerations of parsimony. It is founded, rather, on the notion that the having of a thought or image 'is not the having of an object before the mind'.

> ...[I]f to have a thought is to have an object 'before the mind', and the identity of the object determines what the thought is, then it must always be possible to be mistaken about what one is thinking. For unless one knows *everything* about the object, there will always be senses in which one does not know what the object is. Many attempts have been made to find a relation between a person and an object which will in all contexts hold if and only if the person can intuitively and said to know what the object is. But none of these attempts has succeeded, and I think the reason is clear. The only object that would satisfy the twin requirements of being 'before the mind' and also such that it determines ... the content of a thought, must, like Hume's ideas and impressions, 'be what it seems and seem what it is'. There are no such objects, public or private, abstract or concrete.[15]

If we imagined that introspecting were a matter of inwardly scrutinizing a mental object, then we should have to suppose that our ability to appreciate the content of introspected thoughts depends on a capacity to 'read off' a thought's content from an inspection of the thought itself. Externalism poses obvious difficulties for such a picture. I have suggested, however, the non-externalist, even Cartesian, accounts of content are equally ill-suited to its requirements. We must understand theories of content as setting out conditions that agents must satisfy if they are to have contentful states of mind. Their satisfying these conditions need not be a matter of their recognizing them to be satisfied. This, I think is, or ought to be, uncontroversial. Anyone who questions it is faced with the spectre

---

[15] Davidson (1987, p. 455).

of regress: if my thought's having a particular content requires that I recognize the obtaining of certain conditions, then it requires my having some other thought with a particular content, one, namely, corresponding to this recognition. But of course, *this* thought would require its own corresponding recognition of the obtaining of appropriate conditions for *its* content, and we are off on a regress.[16]

If we are willing to allow the regress-blocking manœuver in the case of ordinary, first-order thoughts, there is no reason to balk at its application to second-order thoughts, introspections. Beliefs about the contents of one's own thoughts, then, need not be based on beliefs about whatever it is that fixes the contents of those thoughts. The contents of second-order thoughts are fixed, just as are the contents of first-order thoughts, by the obtaining of appropriate conditions.

This simple point will be difficult to appreciate, however, so long as we cling to what Davidson calls 'a faulty picture of the mind', a picture in which knowledge of the contents of one's thoughts is caricatured as a species of inner perception. The conception of the mind as a place where specialized mental objects are housed ceased long ago to carry philosophical conviction. It survives, however, at least implicitly, in conceptions of the access we have to our own mental contents. My aim has been to show that it need not.

REFERENCES

Alston, W. P. 1971. Varieties of Privileged Access. *American Philosophical Quarterly*: 223–41.

Burge, T. 1986. Intellectual Norms and the Foundations of Mind. *Journal of Philosophy*: 697–720.

Davidson, D. 1984. Thought and Talk. Pp. 155–70 in *Inquiries Into Truth and Interpretation*. Oxford: Oxford University Press.

———. 1987. Knowing One's Own Mind. Pp. 441–58 in *Proceedings and Addresses of the American Philosophical Association*. Chapter 3 in this volume.

---

[16] An account of content with an epistemic component can perhaps avoid a regress, though only by incorporating a commitment to an externalist account of knowing, one that enables agents to know that something is so even when they are not, in the usual sense, justified in believing that it is so. see n. 11.

Heil, J. 1982. What Does the Mind's Eye Look At? *Journal of Mind and Behavior.* 143–9.

———. 1988. The Epistemic Route to Anti-Realism. *Australasian Journal of Philosophy.* 161–73.

Kosslyn, S., S. Pinder, G. Smith, and S. Schwartz. 1979. The Demystification of Mental Imagery. *The Behavioral and Brain Sciences.* 535–81.

Searle, J. R. 1985. *Minds, Brains, and Science.* Cambridge, MA: Harvard University Press.

Part III: Externalism and Authoritative Self-Knowledge are Incompatible

6

Content and Self-Knowledge

Paul A. Boghossian

Introduction

I. This paper argues that, given a certain apparently inevitable thesis about content, we could not know our own minds. The thesis is that the content of a thought is determined by its relational properties.

The problem can be stated roughly, but intuitively, like this. We sometimes know our thoughts directly, without the benefit of inference from other beliefs. (Indeed, given a plausible internalism about justification, this claim is not merely true but necessary.) This implies that we know our thoughts either on the basis of some form of inner observation, or on the basis of nothing. But there is a difficulty either way. On the one hand, given that the content properties of thoughts are individuated in terms of their relational properties, we could not know what we think merely by looking inwards. What we would need to see, if we are to know by mere looking, is not there to be seen. And, on the other, there appear to be serious objections to the suggestion that we may know our thoughts on the basis of nothing.[1]

---

[1] How a contingent proposition might be known on the basis of nothing will be explained in part III. A word also about 'inner observation': It makes no difference to the argument of this paper if you think of inner observation as amounting to traditional introspection, or if you think of it as amounting to the operation of some Armstrong-style 'brain-scanner'. What *is* crucial to inner observation models of self-knowledge is the claim that beliefs about one's own thoughts are justified by the deliverances of some internal monitoring capacity, much like beliefs about the external environment are justified by the deliverances of an external monitoring capacity (perception).

For 'brain-scanners' see Armstrong (1968). For a useful survey of various conceptions of introspection see Lyons (1986).

The paper proceeds as follows. Part I explains why we could not know our thoughts on the basis of reasoning or inference. Part II explains why we could not know them on the basis of looking. And Part III explains why we could not know them on the basis of nothing.

I consider the skeptical claim about self-knowledge to have the status of a paradox: apparently acceptable premises lead to an unacceptable conclusion. For I do not seriously envisage that we do not know our own minds. Our capacity for self-knowledge is not an optional component of our ordinary self-conception, a thesis we may be able to discard while preserving all that really matters. It is a fundamental part of that conception, presupposed by some of the very concepts that constitute it (consider intentional action). So long as we are not able to see our way clear to abandoning that conception – and I am assuming that we have not yet been shown how to do so – there can be no question of accepting the skeptical claim.[2]

The point of advancing it, then, is not to promote skepticism but understanding: I hope that by getting clear on the conditions under which self-knowledge is not possible, we shall better understand the conditions under which it is. I have to confess, however, that at the present time I am unable to see what those conditions might be.

A couple of preliminary remarks before we proceed. First, I propose to be reasonably serious in the use of the term 'knowledge': by 'self-knowledge' I shall mean not just a *true* belief about one's own thoughts, but a *justified* one. (I do not, however, propose to be so serious as to worry about the complexities induced by Gettier-style counterexamples.) Second, I want to keep the discussion as free as possible of problematic auxiliary assumptions about the nature of thought. In particular, I do not want to assume a 'language of thought' model of thinking. I hope one of these days to write a paper entitled "The Language of Thought Hypothesis in the Philosophy of Mind." It would argue that, contrary to what many people seem to believe, a language of thought model has profound and unexpected implications for the way we think about most mental phenomena. Issues about self-knowledge, in particular, are transformed by its assumption. The reason should be evident: a language of thought model implies that there are *type–type* correlations between certain purely formal and intrinsic properties of thoughts and their semantic properties. This is a heady assumption that stands to profoundly affect the account we are

---

[2] For arguments in support of the indispensability of the ordinary conception, see Boghossian (1990).

able to give of our capacity to know the semantic properties of thoughts. Too heady, I think, to be assumed uncritically and, hence, too heady for the purposes of this paper.

I

The Character of Self-Knowledge

Inference and Self-Knowledge.

2. Many extravagant claims have been made about our capacity to know our own minds. Descartes, who was responsible for the worst excesses, taught many subsequent generations of philosophers that self-knowledge was both infallible and exhaustive. In contrast with our knowledge of other people's minds, Descartes held, our access to our own contemporaneous mental states and events could issue neither in false belief nor in ignorance.

These famous Cartesian claims are not, of course, wholly without substance; for a certain restricted class of mental events – namely, sensations – they may even be true. For it does seem constitutive of, say, an occurrence of pain, that it register with us precisely as an occurrence of pain. And so, it seems not conceivable, in respect of facts about pain, that we should be either ignorant of their existence or mistaken about their character, just as the Cartesian doctrine requires.

But the corresponding theses about contentful or representational states carry little contemporary conviction. That we harbor a multitude of thoughts of whose existence we are unaware is a presupposition not only of Freudian theory, but of much of present-day cognitive science. And phenomena that are intelligible only if infallibility is false – self-deception, for instance – seem pervasive.

3. A Cartesian account, then of the distinction between first-person and third-person knowledge of mind must be rejected. But we should be wary, in correcting for Cartesian excess, of recoiling too far in the opposite direction. For there remains, even after we have discarded the problematic Cartesian claims, a profound asymmetry between the way in which I know my own thoughts and the way in which I may know the thoughts of others. The difference turns not on the epistemic status of the respective beliefs, but on the manner in which they are arrived at, or justified. In the case of others, I have no choice but to *infer* what they think from observations about what they do or say. In my own case, by contrast, inference is

neither required nor relevant. Normally, I know what I think – what I believe, desire, hope or expect – without appeal to supplementary evidence. Even where such evidence is available, I do not consult it. I know what I think directly. I do not defend my self-attributions; nor does it normally make sense to ask me to do so.[3]

Ryle attempted to deny all this.[4] He tried to defend the view that there is no asymmetry between first-person and third-person access to mental states. In both cases, he maintained, the process is essentially the same: ordinary inspection of ordinary behavior gives rise to the discovery of patterns in that behavior, which in turn leads to the imputation of the appropriate propositional attitudes.

The claim carries no conviction whatever. The trouble is not merely that it runs counter to all the relevant appearance, offering an implausible explanation for the knowledge we have of our thoughts. The trouble is that, for much of what we do know about our own thoughts, it can offer no explanation at all. Consider an act of entertaining a particular proposition. You think: Even lousy composers sometimes write great arias. And you know, immediately on thinking it, that that is what you thought. What explanation can the Rylean offer of this? The difficulty is not merely that, contrary to appearance and the canons of epistemic practice, he has to construe the knowledge as inferential. The difficulty is that he has to construe it as involving inference from premises about behavior that you could not possibly possess. Your knowledge of that occurrent thought could not have been inferred from any premises about your behavior because that thought could not yet have come to have any traction on your behavior. So it's not merely that, on the Rylean view, you would have to know inferentially what you appear to know noninferentially. It's that you would not know at all what you seem to know unproblematically.

Any inferential conception is likely to succumb to this sort of objection. Since the epistemic norms governing ascriptions of self-knowledge do not require possession of supplementary evidence, for any item of evidence insisted on by an inference-based account – whether it involve behavior or the environment or even the causal properties of thoughts – it should be possible to describe a situation in which you know your thoughts but you do not know the item in question.

---

[3] Many philosophers have pointed this out. See for example, Davidson (1986, p. 441–42).

[4] See Ryle (1949).

Internalism and Inferential Self-Knowledge

4. It is, actually, surprisingly little noticed that on an *internalist* conception of justification – a conception to which many philosophers remain profoundly sympathetic – knowledge of one's own mental states *has* to be non-inferential. On this view, the alternative is not merely implausible; it is incoherent. I shall explain.

The intuition that fuels internalism in the theory of justification is the thought that someone cannot count as justified in holding a certain belief if, judged from the standpoint of his own subjective conception of the situation, he may appear epistemologically irresponsible or irrational in accepting that belief. The intuition is effectively triggered by various examples in which, although a person's belief satisfies basic externalist demands – the belief is formed by a reliable belief-forming mechanism and so on – the person does not count as epistemically justified because, as far as he concerned, he has no reason for accepting the belief and may, indeed, have reasons for rejecting it.

Consider Sam.[5] Sam believes himself to have the power of clairvoyance, though he has no reason for the belief, and some evidence – in the form of apparently cogent scientific results – against it. One day he comes to believe, for no apparent reason, the President is in New York City. He maintains this belief, appealing to his alleged clairvoyant power, even though he is at the same time aware of a massive amount of apparently cogent evidence, consisting of news reports, allegedly live television pictures, and so on, indicating that the President is at that time in Washington, D.C. Now the President is in fact in New York City, the evidence to the contrary being part of an official hoax. Moreover, Sam does in fact have completely reliable clairvoyant power under the conditions then satisfied, and his belief about the President did result from the operation of that power.

Is Sam justified in his belief about the President? Basic reliabilist demands are met; but the intuition persists that the belief cannot be epistemically justified because, judged from the standpoint of Sam himself, it is epistemically thoroughly irrational.

Examples such as this are at the heart of internalist dissatisfaction with externalist conceptions of justification; they motivate the requirement that, if a belief depends upon evidence, "the knower [must] grasp the con-

---

[5] The example is adapted from L. Bonjour (1985, p. 38–40).

nection between the evidence and what it is evidence for," if his belief is to be justified.[6]

Suppose, then, that the proposition that p depends on the proposition that q. According to internalism, if I am to be justified in believing that p, I must believe that p as a result both of my recognition that I believe that q, and that a belief that q justifies a belief that p. Spelling this out in explicit detail, we have:

1. I believe that p.
2. I believe that q.
3. The proposition that q justifies the proposition that p.
4. I know that I believe that q.
5. I know that a belief that q justifies a belief that p.
6. I believe that p as a result of the knowledge expressed in 4 and 5.

5. Now, there is, of course, a *standard* problem in holding that all knowledge of empirical propositions is inferential, that all beliefs can be justified only by reference to other beliefs. This is the problem of the regress of justification: If the belief that p is to count as justified, then the belief that q on which its justification depends must itself be justified. But if *all* beliefs can be justified only by reference to other beliefs, then the belief that q must itself be justified by reference to other beliefs. And this threatens to lapse into a vicious regress.

And theory of justification must confront this problem. The available non-skeptical options – Foundationalism and Coherentism – are well known and need not be rehearsed here.

The point I wish to make, however, is that there is a *special* problem sustaining a thoroughly inferential conception of *self-knowledge*, one that is independent of the *standard* problem of the regress of justification.

6. In order to bring it out, waive the standard problem: let us not require that if the non-intrinsically credible proposition that p is to be justifiably believed, then it has to rest on a belief that q that is itself justified;

---

[6] D. J. O'Connor and B. Carr (1982, p. 75). Of course, there are responses available to the externalist. I am not going to consider them here because I am not here trying to *argue* for internalism; I am just describing it. Again, for detailed discussion see Bonjour, (1985).

let us simply require that the belief that p be justified *relative* to the belief that q, in accordance with standard internalist requirements.

Where the subject matter of concern is knowledge of one's own beliefs, the belief that p will be a belief to the effect that I have a certain belief, say, that I believe that r. Since we are supposing that all self-knowledge is inferential, there must be a belief on which this belief rests. Let that be the belief that s. Now, what would have to be true if I am to be justified in believing that I believe that r?

1'. I believe that I believe that r.

2'. I believe that s.

3'. The proposition that s justifies the proposition that I believe that r.

4'. I know that I believe that s.

5'. I know that a belief that s justifies the belief that I believe that r.

6'. I believe that I believe that r as a result of the knowledge expressed in 4' and 5'.

The problem is transparent. In order to be justified in believing that I have a certain belief, I must already know that I have some other belief (4'): In order to know that I believe that r, I must antecedently know that I believe that s. But how was knowledge of *this* belief acquired? On the assumption that all self-knowledge is inferential, it could have been acquired only by inference from yet other known beliefs. And now we are off on a vicious regress.[7]

The problem with sustaining a thoroughly inferential conception of *self-knowledge* should have been evident from the start. For the ordinary notion of being justified in believing a non-intrinsically credible empirical proposition *presupposes* self-knowledge. For it presupposes that one has grasped the fact that one's belief in that proposition bears some appropriate epistemic relation to one's other beliefs. In ordinary epistemological discussions this does not emerge as a problem because those discussions tend to focus exclusively on the justification of belief concerning the external world; they tend, understandably, to take knowledge of the

---

[7] The regress does not particularly depend on the fact that the relation between the beliefs consists in *inference*. There are possible coherentist views according to which mediated justification consists not in inference but in "membership" in an appropriate system of beliefs. All such views, applied to self-knowledge, are subject to the regress outlined in the text, given internalist assumptions. (I am indebted here to Crispin Wright.)

beliefs themselves for granted. When such knowledge is not taken for granted, however, it emerges very clearly that not *all* knowledge of one's beliefs can be inferential. On pain of a vicious regress, it must be possible to know the content of some mental states non-inferentially.[8]

7. The intuitive epistemic facts indicate that knowledge of one's mental states is direct. And an internalist conception of justification implies that it has to be. There are two ways to accommodate this claim.

We may conclude, on the one hand, that self-knowledge is not inferential because it is based on some form of inner observation; or, on the other, that is not inferential because it is based on nothing – at any rate, on nothing empirical.

How might a contingent fact be known on the basis of nothing empirical? We shall consider that question in part III. Before that, however, I want to turn to asking whether we could know our thoughts on the basis of inner observation.

II

Content and Knowledge of Content

8. The suggestion that I know about my thoughts by being introspectively aware of them seems, from a phenomenological standpoint anyway, overwhelmingly plausible. It is not simply that I have reliable beliefs about my thoughts. I catch some of my thoughts in the act of being thought. I think: If she says that one more time, I'm leaving. And I am aware, imme-

---

[8] I am inclined to believe that (at least part of) which is going on in the famous passage that concludes Wittgenstein's discussion of rule-following in his *Philosophical Investigations* is an argument to this effect. The passage reads:

> It can be seen that there is a misunderstanding here from the mere fact that in the course of our argument we give one interpretation after another; as if each one contented us at least for a moment, until we thought of yet another standing behind it. What this shows is that there is a way of grasping a rule that is *not* an *interpretation*. (*PI*: 201)

The textual evidence strongly indicates that Wittgenstein uses the term "interpretation" to mean "hypothesis as the meaning of." Read this way, the passage says that the moral of the rule-following "paradox" is that there must be a way of grasping the content of a mental event without having to form hypotheses as to its content.

This is not the occasion to say what else might be going on in that passage or to defend this reading in greater detail.

diately on thinking it, that that is what I thought. Can 'inner awareness' provide the right explanation for how I know my thoughts?

There are many aspects to this question. An exhaustive treatment would distinguish carefully between occurrent events – fleeting thoughts, sudden fancies – and standing states – fixed beliefs, stable desires – and would worry about the epistemological ramifications of that distinction. It would also distinguish between the distinct attitudes that one may sustain toward a given content – judging, believing, desiring, entertaining – and explore any corresponding epistemic differences. Here, however, I shall not be concerned with these important nuances. For my worry is that, given certain currently prevailing orthodoxies about content, it is impossible to see how *any* contentful state could be known on the basis of inner observation.

The difficulty stems from the contemporary commitment to a relationist conception of content: the view that the content properties of mental states and events are determined by, or supervenient upon, their *relational* properties. Intuitively, the difficulty seems clear: how could anyone be in a position to know his thoughts merely by observing them, if facts about their content are determined by their relational properties? Articulating the intuitive problem in explicit detail is the task of the present part.

Anti-Individualism and Self-Knowledge

9. The commitment to relationism is evident, of course, in *wide* or *anti-individualistic* conceptions of thought content. According to such views, many of a person's thought contents are necessarily dependent on relations that that person bears to the physical or, in some cases, social environment. The view is supported by a series of now-famous thought experiments. Their strategy is to show that two individuals who are molecule-for-molecule duplicates of each other, may nevertheless think different thoughts if their environments differ from each other in certain specified ways. Thus, Putnam has argued that *part* of what makes it true that some of my thoughts involve the concept *water*, is that it is typically *in re* H_2O that I token those thoughts; a duplicate of mine, who grew up in an indistinguishably similar environment, except that in it the liquid that filled the lakes and swimming pools consisted of XYZ and not H_2O, would not have the concept water but some other concept, *twater*. Similarly, Tyler Burge has argued that part of what makes it true that some of my thoughts involve the concept *arthritis* is that I live in, and defer to, a community in which the concept of arthritis is used in a certain way, a

duplicate of mine, who grew up in an indistinguishably similar community except that in it the use of the concept was extended so as to cover all rheumatoid ailments, would not have the concept *arthritis* but some other concept, *tharthritis*.

10. Now, doesn't it follow from such anti-individualistic views that we cannot know our thoughts in a direct, purely observational manner? The following line of reasoning might seem to lead rather swiftly to that conclusion. To know my water thoughts, I would have to know that they involve the concept *water* and not the concept *twater*. But I could not know whether my thought involves the concept *water* or the concept *twater* without investigating my environment. For what I would need to know is whether it was typically *in re* H_2O or typically *in re* XYZ, that I token my thoughts; and I certainly would have to investigate my environment in order to know that. I could hardly know such facts by mere introspection. It would seem to follow, therefore, that I could not know the contents of my thought purely observationally: I would have to *infer* what I think from facts about my environment.

This line of reasoning is no doubt too swift. As it stands it appears to be making problematic assumptions about the conditions required for knowledge.[9] Consider perceptual knowledge. Someone may know, by looking, that he has a dime in his hand. But it is controversial, to put it mildly, whether he needs to know all the conditions that make such knowledge possible. He need not have checked, for example, that there is no counterfeit money in the vicinity, nor does he need to be able to tell the difference between a genuine dime and every imaginable counterfeit that could have been substituted. The ordinary concept of knowledge appears to call for no more than the exclusion of "relevant" alternative hypotheses (however exactly that is to be understood); and mere logical possibility does not confer such relevance.

Similar remarks apply to the case of self-knowledge. And so, since under normal circumstances the *twater* hypothesis is not a relevant alternative, we ought not to assume, as the swift argument evidently does, that we could not know our actual thought contents unless we are able to discriminate between them and their various twin counterparts.

11. The swift argument, however, suggests a slower and more convincing argument for the same conclusion. For it seems fairly easy to describe scenarios in which the twin hypotheses *are* relevant alternatives, but in

---

[9] This point is made in Burge (1988, pp. 654–655).

which they are, nevertheless, not discriminable non-inferentially from their actual counterparts.

Imagine that twin-earth actually exists and that, without being aware of it, S undergoes a series of switches between earth and twin-earth. Most anti-individualists agree that, if a person were to remain in each situation long enough, that person would eventually acquire the concepts appropriate to that situation.[10] There are two ways to imagine the final outcome. On the one hand, we may imagine that after a series of such switches, S ends up with *both* earthian and twin-earthian concepts: thoughts involving both *arthritis* and *tharthritis* are available to him. Or, alternatively, we may imagine that with every such slow switch a wholesale displacement of S's resident concepts takes place, so that at any given time either the earthian or the twin-earthian concepts are available to him, but not both.

The story is usually told, I believe, in the second of these two ways; though so far as I can tell, it is perfectly coherent – and a lot more interesting – to tell it the other way. Still, in the interests of keeping matters as simple as possible, I shall follow tradition and imagine only the second version.[11] I invite you to consider, then, a thinker S, who, quite unawares, has been shuttled back and forth between earth and twin-earth, each time staying long enough to acquire the concepts appropriate to his current situation, and at the expense of the concepts appropriate to his previous situation.

What does S know? By assumption, he is not aware that the switches have taken place and nothing about his qualitative mental life or his perceived environment tips him off. Indeed, S may not even be aware of the existence of twin-earth or of the dependence of content on environment.

---

[10] Burge and Davidson are explicit about this.

[11] The first version of the slow switching story involves questions that admit of no easy answer. Suppose both earthian and twin-earthian thoughts are simultaneously available to you. And suppose you think a thought that you would express with the words "I have arthritis." How is it determined whether this particular thought token involves the concept *arthritis* or the concept *tharthritis*? (This is not a question about how you would *know* whether it involved the one or the other; it's a question about what *makes it true* that it involves the one and not the other.) There seems to be no simple answer. It certainly does not seem right to say, for reasons that underlie the intuition that quick switching wouldn't suffice for change of content, that it is simply a function of the environment in which the thought is tokened. Nor are there other obvious dimensions of difference to appeal to: *ex hypothesi*, thoughts with the different contents would have exactly the same functional roles, the same linguistic expresion and the same associated qualitative episodes (if any).

As far as S is concerned, he has always lived on earth. If someone were to ask him, just after one set of twin-earthian concepts has been displaced by a set of earthian ones, whether he has recently thought thoughts involving an arthritis-like concept distinct from *arthritis*, S would presumably say "no." Any yet, of course, according to the anti-individualist story, he has. His knowledge of his own past thoughts seems very poor, but not presumably because he simply can't *remember* them. Could it be because he never knew them?

Let us in fact confront that question directly. Does S know what he is thinking while he is thinking it? Suppose he is on twin-earth and thinks a thought that he would express with the words "I have arthritis." Could he know what he thought? The point to bear in mind is that the hypothesis that he thought *I have arthritis* is now a relevant alternative. He, of course, is not aware of that, but that doesn't change matters. Epistemic relevance is not a subjective concept. Someone may not be aware that there is a lot of counterfeit money in his vicinity; but if there is, the hypothesis that the dime-looking object in his hand is counterfeit needs to be excluded before he can be said to know that it is a dime. Similarly, S has to be able to exclude the possibility that his thought involved the concept *arthritis* rather than the concept *tharthritis*, before he can be said to know what he thought is. But this means that he has to *reason* his way to a conclusion about his thought; and reason to it, moreover, from evidence about his external environment which, by assumption, he does not possess. How, then, can he know his thought at all? – much less know it directly?[12]

Individualist Content and Self-Knowledge

12. Ever since Putnam first invented twin-earth, philosophers have expressed concern about the compatibility of wide individuation with the direct character of self-knowledge.[13] In the previous section I have tried

---

[12] It is no objection to this argument to point out that, on *this* way of telling the switching story, S cannot even frame the hypothesis he is called upon to exclude. Someone may not have the concept of counterfeit money, but if there is a lot of counterfeit money in his vicinity, then he must be able to exclude the hypothesis that the coin in his hand is counterfeit before he can be said to know that it is a dime. The fact that he cannot so much as frame the relevant hypothesis does not absolve him of this requirement. In any case, any residual worries on this score can be averted, if necessary, by telling the switching story in the alternative way outlined in the text.

[13] See, for example, Andrew Woodfield's remarks in the "Introduction" to his collection (Woodfield 1982, p. viii). See also, Brueckner (1986).

to show that these concerns are in order, that there is indeed a problem reconciling the thesis with the intuitive facts. As I shall try now to explain, however, the problem about self-knowledge was there all along and the recent emphasis on *widely* individuated content betrays a misunderstanding: even if no external factors were involved in fixing mental content, on any currently acceptable account of the internal determinants, the difficulty about self-knowledge would still remain.

The point is that according to currently prevailing orthodoxy, even the internal (or narrow) determinants of a mental event's content are relational properties of that *event* (although they are, of course, intrinsic properties of the *thinker* in whom the events occur.)

An example of a properly non-relationist conception of content is provided by the imagistic theory of the British Empiricists. According to this theory, thinking the thought that p involves entertaining an image that represents that p. And the facts in virtue of which an image represents a particular state of affairs are said to depend exclusively on the intrinsic properties of the image. Neither tenet is considered plausible today. Thinkings are not imaginings; and, in any case, the representational properties of images are not determined by their intrinsic properties.

Indeed, according to contemporary conviction, there is *no* property intrinsic to a mental event – certainly no *naturalistic* intrinsic property – that could serve as the complete determinant of that event's representational content. In effect, the only idea around about what narrow properties of an event might fix its content is the suggestion that it is some subset of the event's *causal* properties. The central functionalist idea here is that the content of a mental event is determined by that event's causal role in reasoning and deliberation and, in general, in the way the event interacts with other events so as to mediate between sensory inputs and behavioral outputs. On the assumption, then, that no external factors are involved in content individuation, the facts in virtue of which a thought is a thought about *water*, as opposed to a thought about *gin*, have to do with the thought's causal properties: thoughts with causal role R are thoughts about water, whereas thoughts with causal role R' are thoughts about gin.

Consider now a particular episode of thinking *water is wet*. How, on the dominant functionalist picture, might I know that that is what I thought? To know that I just had a *water* thought, as opposed to a *gin* thought (which, unlike a *twater* thought counts as a relevant alternative even in the absence of special circumstances) I would have to know, it seems, that my thought has the causal role constitutive of a *water* thought, as opposed to one constitutive of a *gin* thought. But is doesn't seem possible to know a thought's causal role directly. The point derives from Hume's observation that it is not possible to ascertain an item's causal properties non-inferentially, by mere inspection of its intrinsic properties; discovering them requires observation of the item's behavior over time.

But, again, this would appear to imply that I would have to *reason* my way to a thought's content; and reason to it, moreover, from facts about its causal role that I do not necessarily possess. How, then, could I know my thoughts at all? – much less know them directly?

Knowledge of Relations

13. It might be suggested that the appearance of a difficulty here is being generated by appeal to a false principle: namely, that in order to know a mental event one must know how things stand with respect to the conditions that individuate that event.[14]

The cogency of the argument would certainly be at risk if such a principle were being assumed. For it is clearly not in general true that to know whether an object x has a property P one has to know how things stand with respect to the facts on which P supervenes. For example, the roundness of this coin in my hand supervenes on a mass of facts concerning the arrangement of molecules at its boundary; but I do not need to know those facts in order to know that the coin is round.

It is fortunate for my argument, therefore, that it assumes no such principle. What it does assume is different and considerably more plausible. Namely this: That you cannot tell by mere inspection of an object that it has a given *relational* or *extrinsic* property. This principle is backed up by appeal to the following two claims, both of which strike me as uncontestable. That you cannot know that an object has a given relational property merely by knowing about its *intrinsic* properties. And that mere inspection of an object gives you at most knowledge of its intrinsic properties.

Uncontestable or not, it may yet seem that there are exceptions to the principle that an extrinsic property can never be detected by mere inspection.

Consider monetary value. Being a dime is not an intrinsic property of an object. For something to be a dime it must bear a number of complicated relations to its economic and social environment. And yet, we seem

---

[14] See Burge (1988a, p. 651) and (1988b).

often able to tell that something is a dime purely observationally, by mere inspection of its intrinsic properties. Counterexample.

Not quite. The reason an extrinsic property seems, in this case, ascertainable by mere inspection, is due to the fact that possession of that property is correlated with possession of an intrinsic property that is ascertainable by mere inspection. The reason that the coin's dimehood seems detectable by mere inspection derives from the fact that it having the value in question is neatly encoded in several of its purely intrinsic properties: in the phrase "ten cents" that is inscribed on it, and in several others of its size, shape, and design characteristics.

To see clearly that it is only because of this feature that we are able to "inspect" the coin's value properties, consider a monetary system in which *all* coins, regardless of value, share their intrinsic properties: they are all minted of precisely the same metal, are all precisely of the same shape, size, and design. As far as their intrinsic properties are concerned, nothing serves to distinguish between coins of different value. Nevertheless, the coins are not all of equal value; and, let us suppose, what determines a coin's value is the mint it was minted at: coins minted at "five cent" mints are worth five cents, those at "ten cent" mints, ten cents, and so on. It should be obvious that the value of *these* coins is not ascertainable by mere inspection; one would have to know something about their historical properties.

If this is right, it shows that our normal ability to "inspect" monetary value cannot help explain our ability to know our thought contents directly. First, because the feature that helps explain our knowledge in the former case – the correlation between the coin's monetary value and possession of certain intrinsic properties – does not obtain in the latter: facts about a thought token's content are not correlated with any of that token's purely intrinsic properties.[15] And second, because even if this were not true, that would still not explain how we might know our thoughts directly. For the process by which we know the coin's value is not really inspection, it's inference: you have to deduce that the coin is worth ten cents from your knowledge of its intrinsic properties plus your

---

[15] This would be false if a language of thought hypothesis were true.

knowledge of how those intrinsic properties are correlated with possession of monetary value. And our knowledge of thought is not like that.

III

Is Self-Knowledge A Cognitive Achievement?

14. Many philosophers would agree, I think, with the conclusion of the previous part: that if we had to know our thoughts on the basis of inner observation, then we couldn't know our thoughts. It has certainly become very popular to claim that an observational model of self-knowledge is mistaken. Thus Burge:

> If one thinks of one's relation to the subject matter of basic self-knowledge on an analogy to one's relation to objects of empirical investigation, then the view that one's thoughts (the subject matter) are dependent for their natures on relations to the environment will make it appear that one's knowledge of one's thoughts cannot be any more direct or certain than one's knowledge of the environment. ... This line of reasoning is deeply misconceived.[16]

Donald Davidson has sounded a similar theme:

> I can tell by examining my skin what my private or 'narrow' condition is, but nothing I can learn in this restricted realm will tell me that I am sunburned. The difference between referring to and thinking of water and referring to and thinking of twater is like the difference between being sunburned and one's skin being in exactly the same condition through another cause. The semantic difference lies in the outside world, beyond the reach of subjective or sublunar knowledge. So the argument might run.
>   This analogy, between the limited view of the skin doctor and the tunnel vision of the mind's eye, is fundamentally flawed.[17]

But it is not as if, in opposing an observational model of self-knowledge, these philosophers are suggesting that knowledge of thought is inferential. The claim is, rather, that the correct way to explain the direct

---

[16] Burge (1988).

[17] Davidson (1986, p. 453).

and authoritative character of self-knowledge is to think of it as based on nothing – at any rate, on nothing empirical.

Cognitively Insubstantial Judgments

Ordinarily, to know some contingent proposition you need either to make some observation, or to perform some inference based on some observation. In this sense, we may say that ordinary empirical knowledge is always a *cognitive achievement* and its epistemology always *substantial*. How could a judgment about a contingent matter of fact count as knowledge and yet not be a cognitive achievement? Or, to put the question another way, how could a contingent proposition be known directly, and yet not through observation?

Consider the judgment *I am here now*. Any token of this contingent judgment would be true and justified. But, in contrast with ordinary empirical judgments, the thinker is not required to possess any evidence for this judgment; he needs only to think it. The judgment is true and justified as soon as thought. The thinker counts as knowing something thanks not to the possession of any empirical evidence on his part, but simply courtesy of the concepts involved.

Consider another example. Suppose that the Kantian thesis, that experience of the world as containing substances is a precondition for experiencing it all, is correct. It would follow, on such a view, (and ignoring for present purposes the distinction between experiencing and knowing), that knowledge that the (experienced) world contains substances is knowledge that is cognitively insubstantial. To know the fact in question a thinker is not required to possess any particular item of empirical evidence; he needs merely to experience. The truth of, and warrant for, the belief are secured, not by evidence, but by the satisfaction of certain very general conditions on experience. The thinker counts as knowing something thanks not to the possession of any evidence on his part, but simply courtesy of those general facts.

A third example. According to some philosophers, certain self-regarding judgments are essentially self-verifying. Antecedent to the judgment that I am jealous, for example, there may be no fact of the matter about whether I am; but thinking it makes it so.[18] The judgment that I am jeal-

---

[18] Jealousy is being used here merely for illustrative purposes. For reasons that are touched upon briefly below (see note 23), I actually rather doubt that judgments about jealousy are self-verifying in the sense bruited in the text.

ous, when made, is, therefore, both true and justified. But, again, no evidence is required for the judgment. To know the fact in question, I am not required to possess any particular item of empirical evidence; I need merely to make the judgment. I count as knowing something thanks not to the possession of any evidence on my part, but simply courtesy of the self-verifying nature of the judgment involved.

These examples illustrate three different kinds of contingent judgment which one may be justified in making even in the absence of any empirical evidence. The warrant for such judgments derives from other sources: from the meanings of the concepts involved, or from the satisfaction of certain general conditions, or from the judgment-dependent character of the phenomena being judged. Whatever the source, no observation, or inference based on observational premises, is required or relevant. These judgments, when known, constitute knowledge that is based on nothing empirical. In my terms, they are not cognitive achievements and are subject, therefore, to an insubstantial epistemology.[19]

The relevance of such judgments ought to be clear. So long as knowledge of thought is construed as dependent on evidence, it seems impossible to understand how we could know our thoughts. That is what the argument of the previous two parts amounts to. If, however, self-regarding judgments could be understood along cognitively insubstantial lines – as the sorts of judgment which, for one reason or another, might be known without empirical evidence – then we might be able to explain how we know our thoughts, consistent with the admission that we do not know them on the basis of observation, or of inference based on observation. Could self-knowledge be, in this way, cognitively insubstantial?

Cognitively Insubstantial Self-Knowledge

15. It is hard to see how it could be. Knowledge that is not a cognitive achievement would be expected to exhibit certain characteristics – characteristics that are notably absent from self-knowledge. For instance, and

---

[19] Wittgenstein remarked, famously, that:

> It cannot be said of me at all (except perhaps as a joke) that I *know* I am in pain. What is it supposed to mean – except perhaps that I *am* in pain? (*PI* 246).

The remark has struck most philosophers as extremely implausible. A truth it may harbor, however, is that if (as seems right) it is constitutive of being in pain that one know that one is, then knowing that one is cannot count as a cognitive achievement; one doesn't count as being in pain unless one knows it. As against Wittgenstein, I am not sure that this point is best captured by denying that judgments about pain constitute 'knowledge'.

unlike ordinary empirical knowledge, you would not expect cognitively insubstantial knowledge to be subject to direction: how much you know about your thoughts should not depend on how much *attention* you are paying to them, if you do not know your thoughts on the basis of evidence. And yet it does seem that, within bounds anyway, self-knowledge can be directed: one can decide how much attention to direct to one's thoughts or images, just as one can decide how much attention to pay to objects in one's visual field.[20]

Or consider the fact that some adults are better than others at reporting on their inner states; and that most adults are better than children. How is this to be explained if self-knowledge is not to be thought of as an information-sensitive capacity that may be subject to cultivation or neglect?

The most important consideration, however, against an insubstantial construal of self-knowledge derives not so much from these observations but from a claim they presuppose: namely, that self-knowledge is both fallible and incomplete. In both the domain of the mental and that of the physical, events may occur of which one remains ignorant; and, in both domains, even when one becomes aware of an event's existence, one may yet misconstrue its character, believing it to have a property it does not in fact possess. How is this to be explained? I know of no convincing alternative to the following style of explanation: the difference between getting it right and failing to do so (either through ignorance or through error) is the difference between being in an epistemically favorable position with relevant evidence – and not. To put this point another way, it is only if we understand self-knowledge to be a cognitive achievement that we have any prospect of explaining its admitted shortcomings.

There is an irony in this, if it's true. Since Descartes, self-knowledge has been thought to present special philosophical problems precisely because it was held to be immune to cognitive deficit. The assumption was that we knew – or anyway had some idea – how to explain *imperfect* cognitive mechanisms; what seemed to elude explanation was a cognitive faculty that never erred. This line of thought seems to me to be exactly backwards. If Descartes' hyperbolic claims were right – if self-knowledge really were immune to error and ignorance – the temptation to explain it in an epistemologically deflationary way would be overwhelming. As it is, how-

---

[20] This observation is made in Mellor (1978).

ever, the Cartesian claims are incorrect and the epistemology of self-knowledge, thereby, substantial.

16. Strange to discover, then, that deflationary accounts of self-knowledge appear to be gaining widespread acceptance.[21] I have already mentioned some general reasons for being suspicious of such accounts. In the remainder of this paper I propose to look at Burge's provocative proposal in detail, outlining the specific ways in which, as I see it, it fails as an account of self-knowledge.

Burge: Self-Knowledge and Self-Verification

17. According to Burge, it is a fundamental error to think that self-knowledge is a species of cognitive achievement. As he puts it, it is a mistake to think that, in order to know a thought, one must know a lot about it. Rather,

> [t]he source of our strong epistemic right, our justification, in our basic self-knowledge is not that we know a lot about each thought we have. ... It is that we are in the position of thinking those thoughts in the second-order, self-verifying way.[22]

How is this to be understood?

Consider the following judgment about what I am thinking:

I judge: I am thinking that writing requires concentration.

In such a judgment, Burge points out, the subject matter of the judgment is not merely contingently related to the thoughts one thinks about it. The judgment is self-referential and self-verifying. The second-order judgment to the effect that I'm thinking that writing required concentration could not exist unless I were to think, through that very thought, that writing requires concentration. The thought I am making a judgment about is self-referentially fixed by the judgment itself; and the judgment is thereby self-verifying. At least in this sort of case, then, it appears that one need know nothing about a thought in order to know that one has thought it; one need only think the thought as part of a second-order thought that

---

[21] See Burge (1988a); Davidson (1986) and Heil (1988).

An interesting proposal, that seems to me to fall somewhere in between a substantial and an insubstantial conception as defined here, is outlined by Crispin Wright (1989). The proposal deserves extensive separate treatment. For a brief discussion see Boghossian (1989).

[22] Burge (1988a, p. 660).

asserts its occurrence. Since such thoughts are, as Burge correctly points out, logically self-verifying, they are guaranteed to be true as soon as thought. Hence, they would appear to constitute authoritative and non-inferential knowledge of thought, the relational character of the properties that determine thought content notwithstanding.

Burge calls this sort of self-verifying, self-regarding judgment *basic self-knowledge*. Let us start with the following question: how much of direct self-knowledge is basic self-knowledge? How well does Burge's paradigm explain the general phenomenon?

18. We may begin by noting that it does not at all explain our knowledge of our *standing* mental states. Judgments concerning such states, for example,

I judge: I *believe* that writing requires concentration

or

I judge: I *desire* that writing require concentration

are not self-verifying. I need not actually believe that writing requires concentration in order to think the first thought, not actually desire that it require concentration to think the second. These self-regarding judgments do not conform to Burge's paradigm. This would appear to be a serious problem. After all, we do know about our beliefs and desires in a direct and authoritative manner, and Burge's proposal seems not to have the resources to explain how.

How does his proposal fare in connection with *occurrent* events? In this domain, too, its applicability seems rather limited. Self-regarding judgments about what I occurrently desire or fear, for example, are manifestly not self-verifying, in that I need not actually desire or fear any particular thing in order to judge that I do. Thus, it may be that

I judge: I fear that writing requires concentration

without actually fearing that it does. The judgment is not self-verifying.

The best possible case for Burge's purposes will involve a self-regarding judgment about a mere thinking or entertaining of a proposition – a judgment of the form.

I judge: I think that writing requires concentration

And even here, the judgment will only prove self-verifying if the time at which the judgment is made is *absolutely coincident* with the time at which the thought being judged about is thought. In other words, the second-order judgment will be self-verifying only if it literally incorporates the very thought about which it is a judgment. It is only under this very special condition that the thinking of the proposition in question is presupposed by the very act of making a judgment about it; and, hence, only under this very special condition that the judgment is self-verifying.[23] If, for example, the judgment concerned an act of entertaining a proposition that preceded the act of making judgment by even the smallest interval of time, as in

I judge: I just now thought that writing requires concentration

then, since it need not be true that I had that thought *then* in order to make this judgment *now*, such a judgment would not be self-verifying and, hence, would constitute a species of self-knowledge that is not subject to Burge's deflationary paradigm.

But is it not precisely knowledge of this form – knowledge of what one has thought immediately after one has thought it – that we think of as central to our capacity for self-knowledge? We are struck by our ability to know, non-inferentially and authoritatively, that a certain mental event has occurred, immediately on its having occurred. We think: Writing requires concentration. And then we know, directly and unproblematically, that that is what we thought. A first-order thought occurs. And we are then able, without the benefit of inference, to form a correct judgment about what thought that was. The second-order judgment in these central cases is not self-verifying. Such cases are not instances of "basic self-knowledge" in Burge's sense. How does his proposal help explain how they are possible? The fact that, *had* the thought been part of a second-order judgment, then that judgment would have been self-verifying, does not help explain how we are able to know what thought it was, given that it *wasn't* part of such a judgment. First-order thoughts that are not part of second-order thoughts are directly knowable. Arguably, acts of knowing

---

[23] This explains why second-order judgments about sudden wants or momentary frights cannot be self-verifying: these events are not mental performatives in the required sense. They cannot be brought about by the mere thinking of a second-order judgment; hence, they cannot be incorporated into a second-order judgment in the way required for self-verification.

such thoughts are paradigm cases of self-knowledge. And Burge's proposal seems incapable of explaining how they are possible.

19. Still, even if Burge's proposal does not explain the central cases, does it not supply us with at least *one* case in which a thought is known directly despite the relational nature of its individuation conditions? And isn't that enough to dislodge our intuition that relationism is irreconcilable with directness?

If Burge's self-verifying judgments were instances of genuine knowledge, then they would indeed dislodge the problematic intuition. But I am convinced that they are.

Consider again the case of the person who undergoes a series of slow switches between earth and twin-earth. Burge observes:

> If the former situation, the person may think "I am thinking that water is a liquid." In the latter situation, the person may think "I am thinking that twater is a liquid." In both cases the person is right and as fully justified as ever. The fact that the person does not know that a switch has occurred is irrelevant to the truth and justified character of these judgments. Of course, the person may learn about the switches and ask "Was I thinking yesterday about water or twater?" – and yet not know the answer. Here knowing the answer may sometimes depend on knowing empirical background conditions. But such sophisticated questions about memory require a more complex story.[24]

These remarks strike me as puzzling. They amount to saying that, although S will not know tomorrow what he is thinking right now, he does know right now what he is thinking right now. For any given moment in the present, say t1, S is in a position to think a self-verifying judgment about what he is thinking at t1. By Burge's criteria, therefore, he counts as having direct and authoritative knowledge at t1 of what he is thinking at that time. But it is quite clear that tomorrow he won't know what he thought at t1. No self-verifying judgment concerning his thought at t1 will be available to him then. To know what he thought at t1 he must discover what environment he was in at that time and how long he had been there. But there is a mystery here. For the following would appear to be a platitude about memory and knowledge: if S knows that p at t1, and if at (some later time) t2, S remembers everything S knew at t1, then S knows that p at t2. Now let us ask: *why* does S not know today

---

[24] Burge (1988, p. 659).

whether yesterday's thought was a *water* thought or a *twater* thought? The platitude insists that there are only two possible explanations: either S has forgotten or he *never* knew. But surely memory failure is not to the point. In discussing the epistemology of relationally individuated content, we ought to be able to exclude memory failure by stipulation. It is not as if thoughts with widely individuated contents might be easily known but difficult to remember. The only explanation, I venture to suggest, for why S will not know tomorrow what he is said to know today, is not that he has forgotten but that he never knew. Burge's self-verifying judgments do not constitute genuine knowledge. What other reason is there for why our slowly transported thinker will not know tomorrow what he is said to know directly and authoritatively today?[25]

In sum, Burge's self-verifying judgments seem to me neither to explain the central cases, nor to provide particularly compelling examples of special cases in which a relationally individuated thought is known non-inferentially.

Conclusion

20. In this paper, I have attempted to map out the available theoretical options concerning self-knowledge. And I have argued that none of the options work. It seems to me that we have a serious problem explaining our ability to know our thoughts, a problem that has perhaps not been sufficiently appreciated. As I said in the introduction, however, the point of the exercise is not to promote skepticism, but understanding. I am confident that one of the options will work; but I think we need to think a lot harder before we are in a position to say which one.[26]

REFERENCES

Armstrong, D. 1968. *A Materialist Theory of the Mind.* London: Routledge, Kegan and Paul.

---

[25] Obviously, this barely scratches the surface of the various issues that crop up here. A proper discussion would include, among other things, an account of what Burge's self-verifying judgments *do* constitute, if not a species of knowledge. Limitations of space prevent me from taking matters further in this paper.

[26] For valuable comments on an earlier draft, or for helpful discussion of the issues, I am very grateful to David Velleman, Stephen Yablo, Barry Loewer, Jerry Fodor, Jennifer Church, and Crispin Wright.

Boghossian, P. 1989. The Rule-Following Considerations. *Mind* 98: 507–49.

———. 1990. The Status of Content. *Philosophical Review* XCIX: 157–84.

Bonjour, L. *The Structure of Empirical Knowledge.* Cambridge, MA: Harvard University Press.

Brueckner, A. 1986. Brains in a Vat. *Journal of Philosophy* 83.3 (March): 148–67.

Burge, T. 1988a. Individualism and Self-Knowledge. *Journal of Philosophy* 85.1 (November): 654–55. Chapter 4 in this volume.

———. 1988b. Cartesian Error and the Objectivity of Perception. *Contents of Thought*, eds. Grimm, R. and D. Merrill. Tucson: University of Arizona Press.

Davidson, D. 1986. Knowing One's Own Mind. *Proceedings of the American Philosophical Association*: 441–58. Chapter 3 in this volume.

Heil, J. 1988. Privileged Access. *Mind* 42.386 (April): 238–51. Chapter 5 in this volume.

Lyons, W. 1986. *The Disappearance of Introspection.* Cambridge, MA: MIT Press.

Mellor, H. 1978. Conscious Belief. *Proceedings of the Aristotelian Society.*

O'Connor, D. J., and B. Carr. 1982. *Introduction to the Theory of Knowledge.* Minneapolis, MN: University of Minnesota Press.

Ryle, G. 1949. *The Concept of Mind.* London: Hutchinson.

Woodfield, A. 1982. *Thought and Object.* Oxford: Clarendon Press.

Wright, C. 1989. Wittgenstein's Rule-Following Considerations and the Central Project of Theoretical Linguistics. Pp. 233–64 in *Reflections on Chomsky*, ed. George, A. Oxford: Blackwell.

7

Anti-Individualism and Privileged Access

Michael McKinsey

It has been a philosophical commonplace, at least since Descartes, to hold that each of us can know the existence and content of his own mental states in a privileged way that is available to no one else. This has at least seemed true with respect to those 'neutral' cognitive attitudes such as thought, belief, intention, and desire, whose propositional contents may be false. The crucial idea is not that one's knowledge of these states in oneself is incorrigible, for surely one can make mistakes about what one believes, intends, or desires. Rather the idea is that we can in principle find out about these states in ourselves 'just by thinking', without launching an empirical investigation or making any assumptions about the external physical world. I will call knowledge obtained independently of empirical investigation *a priori* knowledge And I will call the principle that it is possible to have *a priori* knowledge of one's own neutral cognitive attitude states, the Principle of Privileged Access, or just 'privileged access' for short.

Although many philosophers would insist that privileged access is undeniable, a series of recent discoveries and arguments in the philosophy of language has, I believe, convinced a perhaps equally large number of philosophers that privileged access is a complete illusion. One of the most persuasive of these arguments was proposed by Tyler Burge (1982) as an application of Putnam's (1975) famous Twin Earth case. Oscar, a resident of Earth, believes that water is wet. On Twin Earth, there is no water; rather there is a qualitatively similar liquid with a different chemical composition, a liquid that we may call 'twater'. Toscar, who is Oscar's identical twin and a denizen of Twin Earth, does not believe that water is wet. For

175

Toscar has no beliefs about water at all; rather, he believes that twater is wet, that twater fills the oceans, etc. Yet Oscar and Toscar, being absolutely identical twins, would certainly seem to be *internally* the same. In Putnam's terminology, Oscar and Toscar would share all the same 'narrow' psychological states. Thus, Burge concludes, Oscar's belief that water is wet must be a *wide* state: it must, that is, 'presuppose' or 'depend upon' the relations that Oscar bears to other speakers or objects in his external environment.

In general, Burge endorses a conclusion something like

(B) Some neutral cognitive states that are ascribed by *de dicto* attitude sentences (e.g. 'Oscar is thinking that water is wet') necessarily depend upon or presuppose the existence of objects external to the person to whom the state is ascribed.

Now (B) might certainly *appear* to conflict with privileged access. For (B) implies that sometimes, whether or not a person is in a given cognitive state is determined by external facts that the person himself could only know by empirical investigation. In such cases, it would seem, the person would therefore not be able to know *a priori* that he is in the cognitive state in question.

But interestingly enough, Burge (1988) has recently urged that despite appearances, his anti-individualism (that is, his conclusion (B)) is perfectly compatible with privileged access. And a similar point of view had earlier been expressed by Davidson (1987). I want to argue here that Burge and Davidson are wrong. Anti-individualism and privileged access as standardly understood are incompatible, and something has to give.[1]

I will first briefly discuss Davidson's defence of compatibilism. Davidson clearly accepts anti-individualism as formulated by (B), and like Burge he accepts (B) in part on the basis of Burge's persuasive application of Putnam's Twin Earth case. But Davidson insists that anti-individualism does not undermine first person authority about one's own mental states. He agrees with the anti-individualist thesis that some *de dicto* attitude ascriptions 'identify thoughts by relating them to things outside the head' ((Davidson 1987), p. 451). But he suggests that philosophers like Putnam who find a difficulty for privileged access in this thesis are in effect

---

[1] I have elsewhere discussed at length the problems for particular forms of anti-individualism that arise from these theses' apparent incompatibility with privileged access. See McKinsey (1978) and (1987).

confusing thoughts with their descriptions. Such philosophers make the mistake, Davidson says, of inferring from the fact that a thought is identified or *described* by relating it to something outside the head, that the thought itself must therefore *be* outside the head and hence must be unavailable to privileged access ((Davidson 1987), p. 451).

Now I do not myself see any reason to believe that Putnam or anyone else has actually made this mistake. Certainly, as we shall see below, the most cogent reason for endorsing incompatibilism does not involve this mistake at all, so that Davidson's diagnosis is inconclusive at best. But what is most disconcerting about Davidson's remarks is the version of privileged access that he apparently takes himself to be defending. He explicitly accepts anti-individualism, understanding it as the thesis that thoughts are often *described* (in attitude ascriptions) by relating them to objects outside the head. Then he (quite correctly) points out that it does not follow from this thesis that the thoughts so described are *themselves* outside the head. But what is the relevance of this point to the issue at hand? Apparently Davidson is saying that since the thoughts in question are inner episodes that exist independently of our means of describing them, we can have privileged access to these episodes, whatever the external implications of our descriptions of the episodes might be.

But if this is what Davidson has in mind, then the version of privileged access that he is defending is too weak to be of much philosophical interest. He wishes to claim, apparently, that one could have privileged access to an episode of thought independently of having privileged access to any particular descriptions that the episode might satisfy. But then what would one have privileged access *to* in such a case? Perhaps one would be privileged to know only that the episode exists; given what Davidson says, there is no reason to suppose that the agent would have privileged access even to the fact that the episode is an episode of *thought*, as opposed to being, say, an episode of indigestion.

But surely, having access of this sort to one's thoughts is not much of a privilege. The traditional view, I should think, is not just that we have privileged access to the fact that our thoughts *occur*; rather the view is that we have privileged access to our thoughts *as satisfying certain descriptions*. In particular, the traditional view is that we have privileged access to our thoughts as having certain contents, or as satisfying certain *de dicto* cognitive attitude predicates. Thus, if Oscar is thinking that water is wet, the traditional view would be that Oscar has privileged access, not just to the fact that some episode or other is occurring in him but to the fact that he is thinking that water is wet. Now apparently, Davidson would just *deny* that Oscar has privileged access to the latter sort of fact, since as he says, the fact relates Oscar to objects outside his head. But if he would deny this, then Davidson's claim to be defending first person authority seems misleading at best.[2]

In contrast to Davidson, Burge clearly means to defend privileged access in its traditional guise. Given what he says in 'Individualism and Self-Knowledge' (Burge (1988)), would maintain that the following three propositions are consistent:

(1) Oscar knows *a priori* that he is thinking that water is wet.

(2) The proposition that Oscar is thinking that water is wet necessarily depends upon E.

(3) The proposition E cannot be known *a priori*, but only by empirical investigation.

(Here I assume that E is the 'external proposition' whose presupposition makes Oscar's thoughts that water is wet a wide state.)

Whether (1)–(3) are consistent is determined by the sense that the phrase 'necessarily depends upon' is taken so have in (2). Unfortunately, Burge never explains or clarifies the concept of necessary dependency that he invokes throughout his paper. I will now argue that Burge is able to make his compatibility thesis appear plausible only by tacitly identifying the dependency relation with *metaphysical* necessity. But this identification is illegitimate in the present context, for a reason that I will explain below.

A clue to what Burge has in mind by dependency is provided by the analogy he chooses to undermine the incompatibilist's reasoning. One who reasons from the assumption that we can know our own mental states *a priori* to the conclusion that these states must be independent of any

---

[2] It is, of course, possible that Davidson would be prepared to defend a view on which all our thoughts that fall under wide *de dicto* descriptions also fall under *other* descriptions of some important kind to which we have privileged access. Perhaps, for instance, he might be willing to say that every thought with a 'wide' content would also have another 'narrow' content to which we have privileged access. (I suggest such a 'two-content' view in McKinsey (1986)) But as far as I know, Davidson nowhere spells out or defends such a view. And, of course, the mere hypothetical fact that Davidson *might* be willing to develop a view on which privileged access compatible with anti-individualism does not by itself provide us with any *argument* in favour of this compatibility.

empirical propositions about physical objects is, says Burge, making the same mistake as was once made by Descartes and diagnosed by Arnaud (Burge 1988, pp. 650–1).

From the fact that he could know directly and incorrigibly the existence of himself and his own thoughts, while consistently doubting the existence of his body and the rest of the physical world, Descartes inferred that it was possible for him to exist as a disembodied mind in a nonphysical universe. But this inference is illegitimate. The fact that Descartes could not correctly *deduce* the existence of the physical world from the existence of himself and his thoughts may show something significant about Descartes' *concepts* of himself and his thoughts. But as Arnaud pointed out, this failure of deduction shows nothing about the *nature* of either Descartes or his thoughts. It is perfectly consistent with this failure of deduction to suppose that both Descartes and his thoughts have an essentially physical nature, and that neither Descartes nor his thoughts could possibly have existed unless certain physical objects, including perhaps Descartes' body, Descartes' parents, and the sperm and egg cells from which Descartes developed, had also existed. For the fact, if it is a fact, that Descartes' existence is dependent upon the existence of these other physical objects would not be something that is knowable *a priori*. It would be a fact that is necessary but only knowable *a posteriori*. (As Kripke (1980) pointed out.) Thus the dependency would be a fact that is not deducible *a priori* from Descartes' incorrigible knowledge of himself and his thoughts.

Since metaphysical dependencies are often only knowable *a posteriori*, propositions that are knowable *a priori* might metaphysically depend upon other propositions that are only knowable *a posteriori*. Thus Oscar might know *a priori* that he exists, and his existence might metaphysically depend upon the existence of his mother, even though Oscar cannot know *a priori* that his mother exists.

The upshot of this discussion is that (1), (2), and (3) are all clearly consistent, provided that 'depends upon' in (2) is interpreted as meaning *metaphysical* dependency. When the material conditional 'if p then q' is metaphysically necessary, let us say that *p metaphysically entails q*. Then our result so far is that (1) and (3) are consistent with

(2a) The proposition that Oscar is thinking that water is wet metaphysically entails E.

Burge's main point in defence of the compatibility of anti-individualism and privileged access, then, seems to be that such triads as (1), (2a) and (3) are consistent. In other words, his point is that our having privileged access to our own mental states is compatible with those states being metaphysically dependent upon facts to which we have no privileged access.

But this point, though correct, is quite irrelevant to the main issue. For anti-individualism is the thesis that some neutral *de dicto* cognitive attitude states are wide states, and to say that a state is wide (not narrow) cannot mean *merely* that the state metaphysically entails the existence of external objects.[3] For if it did, then given certain materialistic assumptions that are pretty widely held, it would follow that probably *all* psychological states of *any* kind would be wide, so that the concept of a narrow state would have no application at all, and anti-individualism would be merely a trivial consequence of (token) materialism.

For instance, it is plausible to suppose that no human could (metaphysically) have existed without biological parents, and that no human could (metaphysically) have had biological parents other than the ones she in fact had. (See Kripke (1980), pp. 312–314.) If this is so, then Oscar's thinking that water is wet metaphysically entails that Oscar's mother exists. In fact, Oscar's having *any* psychological property (or any property at all) would metaphysically entail the existence of Oscar's mother. Thus if metaphysical entailment of external objects were what made a psychologi-

---

[3] Here I assume that, for Burge, metaphysical entailment of external objects must be a logically *sufficient* condition for a state to be wide. Perhaps it might be objected that this is unfair to Burge, since all he really needs is the assumption that metaphysical entailment of external objects is a *necessary* condition of wideness. But this objection is misconceived. Burge is trying to show that such triads as (1), (2), and (3) are consistent. His argument is that this is so because (1), (2a), and (3) are consistent. But this argument requires the assumption that (2a) – the claim concerning metaphysical entailment – is logically *sufficient* for (2) – the claim concerning wideness, or necessary dependency. For unless (2a) is sufficient for (2), the fact that (1), (2a), and (3) are consistent is quite irrelevant to the conclusion that (1), (2), and (3) are consistent. (The correct general principle for proving consistency is that, if *p* and *q* are consistent, and *q* logically implies *r*, then *p* and *r* are consistent. Note the difference between this principle and the false principle that if *p* and *q* are consistent and *q* is logically implied by *r*, then *p* and *r* are consistent: this is wrong, since *r* might for instance be an explicit contradiction that logically implies the consistent *q*.)

cal state wide, then probably *all* of Oscar's – and everyone else's – psychological states would be wide.

But this is obviously *not* the sense of 'wide psychological state' that philosophers like Putnam and Burge have had in mind. While it may be true that Oscar's thinking that water is wet entails the existence of Oscar's mother or the existence of the egg from which Oscar developed, it would nevertheless not be for *this* kind of reason that Oscar's mental state is wide! Clearly, to say that the state in question is wide is not to say something that is true by virtue of Oscar's *nature* or the *nature* of the particular event that is Oscar's thought that water is wet. Rather it is to say something about the *concept*, or property, that is expressed by the English predicate 'x is thinking that water is wet'; it is to say something about what it *means* to say that a given person is thinking that water is wet.

Let us say that a proposition *p conceptually implies* a proposition *q* if and only if there is a correct deduction of *q* from *p*, a deduction whose only premises other than *p* are necessary or conceptual truths that are knowable a priori, and each of whose steps follows from previous lines by a self-evident inference rule of some adequate system of natural deduction. I intend the relation of conceptual implication to be an appropriately *logical*, as opposed to a metaphysical, relation.

Our discussion shows, I believe, that the thesis of anti-individualism should be stated in terms of conceptual implication rather than metaphysical entailment.[4] In this connection, it is worth noting that when Putnam originally introduced the notions of narrow and wide psychological states, he did so in terms of *logical* possibility (Putnam 1975, p. 141). Moreover, he introduced these notions as explicitly *Cartesian* concepts. Thus a narrow state should be (roughly) a state from which the existence of external objects cannot be *deduced*, and a wide state would be one from which the existence of external objects *can* be deduced.

On my proposal, Burge's thesis of anti-individualism should be understood as

3a) Some neutral cognitive states that are ascribed by *de dicto* attitude sentences (e.g., 'Oscar is thinking that water is wet') conceptually imply the existence of objects external to the person to whom the state is ascribed.

---

[4] In McKinsey (forthcoming) I give a more thorough and detailed defence of the thesis that the concepts of narrow and wide psychological states must be understood in terms of conceptual implication rather than metaphysical necessity.

But of course, now that we have made anti-individualism into the conceptual thesis that it should be, we also have our contradiction with privileged access back again.

For instance, (2) must now be understood as

(2b) The proposition that Oscar is thinking that water is wet conceptually implies E,

and it is easy to see that (1), (2b), and (3) form an inconsistent triad. The argument is this. Suppose (1) that Oscar knows a priori that he is thinking that water is wet. Then by (2b), Oscar can simply *deduce* E, using only premisses that are knowable a priori, including the premiss that he is thinking that water is wet. Since Oscar can deduce E from premisses that are knowable a priori, Oscar can know E itself a priori. But his contradicts (3), the assumption that E *cannot* be known a priori. Hence (1), (2b), and (3) are inconsistent. And so in general, it seems, anti-individualism is inconsistent with privileged access.

It is worth keeping the structure of this simple argument in mind, so as not to confuse it with another (bad) argument that Burge frequently alludes to in his paper (Burge 1988). Burge sometimes characterizes the person who thinks that anti-individualism is inconsistent with privileged access as reasoning on the basis of the following sort of assumption (see for instance (Burge 1988), p. 653):

(4) Since the proposition that Oscar is thinking that water is wet necessarily depends upon E, no one, including Oscar, could know that Oscar is thinking that water is wet without first knowing E.

One who assumes (4) could then reason that (1), (2), and (3) are inconsistent, as follows. (2) and (4) imply that Oscar could not know that he is thinking that water is wet without first knowing E. But by (3), E is not knowable a priori. Hence, Oscar could also not know a priori that he is thinking that water is wet. But this contradicts (1). Hence, (1), (2), and (3) are inconsistent.

Burge is certainly right when he objects to this line of reasoning. The reasoning is obviously bad when necessary dependency is interpreted as metaphysical entailment. For then, one would be assuming (4) on the basis of the principle that

(5) If p metaphysically entails q, then no one could know that p without first knowing that q.

But (5) is obviously false. For instance, even if Oscar's existence meta-physically entails the existence of Oscar's mother, Oscar can surely know that he exists without first knowing that his mother does!

Even when necessary dependency is interpreted as conceptual implication, the reasoning is bad. In this case, (4) would be assumed on the basis of

(6) If p conceptually implies q, then no one could know that p without first knowing that q.

But, of course, it is a well known fact that closure principles like (6) are false: certainly with respect to any proposition p that can be known at all, it is possible to know p without first knowing each of (the infinite number of) p's logical consequences.

So Burge was certainly right to object to the kind of reason he imagined one might have for believing that anti-individualism and privileged access are incompatible. But, of course, this does not show that no good reason for the incompatibility can be given. The simple argument I gave above is in fact such a good reason, and it does *not* depend on any suspicious closure principles like (5) and (6).

Rather, the argument is much more straightforward. In effect it says, look, if you could know a priori that you are in a given mental state, and your being in that state conceptually or logically implies the existence of external objects, then you could know a priori that the external world exists. Since you obviously *can't* know a priori that the external world exists, you also can't know a priori that you are in the mental state in question. It's just that simple. I myself find it hard to understand why Burge and Davidson will not just accept that obvious and compelling line of reasoning.

REFERENCES

Burge, T. 1982. Other Bodies. *Thought and Object: Essays on Intentionality,* ed. A. Woodfield. Oxford: Oxford University Press.

———. 1988. Individualism and Self-Knowledge. *Journal of Philosophy* 85: 649–63. Chapter 4 in this volume.

Davidson, D . 1987. Knowing One's Own Mind. *Proceedings and Addresses of the American Philosophical Association* 60: 441–58. Chapter 3 in this volume.

Kripke, S. 1980. *Naming and Necessity.* Oxford: Basil Blackwell.

McKinsey, M. 1978. Names and Intentionality. *Philosophical Review* 87: 171–200.

———. 1986. Mental Anaphora. *Synthese* 56: 159–75.

———. 1987. Apriorism in the Philosophy of Language. *Philosophical Studies* 52: 1–32.

———. The Internal Basis of Meaning. Forthcoming.

Putnam, H. 1975. The Meaning of "Meaning". *Philosophical Papers Vol. 2*. Cambridge: Cambridge University Press.

8

The Incompatibility of Anti-Individualism and Privileged Access

Jessica Brown

Michael McKinsey (1991) has provided a general argument for the claim that any version of anti-individualism is incompatible with the Principle of Privileged Access, viz. the principle that each subject can know his thought contents without having undertaken an empirical investigation. McKinsey applies the term 'a priori' to knowledge that is obtained independently of empirical investigation. This use of 'a priori' is not entirely happy,[1] but I will follow McKinsey's terminology in this paper. The structure of McKinsey's argument is as follows. According to anti-individualism, the environment of a subject partly individuates some of his thought contents. A subject need not know the conditions which individuate his thoughts in order to have those thoughts. However, a subject who knows the arguments for anti-individualism may know a priori that if he has a certain thought content, then certain environmental conditions obtain. A subject could use this philosophical knowledge and his a priori knowledge of his thought contents to gain by inference the a priori knowledge that those environmental conditions obtain. However, it is plausible that a subject cannot have a priori knowledge of the way his environment is. So,

---

[1] Some have claimed that x knows that p a priori if and only if x knows that p merely in virtue of understanding the concepts contained in p and knowing the laws of logic. The use of 'a priori' to describe a subject's knowledge of his thought contents is not entirely happy since one does not know the proposition that one has a certain thought content merely in virtue of understanding the concepts involved in it, and knowing the laws of logic.

it seems that anti-individualism and the Principle of Privileged Access are incompatible.

McKinsey (1991) argues that Burgian anti-individualism, in particular, is incompatible with the Principle of Privileged Access. McKinsey claims, and I agree, that Burge is committed to the following three propositions:

(a) Oscar knows *a priori* that he is thinking that water is wet.

(b) The proposition that Oscar is thinking that water is wet necessarily depends upon E.

(c) The proposition E cannot be known *a priori*, but only by empirical investigation. ((1991), p. 12)[2]

where E stands for the proposition which asserts the existence of the entities which are entailed by Oscar's having the thought that water is wet. Burge holds that (i) subjects know some of their thought contents in a direct non-empirical manner, (1988, pp. 649–50); (ii) '[i]n some instances, an individual's having certain *de dicto* attitudes *entails* the existence of entities other than himself and his attitude contents,' (1982, p. 117); and, (iii) a subject has only empirical knowledge of the environmental facts which individuate his thoughts, (1988, p. 650).

If (b) is knowable a priori, then (a)–(c) are inconsistent. Since Oscar knows a priori that he is thinking that water is wet, if he knows (b) a priori, he can know E a priori. But, by (c), E cannot be known a priori. McKinsey argues that (b) is knowable a priori and, hence, that Burge's position is inconsistent. Further, he claims that Burge is right in thinking that a subject cannot know a priori of the existence of the entities entailed by his thought contents. Thus, he claims that anti-individualism and the Principle of Privileged Access are incompatible.

McKinsey argues for the claim that (b) is knowable a priori by arguing that in (b) the notion of necessary dependence must be construed as the notion of conceptual implication. McKinsey claims that anti-individualism must be the thesis that the possession of certain mental properties (e.g., the property of thinking that water is wet) conceptually implies the existence of objects external to the person who has the mental property. Otherwise, he says, anti-individualism would be an uninteresting, trivial

---

[2] In (a)–(c), Oscar is an English speaking Earthian who does not himself know the chemical composition of water, but is part of a community some of whose members do know the chemical composition of water.

thesis, (1994, pp. 125–6). 1 am not concerned to defend McKinsey's trivialization argument, or the claim that (b) involves the notion of conceptual implication. Instead, I argue directly that on Burge's position there is some E such that (b) is knowable a priori and E is knowable only empirically.[3] (McKinsey does not discuss what particular proposition E stands for.)

In Burge (1982), Burge discusses what proposition is entailed by the fact that Oscar is thinking that water is wet. Burge argues that Oscar could think that water is wet even if no water exists, or if no other people exist. However, he denies that Oscar could think that water is wet if neither water nor other people exist:

> What seems incredible is to suppose that [Oscar], in his relative ignorance and indifference about the nature of water, holds beliefs whose contents involve the notion, even though neither water nor communal cohorts exist. (1982, p. 116)

Burge argues that, since Oscar does not know that water is H_2O, without the existence of water or other speakers there would be nothing to determine that Oscar's thoughts are water thoughts as opposed to twater thoughts, (1982, p. 115).

Burge's argument for the claim that Oscar could not have a water thought unless either water or other speakers exist depends on the fact that Oscar does not know the chemical composition of water. This suggests that Burge may hold that a subject who theorizes that H_2O exists could have water thoughts even if neither water nor other speakers exist, (although Burge does not explicitly address this issue). It seems that, according to Burge, the mere fact that a subject has a water thought does not entail any proposition about the environment.[4]

---

[3] Brueckner (1992) argues that there is no clearly empirical proposition entailed by Oscar's thinking that water is wet such that, if anti-individualism were true, Oscar could come to know that proposition a priori by inference from his thought content. I think that Brueckner has failed to consider all the entailments which, on Burge's position, hold between mind and world.

[4] Burge may hold that there is an entailment from the fact that a subject has a water thought to a proposition partly about the environment and partly about the subject of the thought. Perhaps, Burge holds the following entailment:

(1): It is necessary that if Oscar has a thought involving the concept of the natural kind k, then either (i) k exists, or (ii) Oscar knows the correct scientific account of k, or (iii) Oscar is part of a community with the concept of k.

Burge's comments on Oscar suggest that he thinks that there are entailments from thought to the world where the antecedent states that a subject has a thought and that the subject is agnostic about the application conditions of one of the concepts in that thought.[5] Oscar is agnostic about the application conditions of water since he has no view about what the necessary and sufficient chemical conditions for being water are. If a subject is to know a priori that there is an entailment between his having a certain thought and the environment's being some way, then the entailment must not use facts about the application conditions of concepts of which the subject is unaware. For example, Oscar does not know that x is water iff x is H_2O. So, he cannot know a priori the following entailment between mind and world:

P: Necessarily, if x has a thought involving the concept of water, and x is agnostic about the application conditions of the concept of water, then either x is in an environment which contains H_2O, or x is part of a community which has a term 'water' which applies to something if and only if it is H_2O.

It is plausible that the consequent of (1) is not knowable a priori. So, (1) might seem a suitable entailment for McKinsey's argument. However, the truth of the consequent does not require the truth of any proposition solely about the environment of the subject. Hence, knowledge that the consequent obtains does not constitute knowledge that the environment of the subject must be some way. By contrast, the entailments I consider in the main text do yield knowledge that the environment of the subject must be some way.

[5] Burge's comments on arthritis suggest that he also holds that there are entailments from thought to the world where the antecedent states that a subject has a thought and that he is *mistaken* (cf. agnostic) about the application conditions of one of the concepts in that thought. Burge argues that a subject who has false beliefs about the application conditions of 'arthritis' may have the concept of arthritis in virtue of being in a community which has that concept, (1979, pp. 77–79). If a subject does have the concept of arthritis despite being mistaken about its application conditions, it seems that this can be so only if he is part of a community with the concept of arthritis. Burge explicitly says (1979, p. 79) that he could have used a natural kind word, instead of 'arthritis', in the arthritis thought experiment. So, it seems that Burge holds that there are entailments between thought and the world where the antecedent of the entailment states: 'x has a thought involving the notion of water, and x is mistaken about the application conditions of water'. I have not used entailments of this form in my argument against Burge since a subject cannot know a priori whether or not a belief of his about the application conditions of some concept is correct.

However, we can formulate an entailment between mind and world knowledge of which does not require a subject to know that water is H_2O[6]:

Q: Necessarily, if x has a thought involving the concept of a natural kind k and x is agnostic about the application conditions of the concept of k, then either x is in an environment which contains k, or x is part of a community with the concept of k.[7]

We need to ask whether, if anti-individualism were true, Oscar could reason to the truth of Q without using the results of empirical investigation. Oscar could employ the reasoning that Burge employs to justify the claim that Oscar could not have water thoughts unless either water or other speakers exist. Burge argues (1982, p. 115) that without water or other speakers there is nothing to show that Oscar has thoughts about water as opposed to any other kind which is superficially indistinguishable from water, e.g., twater. In his reasoning Burge uses the empirical fact that on Earth 'water' applies to x if and only if x is H_2O. However, this is inessential for the purpose of justifying Q. One could reformulate the argument as follows. Where k and k^* are superficially indistinguishable but distinct natural kinds, if (1) a subject x does not know the scientific account of k; (2) there is no k in x's environment; and (3), there are no other speakers beside x, then there seems no ground for saying that a term, t, in x's repertoire means k, as opposed to k^*. If x does not have any contact with k or with anyone who does have contact with k, it is difficult to see how x could have acquired the concept of k. In conclusion, it seems that Burge should

---

[6] We can compare the entailment Q with the entailments which Brueckner (1992) considered as possible premises of McKinsey's argument. Three of the entailments which Brueckner considered used the fact that water is H_2O and, hence, could not be known a priori by Oscar who does not know that water is H_2O. (According to the fourth and last entailment Brueckner considered, Oscar's having the thought that water is wet entails the existence of some physical entities distinct from Oscar. Brueckner argued (1992, p. 118) that since the consequent of this entailment does not state any particular fact about the physical world, the consequent is not clearly knowable only empirically. By contrast, the consequents of the entailments I consider do state particular facts about the world.)

[7] For the purposes of this definition, knowing that x is water if and only if x is water, does not count as knowing the application conditions of the concept water.

accept that Oscar can know Q a priori since Burge has himself provided the materials for an a priori justification of Q.

It might be objected that it is illegitimate to assume that Oscar knows Burge's argument. After all, Oscar might never have attended a philosophy course, or read a philosophy book. However, this objection has no force. Clearly, a subject need not know anti-individualist arguments in order to have thoughts which are individuated in terms of his environment. However, if anti-individualism is true, then a subject who does know anti-individualist arguments could use these arguments to acquire a priori knowledge of entailments between his thoughts and the world. If just one subject knows a priori an entailment from his thoughts to the world, then he can know a priori a proposition about his environment which Burge claims cannot be known a priori. The fact that not all subjects know philosophy is no objection to McKinsey's argument.

So far we have considered what facts about the world are entailed by a subject's having a thought involving a natural kind concept. Now we should consider what facts about the world are entailed by a subject's having a thought involving a non-natural kind concept. Burge's argument for the claim that Oscar could not have a water thought unless water or other speakers exist, seems applicable to thoughts involving non-natural kind concepts. Imagine that Oscar is agnostic about the application of the word, 'sofa'. For example, he may apply it firmly and correctly to what we call 'sofas', but be unsure about whether it also applies to broad single seat armchairs. According to Burge, if Oscar is part of an English speaking community then, despite his agnosticism, he has thoughts involving the concept sofa. But if, counterfactually, Oscar had been part of a community in which 'sofa' is applied both to what we call 'sofas' and to broad single seat armchairs, then Oscar would have had chofa thoughts, where the concept of a chofa applies both to what we call 'sofas' and to broad single seat armchairs, (1979, pp. 77–83). Now imagine that there are no other speakers in Oscar's environment. How could Oscar have propositional attitudes involving the concept of sofa? Since sofa is not a natural kind concept, Oscar's natural environment cannot help him to acquire the concept. There are no other speakers. Nothing seems to show that his attitudes involve the concept of sofa as opposed to chofa.

It seems, then, that besides Q Burge should endorse the following principle, R:

R: Necessarily, if x has a thought involving a non-natural kind concept, c, and x is agnostic about the application conditions of c, then x is part of a community which has the concept c.[8]

Oscar could know the truth of R a priori by using the argument of the last paragraph reformulated so that it does not involve the empirical fact that, on Earth, 'sofa' is applied to something only if it is a two, or more, seat upholstered piece of furniture.

In order to use Q or R to gain a priori knowledge of the world, Oscar needs to know a priori that the antecedents of Q and R are true when x is replaced by 'I', k is replaced by 'water', and c is replaced by 'sofa'. Given that Burge holds that a subject can seriously misunderstand a concept and still have that concept, (e.g. see 'orang-utan', 1979, p. 91), it seems that a subject could be mistaken about whether a concept is a natural kind concept and still have that concept.[9] For example, Oscar might mistakenly think that jade is a natural kind concept.[10] If Oscar thinks that jade is a natural kind concept, then he is not in a position to know a priori that jade is a non-natural kind concept: in order to find this out, Oscar would need to undertake an empirical investigation into the way 'jade' is used.

Given that a subject can be wrong about whether a concept is a natural kind concept, it might be thought that it is impossible to know a priori whether or not a concept is a natural kind concept. If this is right, then Oscar cannot use either Q or R to deduce a priori knowledge of the world. However, Oscar could use Q and R to deduce a priori knowledge of a new principle, S:

S: Necessarily, if x has a thought involving a concept c, and x is agnostic about the application conditions of c, then either x is in an environment which contains instances of c and c is a natural kind concept, or x is part of a community which has the concept c, whether or not c is a natural kind concept.[11]

---

[8] Note that R has been formulated in such a way that having a priori knowledge of R does not require a subject to have a priori knowledge of the application conditions of the concept c.

[9] Being mistaken about whether a concept is a natural kind concept is distinct from being mistaken about whether a term for a supposed natural kind does name a natural kind. Mistakenly thinking that jade is a natural kind concept is distinct from mistakenly thinking that 'phlogiston' names a natural kind.

[10] 'Jade' applies to two chemically distinct minerals – jadeite and nephrite.

[11] The fact that Burge thinks that content depends on social and natural facts makes the consequents of Q and S complex. However, if an anti-individualist holds that content depends on either social or natural facts, bur not both, then the consequents of the entailments between mind and world would not be disjunctive.

In order to know a priori that the antecedent of S is true when *x* is replaced by 'I', and *c* by some concept he has, Oscar does not need to know a priori whether or not *c* is a natural kind concept. All that Oscar needs to know a priori is that he has a thought involving *c* and that he is agnostic about the application conditions of *c*. Oscar can know a priori that he has a thought involving the concept c in virtue of having privileged access to his thought contents. Oscar can know a priori that he does not have any belief about the chemical composition of water; and, Oscar can know a priori that he is unsure about whether 'sofa' applies to large single seat armchairs.

Given that Oscar can know a priori that the antecedent of S is true, Oscar can use S to deduce a priori knowledge of the world. For example, from the fact that he knows a priori that he has a thought involving the concept of water, he could come to know a priori that (either his environment contains water and the concept of water is a natural kind concept, or he is part of a community which has the concept of water). But this conflicts with Burge's claim that we can have only empirical knowledge of the external facts which individuate our thought contents, (see (Burge, 1988)). Burge's position is inconsistent. Burge claims that anti-individualism and the Principle of Privileged Access are both true, and denies that subjects can have a priori knowledge of the external facts which individuate their thoughts. But, if Burgian anti-individualism and the Principle of Privileged Access are both true, then subjects can have a priori knowledge of the external facts which individuate their thoughts.

Could Burge drop his claim that a subject can have only empirical knowledge of the external facts which individuate his thought contents? It seems not. Such propositions as (either my environment contains water and the concept of water is a natural kind concept, or I am part of a community which has the concept of water) give specific information about the world. Even if a subject can have a priori knowledge of such anti-sceptical propositions as the proposition that there is an external world, it is not plausible that a subject can have a priori knowledge of more specific facts about the world. Thus, it seems that Burgian anti-individualism and the Principle of Privileged Access are incompatible.

McKinsey's argument can be applied not only to Burgian anti-individualism, but to any form of anti-individualism. In this paper, I have discussed how the argument applies to the claim that what natural kind concepts a subject has depends on his natural and/or social environment, and to the claim that what non-natural kind concepts a subject has depends on his social environment. It could also be applied to the claim that some singular thoughts are object-involving – the argument presents a general and acute problem for any form of anti-individualism. McKinsey's argument for the incompatibility of anti-individualism and the Principle of Privileged Access is not addressed by the accounts of privileged access given by anti-individualists.[12]

REFERENCES

Brueckner, A. 1992. What an Anti-Individualist Knows *A Priori. Analysis* 52:111–18. Chapter 9 in this volume.

Burge, T. 1979. Individualism and the Mental. *Mid West Studies in Philosophy* 4: 73–121. Chapter 2 in this volume.

———. 1982. Other Bodies. Pp. 97–120 in *Thought and Object: Essays on Intentionality,* ed. A. Woodfield. Oxford: Oxford University Press.

———. 1988. Individualism and Self-Knowledge. *Journal of Philosophy* 85: 649–63. Chapter 4 in this volume.

McKinsey, M. 1991. Anti-Individualism and Privileged Access. *Analysis* 51: 9–16. Chapter 7 in this volume.

———. 1994. Accepting the Consequences of Anti-Individualism. *Analysis* 54: 124–28.

---

[12] I would like to thank Martin Davies for helpful comments on an earlier draft of this paper.

Part IV: The Compatibilists Respond

9

What An Anti-Individualist Knows *A Priori*

Anthony Brueckner

Michael McKinsey argues in (McKinsey 1991) that the anti-individualist theory of content has the obviously false consequence that one has *a priori* knowledge of the external facts which, according to the theory, help determine the content of one's mental states. Most of McKinsey critical efforts are directed against the views of Tyler Burge, and I will argue that the criticisms rest upon a misunderstanding of these views.

According to McKinsey, Burge (1988) is concerned to defend the consistency of these three propositions:

(1) Oscar knows *a priori* that he is thinking that water is wet.

(2) The proposition that Oscar is thinking that water is wet necessarily depends upon E.

(3) The proposition E cannot be known *a priori*, but only by empirical investigation (McKinsey 1991, p. 12).

E is some 'external proposition' describing 'the relations that Oscar bears to other speakers or objects in his external environment' (McKinsey 1991, p. 10). McKinsey's main criticism of Burge is as follows. Burge's defence of privileged access commits him to (1), and his anti-individualist theory of content commits him to (2) and (3). But (2) has the consequence that Oscar *can* know E *a priori*. Not only does this consequence contradict (3), but, further, it embodies a claim about *a priori* knowledge which is obviously false on anyone's view.

To see whether this criticism of Burge is sound, we must first look at McKinsey's grounds for attributing (1) to (3) to Burge (or, more generally, to a theorist sympathetic to the main ideas of anti-individualism about content). The attribution of (1) is straightforward, given that McKinsey understands *a priori* knowledge to be 'knowledge obtained independently of empirical investigation' (McKinsey 1991, p. 9). On Burge's view, one's knowledge of the content of one's own states has a special self-verifying character. Such knowledge is not, and need not be, based upon any kind of empirical investigation of one's external environment, on Burge's view (see Burge 1988).

The question whether the anti-individualist theory of content commits Burge to (2) and (3) obviously depends upon what the proposition E is. McKinsey is rather vague on this question, and we must proceed carefully if we are to arrive at an accurate assessment of the force of his criticism. Anti-individualism is, roughly, the view that environmental factors external to the individual subject of mental states figure in the individuation of the contents of those states. It is therefore quite natural to suppose that McKinsey's proposition E describes these external, environmental factors. To get clearer on this, let us consider, as McKinsey does, the Twin Earth case originally described by Putnam (1975) and subsequently interpreted by Burge (1982) as bearing on the theory of content. Oscar and his counterfactual twin Toscar 'have the same qualitative perceptual intake and qualitative streams of consciousness, the same movements, the same behavioural dispositions and inner functional states (nonintentionally and individualistically described)', and with one exception involving the ingestion of liquid, 'we might even fix their physical states as identical' (Burge 1982, p. 100). But their environments differ in respect of the chemical composition of the clear liquid filling the oceans, lakes, bath tubs, etc. in their respective worlds. The liquid in Oscar's Earthly environment is H_2O, while the twin liquid in Toscar's Twin Earthly environment is XYZ, a liquid which, according to the anti-individualist, is not water (though it is superficially indistinguishable from water; we will call it 'twater'). When Oscar says 'water is wet, this sentence expresses his thought that water is wet, but when Toscar uses the same sentence, it expresses his thought that twater is wet. The difference in content between the two thoughts is due to the difference between the two thinkers' environments, says Burge. Obviously, the fact that Oscar's environment contains H_2O and not XYZ is not knowable *a priori* by Oscar or anybody else: empirical investigation of Oscar's environment a required for knowledge of that external content-determining fact.

At this point, it is natural to suppose that McKinsey's proposition E, which, according to (3), cannot be known *a priori* but only by empirical investigation, is a proposition describing the recently mentioned external, content-determining fact:

(E1) Oscar inhabits an environment containing H_2O and not XYZ.

Assuming for now that E1 is the proposition McKinsey had in mind, what are we to make of his attribution of (2) to Burge? Here is the only passage in (Burge 1988) in which Burge uses the language of 'necessary dependence': 'My view ... is that many thoughts are individuated non-individualistically: individuating many of a person or animal's mental kinds – certainly including thoughts about physical objects and properties – is necessarily dependent upon relations that the person bears to the physical, or in some cases social, environment (Burge 1988, p. 650).[1] He then proceeds to give an abstract characterization of the sort of thought experiment we have just reviewed. Thus the sense in which, for Burge, the proposition that Oscar is thinking that water is wet *necessarily depends upon* E (interpreted now as E1) is this: the thought experiment involving Toscar establishes that if E1 had been false and, instead, Oscar had inhabited a twin environment containing XYZ instead of H_2O, and if Oscar's phenomenology, functional structure, behaviour, etc., had been held fixed, then some of Oscar's thoughts would have differed in content (he would have thought that twater is wet rather than that water is wet). A thought experiment reveals this counterfactual dependence of content upon E1, and thus we can say that it is necessary that such dependences hold.[2] This necessity is 'indicative of underlying principles for individuating mental kinds' (Burge 1988, p. 656).

McKinsey's criticism of Burge rests upon his attribution of (2) to Burge and his reading of (2) as asserting an *entailment* or *implication* of E by the proposition that Oscar is thinking that water is wet. He holds that the implication is conceptual in nature, where *p conceptually implies q* if and

---

[1] McKinsey says, 'Unfortunately, Burge never explains or clarifies the concept of necessary dependency that he invokes throughout his paper' (McKinsey 1991, p. 12). As just noted, Burge in fact uses the language of 'necessary dependence', only once in that paper (in the passage just quoted in the text). As will become apparent, it is fairly obvious what Burge has in mind when he says that the individuation of content necessarily depends upon relations between thinkers and their environment.

[2] That is. for every possible thinker of water-thoughts in a world relevantly similar to Oscar's, a similar counterfactual dependence holds.

only if 'there is a correct deduction of q from p, a deduction whose only premisses other than p are necessary or conceptual truths that are knowable *a priori*, and each of whose steps follows from previous lines by a self-evident inference rule of some adequate system of natural deduction' (McKinsey 1991, p. 14). McKinsey accordingly interprets (2) as

> (2b) The proposition that Oscar is thinking that water is wet conceptually implies E.

Now if (2b) is true, and if we interpret E as E1, then given that Oscar knows *a priori* that he is thinking that water is wet, it appears to follow that Oscar can know *a priori* that E1 is true. But since Burge accepts (3), he must *deny* that Oscar can know *a priori* that E1 is true. Thus Burge cannot consistently hold (1)–(3) if (2) is interpreted as (2b) (as McKinsey requires) and if E is interpreted as E1 (as we are supposing). Further, it is obviously false on anyone's view that Oscar can know *a priori* that he inhabits an environment containing H_2O and not XYZ.

But if E is interpreted as E1, then McKinsey's (2b) is clearly not a consequence of Burge's anti-individualism, according to which the 'necessary dependence' of Oscar's thoughts upon E1 amounts to the counterfactual dependence of those thoughts' contents upon the environmental factors described by E1. Thus, Burge's anti-individualism does not commit him to the obviously false claim that Oscar can know E1 *a priori*. An anti-individualist can hold that (a) Oscar would not have been thinking that water is wet had he been in a Twin Earthly environment containing XYZ instead of H_2O, while denying that (b) every world in which Oscar thinks that water is wet is a world containing H_2O (i.e., while denying a consequence of the *much stronger* (2b)). Burge explicitly makes such a denial in the paper (Burge 1982) McKinsey cites as the source of Burge's view about Twin Earth's ramifications for the theory of content. When it comes to questions about what is *conceptually implied* by one's thinking that water is wet (or necessitated by such thinkings in a manner knowable *a priori*), Burge is rightly cautious. This is because such questions concern the possibility of a Kantian transcendental argument against scepticism proceeding from the assumption of anti-individualism about content.

Before discussing the relation between anti-individualism and such transcendental arguments, let us consider a way in which McKinsey's objection might be recast in the light of the foregoing criticisms. One might hold that reflection upon Burge's thought experiment affords Oscar *a priori* knowledge about such counterfactual dependences as this:

(2c) If Oscar's environment had been sufficiently different from the way it in fact is (for example, if it had contained XYZ instead of H_2O), then, even holding fixed Oscar's phenomenology, functional structure, behaviour, etc., Oscar would not have been thinking that water is wet.

Oscar knows *a priori* that he is thinking that water is wet. If he also knows (2c) *a priori* on the basis of a thought experiment, then he can know *a priori* that his environment does not contain XYZ instead of H_2O. Thus it appears that Burge's anti-individualism even when viewed correctly as a theory about the counterfactual dependence of content upon the environment, still yields unacceptable consequences about *a priori* knowledge.

The recast objection fails, though. The anti-individualist does not hold that (2c) is knowable *a priori*. (2c) can be decomposed into

(2c1) If Oscar's environment had been sufficiently different from the way it in fact is, then, even holding fixed Oscar's phenomenology, functional structure, behaviour, etc., Oscar would not have been thinking that water is wet.

and

(2c2) Oscar's environment in fact contains H2O instead of XYZ.

Of (2c1) and (2c2), (2c1) may be knowable *a priori* on the anti-individualist theory of content-determination, given various thought experiments involving counterfactual variations from stipulated actual circumstances. (We will return later to the *a priori* commitments, if any, of anti-individualism.) But (2c2) is clearly not knowable *a priori*. So even if Oscar does have *a priori* knowledge of (2c1), this nevertheless does not allow him to deduce anything of interest from his *a priori* knowledge that he is thinking that water is wet, He can at best infer to the *a priori* knowledge that his environment is not different from the way it in fact is.[3]

---

[3] I would like to thank Peter Smith for discussion of the foregoing recast objects and the response to it.

Let us return to the connection between anti-individualism and transcendental arguments. In Burge 1982 (the only paper where Burge discusses Kantian-style anti-sceptical arguments at any length), Burge maintains that 'it is logically possible for an individual to have beliefs involving the concept of water ... even though there exists no water ... of which the individual holds those beliefs'. Otherwise the individual's beliefs would not be *de dicto* in the first place. He says, further, that 'it is logically possible for an individual to have beliefs involving the concept of water ... even though there exists no water' (Burge 1982, p. 114). In such a situation, though, there is the *prima facie* worry that there is nothing licensing the attribution of water-thoughts, rather than twater-thoughts, to the individual. But if the individual is part of a community of language-users, 'there might still be enough in the community's talk to distinguish the notion of water from that of twater and from other candidate notions'. The deluded, waterless community would still have its 'chemical analyses, despite the illusoriness of their object'. However, in such a situation, the existence of water-thoughts would be contingent upon the assumption that 'not *all* of the community's beliefs involve similar illusions' (Burge 1982, p. 116). Burge's idea seems to be that in such a waterless world, there must exist enough physical entities to fix an appropriate content for the community's (false) theoretical sentences.[4] In the case in which one is *alone* in a waterless world, one's solo chemical theorizing might well suffice for a correct attribution of water-thoughts, just as in the communal-illusion case (though Burge does not explicitly say this). But it 'seems incredible' to Burge 'to suppose that ... [a thinker], in his relative ignorance and indifference about the nature of water, holds beliefs whose contents involve the notion [of water], even though neither water nor communal cohorts exist' (Burge 1982, p. 116).

So Burge's view seems to be that it is impossible for Oscar to think that water is wet in a world in which no water exists and in which neither he nor a community of speakers propounds a mistaken chemical theory according to which H_2O exists. This is the view that

(N) It is necessary that if Oscar is thinking that water is wet then either (i) water exists, or (ii) Oscar theorizes that H_2O exists, or

---

[4] Burge's idea may be that there must be enough physical entities to guarantee that some theoretical sentence expresses, e.g., the content that *compounds of two parts hydrogen and one part oxygen exist,* rather than some 'twin' content which is irrelevant to the thinking of water-thoughts (say, a content involving the notion of twhydrogen).

(iii) Oscar is part of a community of speakers some of whom theorize that H_2O exists.[5]

What sort of necessity is involved in (N)? Burge does not explicitly say in the passages in Burge (1982) from which (N) is extracted. But he nowhere maintains that he has in mind a *conceptual* necessity which is knowable *a priori*. Further, since the conditions (ii) and (iii) which figure in the consequent of (N) are derived from the principle that *chemical theory* reveals the nature of water, it is clear that (N) is intended to have the status of a *metaphysical* necessity. Unlike conceptual necessities, some metaphysical necessities are only knowable *a posteriori*. Knowledge that (N), in particular depends upon *a posteriori* knowledge concerning the connection between chemical analysis and the nature of water.

Thus, Burge's anti-individualism does not commit him to the view that Oscar can know *a priori* that *either (i), or (ii),* or *(iii) is true* even if Burge's theory does have the consequence that the disjunction in question is metaphysically necessitated by the proposition (knowable *a priori* by Oscar) that Oscar is thinking that water is wet.[6] Given anti-individualism, though, is there some interesting substantive proposition, 'weaker' or less specific than the disjunction in question, which *is* knowable *a priori* by Oscar, assuming that he knows *a priori* what he is thinking? This is a difficult question, since it is hard to tell how much of anti-individualist theory is derived from *a posteriori* considerations. The theory tells us, quite generally, that in order for Oscar to have water-thoughts, there must be enough in Oscar's world (*whatever* it is like) to rule out the attribution to him of various 'twin' thoughts (such as twater-thoughts). Maybe this is knowable *a priori* if anti-individualism is true (though there is the worry

---

[5] Prior to the publication of McKinsey's paper, Paul Boghossian suggested to me that Burge's theory has the unpalatable consequence that something like (N) is knowable *a priori*. This objection is subtler than McKinsey's and is not marred by any of the misunderstandings of Burge I have attributed to McKinsey. But I think that it can be answered by the considerations which follow in the text.

[6] McKinsey considers the possibility that Burge's anti-individualism gives rise to metaphysical necessities which are not knowable *a priori* (McKinsey 1991, pp. 12-14). Instead of (N), though, he considers the metaphysical necessity that if Oscar is thinking that water is wet, then some external objects exist. He then argues that since this metaphysical necessity could be embraced by an individualist (e.g., one who accepted both materialism and certain Kripkean claims about the necessity of origin), the necessity in question cannot be definitive of anti-individualism. But, as we have seen, the metaphysical necessity McKinsey considers is not put forward as definitive of *anti*-individualism.

that the notion of a 'twin' thought is introduced in the course of thought experiments involving *a posteriori* considerations which concern chemical theory). Anti-individualist theory also seems to tell us, quite generally but more substantively, that the candidates for such content-determining states of affairs are physical in nature and are distinct from the individual subject of contentful states (e.g., liquids with which a speaker causally interacts, speech communities, physical entities sufficient to fix appropriate contents for false theoretical sentences). Thus, it may be that the following *a priori* consequence can be distilled from anti-individualist theory:

> (P) It is necessary that if Oscar is thinking that water is wet, then there exist some physical entities distinct from Oscar.

Suppose (P) is knowable *a priori*, on the basis of reflection on the mind and of language. Then, given Oscar's *a priori* knowledge of what he is thinking, he can know *a priori* that there exist some physical entities distinct from himself. Supposing that Oscar can know this much *a priori*, would this mean that he can know anything *a priori* about the character of his physical environment? It seems that he can at best know that it contains physical entities sufficient to fix the contents of his thoughts. *Which* sorts of entities are required is an *a posteriori* matter.

It is far from clear that (P) is something which an anti-individualist knows *a priori*. There is not space to consider the question whether claims about the pertinence of physical environment to the determination of content are, if true, knowable *a priori*. We would need to consider the difficult question whether such claims, if true, are knowable only on the basis of *a posteriori* knowledge about causal relations between language and the physical world, and about the social character of language. But even if anti-individualism does afford *a priori* knowledge of (P), is this a problem for the theory?[7]

Is it obviously wrong to suppose that one can know *a priori* that there exist some physical entities distinct from oneself? Towards the end of his paper, McKinsey takes to construing his proposition E as the proposition

---

[7] In (Burge 1988, p. 655, n. 6) Burge rejects the suggestion that 'if anti-individualism and the authority of self-knowledge are accepted, then one would have an anti-sceptical argument.' He says that 'there is no easy argument against scepticism from anti-individualism and authoritative self-knowledge'. This suggests that he does not endorse the view that anti-individualism affords *a priori* knowledge of (P), since if it *did* this would make possible an *a priori* argument against certain forms of scepticism.

that 'the external world exists', and he says that 'you obviously *can't* know *a priori* that the external world exists (McKinsey 1991, p. 16). This does seem obvious if the alleged *a priori* knowledge is said to contain much detail concerning the character of the external world distinct from oneself. But if the alleged *a priori* knowledge is simply knowledge that something or other physical exists distinct from oneself, it is not obvious that such knowledge is impossible. McKinsey's mere assertion of such an impossibility is plainly not enough to prove the impossibility of a successful Kantian transcendental argument. Such arguments must be examined individually on their merits, not rejected *a priori* simply on the basis of their ambitions.

REFERENCES

Burge, T. 1982. Other Bodies, in *Thought and Object: Essays on Intentionality* A. Woodfield, ed. Oxford: Oxford University Press.

————. 1988. Individualism and Self-Knowledge. *Journal of Philosophy* 85: 649–63. Chapter 4 in this volume.

McKinsey, M. 1991. Anti-Individualism and Privileged Access. *Analysis* 51: 9–16. Chapter 7 in this volume.

Putnam, H. 1975. The Meaning of "Meaning". In his *Philosophical Papers* Vol. 2. Cambridge, UK: Cambridge University Press.

10

The Brown–McKinsey Charge of Inconsistency

Brian McLaughlin and Michael Tye

Both McKinsey (1991) and later Brown (1995) charge that Burge is committed to a version of externalism that implies, for certain Ps, that if one is thinking that P, then E – where E cannot be known a priori. This charge is made as part of an ad hominem argument against Burge. For Burge (1988) explicitly endorses privileged access.[1] Thus, it is argued that he holds two incompatible theses.[2]

As has been correctly pointed out by Brueckner (1992), McKinsey offers no textual evidence for this charge of inconsistency. However, Brown does. She does not claim that Burge's own Twin-Earth thought-experiment alone commits him to an externalist thesis incompatible with privileged access. Nor does she maintain that Burge's interpretation of Putnam's Twin-Earth thought-experiment alone commits him to such an externalist thesis. Rather, Brown cleverly combines a Burge-type Twin-Earth thought-experiment with Burge's interpretation of Putnam's Twin-Earth thought-experiment to argue (on McKinsey-type grounds) that Burge is indeed committed to an externalist thesis that is incompatible with privileged access. We will argue that Brown fails to show that Burge is so committed.

---

[1] For a precise statement of the privileged access thesis, see McLaughlin and Tye, forthcoming.

[2] The authors don't say which of the two theses he should reject or whether he should reject both.

The textual evidence that Brown cites occurs in the context of Burge's (1982) discussion of what is and what is not required for having thoughts that involve the exercise of the concept of water. Let us begin by looking at Burge's own discussion.

Burge argues that it is possible to have water-thoughts (thoughts involving the exercise of the concept of water) without the existence of water. He argues that an individual in a possible world in which there is in fact no water can, nevertheless, possess the concept of water, and thus have water-thoughts such as the thought that water is wet. He asks us to imagine a world in which an individual, Adam, is a member of community that is under the grand illusion that there is a certain liquid with such-and-such phenomenal properties (the phenomenal properties of water) that fills their oceans and lakes, flows in their rivers and streams, that often falls from the sky, that can freeze solid or be heated into a gaseous state, and so on, and so forth. (Fill in the 'so on and so forth' with general nonexpert beliefs that match a vast range of the general nonexpert beliefs we have about water that do not themselves involve the exercise of the concept of water.) Such a widespread illusion is certainly possible. Burge goes on to tell us that the experts in Adam's community theorize that the (illusory) liquid, which they and Adam intend to call 'water', is H_2O. That requires, of course, that they have the concept of H_2O. But the concept of H_2O is a descriptive concept that it is possible to possess even if there is no H_2O, and thus no water.[3] Burge plausibly claims that Adam counts as having the concept of water.[4]

Notice that in the world in question, people other than Adam exist. Does having water-thoughts require the existence of other people? Surely not. As Burge correctly notes, one might causally interact with water and, as a result, form the concept of water, even if there were no other people. Just imagine Adam alone in a world, but causally interacting with water and forming beliefs about it.

Thus, it is possible for Adam to have the concept of water, even if there are no other people in Adam's world. And it is possible for Adam to have the concept of water even if there is no water in Adam's world. Is it, how-

---

[3] The concept of H_2O is (roughly) the concept of something made up of two hydrogen atoms and one oxygen atom.

[4] Adam need not have the concept of H_2O, however. In Burge's view (and in ours), the concept of water is not the same as the concept of H_2O, even though water, in fact, is H_2O.

ever, possible for Adam to have water-thoughts without *either* water *or* other people existing? It certainly seems so. Moreover, Burge convincingly argues that it is possible. Suppose that Adam is under the illusion that there is a liquid with such-and-such phenomenal properties (the phenomenal properties of water) that fills the oceans and lakes, flows in rivers and streams, etc, etc., and that he intends to call 'water'. Suppose further that Adam, who knows a considerable amount of chemical theory, theorizes that the liquid is H_2O. Adam, Burge plausibly claims, would have the concept of water. These suppositions are consistent with Adam's being in a world without either water or other people. In this way, then, Burge plausibly argues that having water-thoughts requires neither the existence of water nor the existence of other people.

Of course, in this last case, Adam possesses the concept of H_2O. Suppose, however, that Adam lacks the concept of H_2O and has no opinion about the necessary and sufficient conditions for being the kind of stuff he believes fills the oceans, and so on; suppose further that there is no water in his world; and suppose finally that there are no other people. In that case, Burge claims that it

> seems incredible ... to suppose that Adam, in his relative ignorance and indifference about the nature of water, holds beliefs whose contents involve the notion, even though neither water nor communal cohorts exist. (1982, p.116)

That strikes us as incredible too. For, as Burge notes, given Adam's ignorance of the nature of water, his lack of any causal interaction with water (since there is no water), and the fact that he is not a member of any linguistic community with a word that means water (since there are no other people), there seems to be nothing that would *make* Adam's thought a water-thought, rather than, say, a twater-thought. It seems reasonable to conclude that Adam lacks the concept of water; and, moreover, that Adam lacks the concept of twater too. More generally, given that water is H_2O, it seems incredible that an individual could possess the concept of water without either having causally interacted with water, or having theorized that there is H_2O, or being a member of a community with experts who have theorized that there is H_2O. Indeed, so far as we can see, that would be impossible; and that it is impossible seems to us knowable a priori. One could not, however, know a priori that the antecedent of the relevant conditional we just embraced is satisfied; for one could not know a priori that water is H_2O.

Citing as evidence the passage we just quoted from Burge, Brown (1995) maintains that Burge is committed to the following thesis:

> *Q*　Necessarily, if *x* has a thought involving the concept of a natural kind *k* and *x* is agnostic about the application conditions of the concept of *k*, then either *x* is in an environment which contains *k*, or *x* is part of a community with the concept *k*. (p.152)

This goes beyond what is actually in the passage. But Burge makes it clear elsewhere that he intends the water example to generalize to any concept that is in fact a concept of a natural kind. So, we will concede, for the sake of argument, that Burge is committed to *Q*– at least where the phrase 'the concept of a natural kind *k*' is understood as Brown intends it, as 'the concept of *k*, where *k* is a natural kind'.

Brown does not attempt to argue that *Q* commits Burge to denying privileged access. The reason is that she recognizes that one cannot know a priori that the concept of *k* is a concept of a natural kind; for one cannot know a priori that *k* is a natural kind. The concept of water, Brown correctly points out, could have turned out to be like the concept of jade (a concept that applies not to a natural kind, but rather to either of two distinct kinds: jadeite and nephrite). Indeed, we ourselves think that it is epistemically possible for the concept of water to prove to be like the concept of phlogiston. We cannot know a priori that water is a natural kind.

Brown goes on, however, to maintain that, in addition to being committed to *Q*, Burge is also committed to a second thesis, *R*, which, in conjunction with *Q*, commits him to denying privileged access. The second thesis is this:

> *R*　Necessarily, if *x* has a thought involving a non-natural kind concept, *c*, and *x* is agnostic about the application conditions of *c*, then *x* is part of a community which has the concept *c*.

This thesis is, we believe, both false and one to which Burge is, in no way, committed. In attributing *R* to Burge, Brown makes a serious mistake. But of this, more shortly.

Brown correctly maintains that the second thesis, *R*, in conjunction with the first thesis, *Q*, implies the following thesis:

> *S*　Necessarily, if *x* has a thought involving a concept *c*, and *x* is agnostic about the application conditions of *c*, then either *x* is in an environment which contains instances of *c* and *c* is a natural

kind concept, or x is part of a community which has the concept c, whether or not c is a natural kind concept. (1995, p.155)

If S can indeed be known a priori, then the thesis of privileged access is false. For the following claims are inconsistent:

A It is knowable a priori by one that one is having a thought involving the concept of c.

B It is knowable a priori by one that one is agnostic about the application conditions of c.

C It is not knowable a priori by one that one is an environment which either contains instances of c and c is a natural kind concept, or one is part of a community which has the concept c, whether or not c is a natural kind concept.

Claims A and B follow from the thesis of privileged access. Given S, they are incompatible with C. So, if S is true, privileged access is incompatible with C. Hence, S is incompatible with C. We thus have, in S, a version of externalism that cannot be squared with privileged access. If Burge really does maintain S, then he cannot consistently maintain privileged access. Brown concludes: "Burge's position is inconsistent … Burgian anti-individualism and the Principle of Privileged Access are incompatible." (1995, p.155)

Consider, again,

R Necessarily, if x has a thought involving a non-natural kind concept, c, and x is agnostic about the application conditions of c, then x is part of a community which has the concept c.

We noted that Burge is in no way committed to R. Why, then, does Brown maintain that he is? We will quote her at length:

Burge's argument for the claim that [Adam, who, you will recall, is ignorant of the nature of water] could not have a water thought unless water or other speakers exist, seems applicable to thoughts involving non-natural kind concepts. Imagine that [Adam] is agnostic about the application conditions of the word, 'sofa'. For example, he may apply it firmly and correctly to what we call 'sofas', but be unsure about whether it also applies to broad single seat armchairs. According to Burge, if [Adam] is part of an English speaking community then, despite his agnosticism, he has thoughts involving the concept sofa. But if, counterfactually, [Adam] had been part of a community in which 'sofa' is applied both to what we call 'sofas' and to broad single seat armchairs, then [Adam] would have had chofa thoughts, where the concept of a chofa applies both to what we call 'sofas' and to broad single seat armchairs. Now imagine that there are no other speakers in [Adam's] environment. How could [Adam] have propositional attitudes involving the concept of sofa? Since sofa is not a natural kind concept, [Adam's] natural environment cannot help him to acquire the concept. There are no other speakers. Nothing seems to show that his attitudes involve the concept of sofa as opposed to chofa. (1995, pp. 153–154)

On the basis of this reasoning, she concludes that Burge is committed to *R*.

We agree with Brown that, in the scenario she describes, "nothing seems to show that [Adam's] attitudes involve the concept of sofa as opposed to chofa." Indeed, there seems to be nothing that makes it the case that Adam's attitudes involve the concept of sofa, and nothing that makes it the case that his attitudes involve the concept of chofa. It seems that Adam lacks both concepts. But in inferring *R*, Brown seems to be tacitly assuming that there is no concept that Adam expresses using his word pronounced /sofa/. We see no justification for that assumption. Why can't an individual have a *non*-natural kind concept and be agnostic about the necessary and sufficient conditions for its application without being a member of a linguistic community? Brown offers not even a hint as to how to answer this question.

We maintain that there is no reason whatsoever to think that one cannot have a non-natural kind concept, be agnostic about the necessary and sufficient conditions for its application, and yet not be a member of any linguistic community. Suppose, for example, having taken oneself to have just learned the concept of a priori knowledge, a concept one recognizes not to be a natural kind concept, one wonders what, exactly, the necessary and sufficient conditions are for its application. Could one, from these considerations alone, without assuming one has actually learned the concept, conclude that other people exist? Surely not. But if *R* were true, one could. So much the worse for *R*.

In fact, the problem for Brown's position is more serious than simply that it is unsupported by her example. In the scenario Brown describes, Adam has a word that he applies "firmly and *correctly* to what we call 'sofas'" (1995, p.153) (emphasis ours). But if the word can be correctly applied, then it expresses a concept. Brown tells us that the word does not express a natural kind concept; the word, then, expresses a non-natural concept. She tells us, moreover, that Adam is not a member of any linguistic community, and that Adam is "unsure whether ['sofa'] applies to broad single seat armchairs," and is thus agnostic about the application conditions of the concept. Thus, it is part of the very description of the case that Adam has a certain non-natural kind concept despite the fact that he is not a member of any linguistic community and is agnostic about the application conditions of the concept. Rather than supporting R, Brown's very example shows that R is false.[5] For Brown has characterized a possible situation in which an individual possesses a non-natural kind concept, is agnostic about its conditions of application, and is not a member of any linguistic community. The example seems perfectly coherent. It itself shows that R is false.

In conclusion, then, the Twin-Earth thought-experiment Brown employs provides no justification for her principle, S, since it provides no justification for R. Indeed, the thought-experiment itself yields a counterexample to R.[6]

REFERENCES

Brueckner, A. 1992. What An Anti-Individualist Knows A Priori. *Analysis* 52: 111–118. Chapter 9 in this volume.

———. Other Bodies. Pp. 97–120 in *Thought and Object: Essays on Intentionality*, ed. A. Woodfield. Oxford: Oxford University Press.

———. 1998. Individualism and Self-knowledge. *Journal of Philosophy* 85: 649–663. Chapter 4 in this volume.

Brown, J. 1995. The Incompatibility of Anti-Individualism and Privileged Access. *Analysis* 53.3: 149–156. Chapter 8 in this volume.

McKinsey, M. 1991. Anti-Individualism and Privileged Access. *Analysis* 51: 9–16. Chapter 7 in this volume.

---

[5] Notice, moreover, that in the scenario Adam has the concept of a word's applying to something; that is a non-natural kind concept; and Adam may well be agnostic about the application conditions for a word's applying to something. If so, it follows, as before, that Brown's case could not possibly support R, for it is inconsistent with R.

[6] For an extended discussion of the question of whether externalism about thought contents is incompatible with privileged access, see B. McLaughlin and M. Tye forthcoming.

McLaughlin, B. and Tye, M. Forthcoming. Externalism, Twin-Earth, and Self-Knowledge. In *Knowing Our Own Minds: Essays on Self-Knowledge*, eds. C. Macdonald, B. Smith, and C. Wright. Oxford: Oxford University Press).

11

Privileged Self-Knowledge and Externalism are Compatible

Ted A. Warfield

Michael McKinsey has argued (McKinsey 1991) that if externalism is true, it follows that we cannot have knowledge of the contents of our thoughts (self-knowledge) that is independent of empirical investigation of our environment. I shall, following McKinsey, refer to this type of self-knowledge as 'a priori' self-knowledge and shall refer to the thesis that a priori self-knowledge and externalism are incompatible as the Incompatibility Thesis. As shall become clear later, there are those who would reserve the label 'a priori' for a different sort of self-knowledge. I shall thus also refer to knowledge of the contents of our thoughts that is independent of our environmental investigation as 'privileged' self-knowledge in order to contrast it later in the paper with this other sense of 'a priori'.

More specifically, McKinsey argues that for appropriate substitutions for 'E' and where 'necessarily depends upon' is understood as 'conceptually implies', the following three propositions are inconsistent:

1. Oscar knows a priori that he is thinking that water is wet.

2. The proposition that Oscar is thinking that water is wet necessarily depends upon E.

3. The proposition E cannot be known a priori, but only by empirical investigation.

Anthony Brueckner (1992) has refuted McKinsey's argument noting that on various possible interpretations, the argument falters in assuming at least one of the following highly questionable propositions:

Al   If externalism is true, then 'a subject is thinking that water is wet' conceptually implies 'there is water in the subject's environment'.

A2   A subject cannot know a priori that the external world exists, whether or not externalism is true.[1]

While agreeing with Brueckner's criticisms of McKinsey, I do not believe that the refutation of McKinsey's argument has closed the books on the question of whether or not the Incompatibility Thesis is true. Indeed, there is another argument due to Paul Boghossian (1989) for this same sceptical conclusion that makes neither of the controversial assumptions for which Brueckner faulted McKinsey.[2]

So while Brueckner has refuted McKinsey, it is open to the defender of the Incompatibility Thesis to point out that Boghossian's argument for this thesis is not vulnerable to Brueckner's criticisms. In this paper I shall block this response, arguing that Boghossian's argument for the Incompatibility Thesis is fallacious. Having done this, I shall conclude the paper with a brief response to an anticipated rejoinder by defenders of the Incompatibility Thesis.

As part of his argument for the Incompatibility Thesis, Boghossian argues (as he must) that externalism is incompatible with a thinker's knowing the contents of his thoughts on the basis of introspection (Boghossian 1989, pp. 11–14). Boghossian's argument for the Incompatibility Thesis can be no better than his argument for the incompatibility of externalism and introspective self-knowledge. Since, as I shall demonstrate, the latter argument is fallacious, it follows that the former argument is unsound.[3]

---

[1] See Brueckner (1992) pp. 113–15 for discussion of Al, and pp. 117–18 for discussion of A2.

[2] Furthermore, the influence of Boghossian's argument is spreading. For example, Bonjour (1991) endorses Boghossian's argument, taking it to be a reductio of externalism (p. 351).

[3] Another reason for focusing on Boghossian's argument concerning introspection is that however, exactly, we are to understand 'introspection', it is, as Boghossian notes, both plausible and intuitively appealing that it is via introspection that we come to form beliefs about the contents of our thoughts.

Why does Boghossian think that externalism precludes introspective self-knowledge?[4] For purposes of leading up to his official argument, Boghossian offers a preliminary argument, the soundness of which he denies. A quick look at this argument will allow us to see the motivation for some of the details of Boghossian's official argument. I formalize this preliminary argument as follows [Let 'P'= 'S's thought is about water', and let S be an actual world individual]:

P1 If S needs to investigate his environment to know that P, then S doesn't know that P by introspection.

P2 To know that P, S must know that his thought is not about twin water [hereafter 'twater'].

P3 To know that his thought is not about twater, S needs to investigate his environment.

C1 So, S doesn't know that P by introspection.

As Boghossian himself points out, this argument is highly suspect given the implausible account of knowledge it presupposes. Specifically, (P2) appears to be highly questionable. To quote Boghossian:

[This argument] appears to make problematic assumptions about the conditions required for knowledge. Consider perceptual knowledge. Someone may know, by looking, that he has a dime in his hand. But it is controversial, to put it mildly, whether he needs to know all the conditions that make such knowledge possible. He need not have checked, for example, that there is no counterfeit money in the vicinity, nor does he need to be able to tell the difference between a genuine dime and every imaginable counterfeit ... The ordinary concept of knowledge appears to call for no more than the exclusion of 'relevant' alternative hypotheses (however, exactly, that is to be understood); and mere logical possibility does not confer such relevance.

Similar remarks apply to the case of self-knowledge. (1989, p. 12)

---

[4] That this is Boghossian's position is clear. Before stating the first of the two arguments I discuss below, he writes (p. 12) 'Now, doesn't it follow from such anti-individualist views [externalism] that we cannot know the contents of our thoughts in a direct, purely observational manner? The following line of reasoning might seem to lead rather swiftly to that conclusion.' Then, before stating the second argument I am considering (the second being the argument Boghossian explicitly endorses) he claims that the first argument 'suggests a ... more convincing argument *for the same conclusion'* (p. 13, emphasis added).

The flaw of Boghossian's swift argument in short (and by his own admission) is that it assumes a problematic account of knowledge, the abandonment of which falsifies (P2) of the argument.

Boghossian, however, far from concluding that externalism and introspective self-knowledge are compatible, believes that the swift argument points in the direction of a successful sceptical argument. Boghossian says that the swift argument suggests

> a slower and more convincing argument for the same conclusion. For it seems easy to describe scenarios in which the twin hypotheses *are* relevant alternatives, but in which they are, nevertheless, not discriminable non-inferentially from their actual counterparts. (1989, p. 13)

Boghossian goes on to describe one such scenario in a thought experiment.

In this thought experiment (call it the Switching Case), we are asked to imagine that S undergoes a series of switches between Earth and Twin Earth, and that his conceptual scheme is (depending on how one reads the case) thereby either flipped back and forth as he flips locations or enlarged to include both Earthian and Twin Earthian concepts. On this story, Boghossian rightly claims, twater is a relevant alternative to water, for relevance is an objective notion and an alternative's being actual is sufficient for the alternative's being relevant But in the Switching Case, as in the actual world, S can't discriminate between the two, so S does not know the contents of his water/twater thoughts.

What bearing does this story have on the issue at hand? Boghossian thinks that the Switching Case provides an argument for the incompatibility of externalism and introspective self-knowledge. I disagree. I formalize the argument as follows [Using 'P' and 'S' as before]:

P1   To know that P by introspection, S must be able to introspectively discriminate P from all relevant alternatives of P.

P2   S cannot introspectively discriminate water thoughts from twater thoughts.

P3   If the Switching Case is actual, then twater thoughts are relevant alternatives of water thoughts

C1   S doesn't know that P by introspection.

This argument, unfortunately for Boghossian, is invalid. All that follows from the premises is the much weaker conclusion:

C1   If the Switching Case is actual then S doesn't know that P by introspection.

But this conclusion is not relevant to the question of the compatibility of externalism and introspective self-knowledge. It is relevant *at most* to the following question:

> Q   Given externalism is it *necessary* that the contents of a thinker's thoughts are knowable to the thinker on the basis of introspection?

Boghossian's argument has not, I maintain, shown *anything* about the compatibility of introspective self-knowledge and externalism. Rather, granting the assumptions that the Switching Case is logically possible and that all three premises are true, it has shown only that the answer to (Q) is 'No'. In closing out my reply to Boghossian, I submit that while he is correct in doubting the soundness of the 'swift' argument, his official argument against the compatibility of externalism and introspective self-knowledge is invalid. Recall that Boghossian's argument for the Incompatibility Thesis can be no better than his argument against the compatibility of introspective self-knowledge and externalism. The latter, I have shown is fallacious; so the former is unsound. Boghossian, I conclude, has not established the Incompatibility Thesis.

I would like to conclude this paper by offering a response to an anticipated rejoinder by defenders of the Incompatibility Thesis.[5] A defender of the Incompatibility Thesis might argue that while perhaps externalism is compatible with 'a priori' self-knowledge on a construal of 'a priori' on which introspective self-knowledge counts as a priori self-knowledge, externalism is not compatible with a priori self-knowledge understood in a stronger sense.

One might think that a priori knowledge, properly so called, is knowledge independent of contingent environmental facts (e.g. whether or not one is in a Switching Case) and one might be convinced (perhaps by Boghossian) that introspective self-knowledge is dependent on such facts. Thus, while leaving open the question of whether externalism and introspective self-knowledge are compatible, one might argue that externalism

---

[5] This response was suggested independently by both Barry Loewer and Brian McLaughlin. Neither, however, should be taken to be committed to the position each suggested.

is *not* compatible with this stricter sort of a priori self-knowledge on which introspective self-knowledge is *not* a species of 'a priori' self-knowledge.[6]

Rather than offering a point by point evaluation of this anticipated rejoinder, I would simply like to point out that the externalist can, if forced, happily accept the conclusion of line of reasoning.

What motivates philosophers to worry about self-knowledge and externalism is the intuition that externalism might imply the seemingly false conclusion that one must investigate one's environment to know the contents of one's thoughts. But even if it were shown that externalism and this strong sort of a priori self-knowledge are incompatible, it would not follow that one has to investigate one's environment to know the contents of one's thoughts. Introspective self-knowledge is knowledge independent of such environmental investigation and our having introspective self-knowledge is consistent with the view that externalism and this strong sense of a priori self-knowledge are incompatible. So, I submit, the motivation for philosophers' worries about externalism and self-knowledge is missing from this hypothetical reply.

The externalist faced with this hypothetical rejoinder could thus simply agree (at least for purposes of discussion) that this strict sort of a priori self-knowledge is incompatible with externalism. The externalist need only, in addition, point out that this conclusion is consistent with the view that externalism and privileged self-knowledge are compatible and that it is privileged self-knowledge that we care about.

A successful argument that externalism and (this sort of) a priori self-knowledge are incompatible would be worrisome only if

(A) there are reasons to think that it is this sort of a priori knowledge (and not 'merely' privileged introspective knowledge) that we have of the contents of our mental states.

OR

(B) there is an independent argument for the incompatibility of introspective self-knowledge and externalism.

Without a defence of (A) or (B), even a sound argument for the incompatibility of externalism and such a priori self-knowledge would pose no threat to externalism.

---

[6] Another way of making this point would be by claiming that in the case of a priori knowledge, properly so-called, *all* logically possible alternatives are relevant alternatives.

I conclude that as things now stand, there is no good argument for the Incompatibility Thesis, nor do other considerations of self-knowledge (e.g., the adoption of a stronger notion of 'a priori') tell against externalism. Privileged self-knowledge and externalism are compatible.[7]

REFERENCES

Boghossian, P. 1989. Content and Self-Knowledge. *Philosophical Topics* 17: 5–26. Chapter 6 in this volume.

Bonjour, L. 1992. Is Thought a Symbolic Process? *Synthese* 89: 331–52.

Brueckner, A. 1992. What an Anti-Individualist Knows A Priori. *Analysis* 52: 111–18. Chapter 9 in this volume.

McKinsey, M. 1991. Anti-Individualism and Privileged Access. *Analysis* 51: 9–16. Chapter 7 in this volume.

---

[7] I would like to thank Brian McLaughlin, Barry Loewer and Frances Egan for helpful discussion of this issue. I would also like to thank Peter Smith for several helpful suggestions.

Part V: Externalism, Self-Knowledge and Epistemic Warrant

12

Externalism, Self-Knowledge, and the Prevalence of Slow Switching

Peter Ludlow

In an influential article, Paul Boghossian (1989) has argued that external-ism about mental content and a priori self-knowledge are incompatible doctrines. Commandeering the slow switching thought experiment intro-duced by Burge (1988) (where an agent unknowingly switches between Earth and Twin Earth), Boghossian argues that it appears possible for an agent S to know his thoughts at time *t*, forget nothing, yet at some time later than *t* (perhaps having been informed that switches were taking place) be unable to say what the contents of his thoughts were at *t*. As Boghossian argues,

> The only explanation, I venture to suggest, for why S will not know tomorrow what he is said to know today, is not that he has forgotten but that he never knew. Burge's self-verifying judgments do not con-stitute genuine knowledge. What other reason is there for why our slowly transported thinker will not know tomorrow what he is said to know directly and authoritatively today? (Boghossian 1989, p. 23).

Ted Warfield has recently offered an objection to Boghossian's argument, suggesting that it is invalid. Warfield begins by formalizing Boghossian's argument as follows. (Warfield 1992, p. 234–235)

> (P1) To know that P by introspection, S must be able to introspec-tively discriminate P from all relevant alternatives of P.

(P2) S cannot introspectively discriminate water thoughts from twater thoughts.

(P3) If the Switching Case is actual, then twater thoughts are relevant alternatives of water thoughts.

(C1) So, S doesn't know that P by introspection

Warfield claims that this argument is invalid, since all that follows is the much weaker (C1')

(C1') If the Switching case is actual, then S doesn't know that P by introspection

As Warfield further argues, (C1') is simply not enough to undermine the authority of our self-knowledge. The mere possibility of a switching case no more undermines our self-knowledge than the possibility of our possessing a counterfeit coin undermines the authority of our knowledge of how much money we have in our pockets. Boghossian's own remarks appear to support precisely this general view about the character of our knowledge.

> Someone may know, by looking, that he has a dime in his hand. But it is controversial, to put it mildly, whether he needs to know all the conditions that make such knowledge possible. He need not have checked, for example, that there is no counterfeit money in the vicinity, nor does he need to be able to tell the difference between a genuine dime and every imaginable counterfeit... The ordinary concept of knowledge appears to call for no more than the exclusion of 'relevant' alternative hypotheses (however, exactly, that is to be understood); and mere logical possibility does not confer such relevance. (Boghossian 1989, p. 12)

Boghossian is apparently hoisted by his own petard. However, I think we can accept this general view about the character of knowledge and yet circumvent Warfield's argument against Boghossian. The trouble lies in premise (P3) which understates the conditions under which there might be relevant alternatives to water thoughts. Much better would be something along the lines of (P3').

(P3')If switching cases in general are prevalent, then there are relevant alternatives of water thoughts.

To appreciate the difference between (P3) and (P3'), consider the following two analogues for the case of knowledge of coins at coin shows.

(A) If counterfeiting is actual at this coin show, then it is a relevant alternative that this is a counterfeit in my hand.

(A') If counterfeiting (in general) is prevalent at coin shows, then it is a relevant alternative that this a counterfeit in my hand.

To the collector who frequents coin shows, A' is the appropriate principle, not A. Likewise, whether or not the water/twater switching case is actual, denizens of worlds where switching cases are prevalent will want to opt for (P3') – in such worlds there really are relevant alternatives of water thoughts (indeed, of all thoughts).

Of course, to rescue Boghossian's argument we still need to add the following premise.

(P4) Switching cases, in general, are prevalent

But are switching cases prevalent? Do we really get spirited off to Twin Earth in our sleep? Do we really spend part of our lives drinking twater?

Of course nothing in (P4) implies that trips to Twin Earth are common (hopefully they are not). What is implied is that we frequently and unknowingly slide from from language community to another. More to the point, as we travel between different circles of acquaintances, the contents of our utterances and thoughts may shift as well.

To illustrate this point, let's consider the case where an agent, Biff, is an international traveler (in a bit we'll consider a case where he is less worldly). Biff, for his job, spends several weeks in England and then several weeks in the United States. He is aware that there are dialectical variations ('gasoline' vs. 'petrol', etc.), but knows also that there is considerable overlap between British and American English.

Biff eschews leafy vegetables. His knowledge of them is partial, and he defers to the linguistic community when he speaks of them. Thus, he knows that chickory and arugula are such vegetables, but he would not be able to distinguish them by sight. Biff imagines that vegetable vocabulary is one area where British and American English overlap. But of course Biff is wrong in this. When Biff uses the term 'chickory' with his British friends (and deferring to them for the individuating conditions) he is speaking of one thing. When he uses the same term with his American friends (and deferring to them for the individuating conditions) he is speaking of another thing.

Towards the end of his visits to England, Biff may entertain thoughts about leafy vegetables. He may, being concerned about his health, wonder if eating some chickory would be a good idea. But when the same internal episode also takes place in the United States (at the end of his stay) then he will be wondering something else altogether. So, Biff has become a victim of a slow switching case. He knows that he has moved between language communities, but he is unaware of the extent of the switch. He is unaware that the contents of some of his mental states are different.

Biff needn't be a world traveler. Suppose that Biff is a Stony Brook philosopher that never leaves New York State. Suppose also that Biff is aware that when he moves from his university life to real life, he in effect shifts between language communities. Biff knows, for example, that in the Philosophy Department, the term 'realist' applies to one thing, but at home applies to something else. (Biff need not even be clear on the individuating conditions of these terms – like leafy vegetables, he eschews metaphysics). Biff also knows, of course, that for the most part these real world and philosophical languages overlap. There may, however, be terms of which Biff has only partial knowledge and which he takes to be overlap terms, but which are not.

Suppose for example that Biff, who knows little of American philosophy, understands that certain of his colleagues are called 'pragmatists'. He may speak of these colleagues at home as pragmatists as well, not knowing that the expression has different meanings in the two worlds that he moves between. During a conversation with one group or another, Biff may even wonder whether a particular member of the group is a pragmatist. Of course the content of that mental episode will depend on Biff's fellow travelers of the moment (assuming he has spent enough time with them). Once again, Biff is an unwitting victim of slow switching.

But this isn't just a story about hapless Biff. We routinely move between social groups and institutions, and in many cases shifts in the content of our thoughts will not be detected by us. (There is, it appears, a little of Biff in all of us). Nor are these cases even limited to obvious cases of movement. It may occur when we routinely cross campus to talk to colleagues in physics or psychology, or even when we pay routine visits to our favorite restaurant.

These cases can be pumped even further when we recognize that they are applicable not just to nouns like 'water', 'chickory', and 'pragmatist', but to a whole host of other expressions. As Burge notes,

The argument [for external content] has an extremely wide application. It does not depend, for example, on the kind of word 'arthritis' is. We could have used an artifact term, an ordinary natural kind word, a color adjective, a social role term, a term for historical style, an abstract noun, an action verb, a physical movement verb, or any of various other sorts of words. (Burge, 1979, p. 79)

In short, as we slide between circles of acquaintance it is not enough to simply be on guard for shifts in the meanings of nouns. Virtually any part of speech is susceptible here.

It is also worth noting that the social groups that we defer to need not be sprawling networks of individuals, but may in fact be very local in scope. Small, localized, circles of individuals may be completely unwilling to defer to others on certain key terms; for example certain cliques may have their own notion of the individuating conditions of derogatory terms like 'fool', and 'bore', and will not defer to persons outside the group in these cases. Moreover, it is entirely possible that the borders between these groups will go undetected by us – that like Oscar, who unknowingly moves between Earth and Twin Earth, we unknowingly cross between localized groups with different individuating conditions for certain key terms. If we defer to the groups for the contents of these terms, then the contents of our words (and ultimately our thoughts) will shift without our ever noticing a linguistic border crossing.

I conclude that, following certain very natural assumptions about externalism (namely that content is socially determined and that the relevant social groups may be highly localized), (P4) is an entirely plausible premise. If Boghossian's argument is recast with the help of (P3') and (P4), then (C1) will follow after all, and Warfield's objection can be circumvented.[1]

REFERENCES

Boghossian, P. 1989. Content and Self-Knowledge. *Philosophical Topics* 17:5–26. Chapter 6 in this volume.

Burge, T. 1979. Individualism and the Mental. *Midwest Studies in Philosophy* 4:73–122. Chapter 2 in this volume.

---

[1] I am endebted to Norah Martin for helpful discussion of these issues.

―――. 1988. Individualism and Self-Knowledge. *Journal of Philosophy* 85: 649–63. Chapter 4 in this volume.

Warfield, T. 1992. Privileged Self-Knowledge and Externalism are Compatible. *Analysis* 52: 232–37. Chapter 11 in this volume.

13

Externalism, Privileged Self-Knowledge, and the Irrelevance of Slow Switching

Ted A. Warfield

Some philosophers think that externalism about mental content is incompatible with what I call *privileged self-knowledge*: the thesis that one's beliefs about the contents of one's thoughts are at least typically instances of direct knowledge. Two main lines of argument have been developed in support of this claim. The first, put forward most forcefully by Michael McKinsey (1991 and 1994) and also supported by, among others, Jessica Brown (1995), argues that the consistency of privileged self-knowledge and externalism would imply the soundness of what, in these philosophers' eyes, is an implausibly strong transcendental anti-skeptical argument. Having had my say about this flawed line of argument elsewhere,[1] I would like to show on the present occasion that the second line of skeptical reasoning is also flawed.

The second line of argument, originally developed by Paul Boghossian and also discussed by Peter Ludlow (1995a and 1995b) and others, uses so called 'slow switching' (Burge 1988) cases in an attempt to illustrate the alleged incompatibility of privileged self-knowledge and externalism.[2]

---

[1] I argue elsewhere (Warfield 1995 and forthcoming) that the transcendental argument in question is sound.

[2] Kevin Falvey and Joseph Owens (1994 pp.111–15) and Max de Gaynesford (1996, pp. 388ff) also use slow switching cases in an attempt to motivate worries about externalism and self-knowledge.

Boghossian asked us to consider an individual slow switched between Earth and Twin Earth and to reflect on the epistemic status of that individual's beliefs about the contents of his 'water' thoughts. Boghossian argued that such an individual, unaware of the switches between Earth and Twin Earth, does not know whether the content of the thought he expresses with the sentence 'water is wet' is *that water is wet* or *that twater is wet* and therefore that such an individual fails to know the contents of his 'water' thoughts. Boghossian concluded from this example that externalism is incompatible with privileged self-knowledge (Boghossian 1989, pp. 13ff).

In an earlier paper (Warfield 1992, see also Warfield 1995), I argued that Boghossian failed to demonstrate the incompatibility of externalism and privileged self-knowledge. Boghossian's story, I claimed, shows at most that individuals who are being slow switched fail to know the contents of some of their thoughts. This shows at most that externalism is *consistent with* a lack of self-knowledge; it does not show that externalism *implies* a lack of self-knowledge.

Now Peter Ludlow (1995a) comes to Boghossian's defense, claiming that Boghossian's general argument for the conclusion that 'externalism and a priori self-knowledge are incompatible doctrines' (p. 45) can avoid my criticism. Ludlow grants my claim that the mere possibility of slow switching cases neither undermines self-knowledge nor shows that externalism and privileged self-knowledge are incompatible (p. 45). But, Ludlow continues, switching cases are not merely possibilities; switching cases are, he contends, quite common. To be sure, he explains, we are not regularly switched back and forth between Earth and Twin Earth, but switching cases can be much simpler than this. Ludlow explains and argues that from the thesis that content is socially determined and the fact that language groups are frequently small and localized it follows that there are many real world slow switching cases in which the slow switching individuals fail to have privileged self-knowledge of at least some of their thought contents (pp. 46ff).

I do not think that actual world slow switching cases are as common as Ludlow claims. I will pass over this minor issue, however, because even granting all of Ludlow's claims about the prevalence of slow switching and the lack of self-knowledge for individuals caught in slow switching circumstances, we still have seen *no reason at all* for thinking that externalism and privileged self-knowledge are incompatible. Slow switching stories (whether fanciful as in Burge and Boghossian or more realistic as in

Ludlow) are simply not relevant to the question of the compatibility of externalism and privileged access.

I fail to see how Ludlow thinks he has improved upon Boghossian's fallacious argument. The most that follows even granting all of Ludlow's claims is that there is a possible world, the actual world, in which externalism is true and individuals lack privileged self-knowledge of some of their thought contents.[3] This, like Boghossian's argument, shows at most that externalism is *consistent with* a lack of self-knowledge. Ludlow's claims do nothing towards showing that externalism *implies* a lack of self-knowledge.

The problem that Ludlow and Boghossian face is not merely a problem of detail. The kind of argument they offer couldn't possibly show that externalism is incompatible with privileged self-knowledge. To show that these doctrines are incompatible one needs to show that *every* possible world in which externalism is true is a world in which individuals do not have privileged self-knowledge. Boghossian shows *at most* that *some* possible worlds are worlds in which externalism is true and individuals lack privileged self-knowledge and Ludlow shows *at most* that *one* world, the actual world, is a world in which externalism is true and (some) individuals lack privileged self-knowledge. The slow switching arguments employed by these philosophers are simply not of the right form to show that externalism and privileged self-knowledge are incompatible.[4]

REFERENCES

Boghossian, P. 1989. Content and Self-Knowledge. *Philosophical Topics* 17: 5–26. Chapter 6 in this volume.

---

[3] Though my purpose on the present occasion is not to argue this claim, even if all of Ludlow's claims are true it wouldn't follow that all actual world individuals lack privileged self-knowledge of all of their thought contents. For all Ludlow has argued, one staying in one's isolated language community (not subjecting oneself to slow switches) will, consistent with Ludlow's claims about the prevalence of slow switching, have externalistically individuated thought contents and privileged self-knowledge of those thought contents. This again illustrates that at most Ludlow has shown that externalism is consistent with individuals not having privileged self-knowledge. Furthermore, as mentioned above, one might dispute Ludlow's claims about the prevalence of actual world slow switching cases.

[4] I thank Peter Ludlow for helpful discussion.

Brown, J. 1995. The Incompatibility of Anti-Individualism and Privileged Access. *Analysis* 55: 149–56. Chapter 8 in this volume.

de Gaynesford, M. 1996. How Wrong Can One Be? *Proceedings of the Aristotelian Society* 96: 387–94.

Falvey, K. and Owens, J. 1994. Externalism, Self-Knowledge, and Skepticism. *Philosophical Review* 103: 107–37.

Ludlow, P. 1995a. Externalism, Self-Knowledge and the Prevalence of Slow Switching. *Analysis* 55: 45–49. Chapter 12 in this volume.

———. 1995b. Social Externalism, Self-Knowledge and Memory. *Analysis* 55: 157–59. Chapter 17 in this volume.

McKinsey, M. 1991. Anti-Individualism and Privileged Access. *Analysis* 51: 9–16. Chapter 7 in this volume.

———. 1994. Accepting the Consequences of Anti-Individualism. *Analysis* 54: 124–28.

Warfield, T. A. 1992. Privileged Self-Knowledge and Externalism are Compatible. *Analysis* 52: 232–237. Chapter 11 in this volume.

———. 1995. Knowing the World and Knowing Our Minds. *Philosophy and Phenomenological Research* 55: 525–45.

———. forthcoming. A Priori Knowledge of the World: Knowing the World by Knowing Our Minds. *Philosophical Studies*.

14

On the Relevance of Slow Switching

Peter Ludlow

Boghossian (1989) argued that slow switching cases in the sense of Burge (1988) might be used to show the incompatibility of externalism and privileged self-knowledge. The argument was structured as a reductio, in which, given the twin assumptions of externalism and authoritative self-knowledge, it was shown that an agent subject to switching cases both did and did not know the content of his mental states.

Warfield (1992) responded that whatever else might be said about Boghossian's argument, it is unsound since it incorrectly assumes that switching cases are epistemically relevant alternatives. Allegedly they are not epistemically relevant alternatives since they are so rare (indeed fanciful). In response (Ludlow 1995a) I argued that slow-switching was altogether commonplace, and that as a consequence switching alternatives are in fact relevant alternatives. I used several down-to-earth examples to illustrate this, among them cases where I defer to one group at work and another at home. Warfield (1997) has subsequently argued that while my arguments may show that there are switching cases in the *actual* world, that is all I have shown. And that is allegedly not enough, for, according to Warfield, it is the incompatibilist's obligation to show that privileged self-knowledge is false in "*every* possible world in which externalism is true." Allegedly, all that I in fact show is that there is at most one world, the actual world, in which externalism is true and some individuals lack authoritative self-knowledge. Hence, my "claims do nothing towards showing that externalism *implies* a lack of self-knowledge."

There are several responses to be made here. First, it does not seem to me a trivial result that either externalism or self-knowledge fail to hold in the actual world. Put another way, that is just to say that one of the doctrines is false, and showing *that* was the motivation for advancing the incompatibilist argument in the first place.

Second, showing that this result holds in the actual world amounts to overkill if anything. I take it that Boghossian's point was that there is at least one world, never mind the actual world, where we cannot square externalism and self-knowledge – where the doctrines lead to contradiction. This is enough to tell us that there is something horribly wrong with either our conception of self-knowledge or the externalist conception of mental content. It shows us that in certain quite conceivable circumstances, our assumptions will lead us to infer a contradiction. But well-honed concepts are not supposed to allow this. If they are serviceable they should not lead to catastrophic results in a nearby world.

In short, Warfield's insistence that I show privileged self-knowledge to be false in *every* possible world in which externalism is true completely inverts the argumentative burden here.

Even if one wishes to stipulate that 'incompatibility arguments' must show incompatibility in every possible world (I have to confess that the point of the stipulation escapes me), there is a ready reply. We simply revise the thesis to the following: externalism, authoritative self-knowledge, and slow switching are mutually incompatible (in the stipulated strong sense of 'incompatible').

The 'incompatibility argument' just proffered would only be applicable in worlds with slow-switching, but that covers quite a few worlds – the actual world for starters. Indeed what kinds of worlds would it not cover? Since, on my view, slow switching can occur anytime we unknowingly slide between social groups, one is hard pressed to think of nearby worlds that are free of widespread slow switching episodes.

REFERENCES

Boghossian, P. 1989. Content and Self-Knowledge. *Philosophical Topics* 17: 5–26. Chapter 6 in this volume.

Burge, T. 1988. Individualism and Self-Knowledge. *Journal of Philosophy* 85: 649–63. Chapter 4 in this volume.

I am indebted to Paul Boghossian and Ted Warfield for discussion of this topic. I should note that while here I am on Boghossian's side, elsewhere (Ludlow 1995b) I have argued that there remain weaknesses in Boghossian's argument.

Ludlow, P. 1995a. Externalism, Self-Knowledge, and the Prevalence of Slow-Switching. *Analysis* 55: 45–9. Chapter 12 in this volume.

———— 1995b. Social Externalism, Self-Knowledge, and Memory. *Analysis* 55: 157–59. Chapter 17 in this volume.

Warfield, T. 1992. Privileged Self-Knowledge and Externalism are Compatible. *Analysis* 52: 232–37. Chapter 11 in this volume.

————. 1997. Externalism, Privileged Self-Knowledge, and the Irrelevance of Slow Switching. *Analysis* 57. Chapter 13 in this volume.

15

Our Entitlement to Self-Knowledge

Tyler Burge

I want to understand our epistemic warrant for a certain range of judgments about our own thoughts and attitudes. I am guided by two hypotheses. One is that there are certain sorts of self-knowledge that are epistemically special. The other is that the epistemic right or warrant we have to these sorts of self-knowledge is, in a sense, environmentally neutral. I want to understand this specialness and this environmental neutrality.

The hypothesis of epistemic specialness will be argued for in this paper. The hypothesis of environmental neutrality is relevant to a project that deals with scepticism and the nature and functions of reason. I will not develop this latter hypothesis in depth here, but I will comment on it for the sake of orientation.

Most of our empirical thoughts and our thoughts about our empirical thoughts depend for their individuation conditions on relations that we bear to a particular environment. But, on my guiding hypothesis, our epistemic warrant for our judgments about our thoughts does not depend on particular relations to a particular environment. It is common to any environment and derives from the nature of the thinker as a critical reasoner. This point is relevant to showing that certain claims to self-knowledge which are among the premises in a certain anti-sceptical argument do not beg the question by depending on presumptions about the environment that the sceptic calls into question. In this paper I will not discuss scepticism. But I begin with the sort of *cogito*-like judgments that figured in traditional anti-sceptical arguments. I believe these judgments relevant not only to scepticism, but to the epistemic specialness of some self-knowledge. Although some striking features of *cogito*-like judgments are not shared by all members of the wider range of judgments about one's thoughts whose epistemic status interests me, *cogito*-like judgments provide a useful paradigm for reflection.

So I begin with some remarks about a judgment that:

(1) I am thinking that there are physical entities.

This judgment is an instance of *cogito*-like thoughts, an elaboration of Descartes' *I am thinking*. Let us construe 'thinking' in (1) minimally – as *engaging in thought* or *having a thought*, regardless of whether it is merely entertaining a thought, making a judgment, or whatever. In this sense, one 'thinks' all propositional components of any thought one thinks (including negated ones, antecedents of conditionals, and so on). (1) is the content of my judgment. I accept it as true. To be true, (1) requires only that I am engaging in some thought whose content is that there are physical entities.

We do not rest this judgment upon any observation or perception such as was traditionally called 'inner sense'. The judgment is direct, based on nothing else. Making the judgment requires sufficient understanding to think (1). But once one makes the judgment, or indeed just engages in the thought, one makes it true. The thought is *contextually self-verifying*. One cannot err if one does not think it, and if one does think it one cannot err. In this sense, such thinkings are *infallible*.

I do not claim that judgments like (1) are indubitable. The scope for human perversity is very wide. One could be so far gone as to think to oneself: 'I do not know whether I am now thinking or not; maybe I am dead or unconscious; my mantra may have finally made me blissfully free of thought'. Such mistaken doubt would evince cognitive pathology, but I think it possible. It is an error, however, that most people would avoid without swerving.

Key features of (1) are shared by judgments of

(2) I judge, herewith, that there are physical entities.

When *judge* in (2) is used to execute not merely describe a judgment, judgments of (2) are contextually self-verifying. (2) is not made true by the mere thinking of it, nor does it have quite the same quasi-logical self-evident status that (1) does. These are subtleties that I will have to discuss on another occasion.

(1) and (2) are not mere philosophical curiosities. I think that they represent the form of many ordinary self-aware judgments (at least when (1) is taken to have the 'herewith' reflexivity of (2).) When one makes a judgment and is conceptually aware of one's so doing, whether or not one spells out this conceptual awareness, one's judgments have a reflexive form like that of (2). Such conceptual self-awareness goes beyond simply consciously thinking a thought, but it is not an unusual phenomenon among people with normal second-order abilities. Thus I believe that *cogito*-like judgments constitute a significant segment of our everyday mental activity.

To remark that (1) and (2) are *contextually self-verifying* is to remark on their truth conditions, not on our justification or epistemic warrant in thinking them. It does seem that understanding (1) suffices for knowing that it is true. And the relevant understanding requires no great perspicacity. But noting that it is self-evidently self-verifying (supposing that this needed no more comment – which of course it would) would not capture fully what is involved in its epistemic status. For I think that *cogito*-like judgments share an interesting epistemic status with a number of types of self-knowledge that are not contextually self-verifying or infallible, and that lack the quasi-logical status of (1). I have in mind a wider class of judgments about states, not just reflexive occurrences – judgments about what one believes, wants, intends.

When we make judgments about many of our mental states and events, our judgments commonly constitute knowledge. I know very well that I believe that there are physical entities – if I judge that I do. Such judgments do not merely evince an inner state in the way that a yelp evinces a pain; nor are they avowals or conventional practices without cognitive value. What is the epistemic status of such judgments? What epistemic warrant do we have to make them?

I take the notion of epistemic warrant to be broader than the ordinary notion of justification. An individual's epistemic warrant may consist in a justification that the individual has for a belief or other epistemic act or state. But it may also be an *entitlement* that consists in a status of operating in an appropriate way in accord with norms of reason, even when these norms cannot be articulated by the individual who has that status. We have an entitlement to certain perceptual beliefs or to certain logical inferences even though we may lack reasons or justifications for them. The entitlement could in principle presumably – though often only with extreme philosophical difficulty – be articulated by someone. But this articulation need not be part of the repertoire of the individual that has the entitlement.

Our epistemic warrant to much of our self-knowledge is of this sort. Most of us have no justifying argument or evidence backing the relevant judgments. The judgments are immediate, noninferential. Although *cogito*-like judgments may count as self-evident or self-verifying, most judgments that interest me do not. Wherein are we being reasonable – in the sense of operating under norms sanctioned by reason – in making judgments about our own minds?

As I have intimated, the remarks about self-verification suggest an initial analogy between *cogito*-like judgments and knowledge of simple logical truths. The truth of judgments of (1) and (2) *is*, in a broad sense, present in the form and logic of the thought. There is something of the same self-evident and obvious features here as there are in simple logical truths. The main differences are that *cogito*-like judgments are dependent on being thought for being true. and are in their specially direct way self-verifying.

Another analogy to knowledge of simple logical truths is this: The key to the epistemic status of *cogito*-like judgments seems to reside in ordinary understanding, not in some mechanism connecting the knower with a sensed object.

This point will be one of the key elements in my account of the environmental neutrality and specialness of self-knowledge. Perceptual experiences particular to a given environment inevitably figure in the acquisition of understanding of almost any given content. But one's epistemic warrant for believing the content may not incorporate the perceptual experiences or beliefs that go into understanding it. This is the traditional view of knowledge of logical or mathematical truths. One may need perceptual experience to come to understand simple logical or arithmetical notions and truths. (This is surely the case with such logical truths as 'nothing is both a dog and not a dog'.) But on the traditional view such experience is not a constituent of one's justification or entitlement in believing simple logical or arithmetical truths.

I am not arguing for the traditional view – just recalling it. The element in it relevant to our purposes is the following. The account of epistemic justification or entitlement may presuppose understanding, which may be dependent on particular perceptual relations to a given environment. But the account need not include perceptual beliefs or experiences as *constituents* in the individual's justification or entitlement. The account can allow attribution of concepts to the individual which could be acquired only in a limited range of possible environments, while itself taking a form that is applicable to any critical reasoner, regardless of the particular environmentally dependent contents of his or her thought.

I want to illustrate the relevance of this idea to our discussion by reconsidering the scenario of one's being switched between different environments unawares – a scenario I discussed in a paper some years back.[1] Let us assume for the sake of argument that my thinking that there are physical entities (hence my thinking that I am thinking that there are physical entities) is the thought that it is because of relevant causal relations I bear to actual physical objects in my environment. Let us also assume that an individual with a chemically identical body could have been brought up in a situation in which such relations were lacking – and in which the concept of physical object could not be acquired – but in which different, counterpart thoughts occurred. (I doubt that *physical object* is a concept universal to all possible critical reasoners; but if one did not doubt, another concept could be chosen.) Finally, let us grant that if at any time one were switched unawares from one's actual situation into such a counterpart situation, one would have no resources that would tip one off to the difference.

Unless memory and learning connections to the original environment were broken, it is hard to describe a switch of actual situations that would produce a new twin set of the concepts, with no residue from the past experiences. So in the case I am imagining one's thoughts do not switch to twin thoughts. Because of a switch one's thoughts might, however, change content, broadening their extensions without one's being aware of their doing so.

I take it that this observation is sufficient to prompt the following question. Given that we are insensitive to such alleged possible changes in content, how can we know what we are thinking?

I will not try to deal with this question in all its ramifications here. But as I noted some years back, some of the negative force of the question can be shown to be illusory by this consideration: There is no way for one to

---

[1] Burge (1988).

make a mistake about the content of one's present-tensed thought in the relevant cases.

Suppose that I think that I am engaging in a thought that there are physical objects. In thinking this, I have to engage in the very thought I am referring to and ascribing to myself. The reference to the content – expressed in the that-clause – cannot be carried out unless I actually engage in the thought. The intentional content mentioned in the that-clause is not merely an object of reference or cognition; it is part of the cognition itself. It is thought and thought about in the same act. If background conditions are different enough so that I am thinking different thoughts, they will be different enough so that the objects of reference and self-ascription will also be different. So no matter how my thoughts are affected, no matter how I am switched around. I will be correct in self-ascriptions of content that are correctly expressed in *cogito*-that-clause form.

It would be a mistake to reply that because one's correct reference does not give one any grasp of what one is referring to, this reference is empty. For to self-ascribe thoughts in the way expressed by that-clauses, one has to understand the thoughts one is referring to well enough to think them. One need not have any more explicatory understanding of one's thoughts than is necessary to think them. One need not master anti-individualism, much less have an empirical mastery of the conditions that have established the identity of the thoughts one thinks. Such mastery is emphatically not guaranteed by mastery of *cogito*-self-ascriptions. But one *is* guaranteed that one ascribes something of which one has the ordinary understanding involved in using concepts and thinking thoughts.

This understanding presupposes the causal-perceptual relations to a particular environment that help determine what content is available for being understood. What one *can* think is partly dependent on relations to one's environment. And one's second-order self-ascriptions inherit both the content and the background environmental content-determining conditions from one's first-order understanding.

I have granted that one need not be sensitive to actual or counterfactual changes in what one understands under transportations into environments where the content of one's understanding changes or would be different. One need not be capable of detecting such changes. But in any situation in which a person can think the relevant *cogito*-like judgments, the person would think them with understanding – and to all appearances, knowledgeably. At any rate, there is no obvious reason why knowledge in such judgments would be prevented by such changes, much less such possible changes.[2] In any such twin situation, the person would understand the self-ascribed contents and would self-ascribe them with a justice and reliability that is equal to that in any ordinary situation. Some entitlement attaching to understanding seems to be what the self-knowledge depends upon, not on some knowledge of what the understanding consists in, or whether it differs from understanding that is past or possible.

The person's epistemic entitlement to the self-ascriptions presupposes understanding. Understanding is, as I have noted, dependent on and local to causal–perceptual relations to a given environment. But the entitlement that underlies knowledgeable *cogito*-like thoughts and other self-ascriptions does not seem local and seems to survive such switches. It seems to be carried somehow by the fact that we correctly self-ascribe any content at all with understanding. Where does the entitlement derive from? And what makes it capable of surviving such environmental switches?

I think that the relevant entitlement derives not from the reliability of some causal–perceptual relation between cognition and its object. It has two other sources. One is the role of the relevant judgments in critical reasoning. The other is a constitutive relation between the judgments and their subject matter – or between the judgments about one's thoughts and the judgments' being true. Understanding and making such judg-

---

[2] Are there switching situations in which one would have reasonable ground for doubting what contents one is thinking, so that a *cogito*-type judgment would not constitute knowledge? This is very complex, but I will make a few remarks here. The self-ascription in the that-clause way cannot involve a mistake about the intentional content. So the possibility of a switch does not threaten a mistake. I think therefore that such possibilities pose no relevant alternative threat to one's entitlement to one's judgment about the that-clause content of one's thoughts. I believe that the relevant minimal understanding suffices for knowledge in *cogito*-like judgments. Even in non-*cogito*-like judgments, switches in content cannot, for the same reason, undermine knowledgeability of the content of self-ascriptions. Cf. Burge (1988, p. 659). A fuller story has to be told about the propositional-attitude concepts in non-*cogito*-like judgments. I think the possibility of switching, or of errors of incomplete understanding, do not by themselves undermine knowledge; but I will have to discuss these matters further elsewhere.

Some worries about switching situations have focused on memory. I think that they tend to confuse preservative memory with memory of objects or with comparisons within memory, and to overrate the extent to which the content retrieved in memory is sensitive to immediate environmental context. For a discussion of preservative memory, see Burge (1993).

ments is constitutively associated both with being reasonable and with getting them right.

Briefly drawn, my line of thought will be this. To be capable of critical reasoning, and to be subject to certain rational norms necessarily associated with such reasoning, some mental acts and states must be *knowledgeably* reviewable.[3] The specific character of this knowledgeable reviewability requires that it be associated with an epistemic entitlement that is distinctive. The entitlement must be stronger than that involved in perceptual judgments. There must be a non-contingent, rational relation, of a sort to be explained, between relevant first-person judgments and their subject matter or truth.

All of us, even sceptics among us, recognize a practice of critical reasoning.[4] Critical reasoning is reasoning that involves an ability to recognize and effectively employ reasonable criticism or support for reasons and reasoning. It is reasoning guided by an appreciation, use, and assessment of reasons and reasoning as such. As a critical reasoner, one not only reasons. One recognizes reasons as reasons. One evaluates, checks, weighs, criticizes, supplements one's reasons and reasoning. Clearly, this requires a second-order ability to think about thought contents or propositions, and rational relations among them.

When one carries out a proof, one checks the steps of the reasoning, making sure that the inferences are valid. Any activity of proof requires some conception of validity, which requires an ability to think of the propositions in a proof as constituting reasons for what follows from them. Indeed, it is arguable that use of *therefore* in reasoning, – deductive or otherwise – constitutes an exercise of this meta-cognitive ability. When one

---

[3] I think that the following necessity also holds: To think the relevant first-person present tense thoughts about one's thoughts and attitudes, one must be capable of critical reasoning. Indeed, I think that to have a fully formed first-person concept or fully formed concepts of propositional attitudes, one must be capable of critical reasoning. To master concepts of propositional attitudes in a suitably rich sense, one must be capable of appreciating the force and relevance of reasons to attitudes as such, which amounts to being able to reason critically about reasons and reasoning. And to master a fully formed first-person concept, one must have concepts of propositional attitudes.

[4] In actual practice, critical reasoning approximates what I call *reflective* reasoning. Reflective reasoning makes use of all the main concepts necessary to a full understanding of essential or fundamental elements in reasoning. Critical reasoning is simply reasoning that is sufficiently articulate to appreciate reasons as reasons and to employ articulated criticism of reasons and reasoning (as reasons and reasoning).

engages in practical deliberation, one articulates and weighs considerations on each side, goes over possible sources of bias, thinks through consequences. Essential to carrying out critical reasoning is using one's knowledge of what constitutes good reasons to guide one's actual first-order reasoning.

A noncritical reasoner reasons blind, without appreciating reasons as reasons. Animals and small children reason in this way. But reasoning under rational control of the reasoner is critical reasoning. Not all reasoning by critical reasoners is critical. Much of *our* reasoning is blind, poorly accessible, and unaware. We change attitudes in rational ways without having much sense of what we are doing. Often we are poor at saying what our reasoning is. Still, the ability to take rational control of one's reasoning is crucial in many enterprises – in giving a proof, in thinking through a plan, in constructing a theory, in engaging in debate. For reasoning to be critical, it must sometimes involve actual awareness and review of reasons; and such a reviewing standpoint must normally be available.[5]

Critical reasoning involves an ability not merely to assess truth, falsity, evidential support, entailment, and nonentailment among *propositions* or *thought contents*. It also involves an ability to assess the truth and reasonability of reasoning – hence *attitudes*. This is not to say that critical reasoning must *focus* on attitudes, as opposed to their subject matter. Normally we reason not about ourselves but about the world or about practical goods. But to be fully a critical reasoner, one must be able to – and sometimes actually – identify, distinguish, evaluate propositions as asserted, denied, hypothesized or merely considered.[6] Such abilities and activities are central to argumentation. Similarly, in critical practical reasoning, one must be able to – and sometimes actually – evaluate propositions conceptualized as expressing pro-attitudes, to distinguish them explicitly from those that express beliefs and to evaluate relations of reason among such

---

[5] I think Kant neglected distinctions between reasoning, critical reasoning, and reflective reasoning. But he clearly saw that it is the possibility of applications of 'I think' to our thoughts – not our being self-aware in this way all the time – that is basic to full reflective rationality. Of course, the form of 'I think' does not by itself make the relevant contribution to reflective rationality. One could dream *cogito*-thoughts. It is the ability to be conceptually aware of oneself as thinking with a certain control and agency that is crucial.

[6] In effect, Frege's use of the assertion sign is an acknowledgment of a minimal use of these abilities. Without an ability to recognize that a proposition should be and is judged to be true, one cannot reason critically. Having a concept of judgment and using it in reasoning meets my requirement.

propositions as so conceptualized. Such evaluation constitutes minimal evaluations of propositional attitudes.

To be a critical reasoner, one must also be able to, and sometimes actually, use one's knowledge of reasons to make, criticize, change, confirm *commitments* regarding propositions – to engage explicitly in reason-induced changes of mind. Critical reasoning here involves an ability to distinguish subjectivities from more objectively supportable commitments and to explicitly alter the former in favour of the latter. Its point is reasonably to confirm and correct attitudes and reasoning (not merely assess propositional connections), by reference to rational standards.

Critical reasoning must be exercised on itself. Any critical reasoning, even about abstract propositional relations or about the reasoning of others, involves commitments by the reasoner. And genuinely critical reasoning requires an application of rational standards to *those* commitments. A being that assessed good and bad reasoning in others or in the abstract, but had no inclination to apply such standards to the commitments involved in those very assessments, would not be a critical reasoner. To reason critically – to consider reasons bearing on the truth of some matter, to suspend belief or desire, to weigh values under a conception of the good – one must treat one's own commitments as matters to be considered and evaluated. Critical evaluation of one's own commitments is central to forming them and to rationally changing one's mind or standing fast.

So critical reasoning requires thinking about one's thoughts. But it further requires that that thinking be normally knowledgeable. To appreciate one's reasons as reasons – to check, weigh, criticize, confirm one's reasons – one must know what one's reasons, thoughts, and reasoning are. One need not always be knowledgeable, or even right. But being knowledgeable must be the normal situation when one reflects on one's reasons in the course of carrying out reasonable inquiry or deliberation. The interest here is less in the requirement of normal knowledgeability – which is shared with other cognitive activities, such as perception. The interest lies in the ground of the requirement. Why must we be normally knowledgeable about our thoughts when we reflect upon them?

I will answer this question in three stages. First, I want to show that to evaluate reasons critically, one must have an *epistemic entitlement* to one's judgments about one's thoughts, reasons, and reasoning. Second, I want to support the stronger thesis that critical reasoning requires that one *know* one's thoughts, reasons, and reasoning. Third, I will try to show that this knowledge must take a distinctive, nonobservational form.

So I begin with the matter of entitlement. The basic idea is simple. Put crudely: since one's belief, or judgments about one's thoughts, reasons, and reasoning are an integral part of the overall procedures of critical reasoning, one must have an epistemic right to those beliefs or judgments. To be reasonable in the whole enterprise, one must be reasonable in that essential aspect of it.

Less crudely, consider the process of reasoning which involves the confirming and weighing of one's reasons. One must make judgments about one's attitudes and inferences. If one's judgments about one's attitudes or inferences were not reasonable – if one had no epistemic entitlement to them – one's reflection on one's attitudes and their interrelations could add no rational element to the reasonability of the whole process. But reflection does add a rational element to the reasonability of reasoning. It gives one some rational control over one's reasoning.

To put the point somewhat more fully: if one lacked entitlement to judgments about one's attitudes, there could be no norms of reason governing how one ought check, weigh, overturn, confirm reasons or reasoning. For if one lacked entitlement to judgments about one's attitudes, one could not be subject to rational norms governing how one ought to alter those attitudes given that one had reflected on them. If reflection provided no reason-endorsed judgments about the attitudes, the rational connection between the attitudes reflected upon and the reflection would be broken. So reasons could not apply to how the attitudes should be changed, suspended, or confirmed *on the basis of* reasoning depending on such reflection. But critical reasoning just is reasoning in which norms of reason apply to how attitudes should be affected partly on the basis of reasoning that derives from judgments about one's attitudes. So one must have an epistemic entitlement to one's judgments about one's attitudes.

I turn now to the stronger thesis. One might imagine some gap between epistemic entitlement and knowledge. Might one have an epistemic entitlement but be systematically mistaken? Or might failure of some third Gettier-type condition (beyond truth and epistemic entitlement) undermine knowledge?

It is possible in given cases for reflection to be disconnected in these ways from the attitudes purportedly reflected upon. But both possibilities if generalized are incompatible with our having the sort of entitlement to the reflection just argued for. That entitlement rested on the assumption that reflection added a rational element to the reasonability of the whole process of critical reasoning – a process whereby object-level attitudes are guided by reflection on their reasonability. If reflective judgments were not normally true, reflection could not add to the rational coherence or add a rational component to the reasonability of the whole process. It could not rationally control and guide the attitudes being reflected upon (even though one could imagine situations in which such disconnected reflection would be mechanically or instrumentally beneficial in forming true or rational beliefs). So reflection would not add in the relevant way to the reasonability of the process, and therefore would not have the source of entitlement just argued for.

The same point applies to the possible failure of some Gettier-type condition. Again, if reflection were connected to the truth of our judgments about our thoughts in an accidental or non-knowledge-yielding way, the reason-guiding and rational-coherence-making functions of rational review would be broken. Since part of our entitlement to reflective judgments about our attitudes derives from their functions in critical reasoning, the entitlement itself would be undermined.

Not only the relevant entitlement to reflective judgments that derives from their functions within critical reasoning, but critical reasoning itself is constitutively dependent on the truth- and Gettier conditions being met. If a being had an epistemic entitlement to its judgments about its attitudes but were systematically mistaken about them – never got them right – it would not be a critical reasoner. Or if our entitlement were always connected to the truth of our judgments about our thoughts in an accidental or nonknowledge-yielding way, critical reasoning would not be possible. For critical reason requires rational integration of one's higher-order evaluations with one's first-order, object-oriented reasoning. The former must be reason-guided and reason-guiding. And they must cement the rational coherence between the two levels. If the two came radically apart, or were only accidentally connected, critical reasoning would not occur.

So if we failed normally to know our thoughts and attitudes, in ordinary reasoning about reasons, either through systematic falsity of our judgments or through systematic mismatch between our entitlement and truth, critical reasoning would not occur among us. Indeed, the entitlement to reflective judgments that derives from those judgments' place in critical reasoning would lapse. But critical reasoning does occur among us; and we are entitled to reflective judgments by virtue of their contribution to the reasonability of critical reasoning. So as critical reasoners we must know our thoughts and attitudes.

Symptomatic of the connection I have noted between the rationality of reflection in critical reasoning and the truth of reflective judgments is the fact there are severe limits on brute errors in judgments about one's present ordinary, accessible propositional attitudes. A brute error is an error that indicates no rational failure and no malfunction in the mistaken individuals.[7] Brute perceptual errors commonly result from misleading natural conditions or look-alike substitutes. One can be perceptually wrong without there being anything wrong with one. Such brute perceptual errors are unremarkable. But errors about what one's thoughts and attitudes are normally seem to involve some malfunction or rational deficiency. There are exceptions – the cases of unconscious, modular attitudes that are not accessible to reflection. One could easily make brute errors about these. There are judgments about one's emotions, character, or deep motives, that seem hard to get right. I leave open whether these might sometimes involve brute errors. But it seems that we make mistakes about many attitudes that are accessible to reflection primarily when we are subject to some are subject to some failure of rationality or defect in our cognitive powers.[8]

I stated that I would argue that the specific role of knowledge of our thoughts in critical reasoning requires that it be associated with a distinc-

---

[7] I introduced the notion of brute error in Burge (1988, p. 657). I intend rational failures to include any failure of entitlement or justification, not just ones that are epistemically culpable. I intend malfunctions to cover not only mechanical or biological failures in, say, the individual's perceptual apparatus, but also failures of normal understanding – as for example when an individual believes arthritis can occur in the thigh. The idea is that a brute error would have occurred even if the individual's epistemic warrants were in order and the individual's perception and ordinary understanding were functioning optimally.

[8] Our epistemic entitlement to judgments about our present attitudes is a general right and is compatible with our making various mistakes about our attitudes even in the course of critical reasoning. (Of course, then we are, in a sense, not critically reasoning *with* the attitudes we are mistaken about.) We make mistakes of haste, bias, and self-deception. Some attitudes are hard to get at, except with discipline, and even maturation or therapy. In some cases, other people are better at knowing our attitudes than we are. So one might demand further specification of our entitlement. One might ask under what conditions it is overturned or insufficient to give us knowledge. And one might inquire in more depth into the conditions under which errors arise. These issues are complex. I think that when our judgments about a certain class of our thoughts and attitudes are in a certain sense immediate (which entails that they are neither inferred nor otherwise biased by other attitudes), and when our minds are not subject to malfunction, we do not make errors. But there is no recipe for insuring that our judgments are immediate or that they are about the relevant class. There is no internal recipe for avoiding error.

tive sort of epistemic entitlement that necessitates a non-contingent, rational relation between the relevant first-person present-tense judgments and their subject matter or truth. Why need self-knowledge be in any way special? Why is it not enough that it be pretty reliable observation? Some knowledge of our own mental states and events is empirical in the sense that it is based either on imaging, remembering, or reasoning about *sensed* inner-goings-on, or on observing our own behaviour and hearing about it from others. Simplicity tempts some to hold that all self-knowledge is like that.

Let me elaborate this temptation. It is commonly held that beliefs about others' attitudes must be based on inferences from or criteria for observation.[9] On the model at issue, beliefs about one's own attitudes differ only in that one need not always infer those beliefs because one is the closest witness. There is no authority in self-knowledge, other than the authority of inner observational presence, practice, and familiarity.

This simple observational model does not account plausibly for *cogito*-like thoughts. Such thoughts are logically special in their self-verification and epistemically special in their clear dependence for entitlement on intellection and understanding, not on any sort of observation. But *cogito* thoughts do not constitute the full range of thoughts that enter essentially into critical reasoning.

The simple observational model is encumbered with the obscurity of the notion of inner observation as applied to thoughts and attitudes. Unlike sensations or images, thoughts and attitudes lack distinctive presentations or phenomenologies. The model is phenomenologically implausible for many immediate judgments about one's own beliefs or current thoughts. But I want to show that there is a deeper problem if the model is taken to cover all cases.[10]

---

[9] I do not accept this view, but I need not question it here. Cf. Burge (1988). Certainly one's beliefs about others' thoughts are often based this way.

[10] Hume is, I think, a proponent of the simple observational model. A more recent proponent is D. M. Armstrong (1968, pp. 323–38). The rationalist tradition, in its emphasis on the role of self-knowledge in rationality, and the role of understanding (not sensory observation) in self-knowledge, is the source of my view. Kant develops this tradition in a particularly deep way, although his epistemology left him with what was, in my opinion, an implausibly restrictive account of cognition of one's own thoughts, one indeed that overrates the role of inner sense. A more recent nonobservational account that emphasizes the role of self-knowledge in reasoning may be found in Sidney Shoemaker (1988).

Before presenting the argument, I will say what I take to be fundamental to the simple observational model. The model need not claim any phenomenological presentation in self-knowledge, though waiving such a claim weakens the analogy to observation. The fundamental claim is that one's epistemic warrant for self-knowledge always rests partly on the existence of a pattern of veridical, but brute, contingent, non-rational relations – which are plausibly always causal relations – between the subject matter (the attitudes under review) and the judgments about the attitudes. This claim is compatible with holding that from the point of view of epistemology, observational judgments are often immediate and noninferential, requiring no background causal hypothesis on the part of the individual about their source.

My view about perceptual entitlement is more specific than the fundamental claim of the simple observational model. I believe that our entitlement rests partly on our being perceivers, which entails that we – or our species-perceptual systems – are or have been in brute, contingent, non-rational but veridical relations to objects of perception, and the kinds that our perceptual judgments specify.[11] It is necessarily constitutive of the content of our observational or perceptual beliefs about physical objects, and of the very nature of our perceptual systems, that we be veridically attuned to the environment through causal relations to it – either in our learning histories or indirectly in the evolution of our perceptual sys-

---

[11] A tempting oversimplification is to claim that these constitutive veridical causal relations are always *reliably* veridical. Such a claim is tempting because in so many cases our perception are reliable. Perhaps many types of perception must be. But the claim is oversimplified because some perceptual intentional types in some perceptual systems are established through the systems' reliable avoidance of false negatives rather than through their reliable achievement of true positives. It is more critical to a hare's perceptual system that it not fail to register a predator when one is there than that it be reliable in its registration of predators. So the system could commonly indicate the presence of predators falsely – and be broadly unreliable in its perceptions – as long as it was reliable in correctly indicating present predators. It remains, however, constitutive of the systems' perceiving predators as predators that some veridical perceptions played a role in the evolution-fashioned function or in the actual use of the system. Of course, reliability is more important for perceptions of safety than for perceptions of danger.

These qualifications on reliability of course, complicate any account of the relation between perceptual-content constitution and perceptual entitlement. For presumably epistemic entitlements are prima facie comprised by constitutively unreliable perceptual deliverances. I believe that a perceptual system in any agent, however, is constitutively associated with reliable perceptions in a range of cases. But these are issues for another occasion.

tems.[12] Entitlement to observational physical object beliefs rests partly on this necessity. But in particular instances of perception, the relations on which one's entitlement to perceptual judgments rests are brute, contingent, non-rational.[13] It is this claim that forms the paradigm for the simple observational model.

The existence of veridical beliefs involving *de re* causally based relations to the environment is necessary to and constitutive of something's being a perceptual system. But the individual relations are brute, contingent, non-rational. The brute contingency of these relations in individual instances of veridical perceptual judgment is fundamental to observation.

---

[12] I am inclined to think that it is a *conceptual* necessity that there be *causal* relations in perception. But for purposes of my argument, the fundamental feature is that the entitlement to observational beliefs necessarily rests on some pattern of brute, contingent. nonrational relations between observed and observer, regardless of whether the contingent relations are causal. It is common to my view and the opposed observational view of self-knowledge that in many of the cases under dispute, there is a causal mechanism that relates attitudes to judgments about them. What is in dispute is the nature of the epistemic entitlement that one has to such judgments, not the existence of a psychological mechanism. On the simple observational model, our entitlement to self-knowledge always rests partly on the brute, contingent, non-rational causal relations. On my view, in some important cases, it does not: Christopher Peacocke has pointed out to me that in some, though I think not all, cases of special self-knowledge, the entitlement may specify some causal relation between subject matter and judgment. But not all causal relations, are brute, contingent, non-rational ones. (For example those involved in a person's deductive inference are not.) Where a causal relation is not merely a background enabling condition, but an element in the relevant entitlement to self-knowledge, it will on my view never be a brute, contingent, non-rational one. It will be associated in the entitlement with norms for transfer of reasons.

[13] The simple observational model is inspired by a comparison of self-knowledge to observational judgments about physical objects. I operate with a commonsensical conception of such judgments. There are non-common-sensical conceptions that take the basic relation that underlies our epistemic right to be one between the observer and some sort of mental item, a sense datum or an appearance. I ignore such theories not because I regard them as mistaken (although I *do* regard them as mistaken). I ignore them because they model observation of physical objects on knowledge of one's mental events. The model I am attacking proposes to illumine self-knowledge through an independent model. I do think that knowledge of our pains and other sensations – as contrasted with knowledge of our propositional states and events – is empirical in the sense that it depends for its entitlement on sensory experience or sensory beliefs. Judgments that constitute such knowledge just are sensory beliefs. Although I believe that brute error is possible in certain judgments of this sort, such cases are marginal. Understanding even these empirical judgments will, I think, owe more to the kinds of considerations I am elaborating than to reflection on ordinary perceptions of physical objects. But I regard knowledge of one's sensations as requir-

Different conditions could have caused a perceptual judgment that was internally-indistinguishable (indeed I think the same judgment-type) but nonveridical, without loss of entitlement, even as the system functioned optimally well.[14] Thus perception is always subject to brute error. The object or conditions of perception could lead us into misperception without there being any failure of entitlement and without there being any malfunction of our cognitive or perceptual systems.

The objectivity of perception depends on the possibility of epistemically entitled misperception. Perceptual justification and criticism necessarily presuppose a distinction between a person's cognitive perspective and the objective, physical subject matter. They further presuppose this unremarkable possibility of contingent mismatches in individual cases that in no way impugn the individual's epistemic entitlements or perceptual-cognitive functioning. Rational and epistemic evaluation fixes on the individual's perceptual judgments and perspective, not on their physical subject matter. For this is only brute contingently related, in individual cases, to epistemic entitlement.

A consequence of interpreting all self-knowledge on the simple observational model is that in any given case brute errors – errors that do not reflect on the rationality or sound functioning of the reviewing judgment

---

ing separate treatment from knowledge of one's thoughts and attitudes.

It is worth noting that a view that we must 'inferentially' base judgments about physical objects on observations of sense data would also normally be committed to holding that one's entitlement to those judgments rests on brute, contingent, non-rational relations to the physical objects that always allow for brute error. The same point applies to inference-

[14] This gloss on the brute *contingency* of the relations, apart from the parenthetical remark, is less committal than my own view of the contingency involved in observational relations. I think the same perceptual object could, with different external auxiliary conditions, have caused a different nonveridical judgment. And I think that a different perceptual object, or perhaps none at all, could have combined with different external auxiliary conditions to cause a perception or perceptual judgment of the same type, though perhaps one with a different token demonstrative element, making it nonveridical. (I do not depend on these views in my argument here.) These different conditions, in individual cases, need not affect the individual's entitlement to the perceptual judgment: nor need they affect the well-functioning of the individual's perceptual-cognitive apparatus. The sense in which the relevant relations are *nonrational* is complex. Perhaps it can suffice here to note that since in the case of ordinary perception the perceptual objects are physical kinds or physical individuals, there can in *that* case be no question of a rational relation between them – which have no intentional content at all – and perceptions or perceptual judgments.

– are possible. I intimated earlier that brute errors do not seem to threaten some instances of judgments about attitudes. I propose to show why this must be so.

Not all one's knowledge of one's propositional attitudes can fit the simple observational model. For general application of the model is incompatible with the function of knowledge of one's own attitudes in critical reasoning. The main idea is that such application would entail a dissociation between cognitive review and the thoughts reviewed that is incompatible with norms of epistemic reasonability that are basic to all critical inquiry, including empirical, mathematical, philosophical, and practical inquiry.

Rational evaluation of attitudes commonly applies to and within a perspective or point of view. The argument will make reference to this fact. Different people have different points of view. My judgment that your beliefs are irrational may be reasonable from my point of view. But it does not follow that there is reason from your perspective to change your beliefs. I may have made some brute error about what your beliefs are, or your perspective may have different associated reasons or background information from mine.

There can be different perspectives or points of view within a given person. What is reasonable for a person at a given time may be different from what is reasonable from the perspective of the person's memory back on that time. What is reasonable on reflection may differ from what is reasonable in modular cognitive processes, or in an instant practical reasoning, or in subconscious reasoning. My argument hinges on how reasons transfer across points of view.

Suppose that all one's knowledge of one's propositional mental events and states fit the simple observational model. Then one's entitlement to instances of such knowledge would always rest on purely contingent relations between any given judgment about one's mental states and the subject matter of the judgment. What is more, brute error would be possible in any given case. Normative evaluations of reasonability and epistemic entitlement in critical reasoning – in checking and evaluating one's reasoning – would apply within the perspective of the judgments, but not immediately within the perspective of the subject matter of the judgments, except insofar as it contingently conformed to those judgments, and except insofar as it happened to be embedded in a perspective relevantly similar to the perspective from which the judgments were made. For the subject matter might, in any given case, fail to conform to the judgments through no failure of justification or entitlement in the judge, and through no malfunction of the relevant faculties.

But this picture is nonsense if it is applied to all judgments about one's own propositional attitudes. For it is constitutive of critical reasoning that if the reasons or assumptions being reviewed are justifiably found wanting by the reviewer, it *rationally follows immediately* that there is prima facie reason for changing or supplementing them, where this reason applies within the point of view of the reviewed material (not just within the reviewing perspective). If the relation between the reviewing point of view and the reasons or assumptions being reviewed always fit the simple observational model, there would never be an immediate rationally necessary connection between justified rational evaluation within the review, on one hand, and its being prima facie reasonable within the reviewed perspective to shape attitudes in accord with that evaluation, on the other. For the relation between the perspective of the review and that of the reviewed attitudes would always be purely contingent, even under canonical descriptions of them, for purposes of rational evaluation. (The attitudes reviewed would be to the reviews as physical objects are to our observational judgments. They would be purely 'objects' of one's inquiry, not part of the perspective of the inquiry.) It would be reasonable for the person from the point of view of the review that a change in the reviewed material be made. But this reason would not necessarily transfer to within the point of view of the attitudes under review, even though that is a point of view of the same person. Its transferring would depend on brute, contingent, nonrational relations between the two points of view.

In critical reasoning, however, the connection is rationally immediate and necessary. Justifiably finding one's reasons invalid or one's thoughts unjustified, is normally *in itself* a paradigmatic reason, from the point of view of the thoughts being reviewed (as well as from the perspective of the review), to alter them.

If in the course of critical reasoning I reasonably conclude that my belief that a given person is guilty rests entirely on unreasonable premises or bad reasoning, then it normally follows immediately both for the perspective of the review and for the perspective of the reviewed belief that it is reasonable to give up my belief about guilt or look for new grounds for it. In such second-order reasoning, I am not normally reasonable in altering my first-order views about guilt or innocence only with the proviso that they are embedded in reasons that contingently match those associated with my reviewing perspective. I do not normally have the sort of excusing condition that allows for rational error that hinges on the contingent relation that the subject matter bears to my judgments about it. Rather my checking my belief and finding it wanting normally *itself* provides immediate prima facie reason to change it from within the perspective of the review. This is because the first- and second-order perspectives are the *same* point of view.

The reviewing of reasons that is integral to critical reasoning includes the review and the reviewed attitudes in a single point of view. The simple observational model treats the review and the system being reviewed as dissociated in a way incompatible with the norms of critical reasoning. It makes the reviewed system an object of investigation, but not part of the investigation's point of view. So the model fails to account for the norms of critical reasoning.

A closely related point centres on epistemic responsibility. We are epistemically responsible only because we are capable of reviewing our reasons and reasoning. And we are paradigmatically responsible for our reasons when we check and review them in the course of critical reasoning. But the simple observational model implies that in carrying out reviews of one's reasoning, one is epistemically responsible not primarily for the thoughts being reviewed but primarily for the review. The model implies that we are in reviewing our reasons only derivatively responsible for objects of review, as one might be responsible for the actions of one's child or dog – but fully and primarily responsible only where one's knowledge and control contingently matched what one is justified in believing about them.

But one is not epistemically responsible for the thoughts one reflects upon in critical reasoning in the way one is responsible for something one owns or parents. One's responsibility in reflecting on one's thoughts is immediately for the whole point of view. The simple observational model fails to account for the fact that critical reasoning is carried out within a single multi-level point of view.

Of course, we are sometimes disunified. Sometimes to our own good and efficiency, sometimes to our misfortune, we fail to know our motives or reasons, or know them only through observation and empirical reasoning. Sometimes from the point of view of our self-conscious reviewing selves, we are indeed epistemically responsible only derivatively for attitudes that we know only empirically. But in these cases, we are not reasoning critically with those aspects of ourselves that we know only in these ways.

Theoretical knowledge of one's modular attitudes is one sort of purely observationally-based 'self-knowledge'. When attitudes *cannot* be known in a direct nonobservational way, one commonly enters some qualification on the sense in which the attitudes are *one's own*. In these cases failure to know the attitudes nonobservationally is no sign of dissociation. But when one knows only observationally unconscious attitudes which are in principle accessible to non-observational self-knowledge, there is some dissociation of self, constituted by a divide between the point of view of one's critical reasoning and the attitude known only observationally.

Knowledge through therapy of one's unconscious, before full integration of that knowledge, provides one sort of example. One may know the attitudes on the basis of observationally based therapy, but the unconscious attitudes may provide a point of view of their own into which the meta-evaluations of them may not transfer. Those evaluations may not speak to unconscious considerations that are integral to the unconscious pathology: or the unconscious point of view may not have 'taken in' matters that are integral to the rationality of the meta-, therapeutic point of view.

Psychoanalytic cases are not the only sort that illustrate the relevant dissociation. One may know from experience or theory that one will act a certain way, and yet rational meta-considerations may not penetrate to the system of attitudes that motivate the action. Some self-admitted compulsions provide examples. One knows one has or will have the relevant intention, but knows the intention only as object; it is then not the product of critical deliberation. Sometimes rational considerations from the meta-point of view may not have the same rational force and relevance within the point of view that includes the observationally known attitudes.

There are cases of knowledge of one's beliefs like this as well. One may know from self-observation that 'underneath' one believes something because one needs to believe it, while feeling sincere rational urges to assert the contrary. The system of underlying practical beliefs that motivate the needed belief may form a point of view that does not recognize as sufficient the rational meta-reasons that one can offer oneself for giving up the need-based belief. The person's meta-perspective may correctly condemn the need-based belief as epistemically irrational. But the belief may be dissociated from the point of view of his observational knowledge of that belief. It may be rational 'overall' for the person to give up the belief, but the practical rationality of the limited need-driven perspective may exclude or outweigh the considerations that count against the belief.

The relevant psychological dissociation is, I think, sometimes partly to be explained in terms of the fact that a second 'point of view', or system of attitudes with its own internal coherence, has gotten set up within the person, in such a way that reasons from the point of view of the person's critical rationality do not automatically transfer to within the second point of view, rather as reasons from my perspective do not always apply as reasons from yours. Being known from the perspective of the critical reasoner *only* as an object, on the basis of observation and theory, is sufficient for an attitude to be dissociated in this way. Attitudes that are part of such a dissociated point of view may provide us with reasons, even operative ones, for doing things. But insofar as we know them only observationally, they are not of our critical reasoning.

Where we know our thoughts or attitudes only by observation, the question of *means* of control – of effective application of reasons to them – arises, at least from the perspective of our observational knowledge. Where we know our attitudes only as empirical objects, not only are our rational evaluations of those attitudes relativized to contingencies associated with the knowledge. But our ability to apply our reasons (those associated with the point of view of the observational knowledge) must acknowledge the contingency of our rational control over those attitudes. We must face a question of how, by what means, to make those reasons effective in view of the contingent relation between the point of view of the self-knowledge and rational evaluation, on one hand, and the observationally known attitudes, on the other. Again, this is not critical reasoning. In critical reasoning, such questions of means and control do not arise, since one's relation to the known attitudes is rationally immediate: they are part of the perspective of the review itself.

Sometimes observation-based self-knowledge enables one to assimilate an attitude into one's critical point of view, and to take direct critical control and responsibility for the attitude. I may learn through observing my behaviour or through reasoning in therapy that I believe that a friend is untrustworthy. I may 'internalize' this belief so that it is no longer merely an object of observational knowledge. This process is sometimes immediate, sometimes hard, requiring deep personal change.

Although much reasoning and rational attitude formation occurs outside the purview of critical self-knowledge, or indeed any self-knowledge, critical reasoning remains central to our identities as persons. So no reasonable account of self-knowledge can ignore the role and entitlements critical reasoning gives to self-knowledge.

The argument I have given against the simple observational model indicates that the relations between knowledge and subject matter on which one's entitlement rests cannot always be causally brute, contingent. nonrational ones. In some particular instances of self-knowledge, the connection must be a rational one. For conclusions about the reasonability of one's thoughts based on self-review *directly* yield reasons within the point of view of those reviewed thoughts to alter or confirm them. The relation between self-knowledge and subject matter is that they must normally and rationally *be part of the same theoretical and practical point of view* – elements of a single theory or plan.

Connections between reviews and thoughts under review that are fully open to reason and that allow immediate transmission of reasons are necessary to the rational coherence of a point of view. A merely observation-based relation between attitudes insures that they are parts of different points of view. Indeed, it is constitutive of a point of view that failure to follow or understand its connections by the holder of the point of view is a failure of rationality. Thus a point of view is not closed under deductive consequence, and contains rational connections other than deductive ones.

So entitlement to knowledge of one's own thoughts and attitudes is not purely a matter of what one does. It has to do with who one is. One's status as a person and critical reasoner entails epistemic entitlement to some judgments about one's propositional attitudes. It entails some non-observational knowledge of them.

Cogito-like thoughts illustrate one non-contingent rational relation between knowledge and subject matter. In those cases, the reviewed thought is simply a logical part of the review. But *cogito*-like thoughts are in many ways special cases. If we are to understand critical reasoning, the entitlement that I have discussed must apply more broadly. It must include judgments about beliefs, intentions, wants, as well as occurrent thoughts.

So far, I have put little weight on the first-person present tense form of the relevant pieces of self-knowledge. Clearly, for the review and the reviewed thoughts to be part of a practice of critical reasoning, the reviewed thoughts must be capable of becoming part of the reasoner's present array of attitudes. And the special features of *cogito* cases do depend on present tense. But much of what I have said about the dependence of an entitlement on its role in critical reasoning, and about the non-observational character of this entitlement, applies to preservative memory – that type of memory that preserves propositions and our commitments to them in reasoning.[15] I think that this sort of memory provides us with some non-observational knowledge of our past mental states and events, and is epistemically underwritten by its role in critical reasoning.

The first-person point of view is clearly basic to self-knowledge in critical reasoning. The self-knowledge that I featured differs from observational knowledge of physical objects in that the first-person point of view is deeply relevant to the epistemic status of the knowledge. In observations of physical objects, anyone could have made substantially the same observation with equal right, if the same angle of perception had been available at the same time. But self-ascriptions constitute an epistemic angle in themselves.

What does this metaphor come to? If the reviewing knowledge is to be integral to critical reasoning, if it is to provide immediate rational ground for change in the reviewed material, the review must take up the same perspective or point of view as the act under review – the reasoner's own object-level point of view. The first-person point of view bears a distinctive relation to the relevance of rational norms to rational activity. For a review of a propositional mental event or state to yield an immediate rational ground to defend or alter the attitude, the point of view of the review and that of the attitude reviewed must be the same and must be first-personal.

In evaluating reasoning critically, one must make commitments to attitudes partly on the basis of critical evaluations of them. If one is to fully articulate the rational basis for the application of rational norms within critical reasoning, the commitments to both reviews and reviewed attitudes must be conceptually acknowledged as one's own. For acknowledging them as one's own *is* taking them as attitudes that one could rationally and directly change or confirm. Acknowledging first-order attitudes as one's own is necessary to articulating the direct rational relevance of one's critical reasons to first-order reasoning (or more generally, reasonable activity). I intend to say more about this matter on another occasion.

I have sketched the environmental neutrality of our entitlement to self-knowledge. The entitlement remains constant under possible unnoticeable variations in environmental circumstances or cognitive content. For

---

[15] Burge (1993).

it does not depend on the empirical content of the judgments. It does not depend on checking whether our judgments meet certain conditions. It depends on the judgments' being instances of a kind essential to critical reasoning. Critical reasoning presupposes that people are entitled to such judgments. Since we are critical reasoners, we are so entitled.

Epistemic entitlement derives from jurisdiction – from the place of the judgments in reasoning. In *cogito*-like thoughts, this place is coded in the content of the judgments themselves. In other relevant sorts of self-knowledge, which are fallible, the entitlement, indeed one's knowledge, depends only on one's not misusing the judgments and on one's remaining a sane critical reasoner.[16]

REFERENCES

Armstrong, D. M. 1968. *A Materialist Theory of the Mind.* London: Routledge & Kegan Paul.

Burge, T. 1988. Individualism and Self-Knowledge. *Journal of Philosophy* 85: 649–663. Reprinted in Quassim Cassam ed. *Self-Knowledge* Oxford: Oxford University Press, 1994. Chapter 4 in this volume.

———. 1993. Content Preservation. *The Philosophical Review* 102 (October): 457–488.

Shoemaker, S. 1988. On Knowing One's Own Mind. *Philosophical Perspectives* 2: 183–209.

---

[16] Versions of this paper were given as the third of six Locke Lectures at Oxford in 1993, and the first of two Whitehead Lectures at Harvard in 1994, as well as on several other occasions. The key idea and first draft of the paper dates from 1985. I am grateful for helpful comments on drafts or talks based on this paper to Robert Adams, Kent Bach, Tony Brueckner, Phil Clark, David Kaplan, Christopher Peacocke, Marleen Rozemond, Hilary Putnam, Nathan Salmon, Houston Smit, Barry Stroud, Patrick Suppes, and Corliss Swain.

16

Our Entitlement To Self-Knowledge: Entitlement, Self-Knowledge and Conceptual Redeployment

Christopher Peacocke

Entitlement, Self-Knowledge and Conceptual Redeployment[1]

In a wide range of cases, we know our own thoughts and attitudes, their contents included, without needing to check first on our environmental relations. This is so even when, as so often, the contents of the thoughts and attitudes in question depend constitutively on our environment (physical, social and linguistic). How is such self-knowledge possible?

A good answer to this simple-sounding, but actually very difficult, question has to develop a theory of our entitlement to these beliefs about our thoughts and attitudes. This theory should have three properties. First, of course, it must explain how, for a subject who is not relying on evidence about his environment, there can so much as be an entitlement to a second-order belief whose truth requires that the subject be embedded in a certain way in an environment of a certain specific kind. Second, the theory must

---

[1] Earlier versions of the sections below on conceptual redeployment were presented in Oxford and Utrecht in 1994; other parts of the material were also presented in a symposium with Tyler Burge at the 1995 meeting of the Pacific Division of the American Philosophical Association in San Francisco. Special thanks to Tyler Burge for many valuable discussions of these issues and extensive comments on an earlier draft; I am also grateful to Bill Child, Donald Davidson Graeme Forbes, Alvin Goldman, James Higginbotham and Jennifer Hornsby for very helpful observations.

be sufficiently general to cover each of the rather different ways in which this distinctive self-knowledge can be achieved. Various special cases have proved more tractable than the phenomenon in general; the treatment of special cases is welcome, but we do need an understanding which applies generally. Third, the theory must make good its claim to be an account of *entitlement*. It must be reasonable to employ the ways of reaching beliefs that the theory describes as entitling, and those ways must be appropriately connected with the truth of the beliefs reached in those ways.

I will in the early sections of this paper develop some parts of an account of entitlement to the relevant second-order beliefs about one's own thoughts and attitudes. From this discussion, it seems to me that there emerges a general explanatory principle about the role of concepts in the ascription of attitudes. I will go on to elaborate this principle, and its widespread consequences for such topics as: the ascription of content; the validity of inferences involving psychological notions; psychological explanation; the theory of conceptual content; and the semantics of propositional-attitude contexts.

The account I shall be giving is congenial at least to the spirit of Tyler Burge's important contributions on externalism and self-knowledge, in that it does attempt to reconcile the externalist insights about intentional content with the existence of a special kind of knowledge about one's own thoughts and attitudes. There are, though, some quite specific divergences from Tyler Burge over the philosophical explanation of the entitlement to self-knowledge, and over one or two other issues, and I will point up these divergences as we proceed.

I

Sensitivity without Inference: Its Requirements, and Conceptual Redeployment. There is a necessary condition for our beliefs about our own thoughts and attitudes to be knowledge. The necessary condition is that the following counterfactual holds: if the thinker's environment were sufficiently different so that the intentional content of his first-order attitudes were different, then in those circumstances, the contents of his second-order beliefs about his first-order attitudes would be correspondingly different too. For example, we require the truth of this counterfactual: had it been twater (Putnam's well-known substance XYZ) in the thinker's environment, so that he had the first-order belief that twater quenches thirst, then his second-order belief would correspondingly be that he believes that twater quenches thirst. We can call these required counterfactuals 'level-linking' counterfactuals, since they link variation in first-order contents to variations in second-order contents. As I say, this is only a necessary condition for the second-order beliefs to be knowledge. There are plenty of examples in the theory of knowledge which show that counterfactual sensitivity, by itself, does not suffice for knowledge. But I expect there would be widespread agreement that if a thinker were to judge that he believes that water quenches thirst, even in the counterfactual circumstances that his first-order belief is a belief that twater quenches thirst, then his actual judgment that he believes that water quenches thirst would not be knowledge. Part of an account of the status as knowledge of our beliefs about our own attitudes must be devoted to explaining why the required level-linking counterfactuals always hold.

In his paper 'Our Entitlement to Self-Knowledge' (1996), and in his earlier paper 'Individualism and Self-Knowledge' (1988), Tyler Burge discharges this obligation for the case of contextually self-verifying self-ascriptions such as 'I judge, herewith, that there are physical objects'. In these cases, making the judgment with a certain first-order content is what makes true the self-ascription. So in environments in which the embedded first-order content is different, so too is the thought I ascribe to myself when I make a judgment of this contextually self-verifying form. But as Burge also notes, many knowledgeable psychological self-ascriptions are not contextually self-verifying. They can certainly still contain externally individuated intentional contents. So a first question we have to ask is this: How is the truth of the level-linking counterfactuals secured for those knowledgeable psychological self-ascriptions that are not contextually self-verifying?

Knowledgeable self-ascriptions which are not contextually self-verifying fall into several different kinds. Suppose you are asked 'Where was Napoleon defeated?'. You try to remember; and memory serves up the information that Napoleon was defeated at Waterloo. Its occurring to you that he was defeated at Waterloo can be a subjective, conscious event which is capable, at least temporarily, of engaging your attention. It is a subjective state lacking in one who is unable to remember (or misremember) where he was defeated. The nature of the conscious state is specified in part by stating which intentional content it is that memory presents as true. A person to whom it occurs that Napoleon was defeated at Blenheim enjoys an event of a different subjective type.

Suppose you make the first-person self-ascription 'I believe that Napoleon was defeated at Waterloo', and make it because (a) you seem to

remember that Napoleon was defeated there, and because (b) you are taking your memory at face value. This self-ascription of a belief is not self-
verifying; nor is it merely a report of the apparent memory. Rather, you are
taking the apparent memory as correct. endorsing it – as you would be
doing if you were to judge, because of the memory, that Napoleon was
defeated at Waterloo. When (a) and (b) explain your self-ascription, the
route by which you come to make the ascription is one which also commits you to believing that Napoleon was defeated at Waterloo. Suppose
your self-ascription is reached by (a) and (b), and you express it in uttering
'I believe that Napoleon was defeated at Waterloo'. If someone then asks
you, 'And was Napoleon defeated at Waterloo?,' to answer, in these circumstances, 'Oh. I'm not going *that* far' would be absurd. The presence
of this commitment is something these cases share with the contextually
self-verifying cases. (Together, these cases contrast with those in which no
such commitment is present, such as that in which one makes a self-ascription of a belief by acting as one's own psychoanalyst, ascribing it to oneself
on the basis of evidence equally available to a third person.)

A crucial point is that, in self-ascribing the belief that Napoleon was
defeated at Waterloo in the way described, you deploy exactly the same
concepts, and the same intentional content built from them, as your
memory represents as correct.One content rather than another features as
the content of the belief self-ascribed because that content is the same as
that of the conscious memory state endorsed as correct. Because of this
identity, the necessary level-linking counterfactual is sustained. If the history and environment of the thinker were sufficiently different that a different first-order content were represented as correct by memory, then in
those circumstances, the second-order self-ascription would be of a belief
with different content in cases of this first kind. It is the redeployment of
the same concepts in the second-order self-ascription that ensures the
truth of the level-linking counterfactual. This redeployment secures the
level-linking counterfactual as effectively as does the special self-verifying
else.

We can call cases of the first kind of case just illustrated 'intermediate
conscious state' cases. In cases of the first kind, there is some conscious
state which is the thinker's reason for making the self-ascription. But in
many cases there does not even need to he an intermediate conscious state
for a self-ascription to be knowledgeable, whilst the self-ascription is still
not contextually self-verifying. If you are asked your name, your address,
your phone numbers, your job, you can often answer without waiting for

a conscious memory representation. The same is true of corresponding self-ascriptions of knowledge of that information. If in some meeting, a practical need emerges to find the phone number of Oxford University, I may think, and/or say, 'I know that the phone number of Oxford University is 270001'. This self-ascription can itself be knowledgeable, but it is not true that it has to be based first on a conscious subjective memory that the number is 270001.

Even in these cases in which there is no intermediate conscious state, however, there is still a form of redeployment of first-order concepts and contents. We have an underlying state with the representational content that p producing in its subject the belief that he believes that p, without the causation proceeding by way of an intermediate conscious state. Such a method of forming beliefs about oneself will persist in a thinker, and no doubt be selected for as a speedier shortcut, provided that the content of the self-ascribed belief, when reached in this way, is the same as would be produced if the underlying state had led in the appropriate way to a conscious state, and thereby to a self-ascription. When this identity of intentional content is part of the explanation of the existence and persistence of this method of reaching a self-ascription, once again we have a type of redeployment. The level-linking counterfactual required for environmentally-neutral entitlements is again ensured. If the underlying informational state had had a different content, so too would the self-ascribed belief reached by this method.

In a third kind of case, there is neither an intermediate conscious state whose content is endorsed, nor a pre-existing underlying state. Rather, the process leading up to the self-ascription is one of making up your mind.[2] When you are asked 'Do you intend to go to next year's Joint Session?', you may be considering that question for the first time. You can answer the question by putting into operation whatever procedure you have for deciding whether to go to next year's Joint Session, and answering 'I do intend to go' if and only if you do then decide to go. If the self-ascription is made by following that procedure, it is ensured that the content of the decision will be the same as the content of any intention self-ascribed by means of that procedure. So again, the level-linking counterfactuals are sustained. This third kind of case also includes that in which you follow the procedure for self-ascription of belief described by Evans

---

[2] Some of the significance of cases of this third kind is well brought out by Richard Moran (1988).

(1982). You answer the question of whether you believe that p by putting into operation whatever procedure you have for answering the question whether p. Being a self-ascription of a belief, rather than a judgment, a self-ascription so reached cannot be assimilated to the class of contextually self-verifying judgments. But the level-linking counterfactuals are still supported when that procedure is followed. If, as a result of environmental or societal differences, the procedures you use for answering the first-order question were to be procedures for answering the question of whether q, rather than the question of whether p, then you would correspondingly be self-ascribing the belief that q (or not, as the case may be), rather than the belief that p.

II

What is the Source of the Entitlement? I turn now to a cluster of issues about a thinker's entitlement to judgments about his own attitudes.

(i) Is there ever a causal element in the correct account of this entitlement?

(ii) If there is, how is that causal element to be reconciled with the widely recognized fact that there are severe limits on the possibility of 'brute' errors about one's own attitudes? Here a brute error is, following Burge, one which involves no failure of rationality and no malfunction on the part of the thinker.

Self-ascriptions of attitudes also feature in critical reasoning, reasoning in which the thinker recognizes and applies to his own thinking and reasoning some assessment or evaluation of reasons and reasoning itself. So our third question is:

(iii) What is the relation between the ability to engage in critical reasoning and the ability to self-ascribe attitudes with entitlement? Is the ability to engage in such reasoning a source of entitlement, or is it consequential upon some entitlement elucidated independently of critical reasoning?

It is very plausible that the entitlement to make at least some self-verifying self-ascriptions has nothing to do with causation at all. The judgment 'I am entertaining the thought that it would be cheaper to live somewhere else' is true whenever it is made, and is appreciable as such by anyone capable of making it. No particular etiology is required of a judgment with that content for a thinker to be entitled to make it. But I think matters are different for self-ascriptions of the three kinds distinguished in the preceding section.

So let us take first the case in which the thinker self-ascribes a belief that *p* because memory represents, or misrepresents, it to him as being the case that·*p*, and because he is taking the deliverances of memory at face value (at least for some kind of content which includes *p*). I see no good reason to deny that the two uses of 'because' which feature in this description of the case both pick out the relation of causation. In ordinary cases of this type, the thinker is entitled to the self-ascription of the belief that *p*, and the self-ascription will constitute knowledge. It seems to me that the judgment's having those particular rational causes has to be mentioned in an account of why the thinker is entitled to it. A further elaboration of the entitlement should emphasize the point that two of the rational causes of the self-ascription, the memory representation and his taking it at face value, taken together are sufficient for his believing the first-order content *p*, that is, are sufficient for the truth of the self-ascription. In cases of this first type, conditions which suffice for the first-order belief are also causes – rational causes – of the self-ascription.

If the thinker had the memory representation and the willingness to take it at face value, but these were not the causes of his self-ascription of belief, then he would not be entitled to the self-ascription just in virtue of having that memory representation and that willingness. (Any entitlement to the self-ascription would have to be underwritten by something else.) This is partially analogous to the entitlement one has in the rather different case in which one is entitled to a belief which is validly inferred from premises to which one is entitled. If one holds the belief, but it is not in fact caused by one's holding of the premises from which it follows, then one would not be entitled to the belief simply in virtue of holding other beliefs from which it follows.[3]

In cases of the second of the kinds distinguished in §I, that in which there is no intermediate conscious state, the self-ascription is made because there is some underlying state with the representational content that *p*. This state, when appropriately activated, produces the judgment that *p* and self-ascriptions of the belief that *p*. It seems that, because it does

---

[3] There are more distinctions to be drawn here. A conscious state can enter the explanation of why someone believes something without being part of his justification for holding, nor part of his entitlement to hold, that belief. This must be the position of anyone who believes that some proofs lead to a priori knowledge, but who also agrees that a person's perception

the former, it is a good candidate for being a belief that p. If it is such a belief, then we have the first-order belief causing the self-ascription of that first-order belief. A plausible approach to this entitlement is to argue that it is not merely the case that the second-order belief is produced by the truth of its content. It is also true that if the procedure did not have that property, the thinker would not employ it. If the deliverances of an 'automatic' procedure diverged from ascriptions based on conscious attitudes, the procedure would be abandoned or modified. If this were not so, it seems there would be no entitlement. On this approach, the account of the entitlement again involves causal relations, both actual and counterfactual.

What of the entitlement in cases of the third sort of self-ascription, those in which the subject makes up his mind on the occasion of the self-ascription? In the example of the self-ascription of the intention to attend next year's Joint Session, I would hold that a full account of the entitlement to the ascription would mention the fact that the ascription is rationally caused by the same states which cause the subject to have the intention to attend next year's Joint Session: and similarly for other cases of the third kind. Again, a causal element is crucial to the entitlement.

Suppose we accept that there is a causal element in a thinker's entitlement to beliefs about his own attitudes in these three kinds of case, and now consider question (ii), about the relation of this causal element to the apparent absence of brute errors in certain self-ascriptions. If there is a causal element in the entitlement, then one of the following alternatives must hold. Either, contrary to appearances, brute error can occur in some

---

of a written proof is part of the explanation of his believing what is stated in its conclusion. The perception of the proof should be treated as an enabling condition, but not as part of the thinker's justification for believing what is stated in its conclusion – the justification is just the proof itself (considered as a tree-structure of contents or, if you like, Fregean Thoughts). Recent treatments of the a priori which endorse this distinction are Burge (1993) and Peacocke (1993b). That perception does not play a justificatory role in these examples of a priori knowledge acquired by proof is evidenced by such facts as the following. Consider a person who, because of an optical illusion, misperceives an array of symbols in such a way that he has a visual experience as of a genuine proof, which he recognizes as a proof. This person can obtain knowledge, indeed a prior knowledge, of what the proof's conclusion states. His justification for his belief is the tree-structure of contents which does indeed prove what is stated in the conclusion (even though some of his beliefs about what is written on the page are false, and that tree-structure is not in fact expressed by the inscribed sentences). In the self-ascription of belief in cases of the first kind, however, the apparent memory and the thinker's willingness to take it at face value are part of the thinker's reasons for making the self-ascription. This is not of course to say that the self-ascription is *inferred* from them. I acknowledge that all these points are controversial, and merit extensive independent discussion.

way corresponding to its acknowledged possibility in perceptual beliefs; or else there must be some special reason why, in the self-ascription of belief, the presence of a causal element in the entitlement is compatible with severe limitations on the range of cases in which brute error is possible. We can call this second alternative 'the compatibilist alternative'.

It seems to me that reflection on the very nature of the examples gives support to the compatibilist alternative. Let us fix on the case in which there is an intermediate conscious state. Here, to repeat, two of the causes of the thinker's self-ascription, viz. its being consciously represented to him as being the case that p and his willingness to take this at face value, are together *sufficient* for his believing that p. This is a major disanalogy with perceptual knowledge. A perceptual experience itself is never sufficient for the correctness of a perceptual belief about the material world, even if the thinker himself is entirely reasonable and is not malfunctioning. The experience can have a false content, as when one looks through an aperture at an Ames room, or when the light rays are bounced off an unnoticed mirror – the cases of strange objects and misleading local conditions, respectively. If one's conscious memory representation were somehow made available to one only through a further layer of experience of the memory, and for which the question of the veridicality of the experience in respect of the memory arises, then there would apparently be a possibility of brute error. But such a description of the situation is nonsense. The conscious memory representation is already, as a conscious state, something capable of giving reasons for forming beliefs. No further layer of experience of the memory exists, and none is necessary. In the presence of a willingness to take its deliverances at face value, a conscious memory representation can make reasonable self-ascriptions of attitudes (as well making reasonable first-order beliefs). For self-ascriptions made in this way, brute error is impossible. It is impossible precisely because, in these psychological self-ascriptions, there is nothing that plays the role that experience plays in genuine observational knowledge of physical objects. This explanation of why brute error is impossible is entirely consistent with the entitlement to the self-ascription containing a causal element.[4]

---

[4] In cases of the second and third kinds of self-ascription, errors must involve either malfunction, or a failure of rationality, or both – that is, they are not brute errors within the meaning of the Act.

The account I have just offered is not merely consistent with, but arguably entails, the noncontingency of certain of the relations between the self-ascription and its subject-matter. If the account I have been giving of self-ascription in cases of the first type is correct, it is noncontingent that if a thinker makes a self-ascription in the circumstances and with the explanation I have described, then his self-ascription will be correct.

It would also be consistent with the presence of a causal element in the entitlement to assert the non-contingency of another relation. It is necessary that if a thinker has the concept of belief, and a proper mastery of the first-person, then, if the question arises, he will judge that he has the relevant first-order belief when in the antecedent circumstances described in cases of the first or second types. I call this modal principle the principle of the transparency of self-ascriptions of conscious belief, or the transparency principle for short. This second non-contingency as formulated in the transparency principle obviously bears on the extent of a thinker's second-order knowledge of his first-order attitudes. A defence of this second non-contingency about self-ascriptions of belief would be one way of explaining the wide scope of critical reasoning about one's own beliefs whilst continuing to accept a partially causal account of the epistemic status of this kind of self-knowledge.

These answers to questions (i) and (ii) are consistent with Tyler Burge's theses. Our question (iii) asked after the relation between the ability to engage in critical reasoning and our entitlement to judgments about our own attitudes. Tyler Burge's view is that the role of self-ascriptions in critical reasoning is one of the sources of a thinker's entitlement to judgments about his own attitudes. He writes: '...our epistemic warrant for our judgments about our thoughts ... derives from the nature of the thinker as a critical reasoner' (Burge (1996, p. 91)). And:

> ...the relevant entitlement derives not from the reliability of some causal-perceptual relation between cognition and its object. It has two other sources. One is the role of the relevant judgments in critical reasoning. The other is a constitutive relation between the judgments and their subject-matter – or between the judgments about one's thoughts and the judgments' being true. Understanding and making such judgments is constitutively associated both with being reasonable and with getting them right. [...] To be capable of critical reasoning, and to be subject to certain rational norms necessarily associated with such reasoning, some mental acts and states must be *knowledgeably* reviewable. The specific character of this knowledgeable reviewability requires that

it be associated with an epistemic entitlement that is distinctive. [...]
there must be a non-contingent, rational relation, of a sort to be explained, between relevant first-person judgments and their subject-
matter or truth. (Burge (1996, p. 98))

I have already committed myself to some of the relations between first-
order beliefs and their self-ascriptions being rational and noncontingent. I
also agree that there are necessary connections between critical reasoning
and the ability to self-ascribe; and further agree that critical reasoning
requires knowledgeable reviewability of first-order attitudes. What I question is the claim that the role of self-ascriptions in critical reasoning is the
source of a thinker's entitlement to make them.

It is one thing to argue that critical reasoning requires an entitlement to
self-ascriptions; it is a further claim that their role in critical reasoning is
the source of the entitlement to self-ascriptions. Since critical reasoning
exists, and requires entitlement to the self-ascriptions, it follows that there
is entitlement to the self-ascriptions. But nothing follows from these
points about *why* we are entitled to the self-ascriptions. It would be
entirely consistent with these points that critical reasoning is made possible in part by some independently explained entitlement to self-ascriptions. On this conception, which is the one I would defend, an
entitlement to self-ascription is one of the sources of critical reasoning,
rather than *vice versa*.

Here is a partial parallel which may be found helpful. We engage in
practical and theoretical reasoning which is aimed at adjusting our relations to things in our environment, and of altering, rearranging, and
designing objects in our environment, in such a way that they do not cause
us pain. When a person knows, from his own experience of pain, that certain circumstances, objects or practices lead to his being in pain, he has
prima facie reason to avoid or to change them. This reason is not merely a
reason relative to the correctness of his beliefs about whether he was in
pain on certain particular occasions. No such relativization is necessary.
This is so because, if someone has the concept of pain, then that person's
being in pain gives a good and conclusive reason for his making the judgment that he is in pain. It is plausible that the relation between being in
pain and the judgment that one is so is non-contingent in both of the
respects we mentioned earlier. When made for that reason, the judgment
cannot be false; and it is part of possession of the concept of pain that the
thinker must be willing to make the judgment, and for that reason, in
those circumstances. All the same, the entitlement a thinker has to beliefs

about his own current pains certainly seems to involve a causal relation. Your judgment that you are now in pain is knowledge in part because it is rationally caused by the pain itself. It is quite implausible to regard the causal relation as merely an enabling condition, with the entitlement lying elsewhere – what could the other entitlement be? Again too, it is the absence of a level of experience intermediate between the pain itself and the thought about the pain which contributes to making brute error impossible, and which allows it in the perceptual cases. There may be a sound argument from features of the practical and theoretical reasoning surrounding pain-avoidance to the conclusion that the relation between judgments about one's pains and the pains themselves must be in certain respects non-contingent. It would not follow that the *source* of one's entitlement to judgments about one's own pains is anything to do with such practical or theoretical reasoning about pain-avoidance, nor that what entitles one to the judgments is not partially a causal matter.

I suggest that critical reasoning as described by Burge should be seen as the result of combining two more primitive capacities. One of these capacities I will call 'second-tier' thought. The term 'critical reasoning' is a term of art, and it is written into Burge's characterization of critical reasoning that the critical reasoner has concepts of propositional attitudes and is capable of self-ascribing attitudes – not least because as characterized, it involves the assessment of reasoning as such. But as Burge notes, much critical reasoning involves thought about the world, rather than about attitudes. I think there is a more primitive kind of reasoning which still involves assessment of relations of support, consequence, and evidence, and can be used by a thinker in revising his beliefs, without the thinker actually exercising or possessing concepts of propositional attitudes.

We can start with a very simple example. Suppose you come home, and see that no car is parked in your driveway. You infer that your spouse is not home yet; you store that information, or misinformation, and move on to think about other matters. Later, you may suddenly remember that your spouse mentioned in the morning that the brakes of her car were faulty, and wonder whether she may have taken the car for repair. At this point, you suspend your original belief that she is not home yet. For you come to realize that the absence of her car is not necessarily good evidence that she is not home. If the car is being repaired, she would have returned by public transport. Then finally you may reach the belief that she is home after all, given your next thought that she would not have taken any risks with faulty brakes. Nothing in this little fragment of thought seems to me to involve the self-ascription of belief. There are initially thoughts about the world; there is then the bringing to bear of additional information; there are thoughts about what would justify what; there is suspension of certain attitudes; and finally some resolution. This is a (modest) piece of reasoning which results in revision of beliefs in the light of thought about relations of evidence and support, but the thoughts it involves all seem to be thoughts about the world, not about the thinker's thoughts. We can call it second-tier thought, since it involves thought about relations of support, evidence or consequence between contents, as opposed to first-tier thought, which is thought about the world where the thought does not involve any consideration of such relations between contents.

In the example of the car, we had a mature thinker, with the conceptual apparatus for self-ascribing beliefs. But it seems to me a four-year old child could engage in the following simple piece of second-tier thought. First he thinks that a particular toy is in the cupboard, because that is where it is normally kept; then he remembers that his aunt is staying with them, and that she puts toys in the wrong place. He realizes that the cupboard's being the normal storage place does not mean the toy is there now, given the presence of Auntie, and so he no longer believes that the toy is in the cupboard.

It seems to me that a thinker can engage in second-tier thought without conceptualizing the process as one of belief-assessment and revision. There are many other cases in which we want to say that a thinker can be sensitive, even rationally sensitive, to a distinction or property without conceptualizing the distinction or property. An example, uncontentious from the standpoint of the issues of this discussion, would be the case of a child who forms beliefs on the basis of his perceptual experiences, but not on the basis of his visual imaginings. He is sensitive to whether his state is one of experiencing or of imagining; but this does not require him to have the concept of experience. It seems to me that second-tier thought can equally be sensitive to, and the second-tier thinker's later patterns of thought be explained by, the fact that q was his reason for believing that p, without his having the ability to self-ascribe beliefs. This seems a possible description of the case of the child and the revision of beliefs about the location of the toy. If we insist that any case of second-tier thought must involve the capacity to self-ascribe, we would make it impossible for a thinker to engage in elementary second-tier thought without the ability to exercise a general concept of belief, something which arguably involves both the ability to self-ascribe and to other-ascribe. Such mastery of the concept of belief seems to me to be an additional layer of cognitive capacities, not necessarily involved in the ability effectively to assess relations of support, evidence and consequence amongst contents concerning the non-psychological world.[5]

Critical reasoning is the result of the combination of the capacity for second-tier thought with the capacity to self-ascribe attitudes, where the entitlement to the self-ascriptions is explained independently of their role in critical reasoning, along the lines discussed earlier in this section. The ability to engage in second-tier thought contributes the capacity to think, on good grounds, that p could well be the case without q being the case; the ability to self-ascribe contributes the capacity to knowledgeably self-ascribe the belief that q, and, with a suitable background of conceptual capacities, the ability to know that one's reason for believing q was that p. When both abilities are present, the subject is in a position to revise his self-ascribed belief that q, in the way Burge describes. On this account of how full-fledged critical reasoning is possible, critical reasoning is explanatorily posterior to these two contributing abilities, rather than being the source of any one of them.

III

The Redeployment Claim: Intuitive Motivation. I have been emphasizing the fact that when a thinker self-ascribes an attitude with an intentional content, he redeploys the very same concepts which are constituents of the intentional content of the first-order attitude. This fact is an instance of a more general phenomenon, which can be captured in what we can call *the Redeployment Claim:*

The concepts (senses, modes of presentation) that feature in first-level thoughts not involving propositional attitudes are the very same concepts which feature in thoughts about the intentional content of someone's propositional attitudes.

In its linguistic version, the Redeployment Claim states that

---

[5] I should add that nothing in Burge's writings commits him to denying the possibility of second-tier thought which is not yet critical reasoning. I am emphasizing the possibility because it is important for a positive elaboration of the nature of critical reasoning on the different account I am developing.

The sense of a word occurring in contexts not involving propositional attitude constrictions is the same sense which is redeployed as that word's *sense* when the word occurs within the scope of propositional attitude verbs.

The Redeployment Claim is a thesis about any propositional attitude ascriptions, of whatever order, whether first, second, or any arbitrary higher order. In effect it says that the sense of an expression in 'direct', nonoblique, contexts is elevated through the hierarchy of orders of propositional attitudes as the one sense of that expression, which remains the same however far up the hierarchy of orders we travel. The Redeployment Claim is put forward as correct regardless of how the ascribee of the attitudes is picked out, whether it be by a first-person or a third-person sense. The Claim is not just that the concepts (understood here as senses) featuring in first-order contents also occur as components of the Fregean Thoughts to which thinkers stand in propositional-attitude relations. That was Frege's claim, and in its linguistic version it is a claim about the reference of expressions within oblique contexts. The Redeployment Claim is rather a claim about the *sense* of expressions in oblique contexts. I believe that the Redeployment Claim is of some general significance for the philosophy of mind and the theory of intentional content. I will proceed by elaborating some of the intuitive grounds for believing it, and then, in the next section, go on to trace out its consequences for four issues in the philosophy of mind and the theory of content.

Something like the Redeployment Claim is accepted by widely diverse thinkers in the philosophy of language who use either the notion of sense, or some surrogate for it. Almost fifty years ago in *Meaning and Necessity* Carnap modestly wrote 'It does not appear, at least not to me, that it would be unnatural or implausible to ascribe its ordinary sense to a name in an oblique context' (1956, §30, p. 129). One quickly reaches the Redeployment Claim if one reflects on the consequences of a semantic theory which insists on an infinite hierarchy not just of objects and senses, but of distinct senses of senses, senses of senses of senses, ... and so on, if it is supposed that there is no determination of a canonical sense of a sense by that latter sense itself. Donald Davidson (1984) was surely right in saying that the truth-conditions for the sentences of a language following this reading of Frege's model would not be generated by a finite set of semantic rules for the atomic expressions, with the consequence that the language would be unlearnable. If the Redeployment Claim is right, there is no such failure of finite generation of the truth conditions of all the sentences of a language which can describe proportional attitudes. In Davidson's own paratactic analysis, a form of the Redeployment Claim is immediately guaranteed (since on that analysis the embedded sentence is mentioned in the attribution of attitudes). So we certainly have a general motivation in the philosophy of language for accepting something like the Redeployment Claim. Michael Dummett, for instance, has been moved to accept it on closely related grounds in the philosophy of language (1973, pp. 267–9). These considerations all seem to me sound in themselves, but they omit the positive, direct grounds for accepting the Redeployment Claim.

Suppose you and your friend are walking at dusk along a narrow city street. You both see a man further down the street, and your friend says to you 'That man is dangerous'. As a result of his saying that, you come to have a belief about your friend's beliefs, viz.

My friend believes that that man is dangerous.

The belief you attribute to your friend is one which has a perceptual-demonstrative mode of presentation of the perceived man in its intentional content. But how do you, the ascriber of the belief, think of the content of your friend's belief? It falls far short to say merely that you believe that your friend has a belief of the person down the street that he is dangerous (a case of Quine's relational belief). As is very familiar, that would be true if the person down the street happened, unknown to your friend, to be Saddam Hussein, whom your friend certainly believes to be dangerous. What we want to capture is your knowledge that your friend believes that that man is dangerous, a belief which, unlike the mere belief that Saddam Hussein is dangerous, will make you turn around and walk the other way.[6]

There is no doubt waiting to be developed a substantive theory of what it is to be employing a perceptual demonstrative. This theory would in some way link thoughts with perceptual-demonstrative contents to fea-

---

[6] It would equally fall short to add to enrich the relational characterization of the belief to 'My friend believes of the person down the street that he is dangerous and is coming towards him', and to offer that as equivalent to the content 'My friend believes that that man is dangerous'. This is not equivalent either. The former would be true if your friend had learned from a message over his mobile phone that Saddam Hussein is coming towards him. We would begin to capture the required content if we added 'and believes of him that he is *over there*'. But this use of *over there* is redeploying the demonstrative your friend would also use, so far from being an alternative theory, the suggestion supports the Redeployment Claim.

tures of the subject's perceptual experience which make such thoughts available to him. The theory would have to talk of certain canonical grounds for accepting or rejecting perceptual-demonstrative thoughts, amongst much else. If we had such a theory, its materials could be used to specify the demonstrative mode of presentation which features in your friend's thought. A certain role would be distinctive of perceptual demonstratives, and we could specify your friend's thought by saying that it is a thought containing a concept with such-and-such role (as specified in the theory), and made available by such-and-such perceptual experience on this very occasion of walking down the street at dusk. You do not, however, have to have any personal-level knowledge of such a theory in order to ascribe the perceptual-demonstrative belief to your friend.

It begins to be very plausible, as the Redeployment Claim proposes, that the correct account of the way in which you think of the intentional content of your friend's belief is that you use the very same perceptual mode of presentation again, *that man* (modulo minor differences in the angle of viewing). In the case of perceptual demonstratives, this has the independently plausible consequence that there is a way of thinking of the intentional content of your friend's belief which is available only to those who are situated, and perceptually equipped, as he is, at the time he has the belief.

The little argument that we have just given for the case of demonstratives is that in thinking about a person's demonstrative propositional attitudes, we employ a way of thinking of their intentional content which is captured neither by purely relational attributions, nor by thought-theoretical characterizations of intentional contents. As far as I can see, this argument is generalizable from demonstratives to any other intentional content which is available in thought both to ascriber and to ascribee. For any such intentional content, the only way which is both correct and generally available for the ascriber to capture the content of the ascribee's attitudes is for him simply to reuse, to redeploy, the intentional content in question. (It is this which makes it possible for an intentional content in a contextually self-verifying self-ascription to be, as Burge says, both thought and thought about in a single performance.)

If the ascribee uses the first person in a thought, such as 'I am hungry', naturally the ascriber cannot redeploy that very mode of presentation in describing the ascribee's thought. The ascriber cannot use the mode of presentation employed by the ascribee at all, in fact, since if he uses the first person, it will refer to himself, not the ascribee. A corresponding point applies to *now*, *here*, and their ilk. Actually, if we are strict, we ought to say that such cases do not form a counterexample to the linguistic form of the Redeployment Claim, since the words employed in ascribing a first-person or present-tense belief to another are not 'I' and 'now', but 'he' or 'he himself' and 'then'. But that they are not counterexamples is no cause for rejoicing. The linguistic version of the Redeployment Claim is simply remaining silent about what happens in these cases, and to leave matters there would hardly be satisfactory.

In fact, there is more of a positive nature to be said about the cases in which the ascriber is not in a position to use the very same concept as the ascribee. Consider the first-person beliefs of the ascribee. As is widely agreed in the literature, the ascriber can know what the ascribee believes, because he can know that the ascribee is thinking a thought of the first-person type. It is, further, true that when you know, that another person is thinking a thought of the first-person type, the way in which you are yourself thinking of that type has the following property: that it is, for you, a priori that your own first-person thoughts are of that same type. Some of the consequences of the Redeployment Claim which I will be elaborating below apply not only to the case in which we have strict identity of concept employed by ascriber and ascribee, but hold also when the ascriber knows himself to be employing an indexical concept of the same type as that employed by the ascribee. I will flag one such point later on.

IV

The Redeployment Claim: Four Further Consequences. I have already argued that the Redeployment Claim contributes to an explanation of how second-order self-ascriptions can be sensitive to the externally individuated contents of first-order attitudes without the thinker having to rely on evidence about his environment. The other consequences of the Redeployment Claim I will be tracing out are, as one might expect, cases in which either we find relations characteristic of concepts as they feature in first-level contents being lifted in certain ways to the level of the ascription of attitudes; or in which we have cross-level interactions resulting from the identity of concepts stated in the Redeployment Claim.

(a) Norms and the Ascription of Content

There is a basic system of normative relations in which content stands, a system of relations which a thinker will respect in his thinking, and basic in the sense that the thinker can respect these relations without yet employing concepts of propositional attitudes. These are the normative relations which specify what justifies acceptance of a content, what justifies its rejection, what partially confirms it; and so forth. These relations will include what I called in *A Study of Concepts* (1992) 'the normative liaisons' of a content. They are the relations which, as Sellars (1963) and McDowell (1994) would say, locate a content in the space of reasons. It is very natural to take these normative relations of a given content as compositionally determined, as flowing from the identity of the concepts in the content together with their mode of combination.

Now consider a thinker who does advance to the stage of reflecting on what are good reasons for his beliefs, and what in turn the contents of his beliefs give good reasons for thinking. This thinker is in a position to know what (for instance) justifies a judgment with a certain content. There are certain justification relations that are not person-relative. The informational and perceptual circumstances of different thinkers may vary, and so may their epistemic daring. But the underlying normative relations will not vary from thinker to thinker. It is the circumstances in which thinkers find themselves that vary, along with their epistemic idiosyncrasies. So, when other things really are equal, what, at this very basic level of justificational relations, justifies acceptance of a content for one thinker will justify it for others. Other things will almost not be equal; some justificational relations will depend on collateral information and others (in my view) will not. But in any case, knowledge about what justifies a judgment of the given content, in given epistemic and perceptual circumstances, is available to our thinker as a principle he can draw upon in the ascription of content-involving attitudes to others. This is possible because, as the Redeployment Claim states, the very same concepts, comprising the content in question, feature both in the thinker's own, base-level thoughts about the world, and in his attribution of attitudes to others I do not say it is impossible to give a theory which accommodates this transfer of normative relations from the base level to the level of attribution while rejecting the Redeployment Claim. I suppose it would be possible to introduce some notion of a special concept of a concept, for which one postulates that the required transfers hold. But in postulating a distinction between a concept and some special concept of that concept, such an approach seems to me to introduce something which is no more than a fifth wheel. Extra axioms about the postulated special concept of a concept would be needed, and they would serve simply to reinstate for the special concept the pattern of normative relations which follow immediately when one accepts the identity asserted by the Redeployment Claim.

It is worth thinking more about what is involved in this lifting of normative relations to the level of ascription. In reflecting on what it is rational for someone employing a given concept to think, you have to think about the *world*. In wondering what would justify another person's application or denial of the concept *square* to an object, you have to engage in such thoughts as 'Would such-and-such be sufficient to establish that it is square? or for establishing that it is not?'. This involves your use of the concept *square* in much the way that would be involved in deciding whether you yourself have sufficient grounds for concluding that the object is square, or for concluding that it is not. The principal difference between the two cases is just that in one of them you yourself are in the relevant evidential states, while in the other you are just thinking about them. In fact, this whole conception would be consistent with the view that in ascribing attitudes to others one draws on tacit knowledge of a normative theory of the justificatory relations in which contents stand (Stone and Davies, 1996). In any case, we seem to have an intertwining of the ascription of content-involving states with both the normative and the externalist character of content.

This lifting of normative relations to the level of ascription is something which can also be present when we have identity only of the type of concept in question, as in the first-person uses by the ascribee which I mentioned above. The ascriber may first reflect that if he himself were in a situation of such-and-such a kind, he would have reason to form the belief, with a first-person content, that he himself is thus-and-so. Suppose he is then prepared to think of the ascribee as in a situation of the same sort as that about which he has just reflected, and that he also has the capacity to think of the first-person type. In these circumstances the ascriber can then, ceteris paribus, be in a position reasonably to attribute to the other a belief, of the first-person type, that he (the other) is thus-and-so. In such cases sameness of type of concept is sufficient in context to provide the bridge from, on the one side, thinking about the world and what would justify certain thoughts about it, to, on the other side, ascription of a particular attitudes to the other person.

So much by way of the lifting of normative relations to the level of ascription.

(b) Cross-Level Interactions: The Case of Inferences

If the same concepts (senses) feature, as used, in both first-order and higher order contents, then we would expect there to be cross-level inferential interactions between the levels, inferences turning on this identity.

One species of cross-level interaction comes across most vividly in the first-person case. Consider someone who has the second-order, first-person belief

(1) I believe that that man over there is French.

Suppose he also believes, on the basis of what he currently sees and hears while in the airport, that

(2) That man over there is speaking with an American accent and is checking in with an American passport.

Our subject who has beliefs with the contents (1) and (2) is someone with a cognitive problem, a problem he can appreciate just from (1) and (2) alone. From the premises (1) and (2) he can rationally infer

(3) There is someone whom I both believe to be French and who is speaking with an American accent and is checking in with an American passport.

(3) is to be understood in such a way that the scope of 'believe' concludes with the word 'French'; the immediately following 'and' has wider scope than 'believes.' The inference to (3) from (1) and (2) seems to be valid. But it is certainly valid only if the expressions 'that man over there' as used in (2) either have the same sense, or at least there is some a priori fixing, available to the thinker, of one of the senses by the other. If they do not express the same sense, or there is no such a priori fixing available to the thinker, there would be a fallacy of equivocation. It is not at all plausible that some suppressed additional premiss of an a posteriori character needs to be made explicit and assumed for the move from (1) and (2) to be valid.

Nor does the validity of the inference turn solely on the identity of the normal, non-oblique references of the expressions in question. Suppose we replace (2) with (2a).

(2a) Bill Smith is speaking with an American accent and is checking, in with an American passport

so that we can then consider the inference from (1) and (2a) to the same conclusion (3). That is a transition that no one would think of as valid. To move from (1) and (2a) to (3) certainly requires the additional a posteriori premiss

(2b) That man over there is Bill Smith.

The overwhelmingly natural response to the original case is to hold that the demonstratives in the premisses (1) and (2) have the same sense, so that the way of thinking the subject employs in thinking about the perceptually given man and the way of thinking he employs when thinking of the content of his first-order belief are one and the same. If we accept this identity, we have a smooth explanation of how second-order beliefs can rationally interact with first-order beliefs when a thinker is evaluating and revising his own propositional attitudes. This is just the kind of rational interaction which occurs in the case in which critical reasoning does involve a thinker's self-ascribing a belief.

Still, someone may object that this cannot be correct, because, 'that man over there' in (1) and 'that man over there' in (2) actually have different references: the former refers to a mode of presentation (viz., itself) and the latter to a man. It will be said that we had better have constancy of reference in a given term if an inference is to be valid! And in any case, how can the modes of presentation be identical if one refers to itself, and the other to a man? Doesn't this just contradict Leibniz' Law?

The answer to this last point is that anyone who accepts the Redeployment Claim will have to use a relativized notion of reference. For both expressions and for modes of presentation, the relation of reference will have to be relativized to a kind of context. For linguistic (or thought-) contexts in which it does not occur within the scope of a propositional-attitude verb or concept, the mode of presentation has its normal reference. In other contexts, it refers to itself. This is a pair of rules which can be part of a finite set of rules which fully determine the truth-conditions of the sentence of a language capable of expressing the propositional attitudes. On this approach, sense does determine reference, but only relative to a particular linguistic (or thought) context. On this, I am entirely, at one with Dummett, who introduces just this relativization (1973 pp. 267–9).

It is worth emphasizing the general nature or this rule for propositional attitude contexts. Consider someone who has mastered this rule, and who then acquires and understands a new expression true or false of things in the world. It is a prediction of this theory that such a person does not need anything new to understand sentences in which the new expression occurs within propositional attitude verbs already in his repertoire. This prediction seems to be correct: there is no question of having further to learn what concept of a concept is expressed by 'electron' as it occurs in 'Bohr believed there are electrons'. One's understanding of 'believes' and of 'electron' unembedded suffice. According to the Redeployment Claim, since the expression still has its normal sense when embedded, one is already in possession of all that is required for understanding such propositional-attitude sentences.

This treatment of the problem may seem to make the original objection – that difference of reference in different contexts will block inferences – all the more forceful. To address this, we can reconsider the inference front (1) and (2) to (3) with an intermediate step made explicit:

(1) I believe that that man over there is French.

(1') That man over there is such that I believe of him that he is French.

(2) That man over there is speaking with an American accent and is checking in with an American passport.

Hence.

(3) There is someone whom I both believe to be French and who is speaking with an American accent and is checking in with an American passport.

(3) follows from (1') and (2) by conjunction-introduction and existential generalization. (1') follows from (1) by exportation, which is valid for this demonstrative concept. The premiss of an exportation inference involves a concept occurring in oblique position, and its conclusion involves the same concept occurring in a direct context, as simply specifying an object about which some relational attitude is ascribed. Exportation is then precisely a principle which crosses levels. In examples in which exportation is valid, the shift of reference does not involve any nonsequitur.

On this treatment of the transition from (1) and (2) to (3), nothing turns on the use of the first person. If all occurrences of 'I' are replaced uniformly by any other singular term or variable, the resulting, inference is also valid.

I do not say the believer in a strict hierarchy of senses, senses of senses, and so forth, could not account for the validity of the inference from (1) and (2) to (3), but it is worth considering what he would have to say to achieve this result. For this strict theorist, there will be a sense of a sense, and this sense of a sense will be expressed by 'that man over there' in (1).

Suppose we follow the convention that pointed brackets around an expression designate that expression's sense, so that '<that man over there>' designates a first-level sense. The believer in a strict hierarchy will then have to say that every first-level sense uniquely determines a second level sense, and he will also have to say that it is a priori that the uniquely determined second-level sense refers to the first-level sense which determines it. For learnability of his language, he would also have to insist on corresponding axioms relating all other pairs of adjacent levels. With these resources in place, he can account for the validity of the inference, provided he is prepared to attribute tacit knowledge of these axioms to ordinary thinkers.

The resulting account does, though, stretch credibility. The fundamental problem is that it seems to be operating with more distinctions than there are differences. This comes out in three ways.

(a) The special properties attributed by the strict hierarchy theorist to his second-level sense would be explained if the first-level sense were simply to be used again, as the Redeployment Claim holds, in oblique contexts. If the advocate of a strict hierarchy means more than can be accounted for by the Redeployment Claim, I do not know what the additional unexplained material might be. If he does not, he may not have any substantive dispute with the Redeployment Claim.

(b) In other examples in which we draw the distinction between an entity (such as the planet Venus) and the various ways of thinking of it (as the Evening Star, as *that planet* given in perception, and so forth), the distinction is forced by reflection on the nature of the mental states which employ those various different ways of thinking, and by the semantical properties of the sentences in which we describe those states. Such motivations seem to be lacking in the distinction between a first-level thought and the proposed canonical sense of that thought which, according to the hierarchy theorist, is required in a theory of second-order ascriptions. In fact, that is to understate the case. Reflection on second-order cases suggests positively that we precisely must not draw the distinction in the second-order cases in question. This moral is implicit in the earlier discussion of particular modes of presentation, but it is also worth reflecting on complete thoughts. Let us take an example of a second-order attribution, drawn from Tyler Burge's discussion of the hierarchy (1979):

(4) Igor believes Bela believes Opus 132 is a masterpiece.

According to the hierarchy theorist, in specifying Igor's belief in (4), we make reference to a certain mode of presentation of (if you like, to a means of ascribing) the belief content which Igor ascribes to Bela, and this is to be distinguished from the content *Opus 132 is a masterpiece* itself. This seems to me an unintuitive description of the ascription. It seems to me that for (4) to be true, Igor must be thinking that one of Bela's beliefs has the content *Opus 132 is a masterpiece*, and in thinking of this content, Igor is employing exactly the same content in thoughts as Bela would if he were to think that Opus 132 is a masterpiece. It is not at all as if Igor is thinking of the content in some indirect way as the first content asserted on such-and-such page of Joseph Kerman's book. If we should distinguish senses only where facts about epistemic possibility or cognitive significance require it, then we should not in these examples postulate a further canonical sense of the content *Opus 132 is a masterpiece*.

(c) Correlatively, the theorist of a strict hierarchy will give an implausibly elaborate account of what certainly appear to be very straightforward inferences. The following certainly seems to be a valid inference:

(4) Igor believes Bela believes Opus 132 is a masterpiece.

(5) It is true that Opus 132 is a masterpiece.

Therefore,

(6) Something which Igor believes Bela believes is true.

On the Redeployment account, this is a straightforward inference by existential generalization, since one and the same content is mentioned, by the same means, in (4) and(5). If 'p' is a variable over Fregean contents, if we use pointed brackets as before, and use '^' for predicational combination of senses, then on the Redeployment account, the inference in question can he regimented thus:

(7) believes (Igor,<Bela>^<believes>^<Opus 132 is a masterpiece>)

(8) true (<Opus 132 is a masterpiece>)

Therefore.

(9) ∃p (believes (Igor, <Bela>^<believes>^p) & true (p)).

The theorist of the strict hierarchy has to offer something much more complicated, since for him (4) involves reference to a mode of presentation of the content <Opus 132 is a masterpiece>, rather than to the content itself. There would have to be additional principles which either state, or entail, a connection between the truth of the content a given under the proposed canonical mode of presentation and the holding of (8). When we are dealing with inferences analogous to (4)–(6), but with multiple embeddings, there will have to be even more additional principles. My own view is that the inference from (4) and (5) to (6) is what it seems to be, a simple application of existential generalization which does not need validation by special additional premisses.

Problems have been raised in the literature for languages of the sort I have defended in tandem with the Redeployment Claim, that is for languages containing expressions whose reference relation is relativized to a linguistic context. These critical arguments are important, both for their intrinsic interest, and for their relevance to the sustainability of the position I have been developing. Since these arguments involve slightly technical issues in philosophical logic and the philosophy of language, and I do not want to lose the interest of those whose main concern is the philosophy of mind. I have placed discussion of them in an Appendix.

(c) Powers of Relational Explanation

A propositional attitude with a first-order content can, when the thinker is in suitable auxiliary states, explain some relational fact about the thinker. A person's having a belief that water is thus-and-so may explain her acting in such-and-such way in relation to quantities of water: a person's seeing that the exit is in *that* direction may explain his walking in that direction: and so on. What is explained in these cases is not just a bodily movement nonrelationally characterized. What is explained is the occurrence of an action with certain relational, environmental properties. These explanations support counterfactuals formulated in environmental terms. It is plausible that the ability to explain relational states of affairs in suitable circumstances is a constitutive property of attitudes to first-order contents. It is also plausible that particular relational explananda are traceable back to the presence of particular conceptual constituents of first-order contents. These are the themes that I developed in a paper 'Externalist Explanation' (1993a). I will henceforth be taking it for granted that such links between relational explananda and first-order contents do indeed exist.

If the Redeployment Claim is correct, we would expect these powers of relational explanation to be elevated to second-order attitudes; and this does seem to be the case. If you think that your friend believes that that (perceptually presented) man is dangerous, and have reason to avoid anyone your friend believes to be dangerous, then we have enough, given a normal background, to explain your avoiding the perceptually presented man.

In that example, your reasoning leading up to your avoidance of the man would run thus. From the premiss that your friend believes that that man is dangerous, you export, and infer that that man is believed by your friend to be dangerous; and then he falls within your reasons which apply to anyone your friend believes to be dangerous. So in this case, the powers of relational explanation associated with the second-order belief about your friend's belief operate via your making an exportation inference, of the sort discussed in (b) above, from your second-order attitude. I conjecture that this phenomenon is quite general. That is, I conjecture that the way in which the powers of relational explanation associated with particular concepts are elevated to second-order attitudes is by way of the thinker's making exportation inferences from second- to first-order attitudes. These first-order attitudes then display the powers of relational explanation already noted. If this conjecture is true, it has the following consequence. Once we have properly accounted for the powers of relational explanation distinctive of certain concepts in first-order attitudes, and have also properly accounted for the validity of the appropriate class of exportation inferences, then we have the powers of relational explanation of the same concepts in second-order attitudes as a by-product.

These points about relational explananda have a special bearing when the second-order attitude is a self-ascription. Suppose you self-ascribe the belief that person over there is French. We can imagine that you are an official acting on the instruction 'Check again on the nationality of anyone you believe to be French'. In this context, your second-order belief can explain your going over to meet that person – a relational explanandum. On this approach, in having second-order knowledge about your own knowledge, you know which things and properties your knowledge is about *in as strong a sense* as that in which you know which person is speaking with all American accent, when you know that that person over there is speaking with an American accent. In manifesting that first-order knowledge about the world, you can identify the person in question by pointing to him, or by engaging in other actions which are explained as bearing certain relations to that person, and no other. But the ability to identify in this sense is also present when the concept *that man over there* features in second-order attitudes too. Everything that you can do in the first-order case you can also do in the second-order case, when you have to answer the question 'Which person around here is the one whom you believe to be French?'. You can point to the person, or generally engage in actions which are explained as bearing certain relations to that person. It is a consequence of the present account that there is no question of a thinker's knowing the material, external objects of his second-order attitudes only indirectly, or obliquely.

(d) The Most Direct Way of Thinking of a Concept

The Redeployment Claim also entails the intuitive proposition that the most direct way of thinking of any given concept is available only to those who already possess the concept and can use it in thinking about the world.

There is a most direct way of thinking about a concept, a way which is intimately related to what makes it the concept it is. It is this most direct way one employs when one thinks of the concept *square* as the concept *square*, rather than as the concept meeting such-and-such conditions. It is natural to compare this with thought about natural numbers. There is a most direct way of thinking of a particular natural number, as when one thinks of the number four as the number four, rather than as the number of the horsemen of the Apocalypse, or as the solution to a certain equation. A plausible account of the intimate relation between this most direct way of thinking of the number four and what makes the number four the number it is would run thus. In thinking of the number as four, one is thinking of it as having a certain place in a particular omega-sequence used for counting. In particular, one is thinking of it as the successor of three, which in turn is thought of as the successor of two...&c.. Possessing the concept *four* involves, as a constitutive matter, implicitly knowing that for there to be four Fs, there must he a one–one relation between the Fs and the given omega-sequence up to the place occupied by the number four. This implicit knowledge is manifested in the counting procedures the thinker employs for determining whether there are four objects of a given kind.

If the Redeployment Claim is correct, the same concept *square* is employed in thinking *the concept square* as is employed in making first-order judgments about the world involving the concept *square*. To make such first-order judgments, one must meet the conditions required for possessing the concept *square*, and this (in my own view) is what individuates the concept *square*. So only those who meet the condition for possessing the concept can think of it in the most direct way, as the concept *square*. The point applies generality to the operator 'the concept___'. Consider someone who has mastered talk about concepts in general, and the definite description operator. The only further ability he then needs to understand the complex term 'the concept ___', where '___' is replaced by some words expressing a concept, and to be thinking thereby of that concept in the most direct possible why, is the capacity to use the expression ___ in first-order judgments in which it expresses that concept.

V

Redeployment and Scepticism about Knowledge of Content. The Redeployment Claim and the other principles I have defended jointly contribute to an explanation of the near-infallibility of a thinker's knowledge of the content of his conscious beliefs. Suppose you were an Evil Demon, aiming to deceive someone – Descartes, let us say – about the content of his own conscious beliefs. What strategies might you adopt?

Since you can tamper with Descartes' memories, you might start by giving him false memories of his earlier judgments. If yesterday Descartes judged that p, you might now give him the false memory impression that yesterday he judged the different content that q. There are then two cases which may arise. Descartes may take his present apparent memory of yesterday's judgment at face value in forming his present first-order beliefs. When asked whether he believes that q, he will also reply that he does; and in this case he will be right in so replying. The other case is that in which, although he has the apparent memory of judging that q, he works out for himself again whether or not it is the case that p. If he is starting from the same resources as yesterday, he again reaches the belief that p, and will correspondingly be willing to self-ascribe it. If he withholds belief in p because of his apparent memory of reaching the belief that q, he will also then not self-ascribe the belief that p. In none of these cases will self-ascription come apart from the first-order beliefs which are currently held. So tampering with the memories of past judgments will not, in these cases, help you, as Evil Demon, deceive Descartes about the content of his current conscious beliefs.

You also have the power to make Descartes think there has been no interruption in his consciousness, when in fact that there has been a massive gap, with transportation or massive changes to his environment. You could certainly make false belief that the liquid in the lakes around him and falling from the skies is water. He would also be wrong in thinking that his beliefs to the effect that water is thus-and-so are beliefs about that liquid which is around him. But none of this would make false Descartes' belief that his first-order beliefs are belief about water – for they still are (to begin with).

You as Evil Demon have difficulties of principle in carrying through the project. Whatever changes you make in Descartes or his environment, as long as he follows the practice of self-ascribing a belief on the basis of one of his conscious, accepted states which represents the content *p* as correct, and reuses the same content *p* in his self-ascription, then any self-ascription so reached will be correct. Your activities as Evil Demon may or may not have altered Descartes' first-order beliefs, but his second-order beliefs will march in step with his first-order beliefs if his self-ascriptions follow this procedure. Not to be willing to follow the procedure is to lose the concept of belief, if the transparency principle is right. If all this is so, certain kinds of errors about the content of your conscious beliefs are indeed impossible. This reasoning is entirely consistent with an externalist theory of the conceptual content of your beliefs.

The question then rises: why should it have ever been thought that externalist theories of content are liable to make a thinker's knowledge of the content of his own thoughts particularly problematic, or even to lead to doubt about the possibility of ordinary self-knowledge? There are several possible reasons.

One reason is a questionable application of a principle about knowledge familiar from discussions of scepticism. I quote Anthony Brueckner's formulation of the principle, where H and SK are hypotheses: 'If my evidence and reasons (and whatever other considerations are available) do not favor H over SK, then I do not have justification for rejecting SK; hence I do not know that not-SK' (1994, p. 333). (I should emphasize this formulation occurs in Brueckner's discussion of a position which attempts to apply this principle to knowledge of contents; Brueckner is not endorsing the application.) Those influenced by this line of thought then argue that an ordinary thinker's evidence, introspections, and everything else he learns about the world, can fail to favour the hypothesis that he is thinking that some water is dripping over the hypothesis that he is thinking that some twater is dripping. They conclude that an ordinary thinker does not know that he is not thinking that some twater is dripping.

This sceptical line of thought is encouraged by those versions of externalism about content which are cast in modal terms, and which further take externalism to be the doctrine that molecule-for-molecule counterparts who are also phenomenologically and introspectively indistinguishable may nevertheless possess different concepts, and have attitudes with different intentional contents.[7] These versions of externalism beg the question against those who think that externally individuated intentional

---

[7] For a characterization of externalism along these lines, see Brueckner (1990), p.447.

contents enter the content of conscious states, and thereby help to specify the subjective character of those states. Take anyone who thinks that at least one externally individuated concept, be it a demonstrative way of thinking of a direction, a shape concept, or any other, enters the intentional content of a conscious state, and helps to specify what it is like to be in that state. Such a theorist is committed to disagreeing with formulations of externalism which always require the possibility of phenomenological sameness across externally different thinkers. There are also, these externalists will note, independent reasons for preferring constitutive to modal formulations of what is involved in externalism (Peacocke 1993a). Finally these externalists may wonder whether the sceptic will end up committed to the implausible view that intentional content is wholly irrelevant to the subjective nature of conscious states.

These points are hardly going to end the argument, though. The sceptic about ordinary knowledge of states with externally individuated intentional contents can certainly refine his position to say which aspects of intentional content do, and which do not, contribute to the subjective character of a mental state. This sceptic can introduce the concept of *relational similarity* of a pair of concepts. For any concept employed by a thinker, there is what we can call its *reference-fixing relation*. This is the three-place relation – between the thinker who employs the concept, the concept itself, and its reference – in virtue of which the concept, as employed by the thinker, has that reference. (In some cases a time-relativization also has to be introduced into the reference-fixing relation.) Concepts *C* and *D* are relationally similar if their reference-fixing relations are identical. Distinct concepts can have the same reference-fixing relations, and it is plausible that the concepts *water* and *twater* comprise just such a pair. Though these concepts and the liquids to which they refer are distinct, the relation which has to hold between a person on twin-earth and the twater around him for him to be thinking of it as twater is exactly the same as the relation that has to hold between a person on earth and the water around him for him to be thinking of it as water. These relations can take into account that twater looks, tastes and feels just like water. It is a fair comment that there will be plenty of theoretical reasons for which we need to employ the notion of relational similarity, notably in explaining patterns of epistemic possibility shared by thoughts with relationally similar constituents. So any objector to this sceptic should not simply reject the notion of relational similarity of intentional contents: They are relationally similar if they are built up from relationally similar constituents, by the same modes of composition.

Our sceptic will now say that an ordinary thinker's evidence and reasons do not favour the hypothesis that he is thinking that p, rather than the hypothesis that he is thinking that q, where p and q are relationally similar intentional contents. In step with this position, he is likely to assert that phenomenological facts cannot discriminate between intentional contents in the same equivalence class defined by the relational similarity. If he proceeds this way, the sceptic can agree that intentional content contributes to phenomenological character, but not in any way which cuts finer than relational similarity.

Actually this sceptic's position is still threatened by instability, for it is not at all clear that there will not still be externalist elements in reference-fixing relations themselves. But let us bracket that important issue in this paper. We can just address the question: is this sceptic right in holding that an ordinary thinker's evidence and reasons do not settle whether he is thinking water-thoughts or is rather thinking twater-thoughts?

I cannot see any good reasons for the sceptic's view, and several against. It is true that for all an ordinary, unscientific thinker knows, it may be XYZ rather than H_2O around him. But from the fact that he doesn't know it is not H_2O, it does not follow that he does not know it is water. He can know it is water without knowing that it is H_2O. If we try to capture the content of beliefs and knowledge by genuinely possible worlds, this may seem problematic, since it seems that a world in which it is not H_2O around him is consistent with his beliefs. My own view is that this is just another argument against trying to capture essentially epistemic notions by metaphysically possible worlds in so simple a fashion. (After all, a world in which it is not H_2O around him is also a world in which it is not water around him, and is that supposed to be consistent with his beliefs?) The case seems entirely analogous to other unproblematic examples for singular terms and objects. You may know your personal physician, Dr. J. White, having met him on many occasions. You acquire many beliefs to the effect that Dr. White is thus-and-so. You may come to learn that Dr. White is one of two twin brothers, John and James, without knowing which of them he is. The fact that I do not know whether it is John or James that I have met does not entail that I do not know that I have met Dr. White.

A normal thinker's knowledge of the content of his own beliefs will ordinarily be reached by endorsing the content of some conscious state which represents a certain content as correct; or will be reached by the route described earlier as not involving any intermediate conscious state; or will result from the thinker's making up his mind at the time. But if pressed, there is a great deal a normal thinker could say in answer to a challenge about whether his beliefs really are beliefs to the effect that water is thus-and-so. He knows (a) that it is the water that he has drunk, seen in showers, rivers, and lakes; and he knows (b) that it is the liquid to which he has stood in all these relations about which he has beliefs. He is in a position to know what is entailed by these known premises (a) and (b). But (a) and (b) together entail that he has beliefs that are about water (more strongly, are water-beliefs). If the thinker's knowledge of (a) is questioned, we have scepticism not just about the content of his attitudes, but about his knowledge of the world. The problem would not then be special to knowledge of the content of mental states. It is also hard to see why the thinker should not know (b). It does not amount to much more than an identity belief which is underwritten by his use of methods of belief-formation appropriate to a way of thinking of a liquid which involves a recognitional capacity. Even though his normal knowledgeable self-ascriptions are not so based, there seems to be a great deal of evidence and many good reasons available to a thinker to establish that he has beliefs to the effect that water is thus-and-so.

There are at least two other reasons which may be influential in producing the impression that externalism about content must lead to scepticism about the possibility of ordinary self-knowledge. One is the idea that we can have noninferential knowledge only of the vehicles, and not the contents of our beliefs. Another is the fear that if ordinary self-knowledge is possible, then there must be a priori arguments from knowledge of content to substantive conclusions about the world around the thinker. All I can do here is to state dogmatically that the first of these ideas does not seem to me to be correct, it understates the extent of our noninferential self-knowledge and is probably based on overly restrictive models of self-knowledge; while the second does not seem to me an objection, but rather to point positively to a promising line for developing contemporary forms of transcendental arguments.

APPENDIX
VI

Redeployment and Truth-Conditional Semantics. Tyler Burge's paper 'Frege and the Hierarchy' (1979) contains one of the most illuminating and thorough treatments of the Fregean hierarchy. In the final section of

'Frege and the Hierarchy', Burge argues that there are obstacles to giving a systematic theory of truth-conditions for languages which formally embody the approach to multiple embedding advocated in the main body of this paper, i.e. one which embraces a context-sensitive relation of denotation (an approach which Burge calls 'Method I'). In this Appendix, I will argue that the problems with the particular truth theories discussed by Burge are not traceable to context-sensitive relations of denotation, but to inessential features of the particular truth-theory he presents. Once we alter these features, the problems disappear. These are not, or not just, matters of detail: some general lessons about sense and truth-conditional theories emerge from reflection on these issues.

Suppose we are concerned with an object-language L in which we can express the content of

(4) Igor believes that Bela believes that Opus 132 is a masterpiece.

Burge considers the following set of axioms. (I have changed the notation slightly, but not in substantive ways.) We suppose a recursive specification of the class O of oblique contexts, and of the class T of direct contexts. A broadly Tarskian approach is followed, with 'val(s, E, O)' meaning the assignment which infinite sequence s of objects makes to the expression E relative to the class of oblique contexts. Truth is satisfaction by all sequences. I use double inverted commas in place of Quine's corner quotes. Burge's axioms are then:

(a) $(x) (x = \text{val}(s,\text{“Igor}_L\text{”}, T) \equiv x = \text{Igor})$

(b) $\text{sat}(s, \text{“Believes}_L (e_1, e_2)\text{”}, T) \equiv \text{Believes}(\text{val}(s, e_1, T), \text{val}(s, e_2, O))$

(c) $\text{val}(s, \text{BelaL”}, O) = \text{sense}(\text{“BelaL”})$

(d) $\text{val}(s, \text{“Believes}_L, (e_1, c_2)\text{”}, O) =$
$$\text{sense}(\text{“Believes}_L\text{”}) \wedge \text{val}(s, e_1, O) \wedge \text{val}(s, e_2, O)$$

(e) $\text{val}(s, \text{“Opus 132}_L\text{”}, O) = \text{sense}(\text{“Opus 132}_L\text{”})$

(f) $\text{val}(s, \text{“Masterpiece}_L(e_1)\text{”}, O) = \text{sense}(\text{“Masterpiece}_L\text{”}) \wedge \text{val}(s, e_L, O)$.

We also assume the laws

(A) $\text{sense}(\text{“}e_1(e_2, e_3)\text{”}) = \text{sense}(e_1) \wedge \text{sense}(e_2) \wedge \text{sense}(e_3)$

(B) $\text{sense}(\text{“}e_1(e_2)\text{”}) \, \text{sense}(e_1) \wedge \text{sense}(e_2)$.

Suppose we want to prove from these axioms and laws some biconditional giving the truth condition of the sentence in this language L which expresses the same as (4). Burge notes that the best we can do is to prove this:

(10) sat (s, "Believes$_L$ (Igor$_L$, Believes$_L$(Bela$_L$, Masterpiece$_L$(Opus 132$_L$,)))") ≡
Believes(Igor, sense("Believes$_L$")^sense("Bela$_L$")^sense("Masterpiece$_L$")^
sense("Opus 132$_L$")).

Of (10) Burge says that although it 'may perhaps describe the truth conditions [of the object language sentence mentioned on its left-hand side –
CP], it does not "give" them' (1979, p. 277). I agree. The right-hand side
of (10) makes reference to the senses of the object-language expressions,
but since it does not say what these senses are, it cannot fully convey the
meaning of the object-language sentence which captures (4).

This result, though, should not surprise us, since nothing in the axioms
and laws (A), (B), and (a)–(f) says what those senses are either. Suppose
we were to adjoin such laws as these:

(g) sense("Bela$_L$") = <Bela>

(h) sense("Masterpiece$_L$") = <Masterpiece>

(i) sense("Opus 132$_L$") = <Opus 132>

(i) sense("Believes$_L$") = <Believes>.[8]

Here, it should be remembered, "<Bela>" is not a definite description of a
sense – it does not mean "the sense of "Bela" in English". (If it were to, (g)
would be a triviality, which it is not.) Rather, we should say this: concerning the sense Σ, which is in fact the sense of "Bela" in English, to understand "<Bela>" one must know that "<Bela>" refers to Σ. (Compare
David Kaplan's "meaning quotes" in his paper "Quantifying In" (1969).)
The same applies to (h)–(j). With the addition of the axioms (g)–(j), it is
just a matter of identity-substitutions to move from (10) to a theorem
which genuinely gives the truth-conditions of the L-regimentation of (4):

(11) sat (s, "Believes$_L$ (Igor$_L$, Believes$_L$(Bela$_L$, Masterpiece$_L$(Opus 132$_L$)))") ≡

---

[8] "Believes$_L$" of the object language and "Believes" of the metalanguage of this theory
have, as Burge notes, different substitution properties. It does not follow that they express
different senses. They do not: They both express the same mode of presentation of a relation between thinkers and contents (Thoughts). They differ just in the additional conventions which govern they way in which one of the expressions with which they are combined
picks out the content (Thought) in question. To fully understand either one of these
expressions, you have to know not only which sense it expresses, but those additional conventions too.

Believes(Igor,<Believes>^<Bela$_L$>^Masterpiece$_L$>^
<Opus 132$_L$>).

Hence it seems to me that the agreed inadequacy of (A), (B) and (a)–(f) as a semantical theory of L is traceable to their failure to include any statement of what the senses of the L-expressions are, rather than to the distinctive, non-hierarchical way in which L handles oblique contexts.

It would, though, be unsatisfactory to let the matter rest with those observations, and for two reasons. The first reason is that for anyone who (like me) accepts a truth-conditional theory of sense, explicit attribution of senses to expressions in a semantical theory should be connected in that theory with the contribution of those expressions to truth-conditions. It would be bizarre to believe in a truth-conditional theory of sense, to give a truth-conditional semantical theory for a particular language, but then in the same theory to add explicit attributions of sense to object-language expressions as an 'add-on', unconnected with the theory of truth and reference. Yet that is what I have done so far, in supplementing the semantical theory for L with axioms (g) through (j).

The second reason we must say more is that the semantical theory does not fully respect the point made in the main text of the paper, that when you understand a set of expressions as they occur in ordinary, direct contexts, and you have an understanding of "Believes$_L$", you have an understanding of "Believes$_L$" applied to sentences built up from those expressions which are understood as they occur in direct contexts. This is an entirely general point, not specific to just some subclass of expressions, and there should be a correspondingly general axiom in the theory of truth. The case-by-case listing we have in axioms (c) through (f) does not capture this generality.

We can address both these problems simultaneously by the following means. We replace (c)-(f) with the single, intuitive and general axiom (c*), which says that for any sequence and for any expression, the assignment by a sequence to an expression relative to an oblique context is its sense:

(c*) val(s, E, O) = sense(E).

We then also have the following rules of proof, SP and SN. SP treats atomic predicates:

SP   For any n-place atomic predicate F, if it is an axiom that sat(s, "F(e$_1$,...,e$_n$)") ≡ A(val(s, e$_1$, T,..., val(s, e$_n$,T)),
then we can infer
sense(F) = <A>

SN does the same for names:

SN For any name N, if it is an axiom that
val(s, N, T) = C,
then we can infer
sense(N) = <C>.

Similarly for opacity-inducing operators like "Believes" (here just for the sake of clarity of illustration I consider the restricted case in which we have one transparent position and one opaque position):

S$ For any operator $, if it is an axiom that
sat(s, "$(e₁, e₂)") ≡ W(val(s, e₁, T), val(s, e₂, O))
then we can infer
sense($) = <W>.

If the axioms of a truth theory have been selected by proper application of some procedure which ensures that the truth-theory is interpretational, then SP, SN and S$ will be sound rules. (In fact, that remark is little more than a restatement of what it means for a truth theory to be interpretational.) There will need to be analogous rules for quantifiers, connectives and other operators in more complex languages.

With (c*) in place of (c)–(f), together with SP, SN, S$ and the other axioms, it is a straightforward matter to derive the desired truth-condition (11). As required, this is a derivation in a theory which treats its explicit assignments of sense as derivative from some canonical assignments of contributions to truth-conditions.

There will also be a general metatheorem provable for truth-theories which adjoin explicit assignments of sense in the way just advocated, that is in a way which includes an appropriate set of rules like SP, SN, S$ and their ilk. The general metatheorem states this: if there is in the theory a canonical proof of a T-sentence of the form

True(S) ≡ *p*

then concerning the sense <*p*>, there will be some description σ of <*p*> for which it will he a theorem that

sense(S) = σ

Theories for which we have such a metatheorem embody precisely Frege's insight in the *Grundgesetze*: the insight that the sense of an indicative sentence is the thought that a certain condition is fulfilled, viz. precisely that condition which the reference-rules for its constituents determine as the condition under which it is true. That condition, for any given sentence S, is just the content p for which there is a canonical proof of the biconditional

$$\text{True}(S) \equiv p.$$

I do not pretend that the notion of sense used in this Appendix is unproblematic. On the contrary, I agree that it needs extensive defence, and that it remains too abstract until it is taken in combination with a substantive theory of grasp of sense. But the theorist of the strict Fregean hierarchy also simply makes use of the notion of sense too. All I have tried to do in this Appendix is argue that there are no insuperable problems unique to Method I, that of context-dependent reference relations, that prevent us from meeting the requirement of giving a semantical theory for languages like L.

REFERENCES

Brueckner, A. 1990. Scepticism about Knowledge of Content. *Mind* 99: 44–51.

——. 1994. Knowledge of Content and Knowledge of the World. *Philosophical Review* 103: 327–43.

Burge, T. 1979. Frege and the Hierarchy. *Synthese* 40: 265–81.

——. 1988. Individualism and Self-Knowledge. *Journal of Philosophy* 85: 649–63. Chapter 4 in this volume.

——. 1993. Content Preservation. *Philosophical Review* 102: 457–88.

——. 1996. Our Entitlement to Self-Knowledge. *Proceedings of the Aristotelian Society* XCVI: 91–116. Chapter 15 in this volume.

Carnap, R. 1956. *Meaning and Necessity: A Study in Semantics and Modal Logic.* Chicago: Chicago University Press.

Davidson, D. 1984. Theories of Meaning and Learnable Languages, repr. in his *Inquiries into Truth and Interpretation.* Oxford: Oxford University Press.

Dummett, M. 1973. *Frege: Philosophy of Language.* London: Duckworth.

Evans, G. 1982. *The Varieties of Reference*, ed. J. McDowell. Oxford: Oxford University Press.

Kaplan, D. 1969. Quantifying In. In *Words and Objections*, ed. D. Davidson and J. Hintikka. Dordrecht: Reidel.

McDowell, J. 1994. *Mind and World.* Cambridge, MA: Harvard University Press.

Moran, R. 1988. Making Up Your Mind: Self-Interpretation and Self-Constitution. *Ratio* 1: 135–51.

Peacocke, C. 1992. *A Study of Concepts.* Cambridge, MA: MIT Press.

———. 1993a. Externalist Explanation. *Proceedings of the Aristotelian Society* XCIII: 203–30.

———. 1993b. How are A Priori Truths Possible? *European Journal of Philosophy* 1: 175–99.

Sellars, W. 1963. Empiricism and the Philosophy of Mind. repr in *Science, Perception and Reality.* London: Routledge.

Stone, T. and M. Davies. 1996. The Mental Simulation Debate: A Progress Report. In *Theories of Theories of Mind*, eds. P. Carruthers and P. K. Smith. Cambridge, UK: Cambridge University Press.

Part VI: Externalism, Self-Knowledge and Memory

17

Social Externalism, Self-Knowledge, and Memory

Peter Ludlow

In Ludlow (1995), I argued that for an externalist, particularly a social externalist, slow-switching should be rather commonplace. Slow-switching (introduced by Burge (1988)) occurs when an agent unknowingly moves between linguistic communities and thereby (unknowingly) adopts the linguistic norms of the new community. So, for example, an agent who is unaware of the individuating conditions of 'chicory' (save that it is a bitter leafy green vegetable) will defer to certain members of his linguistic community for those individuating conditions. The agent may, however, come to defer to new individuals, unaware that those new individuals have altogether different individuating conditions for 'chicory'.

Paul Boghossian (1989) has argued that the possibility of slow-switching can be used to show the incompatibility of externalism and self-knowledge. For example, it appears possible for an agent S to know his thoughts at time *t*, forget nothing, yet at some time later than *t* (having been informed of the possibility or prevalence of slow-switching) be unable to say what the contents of his thoughts were at *t*. As Boghossian argues,

> The only explanation, I venture to suggest, for why S will not know tomorrow what he is said to know today, is not that he has forgotten but that he never knew. Burge's self-verifying judgments do not constitute genuine knowledge. What other reason is there for why our slowly transported thinker will not know tomorrow what he is said to know directly and authoritatively today? (Boghossian 1989)

At this level of abstraction the argument is breathtakingly simple:

(1) If S forgets nothing, then what S knows at t_1, S knows at t_2,

(2) S forgot nothing,

(3) S does not know that P at t_2;

(4) therefore, S does did not know that P at t_1.

The natural place to focus an attack is on premise (3), and indeed, a number of efforts have been aimed at undermining just this premise, but for the most part it seems to me that these attempts have fallen short (see for example (Ludlow 1995)).

In this note I want to suggest an alternative line of attack against Boghossian's argument from slow-switching and memory. In particular, I will argue that Boghossian's argument turns on an individualistic assumption about the nature of memory – an assumption that the careful social externalist would not accept. In effect, I will argue that the weak premise in Boghossian's argument is premise (1).

What should an externalist say about memory? It seems natural for the externalist to reason that if the contents of our mental states are determined by external conditions, then the contents of our memories are subject to the same external conditions. Accordingly, it is possible to construct twin cases in which two physiologically identical agents have different memories (say one has memories of drinking water, and one has memories of drinking twater).

Likewise, if (following Burge (1979)) the contents of our mental states are determined by our social environment, it is natural to suppose that the contents of our memories will depend upon our social environment. So, for example, the memory I have of eating chicory in my youth will be a memory about chicory, even if I remain unclear about the individuating conditions of chicory (e.g. if I know only that it is a bitter tasting leafy green vegetable). This is so, for I am prepared to defer to the members of my linguistic community for the content of 'chicory' and this deference applies likewise to my memories.

Now comes the interesting question. Is the content of my memory fixed at the time of my initial chicory encounter, or is it fixed many years later when I recall that encounter? The consistent social externalist is bound to say that the content of a memory is fixed at the time recollection takes place – for it is the embedding circumstances of that memory which are crucial to the fixing of its content. The idea that there be some content which is determined at some initial time and then remains frozen up to some later moment of recollection seems wrongheaded. After all, what would it mean to say that the contents of our memories are fixed by our social environment if in fact those contents, once fixed, are totally inert to all environmental changes?

This view of memory, although natural for a social externalist, has strong consequences. It implies that the contents of our memories may well shift over time as the fabric of our linguistic community changes. So, for example, changes could take place in my linguistic community (unnoticed by me) in which the individuating conditions of chicory will shift underneath me. Early memories of a single chicory experience may have different contents from later memories of the same experience. Notice that these shifts in content take place without my learning anything new about chicory, or forgetting anything about chicory. They are simply changes in content due to changes in my environment.

The same applies to my memories of particular episodes of self-knowledge. I may one day think that chicory is bitter. Years later, having come to appreciate chicory, I may recall having had that initial uncharitable thought about chicory. But notice that that recollection will have its contents fixed by *current* environmental conditions. As those environmental conditions shift, the content of my memory of this second-order mental episode will shift (just as the contents of memories of first order thoughts shift).

Turning now to Boghossian's argument, it is immediately apparent where he missteps. Even if I am informed that the content of 'chicory' has changed because of changes in my social environment (in effect, that I have become a unwitting victim of slow-switching) it does nothing to undermine my self-knowledge. The changes need not concern me, for the content of my memory is determined by *current* environmental conditions.

Speaking directly to the argument, let's say that at time t_1 I know that I am thinking that chicory is bitter. Suppose that at time t_2 later than t_1, I recall that initial thought about chicory, but, due to undetected changes in my linguistic community, the content of my thoughts about chicory have shifted. Boghossian is arguably correct in asserting that I do not know at t_2 what I knew at t_1, but he is incorrect in supposing that "the only explanation" for this is that I "never knew" my thoughts in the first place. It is entirely consistent with the social externalist view of memory that I forgot nothing, but that the contents of my memories have nonetheless shifted. Indeed, this is not only *possible* according to social externalism, but given the prevalence of slow switching it should be a rather common state of affairs.[1]

REFERENCES

Boghossian, P. 1989. Content and Self-Knowledge. *Philosophical Topics* 17:5–26. Chapter 6 in this volume.

Burge, T. 1979. Individualism and the Mental. *Midwest Studies in Philosophy* 4:73–122. Chapter 2 in this volume.

————. 1988. Individualism and Self-Knowledge. *Journal of Philosophy* 85:649–63. Chapter 4 in this volume.

Ludlow, P. 1995. Externalism, Self-Knowledge, and the Prevalence of Slow-Switching. *Analysis* 55: 45–49. Chapter 12 in this volume.

---

[1] Tony Brueckner has correctly observed that in this essay I was careless in speaking of having chicory memory after the switch – post-switch memories are of course twicory memories. The talk of post-switch memories ought to be done in scare quotes ("chicory" memories) to reflect the shift in content. This of course leads to the question of whether they are the same memory at all – an issue taken up in subsequent essays in this volume.

18

Social Externalism and Memory: A Problem?

Peter Ludlow

In a recent paper (Ludlow 1995b) I argued that certain problems about social externalism and self-knowledge might be avoided if one adopted an externalist view about the nature of memory. Since then, Hofmann (1995) has observed that the view of memory I suggested itself gives rise to a number of unwelcome consequences. In this note, I want to comment on these alleged consequences, and to offer one possible solution. First, however, a brief review of the background literature may be in order.

Due to important papers by Burge (1988) and Putnam (1979), one of the leading issues in the philosophy of mind has been the question of whether the content of our mental states depends solely on facts about us in isolation (i.e. on what takes place in our heads), or whether the contents of our mental states depend at least in part on relations between ourselves and the environment. This latter view has come to be known as the doctrine of "externalism".

Much has been written in attempt to show that externalism in general is either true or false, and while this work has been useful at times, it seems to me that it is much more interesting to pursue some of the consequences of externalism (setting aside the question of its truth or falsity). One of the most interesting threads in this pursuit has been the question of what consequences externalism may have (if any) for the doctrine that we have a priori knowledge of our mental states.

To some authors it has appeared that externalism and a priori self-knowledge are incompatible. In their view, if externalism is correct then it follows that we shall have to investigate our environment to truly know the content of our mental states. For example, to know whether we are having water thoughts or twater (twin-earth "water") thoughts we may have to conduct an investigation into the chemical composition of the stuff we call 'water'. If this is the case, then there is little hope that we can hang onto the doctrine that we have a priori knowledge of our mental states.

There are a couple of possible answers to the above dilemma, both of which are consistent with the doctrine of externalism. The first is simply to give up the doctrine of a priori self-knowledge, and to argue that self-knowledge is in fact the product of a sometimes empirical investigation. On this view, argued for example by Martin (1994), knowledge of our mental states may be partial, and may be in error at times, but we are nevertheless in a kind of privileged relation towards our mental states because we are usually in a better position than others to investigate our own mental states.

Others have held that despite appearances there is no real tension between externalism and self-knowledge – that the doctrines are compatible. This line has been taken by Davidson (1987), Burge (1988), and by Heil (1988). Although there are important differences between their positions, there is one thread that connects them – the observation that a second-order thought (e.g. the thought that I am thinking that water is wet) will itself have its content fixed by the environment. Accordingly, my second-order thought will be either about a water thought or a twater thought depending upon my environmental conditions.

Several authors have challenged this compatibilist line, but for current purposes the challenge that interests me the most comes from Boghossian (1989). One of the arguments offered by Boghossian is that the possibility of slow-switching can be used to show the incompatibility of externalism and self-knowledge.

Slow-switching is a situation in which an agent unknowingly switches environments, and remains in the new environment long enough so that the new environment lays claim to the contents of the agent's mental states. To illustrate with a science fiction example, we can imagine an agent who is transported from Earth to Twin-Earth without knowing it. After sufficient time has passed on Twin-Earth, water thoughts should give way to twater thoughts.

Examples of slow-switching need not be restricted to crazy science fiction cases. Indeed, as I argued in (Ludlow 1995a) they may be altogether commonplace. To see this, just consider the case of someone who defers to his language community for the individuating conditions of the word 'chickory' and who moves from England to the United States without realizing that 'chickory' has a different meaning in those two locations. Then, as the agent continues to defer to his immediate language community, the content of the term 'chickory' will shift. Or consider the case of an agent who defers to his friends for the individuating conditions of the term 'bore'. As he moves among his circles of friends he may not realize that they attach rather different meanings to the term and thus he may not realize that the content of 'bore' has shifted beneath him. The agent has become an unwitting victim of slow-switching.

How can slow-switching be used to undermine the compatibility of externalism and self-knowledge? Boghossian observes that it appears possible for an agent S to know his thoughts at time t, forget nothing, yet at some time later than t (having been informed of the possibility or prevalence of slow-switching) be unable to say what the contents of his thoughts were at t. As Boghossian argues,

> The only explanation, I venture to suggest, for why S will not know tomorrow what he is said to know today, is not that he has forgotten but that he never knew. Burge's self-verifying judgments do not constitute genuine knowledge. What other reason is there for why our slowly transported thinker will not know tomorrow what he is said to know directly and authoritatively today? (1989)

In Ludlow (1995b), I reconstructed the above argument as follows:

(1) If S forgets nothing, then what S knows at t1, S knows at t2

(2) S forgot nothing

(3) S does not know that P at t2

(4) therefore, S does did not know that P at t1

The question naturally arises as to where one might best attack this argument, and most efforts have centered on premise (3), but in previous work (see for example Ludlow (1995a)) I have been skeptical of efforts to center the attack here. As an alternative, in Ludlow (1995b) I argued that that Boghossian's argument turns on an individualistic assumption about the nature of memory, and I argued further that this is an assumption that the careful social externalist would not accept. In doing so, I was suggesting that the weak premise Boghossian's argument is premise (1).

What should an externalist say about memory? It seems natural for the externalist to reason that if the contents of our mental states are determined by external conditions, then the contents of our memories are subject to the same external conditions. Accordingly, it is possible to construct twin cases in which two physiologically identical agents have different memories (say one has memories of drinking water, and one has memories of drinking twater).

The reasoning here is that if (following Burge (1979)) the contents of our mental states are determined by our social environment, it is natural to suppose that the contents of our memories will depend upon our social environment. As we move from one environmental condition to another (perhaps without even noticing the environmental change), the contents of our memories will shift accordingly. In Ludlow (1995b), I applied this line of reasoning to Boghossian's argument in the following manner.

> ...let's say that at time t1 I know that I am thinking that arugula is bitter. Suppose that at time t2 later than t1, I recall that initial thought about arugula, but, due to undetected changes in my linguistic community, the content of my thoughts about arugula have shifted. Boghossian is arguably correct in asserting that I do not know at t2 what I knew at t1, but he is incorrect in supposing that "the only explanation" for this is that I "never knew" my thoughts in the first place. It is entirely consistent with the social externalist view of memory that I forgot nothing, but that the contents of my memories have nonetheless shifted. Indeed, this is not only *possible* according to social externalism, but given the prevalence of slow switching it should be a rather common state of affairs.

So goes the argument, but Hofmann (1995) has observed that there are a number of peculiar consequences to this view of memory. The first problem is that this view of memory (in conjunction with the prevalence of slow-switching) seems to entail that one can seldom remember the thought one had earlier. As Hofmann puts the problem:

> ...if [the circumstances of recollection] determine memory content, then memory turns into an empty, absurd faculty. This is so, since memory no longer can do what it is supposed to do, namely, to recall the very same thoughts one earlier on had entertained. If Peter had come to believe at t1 somehow that arugula only grows in mediterranian climate, and now, at t2, recalls this thought, then what he recol-

lects will not be the same thought about arugula, but some other thought about, say, tarugula – according to the newly adopted individuating conditions.

A second, related difficulty is that the externalist view of memory I proposed would undermine the important role that memory plays in epistemology.

Furthermore, and equally embarrassing, the truth values of the memories will have changed. So, for example, Peter's belief at t1 that arugula only grows in mediterranian climate will now, when recollected, turn into a falsehood. [...] For, at time t2 it will be a thought about tarugula which is a vegetable (let's assume) that grows only in tropical climates. Even worse, if Peter recollects that he had had, at t1, some arugula experience, then also this memory has turned by now into a falsehood, since it has become a memory-thought about tarugula which (let's assume) Peter never has had any direct encounter with. And, all of this has occurred without Peter being able to introspectively become aware of it. Memory, as social externalism will have it, has 'turned pseudo'. It is no longer a source of knowledge.

What can we say about these arguments? If memories are individuated by their contents, then there are in fact different memories at t1 and t2. And if slow switching is really as prevalent as I suggested in Ludlow (1995a), then one would have a kind of heraclitian theory of memory ("you can't have the same memory twice"). This is an exaggeration, of course. The key (serious) idea is that as you undergo environmental changes, you get different memories.

If the externalist takes this path, then the epistemological worries expressed by Hofmann evaporate. A single memory does not flip-flop back and forth from being true to false. Rather a single memory will be replaced by another memory having another content. Such memories, although possibly transient, would not be unreliable as sources of knowledge. To the contrary, there is no reason at all why they cannot be completely reliable in those environmental conditions in which they occur.

For example, suppose that at time t0 I come to know that water is wet. At time t1, before I shift environments, I may recall that water is wet. Later, at t2, due to undetected environmental changes, I may have the recollection that twater is wet. Is this second episode of memory less reliable than the first? It is difficult see why.

Of course it might seem easy to construct examples in which an initial true memory might be "switched" with a later false memory. Suppose that at t0 I am informed by a reliable source that water contains hydrogen. At t1 (before environmental changes) I recall that water contains hydrogen. Later, at t2 (after slow-switching), I now have the recollection that twater contains hydrogen. This new recollection contains false information of course – twater contains no hydrogen. So it appears that on the externalist theory of memory, memory can easily let us down.

But this line of reasoning is flawed. Slow-switching cases are by definition those cases in which my personal knowledge of the individuating conditions of water is not sufficient to distinguish it from twater. So by hypothesis in a switching case I would not know that water contains hydrogen. Indeed, if my knowledge of the individuating conditions of water were robust enough, I might rely on my memory to help me detect a change in environment. But such cases are not cases of genuine slow-switching.

There is, however, a residual objection. One might suppose that among other things, we rely upon memory to accurately record the contents of our past mental states. But then it seems that the externalist account of memory gives rise to a problem. Suppose that mental episodes at t1 and t2 are both memories of an initial mental episode which took place at time t0. If the contents of my memories at t1 and t2 are not the same (because of slow-switching), then clearly *both* of them cannot accurately record the content of the mental episode which took place at t0.

But is there any reason to suppose that it is the job of memory to "record the contents" of past mental episodes? On the face of it, this assumption begs the central question at issue. According to the externalist conception of memory that I have proposed, it is not the job of memory to record contents, but rather to provide information about past episodes relative to current environmental conditions. Even if there were a mechanism which could, as it were, freeze the contents of an initial mental episode and carry it in memory indefinitely, I'm not sure that it would have any utility. Indeed, it would be a way of preserving the content of a thought which we could no longer have (if, as the externalist supposes, the contents of our current thoughts are determined by our new environment). In short, to undermine the externalist view of memory one has to show that there is a greater epistemological advantage to a faculty that could record the contents of initial mental episodes than there is to a faculty which provides a priori information about past episodes, but relative to current environmental conditions. I for one cannot imagine what the advantage could be.

In sum, it seems to me that the externalist can easily parry Hofmann's objections that the externalist view of memory I proposed turns memory into a "empty absurd faculty," and it likewise seems to me that the externalist is not committed to the consequence that memory is "no longer a source of knowledge." It is certainly true that the nature of memory will be quite different on the externalist picture, and it is also true that there will be strong consequences for the role of memory in epistemology. But rather than being cause for rejecting the externalist view of memory, it seems to me that this is rather an excuse to pursue the consequences of externalism even further.

REFERENCES

Boghossian, P. 1989. Content and Self-Knowledge. *Philosophical Topics* 17:5–26. Chapter 6 in this volume.

Burge, T. 1979. Individualism and the Mental. *Midwest Studies in Philosophy* 4:73–122. Chapter 2 in this volume.

———. 1988. Individualism and Self-Knowledge. *Journal of Philosophy* 85:649–63. Chapter 4 in this volume.

Davidson, D. 1987. Knowing One's Own Mind. *Proceedings of the American Philosophical Association* 60: 441–58. Chapter 3 in this volume.

Heil, J. 1988. Privileged Access. *Mind* 98: 238–51. Chapter 5 in this volume.

Hofmann, F. 1995. Externalism and Memory. Manuscript, Dept. of Philosophy, University of Tuebingen, Germany.

Ludlow, P. 1995a. Externalism, Self-Knowledge, and the Prevalence of Slow-Switching. *Analysis* 55: 45–9. Chapter 12 in this volume.

———. 1995b. Social Externalism, Self-Knowledge, and Memory. *Analysis* 55: 157–9. Chapter 17 in this volume.

Martin, N. 1994. An Externalist Account of Self-Knowledge and Its Implications. PhD thesis, Dept. of Philosophy, SUNY Stony Brook.

Putnam, H. 1975. The Meaning of 'Meaning'. Pp. 131–93 in Gunderson ed., *Language, Mind and Knowledge. Vol. 7, Minnesota Studies in the Philosophy of Science*. Minneapolis: University of Minnesota Press.

19

Externalism and Memory

Anthony Brueckner

Introduction

Paul Boghossian has presented an influential argument against Tyler Burge's account of *basic self-knowledge*. This argument has been frequently discussed but, I think, never satisfactorily analyzed and answered. That is the task of this paper.[1]

According to Burge, the judgment expressed by my utterance of, e.g., 'I am thinking that water is clear' is *self-verifying*: "the content that I am making a judgment about is self-referentially fixed by the judgment itself".[2] Suppose that the expressed judgment is that I am thinking that water is clear. In order to be making that judgment at t, I must be thinking at t that water is clear. The second-order content of the judgment *contains* the first-order content in such a way as to make the judgment true.[3] Cases of basic self-knowledge, then, are those involving such self-verifying judgments.

Boghossian's argument against Burge's account focusses upon the fact that the account at best explains how one knows at t what one thinks at t: one thinks a thought of the form 'I am now thinking that P' at t, and this thought, since it is self-verifying, is guaranteed to be true. Boghossian

---

[1] For Burge's account, see Burge (1988). For Boghossian's argument, see Boghossian (1989).

[2] Burge (1988).

[3] According to Burge, the judgment expressed by 'I believe that water is clear' is not self-verifying, because it is possible to judge that I believe that water is clear without having that belief. But if I judge that I am thinking that water is clear, then it follows that I am at least entertaining the thought that water is clear.

attempts to exploit this limitation (acknowledged by Burge) in such a way as to show that Burge's account cannot even establish that one knows one's current thoughts.[4]

Boghossian's Argument

Let us now turn to Boghossian's argument. Following Burge's lead, Boghossian considers a 'slow-switching' scenario. Suppose that I have been stealthily switched from Earth to Twin Earth (viewed as two parts of a single possible world) and that I have resided there for many years. Assume further that *externalism* about the content of intentional mental states is correct, and that, accordingly, my word 'water' has come to express the concept *twater* (instead of the old Earthly concept).[5] The switches continue. I learn in a general way about what has been happening to me, without learning about the timing of the switches. Regarding some earlier time, I ask, 'Was I then thinking about water or twater?'. According to Burge, I may well "not know the answer". Burge continues,

> Here knowing may sometimes depend on knowing empirical background conditions. But such sophisticated questions about memory require a more complex story.[6]

Boghossian now argues as follows.

---

[4] Others have proposed related accounts of knowledge of one's beliefs, taking their lead from Donald Davidson's remark that "what determines the contents of thoughts also determines what the thinker thinks the contents are". See Davidson (1988). Some writers whose strategies are in the spirit of Davidson's remark: John Heil (1988); Christopher Peacocke (1996); Sydney Shoemaker (1994). See also Paul Boghossian (1992), and Brueckner (1995), for critical discussions of the Davidsonian strategy.

The basic idea of this strategy is that the content of a second-order belief expressed by my utterance of 'I believe that water is clear' covaries with the content of the first-order belief expressed by 'Water is clear'. Suppose, e.g., that the content of the first-order belief is *that twater is clear*, in virtue of my being in a Twin Earth environment. Then the content of the second-order belief, formed in that same environment, is *that I believe that twater is clear*. Since I do believe the first-order content, the second-order belief correctly represents me as believing what I in fact believe.

Boghossian's anti-Burge argument, if successful, would apply equally to the strategies that are in the spirit of the Davidsonian remark. This is because these 'covariation' strategies, like Burge's, at best yield knowledge about what one currently believes.

[5] I assume familiarity with externalism and its motivating thought experiments.

[6] See Burge (1988, p. 659).

For any given moment in the present, say t1, S is in a position to think a self-verifying judgment about what he is thinking at t1. By Burge's criteria, therefore, he counts as having direct and authoritative knowledge at t1 of what he is thinking at that time. But it is quite clear that tomorrow he won't know what he thought at t1. No self-verifying judgment concerning his thought at t1 will be available then. Nor, it is perfectly clear, can he know by any other non-inferential means. To know what he thought at t1 he must discover what environment he was in at that time and how long he had been there. But there is a mystery here. For the following would appear to be a platitude about memory and knowledge: if S knows that p at t1, and if at (some later time) t2, S remembers everything he knew at t1, then S knows that p at t2. Now, let us ask: *why* does S not know today whether yesterday's thought was a *water* thought or a *twater* thought? The platitude insists that there are only two possible explanations: either S has forgotten or he *never* knew. But surely memory failure is not to the point. In discussing the epistemology of …[externalistically] individuated content, we ought to be able to exclude memory failure by stipulation. It is not as if thoughts with …[externalistically] individuated contents might be easily known but difficult to remember. The only explanation, I venture to suggest, for why S will not know tomorrow what he is said to know today, is not that he has forgotten but that he never knew.[7]

Before seeing how this reasoning might be answered, we should clear up one small difficulty. Boghossian (following Burge) sets the times involved in the reasoning – t1 and t2 – at one day apart. This is rather odd, because Burge himself originally presents the slow-switching scenario in such a way that it takes far more than a single day for a switching-victim's concepts to shift.[8] So one need not wonder what one's concepts were *yesterday*: even if one has been switched overnight from one habitat to another, one's concepts are intact. Instead, the times t1 and t2 involved in Boghossian's argument must be chosen so that it makes sense to suppose that a concept-displacement could have occurred between the times. From now on, let us suppose that the reasoning focusses upon times that are appropriately far apart.

---

[7] See Boghossian (1989, pp. 22–3).

[8] See Burge (1988, pp. 652–3).

Actual Switching Versus Possible Switching

I will now turn to a response to Boghossian's reasoning which, I think, fails to get to the heart of the matter. Ted A. Warfield maintains that the reasoning does not establish that if externalism is true, then we lack self-knowledge.[9] This is because the reasoning only applies to situations in which thinkers are victims of slow-switching. Unless *our* actual situation involves slow-switching, the reasoning is simply irrelevant to the question of whether we have self-knowledge if externalism is true.

I think that Warfield has misconstrued the goal of Boghossian's argument. He is not trying to prove a conclusion about our general failure to know (given externalism) the contents of our thoughts. Rather, he is arguing that Burge's attempt to secure basic self-knowledge via the mechanism of self-verification is a failure.[10] In order to achieve his goal, it is sufficient to consider merely possible situations involving slow-switching (which may well be quite different from our actual situation). Suppose that Boghossian can show that in those situations, a thinker who starts out on Earth does not know at t, via Burge's mechanism, what he is thinking at t, in virtue of the *subsequent* switches and the application of the reasoning about memory. It would then be extremely odd to suppose that the mechanism of self-verification is *ever* sufficient to secure knowledge of what one is thinking when one is thinking it. Assume that in our actual situation, none of us has been switched. Burge could not reasonably hold that (a) we now (at t) possess basic self-knowledge via the mechanism of self-verification, but (b) if we are subsequently switched, it will no longer be true that we possessed basic self-knowledge at t. That seems to be a flat-out contradiction. Granting the success of Boghossian's reasoning about merely possible switching situations, the only alternative for Burge regarding the actual situation would appear to be this: if we are switched at some future time, then we never did have basic self-knowledge in the first place; if we are not switched, then we did have basic self-knowledge after all. I do not have an argument against this alternative, but it seems quite implausible. Future developments can determine whether my current belief about the future turns out to amount to knowledge, in virtue of the truth condition for knowing. Future developments can also determine whether I continue to possess some knowledge I currently possess.

---

[9] See Warfield (1992).

[10] If Boghossian is right, then all the covariation strategies will fail for the same reason.

For example, I may come to possess some information that defeats my current justification for believing something. But it seems implausible to suppose that future developments can determine whether my current belief about what I am currently thinking now amounts to knowledge. So if Boghossian's argument succeeds in showing that Burge's account of basic self-knowledge fails in switching situations, then it shows that the account fails in all situations.[11]

Shifting Memory-Content

Peter Ludlow provides an unsuccessful answer to Boghossian.[12] But the way in which it fails is illuminating and points us towards a better answer. Ludlow reconstructs Boghossian's argument from slow-switching as follows, letting 'P' stand for the proposition that S thinks at t1 that chicory is bitter:

(1) If S forgets nothing, then what S knows at t1, S knows at t2,

(2) S forgot nothing,

(3) S does not know that P at t2;

(4) therefore, S...did not know that P at t1.[13]

Ludlow grants (2) and (3). His strategy is to attack premise (1) by appealing to the point that if the contents of the thoughts S expresses using a

---

[11] Peter Ludlow has responded to Warfield by claiming that situations similar to slow-switching actually do occur. See Ludlow (1995a). The considerations in the text show that Boghossian's argument does not need the sort of protection offered by Ludlow.

[12] See Ludlow (1995b) where Ludlow tries to refute the Boghossian argument that he earlier defended from Warfield's objection.

[13] See Ludlow (1995b, p. 157). Boghossian's argument concerns propositional knowledge that is based on memory. Accordingly, I will focus upon memory-claims of the form 'S remembers that Φ' (as does Ludlow), rather than those of the form 'S remembers the F' (e.g., 'Charles remembers the address', and 'Maria remembers the shooting'). True memory-claims having the propositional form can be divided into two categories: (I) claims where the fact that makes Φ true involves an event that S perceived or introspected (e.g., 'S remembers that he hit the bullseye' and 'S remembers that he felt queasy'), and (II) claims where the pertinent fact was not perceived or introspected by S (e.g., 'S remembers that Lincoln was assassinated' and 'S remembers that the parallel postulate is independent of the rest of the Euclidean postulates'). The memory-claims under discussion in this paper are of category (I), but the principle (1) in the text is meant to apply to all propositional memory-claims.

term shift in virtue of slow-switching, then so do the contents of the *memories* S expresses using the term. For example, suppose that my uses of the term 'chicory' express the concept of chicory at t1, while at t2 (after slow-switching), my uses of 'chicory' express a different concept (say, the concept of *twicory*, whose application-conditions differ from those of the concept of chicory; the concepts apply to distinct sorts of leafy vegetable).[14] Ludlow says that, concomitantly, "Early memories of a single chicory experience may have different contents from later memories of the same experience".[15] Part of what Ludlow is claiming here (the unproblematic part) is this: before the switch, when I say 'I remember that I ate chicory from Mary's garden', my sentence expresses a content involving the concept of chicory; but when I utter the same sentence after the switch, the content shifts (the post-switch content instead involves the concept of twicory).

How does Ludlow's point about memory affect Boghossian's argument? Ludlow maintains that it provides a refutation of premise (1). He says that in the slow-switching case involving 'chicory', I know at t1 that P (where P is the proposition that I think at t1 that chicory is bitter), I forgot nothing between t1 and t2, but I do not know at t2 that P.[16] He justifies this rejection of (1) as follows:

> Boghossian is arguably correct in asserting that I do not know at t2 what I knew at t1, but he is incorrect in supposing that 'the only explanation' for this is that I 'never knew' my thoughts in the first place. It is entirely consistent with the social externalist view of memory that

---

[14] Ludlow holds that the situation with respect to 'chicory' is parallel to that involving 'water' in Burge's slow-switching example. S's thought-contents shift when he is switched from an American-English-speaking community to a British-English-speaking one, according to Ludlow (see Ludlow (1995a, p. 47)), and I assume that this is because 'chicory' contributes different concepts to S's thought-contents before and after switching. Ludlow is rather careless in his reporting of shifts in content, *using* 'chicory' in reporting both the pre-switch content and the distinct post-switch content. Just as an English speaker cannot correctly characterize the Twin Earthians as believing that *water* is wet, an American English speaker (like me) cannot correctly characterize Britons as thinking that *chicory* is bitter. In the text, I use the made-up term 'twicory' to express the post-switch concept, since, even after consulting the *O.E.D.*, I do not know whether there is an American English term that expresses whatever concept is expressed by 'chicory' as it is used in British English.

[15] See Ludlow (1995b, p. 158).

[16] See Ludlow (1995b, p. 159)

I forgot nothing, but that the contents of my memories have nonetheless shifted.[17]

The clear implication is that I have a memory at t2 of the thought I had at t1: I have forgotten nothing –it's just that my memories' contents have shifted since t1. Ludlow says, "…at t2…I recall that initial [t1] thought about chicory, but, due to undetected changes in my linguistic community, the contents of my thoughts about chicory have shifted".[18]

Now if it turns out that Ludlow's externalism about memory implies that by t2 I forgot something I knew at t1, then his objection to premise (1) fails. To see that this implication does indeed hold, let us begin by supposing that at t2, I utter the sentence

(M) I remember that I was thinking at t1 that chicory is bitter.

In order for my utterance of (M) at t2 to be true (in order for it to express a genuine memory of what I thought at t1), it must be the case that at t1, I had a thought with the content expressed by the final 'that'-clause in my t2 utterance of (M). However, according to Ludlow's externalism about memory, the content of my thought at t1 (a content involving the concept of chicory) is different from the content expressed by the final 'that'-clause in my t2 utterance of (M) (a content involving the concept of twicory). In other words, I did not think at t1 the thought that my t2 utterance of (M) represents me as having thought. At t1, I thought *that chicory is bitter*, but my utterance of (M) represents me as having thought *that twicory is bitter*. Thus, my t2 utterance of (M) is false and does not express any genuine memory. So it is hard to see how Ludlow's externalism about memory shows that from t1 to t2, "I forgot nothing". The externalism about memory establishes exactly the opposite. It establishes that at t2, I *fail to remember* what I thought at t1. Thus if at t1 I knew what I was thinking (as Ludlow maintains), then by t2 I forgot something I knew at t1.

Ludlow's position is rather curious. If I indeed *do* remember at t2 what I was thinking at t1, then presumably I thereby *know* at t2 (via memory) what I was thinking at t1. But then (1) would not be refuted and (3)

---

[17] See Ludlow (1995b, p. 159).

[18] See Ludlow (1995b, p. 159). This is an example of careless reporting of content. The post-shift content expressed using 'chicory' is not *about chicory*, just as a Twin Earthian's content expressed using 'water' is not *about water*.

would be false, contrary to Ludlow's intended strategy. On the other hand, if, as I have argued, externalism about memory implies that I do *not* remember at t2 what I was thinking at t1, then Ludlow's considerations about memory seem irrelevant to Boghossian's argument, since they do not refute (1).

Forgetting

Let us take stock of the position we have reached in considering Ludlow's objection to Boghossian. In the slow-switching case we have been discussing, I do not at t2 remember what I was thinking at t1, in virtue of the shift in my concepts between those times. So I do not at t2 *know* what I was thinking at t1 (we assume that there is no avenue other than memory through which I have the knowledge). On the assumption that I *did* at t1 know what I was then thinking, it would seem to follow that at t2 I have forgotten something I knew at t1.[19] This would follow given the following assumption:

> (*) At t, S has forgotten that P iff (i) at t, S does not remember that P, and (ii) for some t' earlier than t, at t', S knew that P.

Now it appears that premise (1) is a trivial consequence of (*). If at t2, S has forgotten none of the things that he knew at t1, then, given (*), it follows that at t2, he remembers all of those things. It is reasonable to suppose that he therefore *knows* all of those things.[20]

So our discussion of Ludlow leaves us affirming premise (1) of the Boghossian argument as indeed having a platitudinous status. But the considerations that have emerged show that premise (2) of the argument is false. In the slow-switching case, at t2, I have forgotten something I knew at t1.

Boghossian sought to *stipulate* that in the cases he wishes to consider, there is no "memory failure", so that at the later time involved in the cases, the thinker has forgotten nothing that he knew at the pertinent earlier time. But that cannot be simply stipulated in the slow-switching cases. It will be helpful to say a bit now about the conditions under which memory failure, or forgetting, can occur. Suppose that S forgets something he knew earlier, say that John solved an equation involving imaginary numbers while eating a pickle (suppose that S observed that event at t). In one

---

[19] This was suggested by Peter Ludlow in correspondence. I found his suggestion to be extremely helpful in sorting out Boghossian's argument.

[20] We will see later that things are not quite this simple.

sort of case, S at t' (later than t) correctly *represents* the past event (e.g., S *believes* that John solved an equation involving imaginary numbers while eating a pickle); but the representation is not properly causally connected to the event (say, S has the belief only because someone told him about the event).[21] Another possibility is that John *misrepresents* the past event. For example, he believes that John solved an equation involving *rational* numbers while eating a pickle. In one version of that sort of case, John continues to possess the concept of an imaginary number but fails to apply it to the past event. In another version, John no longer possesses the concept; he uses the words 'imaginary number' but firmly believes that they refer to the negative integers. The slow-switching case involves that sort of memory failure: I misrepresent a past event (a thinking of a *chicory*-thought) in virtue of applying the wrong concept to it while lacking the right one (the one that correctly applies to the event).

So there is no bar to rejecting Boghossian's argument by accepting premise (1) while denying premise (2). In the slow-switching cases so far under discussion, it can plausibly be maintained that there *is* memory failure.[22]

---

[21] One might think that if S has forgotten that P, then it must be the case that S is unable to confidently and correctly answer appropriate questions regarding P. For example, if S has forgotten that Richard Nixon was Eisenhower's last Vice-President, then it must be the case that S cannot confidently and correctly answer questions like 'Who was Eisenhower's last Vice-President?'. On this view, S can fail to remember that P (which he knew earlier) *without* forgetting that P. In the example in the text, S fails to remember in virtue of failing to satisfy a causal condition on remembering; however, S (we can suppose) confidently and correctly answers questions like 'What was John eating when he solved the equation, and what sort of equation was it?' (his confidence and correctness deriving entirely from a friend's recent recounting of the events). So on the conception of forgetting under discussion in this footnote, S has *not* forgotten. I will continue to equate *forgetting something* with *failing to remember something one knew earlier*. Even on the alternative conception just sketched, S has forgotten at t2 that he was thinking at t1 that chicory is bitter, since, lacking the concept of chicory, he cannot *correctly* answer appropriate questions regarding his earlier thought.

[22] In a later paper ("Externalism and Inference") Boghossian holds that a victim of slow-switching can possess two sets of twin concepts simultaneously. (Burge suggested this in "Individualism and Self-Knowledge".) I leave it to the reader to work out the implications of this view for a Boghossian-style memory argument.

Remembering without Knowing

But this is not the end of the story. Let us look at the sort of case that Burge focussed upon in the above-quoted passage that elicited Boghossian's argument. I have been switched repeatedly, and at t2 I utter

> (M) I remember that I was thinking at t1 that chicory is bitter.

Then I am informed of the switching, without being told which situation I occupy at t2. Suppose that I am, at t2, in one of the *chicory*-thought phases. Does (M) express a truth? Unlike in the case we discussed earlier, I correctly represent, at t2, what I thought at t1 (as before, a *chicory*-thought), and there is a causal link between that thinking and my representation of it at t2.[23] So it might well be true that I remember that I was thinking at t1 that chicory is bitter.[24] However, as Burge's remarks in the passage suggest, it seems that I do not *know* that I thought at t1 that chicory is bitter. This may be a case in which S remembers that P but does not know that P on the basis of that memory. In the current case, the information about switching defeats my justification for believing that I thought at t1 that chicory is bitter. It seems plausible to hold that in general, S knows that P on the basis of remembering that P only if S has no reason to doubt the accuracy of his apparent memory that P.[25]

This case suggests that (1) might not be true after all: it might not correctly express a "platitude" about memory. To say that at t2, s has forgotten nothing that he knew at t1 is to say that at t2, S remembers everything that he knew at t1. But it does not follow that at t2, S *knows* everything that he knew at t1. This is because for some P that he knew at t1, he may remember at t2 that P while failing to know at t2 that P, say, because of some defeating information that he has learned between t1 and t2. Maybe (1) could be revised as follows:

> (1') If at t2, S has forgotten nothing that he knew at t1, and S has no reason to doubt the accuracy of his apparent memories

---

[23] The causal link is unusual, in virtue of the comings and goings of one of the concepts involved in the memorial representation. If this implies that the causal conditions for memory are not satisfied, then for that reason (and not for the more complex one to be discussed in the text), there is memory failure in the current case.

[24] I am assuming that S remembers that P if S satisfies appropriate representation and causal conditions.

[25] See Carl Ginet (1975, chapter VII) for a helpful discussion of memory knowledge.

regarding propositions that he knew at t1, then what S knows at t1, S knows at t2.[26]

Let us now try to apply a Boghossian-style argument to the current case, in which I am informed of the switching regime. We can now see that the antecedent of the premise that would be based upon (1') will not be available for use in the desired argument. This is because in the envisaged case, I *would* have reason to doubt the accuracy of my memories. So a Boghossian-style cannot get off the ground in the present case, since the appropriate analogue to premise (2) in the original argument is not true.

Let us conclude by considering a case in which I am *completely unwittingly* involved in switching and in which I utter (M) during one of my *chicory*-thought phases. As in the previous case, it is plausible to hold that my utterance expresses a true memory-claim. Do I know, though, on the basis of memory, what I was thinking at the earlier time? Burge's remarks in the passage quoted earlier do not commit him to an answer to this question. Suppose that he were to deny that I have knowledge of the past thought in the case at hand. Would a successful Boghossian-style argument then be possible? Unlike in the previous case, the antecedent of the appropriate (1')-based premise *would* be available: since I am unaware of the switches, I have no reason to doubt the accuracy of my memory. However, to the extent that one is inclined to deny that I have knowledge in the case, one will be inclined to suppose that I fail to satisfy some necessary condition for having knowledge that is based on memory.[27] When S remembers that P, he must satisfy some further conditions if he is to know that P on the basis of memory. One condition, as we have seen, is that embodied in the second conjunct of (1')'s antecedent. Another condition is that S must believe that P (since S might, for a variety of reasons, lack confidence in the deliverances of his memory); and S must have this belief *because* he remembers that P.[28] In addition, a piece of memory-based

---

[26] See Robert Audi (1995), for a critical discussion of the view that the justification of memory beliefs derives entirely from their reliability. On this reliabilist approach, memory-based beliefs *automatically* amount to knowledge so long as the relevant memorial process has a sufficiently high truth ratio.

[27] We are assuming that in the current case, I remember that I was thinking at t1 that chicory is bitter.

[28] See Ginet (1975, Chapter VII).

knowledge must satisfy all further conditions that are necessary conditions for knowing in general.

If one thinks that I lack knowledge in the case at hand (involving unwitting switching and successful remembering), then this may well be because one holds some sort of relevant alternatives view of knowledge. That is, suppose that one holds, in general, that if S knows that P, then S must be in a position to rule out the relevant alternatives to P. For example, for S to know that he is seeing a barn while in a countryside strewn with barn facsimiles, he must be able to rule out the possibility that he is looking at a facsimile. On this view, one might well maintain that I lack memory-based knowledge in the current case, since I have no way of ruling out the possibility that I have been switched between t1 and t2 (short of doing research on my linguistic history). In view of my switching history, that possibility (though non-actual in the case) is a relevant one, and if it were the case, then I would not be remembering what I thought at t1.

The upshot is that (1') should be amended. Let us say that an *m-condition* is one that S must satisfy if he is to know that P on the basis of his memory that P. Let us revise (1') as follows:

(1'') If at t2, S has forgotten nothing that he knew at t1, and if S satisfies all the m-conditions for memory knowledge of those propositions S knew at t1, then what S knows at t1, S knows at t2.

This does seem to be a genuine "platitude" about memory. But it cannot be used in a Boghossian-style argument in the current case. If one holds that I do not know at t2 what I was thinking at t1 (in virtue of the stealthy switching regime), then presumably one will also hold that I fail to satisfy some pertinent m-condition (such as a relevant alternatives condition). But then (1'')'s antecedent will be unavailable for use in the argument: the appropriate (2)-like premise is not true.

I conclude that no Boghossian-style argument succeeds in refuting Burge's account of basic self-knowledge.[29][30]

---

[29] The covariation strategies are untouched as well.

[30] I have reservations about all these approaches to self-knowledge, but they have nothing to do with Boghossian's argument. See Brueckner (1995, 1992).

REFERENCES

Audi, R. 1995. Memorial Justification. *Philosophical Topics* 23.

Boghossian, P. 1989. Content and Self-Knowledge. *Philosophical Topics* 17. Chapter 6 in this volume.

———. 1995. Externalism and Inference. In *Rationality in Epistemology,* ed. Enrique Villanueva. Atascadero, CA: Ridgeview Publishing Company.

Brueckner, A. 1995. Trying to Get Outside Your Own Skin. *Philosophical Topics* 23.

———. 1992. Semantic Answers to Skepticism. *Pacific Philosophical Quarterly* 73.

Burge, T. 1988. Individualism and Self-Knowledge. *Journal of Philosophy* 85. Chapter 4 in this volume.

Davidson, D. 1988. Reply to Burge. *Journal of Philosophy* 85. Chapter 4 in this volume.

Ginet, C. 1975. *Knowledge, Perception, and Memory.* Boston: D. Reidel Publishing Company.

Heil, J. 1988. Privileged Access. *Mind* 97. Chapter 5 in this volume.

Ludlow, P. 1995a. Externalism, Self-Knowledge, and the Prevalence of Slow Switching. *Analysis* 55. Chapter 12 in this volume.

———. 1995b. Social Externalism, Self-Knowledge, and Memory. *Analysis* 55. Chapter 17 in this volume.

Peacocke, C. 1996. Entitlement, Self-Knowledge and Conceptual Redeployment. *Proceedings of the Aristotelian Society* 96. Chapter 16 in this volume.

Shoemaker, S. 1994. Self-Knowledge and 'Inner Sense'. *Philosophy and Phenomenological Research* 54.

Warfield, T. 1992. Privileged Self-Knowledge and Externalism are Compatible. *Analysis* 52. Chapter 11 in this volume.

20

Self-Knowledge and Closure

Sven Bernecker

If 'privileged self-knowledge' means knowledge that is not based on investigations of one's environment, we certainly seem to possess privileged self-knowledge of some of our conscious and occurrent thoughts. Nevertheless, some have questioned our ability to authoritatively know our mental states. One reason for doing so derives from externalism (or anti-individualism), the view that the content of an intentional state is fixed in part by the environment external to the believer. Because mental content supervenes on extrinsic relations it is called 'broad' or 'wide' content. The leading argument for the incompatibility of privileged self-knowledge and externalism claims that privileged self-knowledge is incompatible with the kind of twinning and switching scenarios on which externalism is based. It is argued that this argument is flawed and that privileged self-knowledge is consistent with externalism.

The advocates of the incompatibilist argument discussed in this paper are, among others, Boghossian, BonJour, Brueckner, and McGinn.[1] The argument proceeds from a slow switching thought experiment introduced by Burge (1988, pp. 652ff.) where an agent, S, is switched from Earth to Twin Earth and remains there for some time. The only difference between the two planets is that Twin Earth doesn't have any water. Instead of water there is a liquid that superficially resembles water but which has the chemical formular XYZ. Practically everyone agrees that after a while (how long is unclear), tokens of 'water' in S's mentalese will

---

[1] Cf. Boghossian (1989, pp. 13–4; 1992, pp. 17–21; 1994, pp. 36–40), BonJour (1991, p. 339), Brueckner (1990, pp. 449–51; 1992, pp. 206–7; 1994), and McGinn (1989, pp. 82–94). For a discussion of other incompatibilist arguments see my 1996a.

cease to mean water (H_2O) but will instead refer to XYZ. If we want to express S's word 'water' in English, we have to coin a word – 'twater', say. The content of the thought S expressed on Earth by saying "I am thinking that water is wet" is different from the thought content he expresses by the same sentence uttered on Twin Earth. However, since nothing internal to S distinguishes the two worlds, he cannot know by introspection which one he is in. But then, doesn't it follow that he lacks privileged knowledge of the content of his thought? Incompatibilists say 'yes' for they maintain that "S has to be able to exclude the possibility that his thought involve[s] the concept [water] rather than the concept [twater], before he can be said to know what his thought is" (Boghossian 1989, p. 14). Since introspection doesn't tell him whether he is entertaining a water thought or a twater thought, he lacks privileged self-knowledge of (some of his) thought contents. And since Twin Earth scenarios are the primary motivation for externalism, it follows that externalism is inconsistent with the doctrine of privileged self-knowledge. This argument can be parsed into the following steps:

(1) S is switched from Earth to Twin Earth. In situations where S used to think water thoughts he now entertains twater thoughts.

(2) Since S is supposed to remain physically identical through the switching, he cannot introspectively discriminate water thoughts from twater thoughts.

(3) Water thoughts and twater thoughts differ in broad content.

(C) Thus, if S has privileged self-knowledge, what he has knowledge of is not broad content.

It is important to realize that the force of this reasoning depends neither on S's being ignorant of the existence of Twin Earth nor on his forgetfulness. Given externalism, it is possible for S to know his thoughts at time t_1 (before the switch), forget nothing, be informed about the switch, and yet at some later time t_2 be unable to know *introspectively* what the contents of his thoughts were at t_1. Boghossian (1989, p. 23) argues "the only explanation [...] for why S will not know tomorrow what he is said to know today, is [...] that he never knew". To know what he thought at t_1, S would have to discover what environment he was in at that time and how long he had been there. But these things cannot be known authoritatively.

Incompatibilists conclude that externalism cannot account for privileged self-knowledge.

As it stands, the incompatibilist argument is invalid. What is missing is an explanation for why being able to distinguish non-empirically water thoughts from twater thoughts should be a necessary condition of privileged self-knowledge. To complete the argument the following premise has to be added:

(4) Privileged self-knowledge is closed under known entailment.[2]

It is the *closure principle* applied to privileged self-knowledge that does all of the work in the above incompatibilist argument. The principle of closure under known implications states that if S knows P, and S knows that P entails Q, then S knows Q. This principle is commonly used to back skepticism regarding our ability to know about the external world: If I know that this is water, I also have to know I am not on Twin Earth. But I don't know that I am not on Twin Earth, since if I were, things would seem exactly as they seem now and this would not be water. It follows that I don't know that this is water. Whereas the Cartesian skeptic employs epistemic closure to undermine knowledge of the external world, Brueckner uses the closure principle to show that, given externalism, privileged self-knowledge is impossible: "[M]y knowing that I am thinking that some water is dripping requires that I know that I am not thinking that some twater is dripping," for self-knowledge implies the ability to rule out counterfactual thought contents. But I don't know authoritatively that I am not thinking that some twater is dripping, for, "if I were a brain in a vat [in a waterless world], things would seem exactly as they now seem (and have seemed)" (Brueckner 1990, pp. 450, 448; cf. 1992, pp. 206–7). Therefore, Brueckner and other incompatibilists conclude, I don't know authoritatively that I am thinking that some water is dripping, i.e., I don't know the content of my thought.

Regarding knowledge of the outside world most epistemologists agree that the closure principle is too strict to be convincing. If knowing that P would require the elimination of *every* alternative to P, as suggested by the closure principle, we could never know anything about the world around

---

[2] Instead of premise (4) some incompatibilists assume the following premise (4'): Privileged self-knowledge of thought contents requires that one can determine non-empirically sameness and difference in thought contents. Since premise (4') is a derivative form of the closure principle it will not be discussed separately. For a good discussion of premise (4') see Owens 1992.

us.[3] A much more plausible view is that knowledge requires the elimination of *relevant* alternatives only. This position is commonly called the '*relevant alternative account of knowledge*'. Which alternatives are relevant? Relevance has to do with the kind of possibilities that actually exist in the objective situation.[4] In an ordinary case of claiming to know that some animals in the zoo are zebras, to use Dretske's example, the alternative that they are cleverly painted mules is not relevant. Thus, one can truthfully claim to know that they are zebras despite one's inability to rule out this fanciful alternative. But in some extraordinary cases, the painted mules hypothesis is a relevant alternative; and then we have to eliminate this alternative to know that what we are seeing are really zebras.

Warfield (1992) has offered an objection to the incompatibilist argument by applying the relevant alternative approach to self-knowledge. Why, he asks, should the conditions of knowledge of one's own thoughts be any stricter than the conditions on knowledge of the external world? If knowledge of the external world isn't closed under known implications, why should privileged self-knowledge be closed? Warfield argues that the incompatibilist reasoning, by itself, fails to rob us of privileged self-knowledge. Only if switching cases were relevant, we would fail to know what it is we are thinking. In ordinary circumstances, however, the mere possibility of switching cases no more undermines my self-knowledge than the

---

[3] This is not the only reason to get rid of the closure principle: Knowledge is closed under known logical implications only if each necessary condition for knowing is so closed. Any correct analysis of knowledge must contain a belief condition and a truth condition. Truth is obviously closed under known implications and belief is arguably too. But what about the justification condition? Assuming that there is a justification condition for knowledge, many epistemologists have maintained some kind of closure principle for justification (cf. Hooker 1973). However, given reliabilism, the proper analysis of knowledge doesn't yield a justification condition. The justification condition is replaced by what might be called the 'reliability condition': a belief that P qualifies as knowledge only if it is a reliable indicator of the truth that P. Advocates of closure would have to show that the reliability condition is closed under known implications; and this seems hard to do.

[4] On the notion of relevant alternatives see Dretske (1981) and Goldman (1976). Apart from the objective reading of relevance there is a subjective reading according to which the attribution of knowledge is relative to the conversational context. For example, the sentence "S knows that he is sitting at his desk" can be true or false depending on whether the claim is taken to imply that S is sitting at his desk (not yours), or that he is sitting at his desk (not standing), or that he is sitting at his desk (not his armchair). The subjective notion of relevant alternative is the basis of contextualism.

mere possibility of me possessing counterfeit coins undermines my knowledge that I have a dime in my pocket.

In response to Warfield, Ludlow (1995a) has argued for the prevalence of switching scenarios. While Twin Earth scenarios are normally about tokens of the same word type having different meanings in different worlds, Ludlow examines the reverse case – tokens of distinct word types having the same meaning in different worlds. And instead of moves between Earth and Twin Earth, Ludlow considers moves between language communities, social groups and institutions: Biff who knows very little about vegetables moves between the United Kingdom and the United States. In the United Kingdom, Biff expresses a particular thought by saying "Chicory is tasty". When the same internal episode takes place in the United States he says "Arugula is tasty". Biff is unaware that the contents of both thoughts are identical. Moreover, this fact isn't detectable purely on the basis of introspection. According to Ludlow, Biff is a victim of a slow switching case. Since we routinely move between social groups and institutions and because Biff-like cases can be applied not only to a wide variety of nouns (e.g., 'chips' and 'crisps', 'gasoline' and 'petrol') but to any part of speech (e.g., 'latino' and 'hispanic'), Ludlow concludes that, contrary to Warfield's contention, slow switching cases are indeed prevalent.

I applaud Warfield's criticism of incompatibilism. Just as in ordinary cases I can know that some animals in the zoo are zebras without having to know that they are not cleverly painted mules, I can normally know that I am having a water thought without being able to rule out the possibility that I am having a twater thought. Since there is no reason to suppose that the requirements for knowledge of one's thought contents are any stricter than those for knowledge of the external world, I claim that, in ordinary cases, self-knowledge isn't closed under known implications. While agreeing with the relevant-alternatives account of knowledge, I think it is unlikely that incompatibilism can be refuted in this way. The dispute on the prevalence of slow switching cases easily degenerates into an idle exchange of burden of proof arguments. Fortunately however, we do not have to enter into the discussion on whether twater thoughts are relevant or irrelevant alternatives, for they aren't (entertainable) alternatives at all. Let me explain.

Burge (1988, 1996) and others have provided a convincing case for the compatibility of externalism and privileged self-knowledge. To know that I am thinking that, say, water is wet, I don't need to first acquire knowledge of either how experts in my community use 'water' (social external-ism) or of the kind of substance I was in contact with when I learned 'water' (causal-essentialist externalism). The reason is that the content of the first-order thought ("water is wet") is automatically contained in the content of the second-order thought ("I believe that water is wet") and the contents of both thoughts are determined by the same causal relations of which one may be ignorant. So no matter which planet one resides on, as long as the first-order thought and the second-order thought are enter-tained simultaneously, the content of the second-order thought cannot come apart from the first-order thought by which it is causally sustained. I refer to this compatibilist line as the '*inclusion theory of privileged self-knowledge*'.

The inclusion theory of self-knowledge relies on a reliabilist conception of knowledge. *Reliabilism* is the view that to know something all that is required is that the belief-fact link is reliable. The subject doesn't need to know that it is reliable. Reliabilism replaces the traditional notion of justi-fication by a nomic (e.g. causal or counterfactual) or other such external relation between belief and truth. Therefore, to have self-knowledge a subject need only, as a matter of fact, stand in some causal relation to his first-order states; he need not know that he does. Reliabilism stands opposed to epistemic internalism, the view that knowledge requires cog-nitive access to the justificatory procedure and evidence on which it is based. Some versions of internalism are committed to the KK-principle, i.e., the view that knowing entails knowing that one knows. Without the assumption of reliabilism, the inclusion theory of self-knowledge might explain why second-order thoughts of the form "I am believing that water is wet" are necessarily true, but it would fall short of accounting for intro-spective *knowledge*.[5]

The combination of reliabilism and the relevant alternative account of knowledge yields a powerful objection to the incompatibilist argument under consideration.[6] Given the inclusion theory of self-knowledge, the

---

[5] Burge endorses reliabilism regarding introspective knowledge, but he doesn't assume it as a general doctrine of knowledge.

[6] Although most reliabilists deny the closure principle, reliabilism and closure are, in princi-ple, compatible. Suppose a version of reliabilism that rests on the following counterfactual condition: If P were false, then S would not mistakenly believe that P. Now suppose S's claim to know logically implies the proposition that S is not a brain in a vat (BIV). If S were a BIV, then, presumably, S would mistakenly believe that he is not a BIV. Hence, he doesn't know that P. Thus, if the belief-forming process counts as reliable iff it actually yields a suf-

hypothesis according to which I am having twater thoughts while think-ing that I have water thoughts simply isn't a (entertainable) possibility. When I am on Earth thinking earthian concepts, I *cannot* believe that I am thinking that twater is wet for I don't have the concept of twater avail-able; so this concept cannot figure in any of my mental states. Analo-gously, when I am on Twin Earth, I *cannot* mistakenly believe that I am entertaining water thoughts. No matter how often I am switched between Earth and Twin Earth, I will never erroneously think that I am having water thoughts while in fact I am having twater thoughts and vice versa. Privileged self-knowledge is therefore immune to skeptical arguments from switching and twinning scenarios.

This is the central compatibilist argument. In the remainder of the paper I will consider three incompatibilist rejoinders, none of which is convincing.

(1) Apparently the compatibilist argument above presupposes that the switching or twinning of an agent S brings about a *complete change* of his concepts and thought contents. For it is claimed that S cannot mistake his twater thoughts for water thoughts and vice versa because on Twin Earth he doesn't have available the concept water and on Earth he doesn't have available the concept twater.

Now Boghossian (1992, pp. 19–21; 1994, pp. 38–9) has challenged the idea that switching and twinning results in a complete change of the agent's concepts and contents. The suggestion is that when on Twin Earth S remembers water thoughts from the time he was living on Earth, then, despite being tokened on Twin Earth, these tokens of 'water' occur-ring in memories retain their earthly interpretation. Thus it is not impossi-ble for S to have available both water thoughts and twater thoughts at the same time. But then switching and twinning hypotheses may indeed rep-resent relevant alternatives to one's privileged self-knowledge. It might happen that what S takes to be a twater thought is in fact a remembered water thought. And since twater thoughts and water thoughts cannot be

---

ficiently high ratio of true beliefs both in the actual and the counterfactual situation, then reliabilism is compatible with closure. Moreover, although most advocates of the relevant alternative account of knowledge endorse reliabilism, the relevant alternative account is, in principle, compatible with epistemological internalism. It is possible to hold a sort of inter-nalist theory of knowledge that highlights the role of evidential justification (and reject reli-abilism) and then go on to deny closure via embracing the notion of a relevant alternative. I owe this point to Tony Brueckner.

discriminated on the basis of introspection alone, S would lack privileged self-knowledge of what he is thinking.

As Ludlow (1995b) has pointed out, this defense of incompatibilism rests on a conception of *memory* which conflicts with the spirit of externalism. Any externalist conception of memory has it that the content of a memory is in part dependent on systematic external relations. But which relations – past or current ones? Boghossian assumes that S's content of his memory fixed at time t_1 remains frozen up to some later moment of recollection. But if externalism is right and mental contents are determined by external facts, why not suppose that the content of a memory is fixed at the time recollection takes place, since it is the embedding circumstances of that memory which are crucial to the fixing of its content? On this view of memory, S's memory of event W at t_1 is different from his memory of W at t_2, if the content-determining environment changes. Just as slow switching can bring about changes in mental content, it can bring about changes in memory content. It is therefore impossible that, while residing on Twin Earth, S's tokens of 'water' occurring in memories can retain their earthly meaning.

Ludlow's externalist notion of memory has met criticism. Burge (1996, p. 97n), for example, has warned against "overrat[ing] the extent to which the content retrieved in memory is sensitive to *immediate* environmental context".[7] The problem some philosophers are having with Ludlow's concept of memory is this: At t_1, while living on Earth, S thinks that water is wet. At t_2, after having been transported to Twin Earth, S thinks "At t_1 I thought that water is wet". How can the thought at t_2 involve the concept twater and, at the same time, express a memory of an earthly thought? For a state to be a memory doesn't its content have to involve concepts that apply to the remembered event? Ludlow's concept of memory is said to be implausible for it suggests that, in an important sense, it is beyond one's control whether or not one can remember one's previous thoughts. Moreover, in conjunction with the prevalence of slow-switch-

---

[7] My emphasis. Cf. Brueckner (1997, pp 5–6.), Hofmann (Mscr.), and Ludlow (1996). Burge's (ch. 21 in this volume) most recent thoughts on preservative memory (which I read after having finished this chapter) support my idea that memory doesn't require the ability to distinguish original thoughts from new twin thoughts.

ing scenarios, Ludlow's notion of memory entails that one can seldom remember one's earlier thoughts.

The problem with this objection to Ludlow's notion of memory is the assumption that a memory state *necessarily* contains the content and concepts of the relevant earlier state. Why should we suppose that our memory is sensitive to twinning scenarios given that water thoughts and twater thoughts are phenomenologically, functionally and introspectively indistinguishable? What would be the evolutionary utility of designing memory in such a way as to make it respond to differences that, introspectively speaking, don't make a difference? What I am suggesting then is that the job of memory, rather than to replay previously recorded contents, is to provide information about past states relative to the present environmental conditions. The transfer of contents and concepts across time might be a sufficient condition for memory but it falls short of being a necessary condition.

Even if there was a strict proof that the content of a memory is fixed at the time recollection takes place, there might still be situations in which an agent possesses both concepts, water and twater, at the same time. Imagine, for example, that while being transported from Earth to Twin Earth S is very thirsty. He continuously thinks "I have been wanting a drink of water for the last two hours". Now it could be argued that once S has reached Twin Earth (and has stayed there for a while) S's term 'water' in "I have been wanting a drink of water for the last two hours" is ambiguous in that it refers to both H_2O and XYZ. But if S can have both concepts – water and twater – at the same time, isn't it then possible that he mistakes his twater thought for a water thought and therefore lacks privileged self-knowledge of his thought contents? And if this is so, doesn't it follow that privileged self-knowledge is inconsistent with switching and twinning scenarios?

For this objection to be convincing the compatibilist argument presented above would have to presuppose that the switching and twinning of an agent S brings about a *complete change* of his concepts and contents. But compatibilism isn't committed to this presupposition. Even if S had available water *and* twater concepts simultaneously, he still couldn't erroneously think that he is having a water thought while in fact he is having a twater thought and vice versa. For given the inclusion theory, if the first-order thought isn't just an object of reference but is part of the higher-order cognition itself, the concepts of the first-order thought cannot come apart from those of the second-order thought. So when S is thinking a water thought, his second-order thought involves the concept water; and when he is thinking a twater thought, his second-order thought involves the concept twater. So no matter what he does, he cannot get his first-order thought wrong.[8]

(2) The inclusion theory of self-knowledge shows no more than that the hypothesis according to which I am having twater thoughts while thinking that I am having water thoughts is not an *entertainable* possibility. In other words, the scenario envisioned by the incompatibilist involves a *pragmatic* contradiction. But this doesn't mean that the scenario could not be true. This would only follow if it contained a *logical* contradiction. The hypothesis that I have alternative contents is indeed possible, although not thinkable. Thus, we are even worse off than we thought. We lack the necessary concept to express what may very well be true, and our causal circumstances make it impossible for us to acquire them.

The incompatibilist could use this reasoning to construct an argument to the effect that our ordinary claims to introspective knowledge are unjustified. He could suggest that the class of relevant alternatives is not restricted to actual thought contents but also includes possible thought contents. The idea is that the unthinkable and thus purely *abstract* possibility of alternative contents is enough to destroy privileged self-knowledge. Even if one cannot coherently think that one mistakes one's present water thoughts for twater thoughts, if one dwells on switching cases long enough, the level of scrutiny will rise and one will find oneself unwilling to claim to know that one is occupying a water thought (as opposed to a twater thought). Self-knowledge can be undermined just by knowing in the abstract that there are alternative contents, without ever knowing what those alternatives are and without ever being able to verify their existence via introspection. The situation is similar to that of a person who has never seen a counterfeit coin and doesn't know what a counterfeit looks like but who, after having read Descartes' *Meditations on First Philosophy*, worries that the dime-like looking object in his pocket is a counterfeit. This person might find himself unwilling to claim to know that he has a dime in his pocket.

To see what is wrong with this incompatibilist rejoinder one needs to realize that there are two very different phenomena that can be thought of as the contextual relativity of knowledge. One characteristic of knowledge is that it is determined relative to the *extra-evidential context* of the sub-

---

[8] I owe this point to John Perry and Ken Taylor.

ject. Subjects living in different environments can possess the same evidence for the truth of a certain proposition P, and one of them knows that P while the other one fails to know it. It is this notion of contextual relativity of knowledge that underlies (my objectivist reading of) the relevant-alternative account of knowledge. An alternative construal of contextual relativity says that knowledge *attributions* are dependent on the *conversational context*. On this view, the attributor's purposes, intentions, and presuppositions of the epistemic subjects play a role in setting the standards of relevance. I could say of someone in one conversational context that he knows that P and could then go to a different conversational context and say of him that he doesn't know that P. The same is said to apply to cases of self-attribution of knowledge. While reliabilism emphasizes the extra-evidential context of knowledge, contextualism stresses the conversational context.[9]

The above incompatibilist rejoinder rests on a confusion of conditions for knowledge attributions with conditions for knowledge. Even if slow switching scenarios destroy one's attributive self-knowledge, they don't thereby destroy the introspective knowledge one has of one's mental condition. For just because one cannot justifiably *say* that one knows what one is thinking doesn't show that in fact one doesn't know what one is thinking. Having reasons for knowing and having reasons for self-attributing knowledge are two quite different things. One might not have reasons for attributing knowledge to oneself and still know. In other words, one can know that one is thinking that P and not be able to justifiably say that one knows what one is thinking. And therefore, the abstract possibility of alternative thought contents is unable to undermine privileged self-knowledge.

(3) Boghossian (1989, pp. 17 ff.; cf. Goldman 1993, p. 25) has argued that privileged self-knowledge must involve '*cognitive achievement*' in the sense of requiring observation or the performance of some inference based on some observation. Self-knowledge is a cognitive achievement because it is subject to direction, is fallible, and incomplete. According to Boghossian, the inclusion theory of privileged self-knowledge cannot account for any of these characteristics and therefore is cognitively insubstantial; it is sham knowledge. The reason it cannot account for these characteristics is that it relies on reliabilism according to which the justifi-

---

[9] Cf. Cohen (1986), Dretske (1970), Lewis (1979). Reliabilism and contextualism are compatible positions.

cation condition for knowledge is replaced by some non-normative notion of evidential support. Boghossian compares Burge's analysis of judgments like "I am thinking that water is wet" to the analysis of logical truths such as "I am here now". Whenever one thinks "I am here now" one thinks a true thought of which one knows that it is true. The judgment is justified not because one possesses special knowledge about oneself, one's location, and time but simply in virtue of the meanings of the indexical elements involved. Mastering the words 'I', 'here', and 'now' is sufficient for knowing that "I am here now" is true. In fact, Burge asserts that *whenever* one thinks about one's occurrent thoughts one is epistemically justified in making a judgment of the kind "I am thinking that P". It is not necessary to ground self-reflexive thoughts on anything else such as other beliefs or observations. Burge writes:

> The source of our strong epistemic right, our justification, in our basic self-knowledge is not that we know a lot about each thought we know we have. [...] Justification lies not in the having of supplemental background knowledge, but in the character and function of the self-evaluating judgments (1988, p. 660).

It is the non-normative notion of evidential support Boghossian quarrels with. A reliabilist notion of self-knowledge, he argues is "based on nothing – at any rate, on nothing empirical" (1989, p. 17). For self-knowledge to be genuine knowledge, it must be justified by observation or inference based on some observation.

This is the most basic of the three incompatibilist objections, since it presents a head-on attack on the epistemology underlying the inclusion theory of self-knowledge. One way to fend off Boghossian's charge would be to come up with a general criticism of the internalist justification condition for knowledge. However, I don't see this strategy getting us very far since a *general* dispute between internalism and reliabilism is unlikely to provide a knockdown argument for the reliabilist treatment of *self*-knowledge.[10] Fortunately, there is another way to demonstrate that the reliabi-

---

[10] It is worth noting that arguably the most powerful internalist objection to reliabilism may apply to knowledge of the external world but doesn't apply to introspective knowledge. The argument says that, according to the reliabilist criteria, a person may be highly irrational and irresponsible in accepting a belief, when judged in the light of his own subjective conception of the situation, and may still turn out to be epistemologically justified and to possess knowledge because the belief is reliably formed. To BonJour (1985, ch. 3) and others this seems highly counterintuitive: If one has good reason to think that one's

list construal of privileged self-knowledge is cognitively substantial. I will neutralize Boghossian's objection by showing that, despite its commitment to reliabilism, the inclusion theory of self-knowledge can account for the three qualities he claims are distinctive of genuine self-knowledge, namely *directability, fallibility,* and *incompleteness.*

Directability. One of the essential properties of self-knowledge, so Boghossian says, is that it is subject to direction: "how much you know about your thoughts should [...] depend on how much *attention* you are paying to them" (1989, p. 19). The inclusion theory, he claims, is incapable of accounting for this feature for, on this picture, "you do not know your thoughts on the basis of evidence". This is false. Nothing prevents the inclusion theory from acknowledging that one can attend to and investigate one's mental states with varying degree of care. Frequently one has to take a second 'look' to find out, say, that the pain one is feeling is of the throbbing rather than the stinging or grinding kind. The inclusion theory can account for this fact in the following way: By attending to one's thought that P one can become a reliable indicator not only of P (pain) but of specific forms of P (throbbing pain). What the inclusion theory denies, however, is that by paying closer attention to one's thought that P one's knowledge of this thought somehow becomes more reliable. Like any other kind of factual knowledge, privileged self-knowledge is an absolute concept. Either I know that I am thinking P or

---

belief isn't reliable, then, even if it is reliable, it doesn't qualify as knowledge. Now this argument doesn't undermine reliabilism regarding privileged self-knowledge. The crucial question is: What could count as reasons for thinking that one's introspective beliefs are unreliable? There are two obvious candidates for such evidence – behavioral evidence and findings of a brain-scanning device. Behavioral evidence doesn't do the job since it is of empirical origin. For the above anti-reliabilist argument to be applicable to privileged self-knowledge, one's reason for thinking that one's second-order belief is unreliable would to be based on non-empirical origin. For the above anti-reliabilist argument to be applicable to privileged self-knowledge, one's reason for thinking that one's second-order belief is unreliable would have to be based on non-empirical evidence. The second candidate, a brain-scanning device, fails to complete the anti-reliabilist argument since the postulation of such a device doesn't hold up to scrutiny (cf. Bernecker 1996a, pp. 127–34; Shoemaker 1994, pp. 249–90). Hence, there is no way to make sense of the idea that one has reason to doubt the reliability of one's introspective beliefs about one's occurrent thoughts. Moreover, given the coherence theory of justification (and other inferential conceptions of self-knowledge), it is not only unreasonable but even impossible to have reason to question the reliability of all of one's self-referential beliefs. On this view, an introspective belief is justified by reference to other introspective beliefs. General doubts concerning the justificatory status of one's introspective beliefs would lead to a vicious regress (cf. Boghossian 1989, pp. 8–11; BonJour 1985, p. 51).

I don't. There is nothing like knowing it better. From an epistemic point of view, my belief that I am in some kind of pain or other is just as good as my belief that I am suffering from intense throbbing pain. The second kind of belief might of course prove to be more useful as it allows a physician to develop a more precise diagnosis of my ailment. But this is beside the point, since whether or not a belief is useful isn't relevant for it qualifying as knowledge.

Fallibility and *Incompleteness*: "The most important consideration", according to Boghossian, "against an insubstantial construal of self-knowledge" is that it cannot account for the fallibility and incompleteness of self-knowledge: "mental [...] events may occur of which one remains ignorant; and [...] even when one becomes aware of an event's existence, one may yet misconstrue its character, believing it to have a property it does not in fact possess" (1989, p. 19). Boghossian doesn't explain why fallibility and incompleteness are supposed to be necessary conditions of knowledge. Presumably he holds that the very concept of knowledge implies the possibility of mistake, and that when there is no possibility of getting things wrong, all talk of knowledge is out of place. Now, I don't see any reason why knowledge cannot be complete and unfailing. But quite apart from this, Boghossian errs in maintaining that the inclusion theory implies that privileged self-knowledge is infallible and complete. This error goes back to Burge himself who holds that the inclusion theory renders self-knowledge "self-verifying (hence infallible)" (1988, p. 658n). Given the inclusion theory, it is true that one cannot be wrong about the fact that one is thinking of P (e.g., water) rather than Q (e.g., twater). However, the inclusion theory is consistent with our ignorance and fallibility regarding other aspects of our mental condition. This needs further explanation.

In (1996b) I have argued that though the inclusion theory explains knowing it is P I am thinking about, it doesn't explain how I can have privileged self-knowledge that the state I occupy is a state of believing rather than, say, a state of doubting, or expecting etc. In other words, the inclusion theory explains privileged access to one's *contents* but not to one's *attitudes*. The reason is that a state's attitude isn't part of its content and it is only the content that is automatically included in the that-clause of a self-referential cognition. Since self-knowledge consists in the identification of the attitude as well as the content, the inclusion theory doesn't provide a complete account of privileged self-knowledge. Moreover given externalism, self-knowledge of the attitudinal component is vulnerable to brute error and doesn't have the same kind of privilege as self-knowledge of content. The suggestion is that because of external determination of attitude concepts such as 'to believe', 'to doubt', and 'to expect', empirical investigation might be needed to know the mode in which one's thought content is realized. The inclusion theory therefore cannot be extended to provide a solution to privileged self-knowledge of attitudinal components, and that there is no indication that there is some other externalist account to be had of this kind of knowledge. Thus, there is at least one respect in which the inclusion theory can allow for privileged self-knowledge to be fallible and incomplete.

Now, Boghossian could turn around and claim that the point about attitude-identification, rather than lending support to the inclusion theory of self-knowledge by rendering it cognitively substantial, works to its disadvantage. The fact that the inclusion theory cannot explain privileged access to one's attitudes doesn't point to a limitation of our capacity to know our own minds, instead it reveals a limitation on the part of the inclusion theory. The notion of self-knowledge underlying the inclusion theory is sham knowledge because it cannot account for privileged access to one's attitudes. Without being able to respond to this challenge in detail, I want to suggest that it is only through the study of externalism that a reasonable notion of self-knowledge emerges. Privileged access to the attitudinal components of one's thoughts is one of the many Cartesian superstitions that the inclusion theory forces us to abandon. But even if it should turn out that attitude-identification is an essential aspect of first-person authority, the particular argument for incompatibilism presented in the beginning of the paper is flawed: Given both reliabilism and the relevant alternative account of knowledge, twinning and switching scenarios pose no problem for the doctrine of privileged self-knowledge of thought content. Moreover, nothing speaks against using reliabilism and the relevant alternative account to analyze privileged self-knowledge. We can conclude that externalism and privileged self-knowledge are consistent.[11]

---

[11] The preparation of this chapter was in part supported by a fellowship from the Stanford Humanities Center. For valuable comments on earlier drafts of this paper, I am grateful to Tony Brueckner, Fred Dretske, Frank Hofmann, Peter Ludlow, Carlos Moya, John Perry and Ken Taylor.

REFERENCES

Bernecker, S. 1996a. Davidson on First-Person Authority and Externalism. *Inquiry* 39: 121–39.

———. 1996b. Externalism and the Attitudinal Component of Self-Knowledge. *Nous* 30: 262–75.

Boghossian, P. 1989. Content and Self-Knowledge. *Philosophical Topics* 17: 5–26. Chapter 6 in this volume.

———. 1992: Externalism and Inference. *Philosophical Issues* 2: 11–28.

———. 1994. The Transparency of Mental Content. *Philosophical Perspectives* 8: 33–50.

BonJour, L. 1985. *The Structure of Empirical Knowledge.* Cambridge, MA: Harvard University Press.

———. 1991. Is Thought a Symbolic Process? *Synthese* 89: 331–52.

Brueckner, A. 1990. Scepticism about Knowledge of Content. *Mind* 99: 447–51.

———. 1992. Semantic Answers to Skepticism. *Pacific Philosophical Quarterly* 73: 200–19.

———. 1994. Knowledge of Content and Knowledge of the World. *Philosophical Review* 103: 107–37.

———. 1997. Externalism and Memory. *Pacific Philosophical Quarterly* 78: 1–12. Chapter 19 in this volume.

Burge, T. 1988. Individualism and Self-Knowledge. *Journal of Philosophy* 85: 649–63. Chapter 4 in this volume.

———. 1996. Our Entitlement to Self-Knowledge. *Proceedings of the Aristotelian Society* 117: 91–116. Chapter 15 in this volume.

———. 1998. Memory and Self-Knowledge. Chapter 21 in this volume.

Cohen, S. 1986. Knowledge and Context. *Journal of Philosophy* 83: 574–83.

Dretske, F. 1970. Epistemic Operators. *Journal of Philosophy* 67: 1007–23.

———. 1981. The Pragmatic Dimension of Knowledge. *Philosophical Studies* 40: 363–78.

Goldman, A. 1976. Discrimination and Perceptual Knowledge. *Journal of Philosophy* 73: 771–91.

———. 1993. The Psychology of Folk Psychology. *Behavioral and Brain Sciences* 16: 15–28.

Hofmann, F. Mscr.: Externalism and Memory. University of Tübingen, Germany.

Hooker, M. 1973. In Defense of the Principle for Deducibility of Justification. *Philosophical Studies* 24: 402–6.

Lewis, D. 1979. Scorekeeping in a Language Game. *Journal of Philosophical Logic* 8: 513–43.

Ludlow, P. 1995a. Externalism, Self-Knowledge, and the Prevalence of Slow Switching. *Analysis* 55: 45–9. Chapter 12 in this volume.

———. 1995b. Social Externalism, Self-Knowledge, and Memory. *Analysis* 55: 157–9. Chapter 17 in this volume.

———. 1996. Social Externalism and Memory: A Problem?. *Acta Analytica* 14: 69–76. Chapter 18 in this volume.

McGinn, C. 1989. *Mental Content.* Oxford: Basil Blackwell.

Owens, J. 1992. Psychological Supervenience. *Synthese* 90: 89–117.

Shoemaker, S. 1994. Self-Knowledge and 'Inner Sense'. *Philosophy and Phenomenological Studies* 54: 249–314.

Warfield, T. 1992. Privileged Self-Knowledge and Externalism are Compatible. *Analysis* 52: 232–7. Chapter 11 in this volume.

21

Memory and Self-Knowledge

Tyler Burge

In "Individualism and Self-Knowledge" I argued that immediate, authoritative, non-empirically warranted self-knowledge is compatible with anti-individualism about the individuation of propositional attitudes. Paul Boghossian uses my slow-switching cases to argue that such self-knowledge and anti-individualism are incompatible. I will try to show why this argument does not succeed.[1]

I postulated as possible a case like this: An individual grows up in an environment like ours with a normal set of experiences of a particular sort of object or stuff, say aluminum. The individual does not know anything about the micro-structural features of metals. But he has seen aluminum and made use of it. Perhaps he has heard things about it from others. The individual grows to maturity with this learning history. The individual has a normal lay concept of aluminum. It applies to aluminum and nothing else. I presumed that the individual believes that look-alike metals can be different metals. So his conception of aluminum allows that something could be superficially indistinguishable from aluminum and not be aluminum.

I then imagined that the individual is switched unawares to another planet (either forever, or gradually back and forth staying at each planet a substantial amount of time before switching). Given what he knows and can discern perceptually, he cannot distinguish the second environment from his home environment. The second environment contains twaluminum in all the places aluminum occupies in the original environment. Aluminum is lacking altogether. Twaluminum is a different metal that is

---

[1] Burge (1988, pp. 649–63), Boghossian (1989, pp. 5–26).

indistinguishable for the individual from aluminum. I claimed that the individual's original concept does not apply to twaluminum. But I claimed that if the individual had enough experiences with the new metal comparable to those of the old, or if the individual interacted sufficiently with a community that had a term that applied to twaluminum, the individual would normally eventually acquire a concept more appropriate to the new environment than the concept of aluminum.

In "Individualism and Self-Knowledge" I assumed that the newly acquired concept would be a "twin" concept. So if one had an aluminum concept in the first environment, one would acquire a twaluminum concept in the second. The twaluminum concept does not apply to aluminum. In these cases, the individual's word-form "aluminum" expresses on different occasions two concepts whose extensions are disjoint. Let use call such cases "*Disjoint Type* cases".

I will continue to suppose that Disjoint Type cases are possible. But they are not the only sorts of cases that can arise. The new set of concepts may be broadenings of the old. Thus the concept in the second environment may apply both to aluminum and twaluminum. One pressure in this direction is that these metals are indistinguishable to the individual, and instances of both (let us assume) enter into normal, paradigmatic perceptual applications of the individual's word-form "aluminum". If the individual's concept broadened in this way, the individual would acquire a non-natural-kind concept rather like our actual concept of jade.[2] Call these "*Amalgam Type* cases".

Whether in slow switching we have an Amalgam Type case depends partly, probably mainly, on how the individual is committed to the standards of the communities in the two environments. The relevant individ-

---

[2] This point does not in the least constitute an admission that in the first environment, apart from actual switching, the individual must express this broadened concept in using the word form "aluminum". The concept is fixed partly by actual causal interactions. I take it that the individual's belief that metals may differ while appearing the same helps prevent his concept from applying from the beginning to just anything that looks to him like aluminum. And in the absence of constraining factors, there is no basis for its applying just to aluminum and twaluminum – as opposed to aluminum and all possible look-alike metals in addition to twaluminum. Before the switches, twaluminum played no more role in the individual's concept acquisition than any other possible metal that might look like aluminum.

These matters are complex, however. Some have held that the individual's future constrains his past, so that if he later comes into contact with twaluminum in such a way as to yield a broadened concept, he always has the broader concept – one that applies to both aluminum and twaluminum. There are interesting questions here about how to determine

ual lacks knowledge of the metals' substructures. In the absence of commitments to communal standards and to communal understanding, and given extensive, prolonged new experiences with twaluminum, the relevant individual will lack the cognitive resources for the referent of his word-form "aluminum" to be fixed as a single natural kind. In the absence of other constraints, only normal experience with metals that are in fact instances of a single natural kind would so fix the referent. In the face of normal, constant perceptual application of the term to different natural kinds (where there is no countervailing pressure having, for example, to do with differential values or purposes to which the metals might be put), the extension will commonly broaden.[3]

The individual's specific intentions may also play a role. The individual might resist such broadening by intentionally and specifically limiting the original concept to the original paradigms in the first environment. Such resistance might yield a Disjoint Type case or even no change at all. But this sort of resistance is certainly not the norm. In the absence of regular application to a single kind, or special intentions by the individual, it appears that something like relations of communal dependence would be needed to prevent the expression "aluminum" from coming, through contact with the second environment, to express a concept that would

---

the limits of normal circumstances. But I do not accept this view as a general analysis. I think there is a constraint in the account of concept determination that for most normal human beings requires a concept to be one of a natural kind if one's experience in normal circumstances is overwhelmingly that of instances of a natural kind. And there is a constraint that allows concepts to change extension with sufficient changes in what is normal within the individual's experience. Allowing the whole future to count in determining an individual's concept would not plausibly accommodate conceptual change through change of normal circumstances. It would also underestimate the role of causation in determining an individual's present cognitive abilities, and would pointlessly complicate accounts of communal sharing of concepts. But I need not go into these matters here. For if the amalgam concept is always the individual's concept, there would be no conceptual change. And this would ease rather than threaten the compatibilist position that I am outlining.

[3] Regular, frequent switching at relatively short intervals – as distinguished from a single switch, or very infrequent switches with long intervals at each place – seem to make Amalgam Type cases more intuitive for some. In effect, such switching might make the conjunction of the two planets seem more plausibly a single "normal" environment. But I think the main issue has to do not with speed or frequency but with whether additional factors, such as communal factors, serve to distinguish the environments in cognitively relevant ways, once the new planet becomes a factor. All of these matters deserve deeper reflection. Needless to say, there will be many don't cares and borderline cases.

apply equally to aluminum and twaluminum. How the individual relates to the two communities bears on whether we have a Disjoint Type or an Amalgam Type case. The relevant parameters are complex and contextual, and I will not try to discuss them here.

In any event, I will suppose that after sufficient switching, it is possible for the individual to have a single concept expressed by the word-form "aluminum" that applies to aluminum and twaluminum. These are Amalgam Type cases.

In both types of case the individual has undergone a conceptual change that is unknown to the individual. In Disjoint Type cases, the individual has taken on two concepts for disjointly different sorts of things without knowing it. In Amalgam Type cases, a concept that comes to be expressed by the individual's word-form includes the extension of the original concept before the switching, but is broader. And again the individual is unaware of the change. I leave open whether in Amalgam Type cases, the individual retains the original concept in his repertoire. In both Disjoint Type and Amalgam Type cases the individual's lack of awareness of the change derives from his inability to distinguish aluminum from twaluminum. The individual cannot explain or articulate a distinction between the concepts in the first and second environments. He is unaware that there are two concepts. So there may be times when the individual is unable to determine whether he was thinking, at some earlier time, about aluminum alone or twaluminum or some amalgam.

Nevertheless, I believe that the individual will commonly have immediate, non-empirically warranted self-knowledge of the form *I think (believe, judge) that p*, where *that p* includes a relevant concept (*aluminum, twaluminum*, or the amalgam concept). Before the switches, the individual might know a *cogito*-like thought in thinking it: *I am hereby thinking that aluminum is a light metal*. And the individual can have self-knowledge of this sort – though the content will be different – after the switches as well. In a Disjoint Type case, for example, the individual can think and authoritatively know after a switch: *I am hereby thinking that twaluminum is a light metal*.

There are many complicated issues associated with this view. I will not go into many of these. And I will not repeat the considerations that support the view, except for one reminder. It is not disputed that the individual can on given occasions think *cogito*- or other self-attributional thoughts with a definite concept, say, the aluminum concept or the twaluminum concept. In relevant self-attributions, the individual simultaneously uses and self-attributes concepts (in the reflexive, that-clause way). In these cases the individual cannot get *the content* wrong.[4] For the attributed intentional content is fixed by what the individual thinks. It is not something that he identifies independently.

Much of the literature on this subject deals with problems that arise from the assumption that we need to *identify* the content of our thoughts in such a way as to be able to rule out relevant alternatives to what the content might be. Boghossian, unlike many of those who write on this subject, seems to recognize that this assumption is not acceptable on my view. One's relation to one's content, when one is non-empirically self-attributing in the reflexive, that-clause way is not analogous to a perceptual, identificational relation to which alternatives would be relevant. In present tense self-attributions of the relevant kind, alternatives are irrelevant. Boghossian's strategy is to consider cases of memory and argue that these cases reflect badly on my views about the present tense cases. Boghossian writes:

[Burge's claims] amount to saying that, although [the subject] S will not know tomorrow what he is thinking right now, he does know right now what he is thinking right now. For any given moment in the present, say t1, S is in a position to think a self-verifying judgment about what he is thinking at t1. By Burge's criteria, therefore, he counts as having direct and authoritative knowledge at t1 of what he is thinking at that time. But it is quite clear that tomorrow he won't know what he thought at t1. No self-verifying judgment concerning his thought at t1 will be available to him then. Nor, it is perfectly clear,

---

[4] Cf. Burge (1996). Boghossian rightly points out what I myself had indicated – that self-verifying judgments are just a small sub-class of the self-knowledge to which we have special authoritative, non-empirical entitlements. I think, however, that they provide a paradigm that is suggestive of many of the key features of the larger class. I have discussed aspects of these matters in the above cited article. All I do here is to deal with his objections to my taking anti-individualism about content to be compatible with seeing self-verifying judgments to be cases of non-observational self-knowledge. But the main line of his argument would apply to all cases of ordinary non-empirical self-knowledge, and my reply does also. So neither my examples of *cogito* thoughts nor Boghossian's remarks about self-verification are central to the main issues about memory that I will be discussing. My points above about the individual's inability to get the content wrong in non-empirical present-tense self-attributions (in the that-clause way) apply not only to self-verifying *cogito* thoughts, but to all non-empirical that-clause type self-attributions. I will argue that the same point carries over to certain types of memory of past self-attributions.

can he know by any other non-inferential means. To know what he thought at t1 he must discover what environment he was in at that time and how long he had been there. But there is a mystery here. For the following would appear to be a platitude about memory and knowledge: if S knows that p at t1, and if at (some later time) t2, S remembers everything S knew at t1, then S knows that p at t2. Now, let us ask: *why* does S not know today whether yesterday's thought was a *water* thought or *twater* thought? The platitude insists that there are only two possible explanations: either S has forgotten or he *never* knew. But surely memory failure is not to the point. In discussing the epistemology of relationally individuated content, we ought to be able to exclude memory failure by stipulation. It is not as if thoughts with widely individuated contents might be easily known but difficult to remember. The only explanation, I venture to suggest, for why S will not know tomorrow what he is said to know today is not that he has forgotten but that he never knew. Burge's self-verifying judgments do not constitute genuine knowledge.[5]

Let the thought *that p* be what individual S believes before the environmental switches occur. For example, S may believe *I am thinking that aluminum is a light metal*. Boghossian's argument is as follows:

(1) If S does not forget anything, then whatever S knows at time t1, S knows at time t2.

(2) In the cases at hand S does not forget anything.

(3) S does not know that p at time t2.

(4) So S does not know that p at time t1.

Let us consider Disjoint Type cases first. So assume that at t2, the individual has a new set of concepts disjoint from the ones that he had before the switching began. He need not have lost the old set, however. I do not concede that the individual "will not know tomorrow what he is thinking right now" (i.e. at t1), at least in the sense of "knowing what" that is relevant to my view. Moving to the other environment and acquiring new concepts will not normally obliterate old concepts or memories that derive from the first environment. If one always lost all past concepts by acquiring new ones after a switch, one would never be able to remember

---

5 Boghossian (1989, p. 22–3).

or report accurately what one had said or thought. The old abilities will normally still be there; and there are situations, such as invocation of memory, or reasoning based on memory, or return to the first environment with acts of deference to its communal norms, that can bring these abilities into play.

Boghossian defends (3) by saying "it is quite clear" that it is true. But it is not clear. In fact, if S has forgotten nothing, I see no reason to think that S will not know (in the relevant sense) at time t2 what he knew at t1. (As I will soon indicate, I think that the phrase "know what he thought" covers two different sorts of "knowing what".) S can at t2 remember his thinking at t1, and his memory can link the content of the earlier thought to that of the memory-induced one, by fixing the memory induced content as that of the remembered one. Merely being in the second environment, with concepts appropriate to that environment, does not prevent him from retaining and thinking thoughts appropriate to the first. Nor does it automatically prevent his retaining knowledge that he had before.

I will concentrate on cases where knowledge is activated through memory. I have maintained that the individual may not know whether yesterday he had an aluminum or twaluminum thought. He does not have discriminative knowledge of this form. But memory need not work by discrimination; it can work through preservation. The memory need not set out to identify or pick out an aluminum rather than a twaluminum thought, trying to find one by working through the obstacles set by the switches. Preservative memory normally retains the content and attitude commitments of earlier thinkings, through causal connections to the past thinkings. That is one of its functions – maintaining and preserving a point of view over time. It need not take a past thought as an object of investigation, in need of discrimination from other thoughts. Memory need not use the form "Yesterday I was thinking a _____ type of thought", where the memory attempts to *identify* the thought content as an object. Again, if it did, the individual might perhaps err by using a thought appropriate to the second environment in making an attribution to a thought event in the first environment.

The memory need not be *about* a past event or content at all. It can simply link the past thought to the present, by preserving it. Such cases involve a particular type and function of memory – preservative memory – which preserves propositional contents and attitudes toward them, rather than *referring* to objects, attitudes, contents, images, or events. The memory content is fixed by the content of the thinking that it recalls. Similarly, the "referent" of the past tense in the memory is fixed not by an independent identification of the past event, but through the memory connection to the event itself. The individual reasons from the past thought, takes it up again, without the memory's taking it or anything else as an object (as, by contrast, the memory does in substantive memory).[6]

There is a broad but qualified analogy between preservative memory and certain aspects of pronomial back-reference. The analogy must be used with caution. I do not model preservative memory on pronomial back-reference. I believe that preservative memory is more basic (both ontogenetically and in explanations of epistemology and rationality) than anaphora in language. In fact, it seems to me that a linguistic theory of anaphora has to be able to account for anaphora supported by preservative memory. Still, the analogy may be helpful in the respects in which it holds.

In using pronouns, the speaker need not be able to identify the referent of a pronoun, or even its antecedent, in order to secure the antecedent. The speaker might get the antecedent or its referent wrong if he were asked to identify it independently of the pronoun. For to secure an antecedent for the pronoun, it is enough for him to rely on chains inherent in the discourse. The causal chains in preservative memory do a similar job in connecting later thoughts, including later self-attributions, to earlier ones. The same faculty is fundamental to ordinary reasoning, which preserves previous steps of reasoning to make the coherence of reasoning possible. Given appropriate reliance upon preservative memory, and given the existence of causal memory chains back to the states which carried intentional content, preservative memory takes up the "antecedent" content automatically, without having to identify it. As with anaphora, the thinker need not be able to identify the antecedent, much less its referent. He may rely on the mechanisms of memory to do the job.

In the case of anaphora the interpretation or referent of the pronoun is not always the same as that of the antecedent. Anaphora is a syntactic device, whose semantic interpretations may vary, depending on the type of anaphora and the linguistic context of the pronoun. To this degree, anaphora and preservative memory differ. Preservative memory is not primarily a syntactic matter. It is a preservation of content, fundamental to the coherence of rational activity. In the memory case, the content and

---

[6] For discussion of the distinction between the different types of memory, see Burge (1993, pp. 457–88). A psychological analog of my distinction can be found in E. Tulving (1972; 1983).

referent of the remembered material is not distinct from that of the antecedent thought content, which in ordinary that-clause-type self-attributions is both thought and referred to. The point of preservative memory is
to fix the content in present mental acts or states as the same as the content
of those past ones that are connected by causal-memory chains to the
present ones.[7] If the individual relies primarily upon preservative memory,
and if the causal-memory chains are intact, the individual's self-attribution is a reactivation of the content of the past one, held in place by a
causal memory chain linking present to past attributions.

Memory could preserve the content of a past thought in either of two
ways. The individual could remember the past thinking as an event; and
only the content of the thinking could be remembered in the preservative
way. His memory would then tie current conceptual use to the concepts of
that past thinking. Here substantive event memory and preservative
memory would work together – the former identifying an event, the latter
preserving the content and attitude-modality of the event. Or, second,
memory could just preserve and bring up the attitudinal-commitment
and the content of the earlier thought, making use of a file that tracks
tenses and indexicals within it, without referring to the past thinking
event. Here the memory is not referentially *of* the earlier event. It simply
carries forward the content and force of the earlier thought for later use.
In neither case need the individual *identify* the *content*. Memory functions
to allow him to employ it again. It preserves the content regardless of
what the individual thinks about it or knows about the world.

When activated, the remembered thought content will no longer be
associated with a cognitive state that is indexed with present tense. And

---

[7] With important qualifications, there is an analogy to pronouns of laziness, pronouns
which can be expanded into rewrites of the antecedent. Just as pronouns of laziness are in
effect exact reproductions of their syntactic antecedents, preservative memory produces an
exact reproduction of its content "antecedent". The difference between syntax and semantics is, however, crucial. Perhaps in thinking about this analogy, it would help to imagine
that the antecedent of the pronoun of laziness is a term that is both used and self-referentially mentioned. So the prounoun as rewritten must do the same. *Ordinary* pronouns of
laziness can, of course, carry different referents from their antecedents, because of contextual or scope elements of the discourse in which the pronoun is embedded. The function of
preservative memory is to preserve content, which is by no means the function of pronouns
of laziness. Pronouns are syntactic devices with a variety of semantic interpretations,
whereas preservative memory is a feature of thought. In fact, preservative memory is typically a reactivation of earlier material not a pronominal shorthand for it. Purely preservative
memory can be expressed in language, of course. But it is not a linguistic device.

any new thought occurrences produced by the memory will not themselves be self-verifying. Thus instead of *I am hereby thinking that aluminum is a light metal,* one would be remembering what can be approximately expressed as *I was thereby thinking that aluminum is a light metal.* But – this is important – the "was" and "thereby" have the special preservative character involved in preservative memory. They relate to elements in the original thought preservatively rather than referentially. There is no independent reference, from the time-perspective of the present memory, to the time of the past thinking. Nor is there independent reference to the act originally expressed in "hereby". The preserved thought content will be preservatively linked to the tense and self-verification of the original thought event.[8]

Despite these differences between the memory and the remembered thought, I have no objections to thinking of the thought content of the memory as being the same content as that of the original self-attribution. At any rate, the memory can remember the self-verification and reflexivity of the original thought. The linkages are made by the cognitive system to the original applications of concepts. They do not depend for their operation – or, I will argue, for their being epistemically warranted – on any new cognitive relations to the environment. The causal-preservative linkages simply allow for redeployment of old concepts.[9]

Boghossian writes:

> Now, let us ask: *why* does S not know today whether yesterday's thought was an [*aluminum*] thought or a [*twaluminum*] thought? The platitude insists that there are only two possible explanations: either S has forgotten or he never knew...

---

[8] There is some analogy between these anaphorical uses of tense and Castenada's "I*". Cf. H.N. Castenada (1967, pp. 85–100; 1968, pp. 439–56). Thus although the preserved thought content no longer picks out the present in its tense, it keeps track of the present-tense character as well as the time of the original thought. In this respect "was" is misleading. Similarly for "thereby" and "hereby". The self-verification of the original thought is preserved, even though the remembering may not itself be self-verifying.

[9] Boghossian appears to place weight on the supposed later unavailability of the self-verification of a self-verifying thought. As noted (note 8), I think the past self-verifying thought is available through preservative memory, even though the activated memory is not itself self-verifying. But self-verification is not a necessary feature of our non-empirical entitlement to self-knowledge. I used *cogito* cases primarily for expositional purposes in the original article; I think that they carry clues to understanding the wider array of non-empirically known self-attributions. In any case, the respects in which self-verification is not re-enacted

Boghossian is asking the wrong question here. So doing yields a misleading application of the "platitude". In preserving knowledge, S (or S's memory) need not be in the third-person position of solving the problem of whether yesterday's knowledge had one content rather than another. That would be to take the past thought as an object of identification. The knowledge to be preserved did not have the form that Boghossian's question implies, something like: *I am thinking that aluminum is a light metal; and the thought just thought is an aluminum thought as distinct from a twaluminum thought.* S did not think a thought that looked on a content from the outside and opened itself to questions of comparative discrimination.

The right question is whether knowledge first expressed by *I am thinking that aluminum is a light metal* can be preserved. I have always maintained that thinking back to yesterday, S might be unable to discriminate the aluminum thought from a twaluminum thought. My view has been that S need not make such discriminations, except insofar as they are made by what he actually thinks – and by what is preserved in memory from those thoughts. If the individual tries to *identify* in memory a past thought as an object of investigation, of course, he may misattribute thoughts appropriate to the second environment to uses in the first.

The form of the question is important. The question to be asked on behalf of the individual's memory is not whether the original thought contained a concept of aluminum (or twaluminum). Such a question takes past thoughts as objects of investigation. The question is whether the original thought or knowledge can be preserved. To connect with my position, Boghossian should have asked why S does not know today that

---

in preservative memory are not respects in which the environment bears on the individual's concepts. Thus the issue of self-verification is irrelevant to the nature of the individual's concept *aluminum*. (Cf. note 4.) That concept is redeployed in preservative memory.

In switching cases, especially if there are multiple switches back and forth, the individual's memory may have difficulty separating the causal-anaphoric files from one another. Many past individual thinkings may be lost to memory for all practical purposes. But insofar as one can remember an individual thinking event through preservative memory, one is in a position to retain the knowledge. Moreover, the beliefs (and other standing attitudes) associated with the thinkings are there to be accessed, and will cause fewer practical problems than remembering individual thinkings in the overgrown past. Here again I am assuming that the individual has not lost the concepts appropriate to the original environment. If the individual has lost those concepts, or if there are problems accessing past thoughts, we cannot assume that the individual has forgotten nothing.

he thought[10] that aluminum is a light metal. I think that S *does* know this insofar as the knowledge derives from preservative memory rather than from a third-person perspective on his past thoughts. If he tried to access the knowledge in the ways Boghossian's question suggests, he might fail to know by failing to identify the right thought. He might lack any special entitlement to his conclusions. When the individual thinks *I thought that aluminum is a light metal,* where a relevant thought is preserved from the original environment, preservative memory, working properly, automatically links the present thought with the remembered thought, with its aluminum concept, in the original environment.[11] It does so by relying on causal-preservative relations to the past thought event.

The differences in the form of the question about the individual's knowledge of his past correspond to two ways of understanding the question of whether the individual "knows what he was thinking yesterday". If one has identification in mind, perhaps it is natural to infer that in the slow switching cases, the individual does not know what he was thinking yesterday, since he cannot discriminate between two seemingly relevant possibilities. One is inclined to think that at least in many relevant switching cases, the existence of alternative contents accessible to the individual will make the alternative contents relevant to whether the individual knows, in the sense of "knows how to pick out", what – that is, which – thought he was thinking.

But identification is not at issue in preservation of self-knowledge, as distinct from third-person identificatory thinking back on it. If the "what" indicates preservation, then where the individual does not forget past thoughts, he will continue to know what he thought. He will continue to know the same content that he knowledgeably thought before.

---

[10] The past tense here refers back, anaphorically, to the time of yesterday's thought. But "yesterday" is not specified as such in the content of the preservative memory. If it were, the individual would go beyond preservation to identification, and would be vulnerable to an error of identification.

[11] It is easy to confuse the situation being discussed with situations in which the individual knows about the switches but does not know when they occurred. This is easy because we who are thinking about the case know about the switches. Where the individual knows about the switches, there are special opportunities for confusion for that individual. He may confusedly despair of relying on memory, for example. But I think that where he does rely upon preservative memory, he will remain epistemically warranted. Since the argument I am considering does not rest on examples in which the individual knows about the switches, I have not gone into them.

Is the individual epistemically entitled to the products of preservative memory? One is, I think, entitled to rely upon such products, as long as it is in fact working properly, except perhaps in certain cases where one has reason to think one's memory is slipping and not maintaining the causal memory chains. To be entitled to rely on such memory, one need not supplement it with discriminatory identifications. One need not be able to defend it against potentially confusing challenges that would require one to distinguish the belief one actually calls up from beliefs that are similar to it. In fact, I think that as long as the causal memory links are in place, preservative memory is authoritative in something like the way much immediate present-tense self-knowledge is.[12]

Perhaps Boghossian thinks that one is not entitled to rely on memory because of one's inability to distinguish original thoughts from the new twin thoughts, or inability to distinguish a thought actually remembered from a twin thought. If so, he needs to argue for this view. For assuming it in effect begs the question. I began with the claim that one need not be able to distinguish aluminum thoughts from twaluminum thoughts to have knowledge in certain self-ascriptions, such as the *cogito*-like judgment of *I am hereby thinking that aluminum is a light metal*. This same view applies to memory, at least purely preservative memory – which works by simply preserving thoughts already thought and making them available for reactivation and reasoning.

Preservative memory is necessary to any reasoning that takes place over time, hence any reasoning. We are as fundamentally entitled to rely upon it as we are entitled to rely upon reasoning. In fact, if we were not entitled to rely upon preservative memory, we would not be entitled to rely upon reasoning.

In the case of preservative memory, as in the case of direct self-knowledge, entitlement depends only on ordinary understanding and on the normal working of one's cognitive faculties. In neither case is discursive defense needed to safeguard the entitlement.

Consider the role of preservative memory in deductive reasoning. Such memory is needed just to carry the argument along over time. Such mem-

---

[12] I think that since we are not dealing with identification, issues about relevant alternatives do not arise in anything like same way that they arise with perception or other forms of identification. As long as preservative memory is working properly, there is no possibility of error. There are no issues about "look alikes", since the memory is not "looking". Several issues here need detailed discussion, but since the argument we are considering does not raise them, I will not go into them on this occasion.

ory does not constitute or enhance the justificational force of the individual's justification for believing a deduced theorem. But the individual must be entitled to rely on preservative memory to be entitled to rely upon the deductive reasoning. One is entitled to rely on one's memory in such reasoning if it is working properly – if the thoughts are preserved in the course of the reasoning. Even if there are alternative thoughts that one cannot distinguish from those one is in fact thinking, one is entitled to the reasoning one is actually carrying out, as long as the reasoning is understood and deductively sound. And one is entitled to rely on the preservative memory on which the reasoning depends – as long as it preserves the thoughts thought earlier in the argument. It does so not by identifying the earlier thoughts or discriminating them from similar thoughts, but simply by preserving them for later employment.

Similarly, the individual may not be very good at distinguishing the content of past events, taken as objects for identification. But purely preservative memory of the past contents remains; and that is sufficient for knowledge through memory. Where self-attributions rely upon preservative memory that is working properly, the content will be knowledgeably preserved. Entitlement to memory-dependent thought or reasoning depends on the proper working of preservative memory, not on the individual's ability to specify what the memory is doing or retrieving, or on the individual's checking to verify that the memory is in good working order.

Considerations about preservative memory help undermine another of Boghossian's criticisms of anti-individualism. This criticism concerns reasoning, not self-knowledge. Boghossian considers some switching cases in which a person has two concepts expressed by the same word-form.[13] He

---

[13] Paul Boghossian (1992a, 1992b). Boghossian claims (1992b, p. 39) that it has been widely overlooked that according to anti-individualism (or "externalism") a thinker might have Earthly and Twin Earthly contents cohabit in his system without there being any internal indication to him that this is so. He even claims that "no one seems to have noticed" the point (1992a, p. 17). In fact, this was the central construal of the switching case I explain in Burge (1988, p. 652). Much of the interest and challenge of the issues about self-knowledge derive from the assumption of cohabitation. In setting up the thought experiment, I wrote about acquiring new concepts in the new situation, and said nothing about losing old ones. Displacement was never part of the switching cases, at least in my understanding of them. Cohabitation was always the assumed case. I did not and do not consider the displacement model (as a general model for switching cases) a plausible account. I did not discuss and criticize the displacement model in the 1988 paper, but largely because I thought it clearly implausible. I did consider it, and I included elements in my account that were meant to suggest its implausibility. Displacement raises obvious prob-

claims that externalism (which we shall not distinguish from anti-individu-alism) opens an unattractive possibility of undetectable equivocations in reasoning. He draws the stronger conclusion that "externalism under-mines our ability to tell apriori whether any particular inference of ours sat-isfies one of [the forms of valid inference]".[14]

Boghossian seems to assume that apriori warrants must be "internally detectable". He seems to assume further that it follows from a certain argument's being vulnerable to possible undetectable equivocation that we can never tell apriori, even in normal cases, that they are justified. I

---

lems about memory in many standard cases. And it has no basis, as far as I know, in our ordi-nary understanding of how concept acquisition works in ordinary "moving" cases, especially among relatively mature language users with good memories and recurrent uses for the old concepts. Merely being switched stealthily from one place to another and gaining new con-cepts will not in general cause one to lose conceptual abilities. Part of the idea behind my postulation of switching was to indicate that the individual would retain a prospective use for direct applications of the old concepts (in addition to being able, I think, to remember objects, events, and thoughts from the departed environment). Concepts mark abilities; *just* moving around and acquiring new concepts will not in general obliterate such abilities, especially given that one still has uses for the old concepts and a perfectly good memory.

I wrote "Now suppose that, after decades of such switches, one is told about them and asked to identify when the switches take place. The idea is that one could not, by making comparisons, pick out the twin periods from the "home" periods." (Burge 1998, p. 653.) One person has thought that only if the concepts are displacing each other will the question *what concepts a person has* track when the switches took place. My supposition was not as fully characterized as it should have been. But this interpretation misses my reasoning. What I think tracks when the switches take place is not what concepts the individual has at given times, but what uses the person makes of the concepts. I assumed that one would mostly use earth concepts on earth and mostly use twin earth concepts on twin earth – once one had acquired each set. So if one knew when the various thinkings took place and if one had some internal sign (which I think we in fact lack) that would enable one to *compare* and distinguish the earth and twin-earth thinkings (concept-uses) in retrospect, one could tell (more or less) when the switches took place. Although there may be some uses on twin-earth of earth concepts, they would not normally be dominant. If one could distinguish in memory ("by comparison") between uses on twin-earth that were governed by memory of earthean uses, on one hand, and twin-earth uses that were more tied to the immediate cir-cumstances (and similarly for uses on earth), one could sort out the differences of location *through* memories of those uses even more exactly. Of course, I think that we cannot do these things. The relevant memory works through preservation, not comparison.

[14] Boghossian (1992a, p.22n).

think that both assumptions are mistaken.[15] But my discussion here challenges even the view that according to anti-individualism we must be subject to possible undetectable equivocations producing invalid reasoning, because of the possibility of switching cases.

An example of Boghossian's argument adapted to our case goes as follows. Assume anti-individualism to be true. Then Alice might remember an event of picking up, and feeling the light weight of, some aluminum on earth, before she was switched; and in remembering the event, she might think correctly that she picked up some aluminum at that time. Then remembering a sample of twaluminum on twin earth that she saw yesterday, she might think that yesterday there was some twaluminum beside her. (Both of these are uses of substantive, object-oriented memory.) She might reason from these premises, fallaciously, to the conclusion that she once picked up the same sort of thing that was beside her yesterday. The word form "aluminum" undetectably expresses for Alice two different concepts. The concepts used in the reasoning are supposed to be different because whereas the earth concept is evoked by the memory of the long past event of picking up aluminum, the twin earth concept is supposed to be evoked by the memory of what is in fact twaluminum on twin earth. The inference appears to Alice to be valid; but because of the switch in concepts, it is invalid.

The weakness of examples of this sort is that they overlook the centrality of preservative memory in reasoning, and fail to note the particular character of the relation between the different concepts within the individual's cognitive system. As Boghossian insists, there is little ground to think that Alice made a mistake in reasoning. But contrary to his claims, there is no necessity on anti-individualistic grounds to attribute one to her.[16]

---

[15] For a discussion of apriority that entails the falsity of both assumptions, see Burge (1993).

[16] Although I do not agree with all of his remarks, Stephen Schiffer seems to me to make essentially the right points in his reply (Schiffer 1992, pp. 29–37). I simply bring out a generalization of Schiffer's points, and invoke the notion of preservative memory. Boghossian claims regarding the second premise of an analog of the example about Alice that it is "entirely independent" of the first premise. But in actual reasoning we typically tie key terms in premises together through preservative memory, as Schiffer in effect points out. Schiffer also shows that various rephrasings of arguments, using relative clauses instead of separate premises, would elicit the non-independence of relevant components of the two premises, given the reasoner's intentions. One might make the same sort of point with respect to other examples by appeal to pronouns. These tyings together are particularly strong in these cases, in view of the fact that the reasoner would, if the opportunity arose, identify the same objects using either concept. But even if an individual does not tie premises together in this way, Boghossian's argument fails, as I shall show.

Alice's argument is carried out in thought. I think it natural to agree with Boghossian's account of the first premise. In determining what Alice is thinking in the second premise, one must remember that both the substantive memory of yesterday's experience, and the preservative memory of the use of the concept in the first premise, are operating in Alice's thinking. What it is to carry out valid arguments in thought is to connect premises, holding them together in a way that supports the conclusion. And preservative memory – even in short arguments that we idealize as occurring in a specious present – is essential to this enterprise. Insofar as we think intuitively that Alice is not making a mistake in reasoning, it is natural, and in most cases I think correct, to take her to be holding constant, through preservative memory within the argument, the concept used in the first premise in her thinking the second premise. The role of the concept aluminum in the reasoning is primary in her thinking, and preservative memory takes the occurrence of the concept in the first premise as a basis for its reuse in the second premise.

Anti-individualism does not say that every thought's content is fixed by the type of object that occasions the thought. Although free-standing memories normally evoke the concepts utilized in or appropriate to the remembered context, the exigencies of reasoning will often take precedence. One commonly utilizes concepts used earlier in an argument to identify objects in memories invoked in later steps.

Given this usage by Alice, the second premise is false: She is mistaken in applying her concept aluminum, preserved from the first premise and originally evoked by her experience on earth, to her experience yesterday on twin earth. She is using the concept obtained from the first premise to *identify* the metal she remembers seeing, as expressed in the second premise. The mistake is a mistake of memory identification, not one of reasoning. Variations on this point apply to all of Boghossian's examples.[17]

---

[17] As I have noted if someone who has undergone switches relies upon memory to *identify* a past object or event – including a past thought – he is subject to error. But supposing that Alice thought yesterday that twaluminum is beside her, she is in a position, relying on *preservative* memory, to remember what she thought then. And if this memory were to generate reasoning, then it would normally be held constant through an argument, and it might generate misidentifications of other past thoughts in later premises. Then although the reasoner knows what those past thoughts were, and could call them up if she relied purely on preservative memory, the reasoner might make mistakes about those past thoughts through reliance on identificatory substantive memory. These cases bring out again that accessing past knowledge in switching cases involves more parameters than in normal cases.

Perhaps there are cases where the reasoner does not tie the parts of an argument together in this way. That is, the reasoner's intended reasoning does not close the question of whether the concepts expressed by the same word-sound in an argument that is otherwise syntactically valid are the same. Insofar as the reasoner's intentions in reasoning are not dominant in requiring "anaphorically" that the same concept be used through the reasoning, and insofar as we think that there is a gap between the premises that the reasoner has not made explicit, it would seem obvious that the reasoner tacitly and mistakenly presupposes that the concepts apply to the same objects. This presupposition is not present in cases of equivocation that occasion invalid reasoning. In such cases the individual overlooks the difference between concepts expressed by the same term, but has no tendency to treat the concepts as interchangeable in general beliefs, and no tendency to apply them to the same objects. So to fully capture the reasoner's cognitive state in a case where the reasoner does presuppose (mistakenly) that the concepts apply to the same objects, one would have to supply for the reasoner the mistaken presupposition that twaluminum is aluminum. Again, there is no mistake in reasoning, only a mistake in presupposition.

I am doubtful that there are any clear cases of invalid equivocation deriving from switching cases. But if there are, they are marginal. And one can avoid any such cases by firmly and intentionally relying upon preservative memory in maintaining the same concepts throughout the course of one's arguments. In view of the fact that switching cases leave one inclined to apply different concepts to the same objects, this intention will accord with both *de re* and general memories, beliefs, and desires involving the different concepts. Applications of concepts governed by connection to other premises may then express misidentifications, or other mistaken beliefs, that the switched individual is already inclined to.

Let us return to self-knowledge. So far I have focused criticism on step (3) of Boghossian's argument: The assumption that in slow switching situations, assuming anti-individualism, we cannot know at the later time, without empirical investigation, what was known at the earlier time. All of my discussion of self-knowledge has simply granted step (2) – that nothing is forgotten. I have granted that the individual has, without realizing it, both the original concept and a new concept after slow-switching. And I have assumed that this situation does not (in general) result in the individual's actually forgetting anything. So the original beliefs are not forgotten. At worst, they can fail to be accessed in certain situations.

But some cases may run contrary to the assumption that forgetting is irrelevant. It may be that in certain Disjoint Type cases, in which an individual does not reactivate the concepts from the original environment (say, if he forgets specific events from the earlier environment), the individual eventually loses the original concept. He loses the ability to think specifically about aluminum. I see no reason to think that in such cases the individual's knowledge of his thoughts before he lost the concept is threatened. The argument Boghossian gives will simply be short-circuited at a different point, step (2).

Let us finally turn to Amalgam Type cases. It will be recalled that these are cases where, in addition to having the original concept, the individual acquires a jade-like concept that applies equally to aluminum and twaluminum. So assume that S has a broadened concept which includes the extension of the original one. If S has not lost the original concept, then the response I gave for Disjoint Type cases reapplies. I see no reason to think that S will ordinarily lose the original concept, even in Amalgam Type cases. Normally S will be able to access through memory the old conceptual ability to think about aluminum, about past-aluminum experiences, or about past aluminum thoughts. But if S does lose the original concept, then a different reply is appropriate. If losing a concept is a form of forgetting, then premise (2) of the argument is mistaken. Clearly if one loses a concept when it is replaced by a new one, and for that reason one has no access to beliefs one once had, one may lose knowledge one once had.[18] Whether (1), (2), or (3) is at fault, I see no reason here to doubt that one's

---

[18] There is reason to think that step (1) is false in any case. There appear to be cases in which one knows something at one time but loses the knowledge at a later time, not because one forgets anything, but because one's original warrant is (misleadingly but reasonably) outweighed by prima facie defeating alternatives that emerge at a later time. Suppose that one has true warranted belief amounting to knowledge at a given time. For example, suppose one sees a lectern and thereby knows that the lectern is in the room. Suppose at some later time one acquires good reason to believe that one's apparent experience of the lectern was or may well have been the product of an illusion-causing hologram. Then even though one had in fact seen the lectern, one could at the later time perhaps lose the knowledge that the lectern was in the room, despite the fact that one forgets nothing. Such cases might seem to be relevant to some of the switching cases at hand. One might think that after the switching, one's original warrant is undermined by relevant alternatives, even though one's original self-knowledge was in place. So one could be prevented from having

authoritative, non-empirically warranted self-knowledge is compatible with the truth of anti-individualism.[19]

REFERENCES

Boghossian, P. 1989. Content and Self-Knowledge. *Philosophical Topics* XVII. Chapter 6 in this volume.

———. 1992a. Externalism and Inference. *Philosophical Issues* 2: 11–28.

———. 1992b. Reply to Schiffer. *Philosophical Issues* 2: 39–42.

Burge, T. 1988. Individualism and Self-Knowledge. *Journal of Philosophy* 85. Reprinted in *Self-Knowledge*, ed. Quassim Cassam. Oxford: Oxford University Press. Chapter 4 in this volume.

———. 1993. Content Preservation. *The Philosophical Review* 102: 457–88.

———. 1996. Our Entitlement to Self-Knowledge. *Proceedings of the Aristotelian Society.* Chapter 15 in this volume.

Castaneda, H. N. 1967. Indicators and Quasi-Indicators. *American Philosophical Quarterly* 4: 85–100.

———. 1968. On the Logic of Attributions of Self-Knowledge to Others. *The Journal of Philosophy* 65: 439–56.

Schiffer, S. 1992. Boghossian on Externalism and Inference. *Philosophical Issues* 2.

Tulving, E. 1972. Episodic and Semantic Memory. In *Organization of Memory*, ed. Tulving and Davidson. New York: Academic Press.

———. 1983. *Elements of Episodic Memory.* Oxford: Clarendon Press.

---

knowledge of one's past (originally known) thoughts, even though one forgets nothing.

I will not discuss here whether there are any such cases in which step (1) fails. I am not inclined to press this point because I believe that in neither the present-tense self-knowledge case nor the case where preservative memory preserves self-knowledge, is the relevant-alternatives epistemology applicable. And whenever preservative memory is relied upon, the original self-knowledge can be retained regardless of what switching has occurred. I am inclined to think that in certain basic epistemic functions, knowledge is immune to threat from alternatives as long as the basic processes are working properly (and perhaps additionally, those processes' proper working is not called specifically and reasonably into question), and as long as those processes are not subverted by irrational interferences from within the cognitive system itself. Authoritative self-knowledge and preservative memory are among these functions. I have not defended this view in appropriate generality. But it has informed my picture of self-knowledge from the beginning, and has so far not been explicitly attacked head-on. In fact, as I have noted, Boghossian's criticism in effect acknowledges the view and tries to defeat my position without questioning it.

[19] Thanks to Glenn Branch and Peter Ludlow for comments on a draft, and to Youichi Matsusaka whose seminar paper on this subject helped clarify a key points.

Supplemental Bibliography

Anderson, C. and J. Owens, eds. 1990. *Propositional Attitudes: The Role of Content in Logic, Language and Mind*. Stanford, CA: CSLI Publications.

Bach, K. 1988. Burge's New Thought Experiment: Back to the Drawing Room. *The Journal of Philosophy* 86: 88–97.

Baillie, J. 1997. Externalism and Personal Identity. *Philosophical Psychology* 10: 323–33.

Bernecker, S. 1996. Davidson on First-Person Authority and Externalism. *Inquiry* 39: 121–39.

———. 1996. Externalism and the Attitudinal Component of Self-Knowledge. *Nous* 30: 262–75.

———. 1997. Die Grenzen des Selbstwissens. *Zeitschrift für Philosophische Forschung* 51: 216–31.

Bilgrami, A. 1985. Comments on Loar. in Grim and Merrill (1988).

———. 1987. An Externalist Account of Psychological Content. *Philosophical Topics* 15: 191–226.

———. 1992. Can Externalism Be Reconciled With Self-Knowledge? *Philosophical Topics* 20: 233–67.

Biro, J. 1992. In Defense of Social Content. *Philosophical Studies* 67: 277–93.

Boghossian, P. 1992. Externalism and Inference. *Philosophical Issues* 2: 11–28.

———. 1992. Reply to Schiffer. *Philosophical Issues* 2: 39–42.

———. 1994. The Transparency of Mental Content. *Philosophical Perspectives* 8: 33–50.

———. 1997. What the Externalist Can Know A Priori. *Proceedings of the Aristotelian Society* 97: 161–75.

Brown, D. 1993. Swampman of La Mancha. *Canadian Journal of Philosophy* 23: 327–48.

Brueckner, A. 1986. Brains in a Vat. *The Journal of Philosophy* 84: 148–67.

———. 1990. Scepticism about Knowledge of Content. *Mind* 99: 447–51.

———. 1992. If I am a Brain in a Vat, Then I Am Not a Brain in a Vat. *Mind* 101: 123–28.

———. 1992. Semantic Answers to Skepticism. *Pacific Philosophical Quarterly* 73: 200–19.

———. 1993. One More Failed Transcendental Argument. *Philosophy and Phenomenological Research* 53: 633–36.

———. 1993. Skepticism and Externalism. *Philosophia* 22: 169–71.

———. 1994. Knowledge of Content and Knowledge of the World. *Philosophical Review* 103: 327–43.

———. 1995. The Characteristic Thesis of Anti-Individualism. *Analysis* 55: 146–48.

———. 1995. Trying to Get Outside Your Own Skin. *Philosophical Topics* 23: 79–111.

Buekens, F. 1994. Externalism, Content, and Causal Histories. *Dialectica* 48: 267–86.

Burge, T. 1982. Other Bodies. in Woodfield 1982 pp. 97–120.

———. 1982. Two Thought Experiments Reviewed. *Notre Dame Journal of Formal Logic* 23: 284–293.

———. 1986. Cartesian Error and the Objectivity of Perception. Pp. 62–76 in Grimm and Merrill (1988).

———. 1986. Individualism and Psychology. *The Philosophical Review* 95: 3–45.

———. 1986. Intellectual Norms and the Foundations of Mind. *The Journal of Philosophy* 84: 697–720.

———. 1988. Reply to Mathews: Authoritative Self-Knowledge and Perceptual Individualism. Pp. 86–98 in Grimm and Merrill (1988).

———. 1989. Individualism and Causation in Psychology. *Pacific Philosophical Quarterly* 70: 303–22.

———. 1993. Content Preservation. *The Philosophical Review* 102: 457–88.

Cassam, Q. 1994. *Self-Knowledge*. Oxford: Oxford University Press.

Christensen, D. 1993. Switched-Worlds Skepticism: A Case Study in Semantical Anti-Skeptical Argument. *Philosophical Studies* 79: 33–58.

———. 1993. Skeptical Problems, Semantical Solutions. *Philosophy and Phenomenological Research* 53: 301–20.

Collier, J. D. 1990. Could I Conceive Being a Brain in a Vat? *Australasian Journal of Philosophy* 68: 413–19.

David, M. 1991. Neither Mentioning 'Brains in a Vat' nor Mentioning Brains in a Vat Will Prove that We Are Not Brains in a Vat. *Philosophy and Phenomenological Research* 51: 891–896.

Davidson, D. 1984. First Person Authority. *Dialectica* 38: 101–11.

———. 1988. Reply to Burge. *The Journal of Philosophy* 86: 664–65.

———. 1989a. What is Present to the Mind? *Grazer Philosophische Studien* 36: 3–18.

———. 1991. Epistemology Externalized. *Dialectica* 45: 191–202.

de Vries, M. 1996. Experience and the Swamp Creature. *Philosophical Studies* 82: 55–80.

Ebbs, G. 1996. Can We Take the World at Face Value? *Philosophy and Phenomenological Research* 56: 499–530.

Edwards, S. 1994. *Externalism in the Philosophy of Mind*. Brookfield: Averbury.

Falvey, K. and J. Owens. 1994. Externalism, Self-Knowledge, and Skepticism. *Philosophical Review* 103: 107–37.

Fodor, J. A. 1982. Cognitive Science and the Twin Earth Problem. *Notre Dame Journal of Formal Logic* 23: 98–118.

Forbes, G. 1995. Realism and Skepticism: Brains in a Vat Revisited. *The Journal of Philosophy* 92: 205–22.

Gallois, A. 1994. Deflationary Self-Knowledge. In M. Michael and J. O'Leary-Hawthorne, eds., *Philosophy in Mind: The Place of Philosophy in the Study of Mind*. Kluwer.

Gallois, A. and J. O'Leary-Hawthorne. 1996. Externalism and Scepticism. *Philosophical Studies* 81: 1–26.

Gauker, C. 1987. Language as Tool. *American Philosophical Quarterly* 24: 47–58.

———. 1991. Mental Content and the Division of Epistemic Labour. *Australasian Journal of Philosophy* 69: 302–18.

Georgalis, N. 1990. No Access for the Externalist: Discussion of Heil's 'Privileged Access'. *Mind* 99: 101–8.

Glock, H. 1995. Externalism and First-Person Authority. *The Monist* 78: 515–33.

Gibbons, J. 1996. Externalism and Knowledge of Content. *The Philosophical Review* 105: 287–310.

Goldberg, S. 1997. Self-Ascription, Self-Knowledge, and The Memory Argument. *Analysis* 57: 211–19.

Gopnik, A. 1993. How We Know Our Own Minds: The Illusion of First-Person Knowledge of Intentionality. *Behavioral and Brain Sciences* 16: 1–14.

Grimm, R. H. and D. D. Merrill, eds. 1988. *Contents of Thought*. Tucson: The University of Arizona Press.

Haldane, J. 1992. Putnam on Intentionality. *Philosophy and Phenomenological Research* 52: 665–82.

Harrison, J. 1985. Professor Putnam on Brains in Vats. *Erkenntnis* 31: 55–57.

Heil, J. 1988. The Epistemic Route to Anti-Realism. *The Australasian Journal of Philosophy* 66: 161–73.

Heil, J. 1992. *The Nature of True Minds.* Cambridge: Cambridge University Press.

Hofman, F. 1995. Externalism and Memory. Manuscript, Department of Philosophy, University of Tübingen, Germany.

Hymers, M. 1997. Realism and Self-Knowledge. *Philosophical Studies* 86: 303–25.

Iseminger, G. 1988. Putnam's Marvelous Argument. *Analysis* 48: 190–95.

LePore, E. 1990. Subjectivity and Environmentalism. *Inquiry* 33: 197–214.

Lewis, D. 1984. Putnam's Paradox. *Australasian Journal of Philosophy* 62: 221–36.

Loar, B. 1987. Subjective Intentionality. *Philosophical Topics* 25: 89–124.

———. 1988. Social Content and Psychological Content. Pp. 99–110 in Grimm and Merrill.

———. 1988. Reply to Bilgrami: A New Kind of Content. Pp. 121–39 in Grimm and Merrill (1988).

Long, D. C. 1992. The Self-Defeating Character of Scepticism. *Philosophy and Phenomenological Research* 52: 67–84.

Ludlow, P. and N. Martin. 1993. The Fallibility of First-Person Intentionality. *Behavioral and Brain Sciences* 16: 60.

Ludwig, K. A. 1994. First Person Knowledge and Authority. In Preyer et al. (1994).

MacDonald, C. 1995. Externalism and First-Person Authority. *Synthese* 104, 99–122.

Malpas, J. 1994. Self-Knowledge and Scepticism. *Erkenntnis* 40: 165–84.

Mathews, R. J. 1988. Comments on Burge. Pp. 77–86 in Grimm and Merrill (1988).

McCulloch, G. 1995. *The Mind and Its World.* New York: Routledge.

McDowell, J. 1992. Putnam on Mind and Meaning. *Philosophical Topics* 20: 35–47.

McGeer, V. 1996. Is Self-Knowledge and Empirical Problem? Renegotiating the Space of Philosophical Explanation. *The Journal of Philosophy* 93: 483–15.

McGinn, C. 1989. *Mental Content.* Oxford: Basil Blackwell.

McIntyre, J. 1984. Putnam's Brains. *Analysis* 44: 59–61.

McKinsey, M. 1987. Apriorism in the Philosophy of Language. *Philosophical Studies* 52: 1–32

——. 1994. Accepting the Consequences of Anti-Individualism. *Analysis* 54: 124–28.

McLaughlin, B. and M. Tye. 1997. Externalism, Twin Earth and Self-Knowledge. In *Knowing Our Own Minds: Essays in Self-Knowledge*, ed. C. MacDonald, B. Smith and C. Wright. Oxford: Oxford University Press, forthcoming.

Miller, R. W. 1997. Externalist Self-Knowledge and the Scope of the A Priori. *Analysis* 57: 67–75.

Millikan, R. G. 1993. *White Queen Psychology and Other Essays for Alice.* Cambridge: MIT Press.

Moore, J. A. 1991. Knowledge, Power, and the Promise of Epistemological Externalism. *Synthese* 101: 379–98.

Owens, J. 1994. Psychological Externalism and Psychological Explanation. *Philosophy and Phenomenological Research* 54: 921–8.

Peacocke, C. 1993. Externalist Explanation. *Proceedings of the Aristotelian Society* 93: 203–30.

Pessin, A. and S. Goldberg, eds. 1996. *The Twin Earth Chronicles.* Armonk: M.E. Sharpe.

Pettit, P. 1983. Wittgenstein, Individualism and the Mental. *Epistemology and Philosophy of Science.* Paul Weingartner and Johannes Czermak, eds. Vienna: Holder-Pichler-Tempsky, 1983.

Pettit, P. and J. McDowell, eds. 1986. *Subject, Thought and Context.* Oxford: Oxford University Press.

Preyer, G., F. Siebelt and A. Ulfig eds. 1994. *Language, Mind and Epistemology: On Donald Davidson's Philosophy.* Dordrecht: Kluwer.

Puhl, K. 1994. Davidson on Intentional Content and Self-Knowledge. In Preyer et al. 1994.

Putnam, H. 1975. The Meaning of 'Meaning', in Putnam (1975a).

——. 1975a. *Mind, Language and Reality.* Cambridge: Cambridge University Press.

——. 1981. *Reason, Truth and History.* Cambridge: Cambridge University Press.

——. 1982. Comment on Fodor's 'Cognitive Science and the Twin Earth Problem', *Notre Dame Journal of Formal Logic* 23: 294–5.

——. 1988. *Representation and Reality.* Cambridge: MIT Press.

——. 1990. *Realism with a Human Face.* Cambridge: Harvard University Press.

———. 1992. Reply to Akeel Bilgrami. *Philosophical Topics* 20: 385–91.

———. 1992. Reply to John McDowell. *Philosophical Topics* 20: 358–61.

Rey, G. 1992. Semantic Externalism and Conceptual Competence. *Proceedings of the Aristotelian Society* 92: 315–33.

Roska-Hardy, L. 1994. Internalism, Externalism, and Davidson's Conception of the Mental in Preyer et al. 1994.

Sartwell, C. 1995. Radical Externalism Concerning Experience. *Philosophical Studies* 78: 55–70.

Schiffer, S. 1992. Boghossian on Externalism and Inference. *Philosophical Issues* 2: 29–37.

Shoemaker, S. 1988. On Knowing One's Own Mind. *Philosophical Perspectives* : 183–209.

———. 1990. First-Person Access. *Philosophical Perspectives* 4: 187–214.

———. 1994. Self-Knowledge and 'Inner Sense'. *Philosophy and Phenomenlogical Research* 54: 249–314.

Smith, P. 1984. Could We Be Brains in a Vat? *Canadian Journal of Philosophy* 14: 115–23.

Stalnaker, R. 1989. On What's in the Head. *Philosophical Perspectives* 3: 287–316.

———. 1993. Twin Earth Revisited. *Proceedings of the Aristotelian Society* 93: 297–311.

Steinitz, Y. 1994. Brains in a Vat: Different Perspectives. *The Philosophical Quarterly* 44: 213–22.

Tye, M. 1998. Externalism and Memory. *Proceedings of the Aristotelian Society*, Supplementary Volume. Forthcoming.

———. (forthcoming). Inverted Earth, Swampman, and Representationalism. *Philosophical Perspectives.*

Warfield, T. A. 1995. Knowing the World and Knowing Our Minds. *Philosophy and Phenomenological Research* 60: 525-45.

Woodfield, A. ed. 1982. *Thought and Object.* Oxford: Clarendon Press.

———. 1982. On Specifying the Contents of Thoughts. in Woodfield (1982).

Wright, C. 1992. On Putnam's Proof that We Are Not Brains-in-a-Vat. *Proceedings of the Aristotelian Society* 92: 76–94.

Wyler, T. 1994. First Person Authority and Singular Thoughts. *Zeitschrift für Philosophie Forschung* 48: 585–94.

Name Index

A

Adams, R. 82, 263
Albritton, R. 82
Alson, W. 129
Armstrong, D.M. 66, 71, 149, 252
Arnauld, A. 113, 179
Audi, R. 329

B

Bach, K. 263
Bell, D. 125
Bennett, J. 70
Bernecker, S. 13–14, 345
Bilgrami, A. 110
Block, N. 66
Boghossian, P. 6, 9, 10, 11, 12, 13,
   14, 150, 168, 203, 216, 217, 218,
   219, 225, 226, 227, 229, 231, 232,
   233, 235, 236, 307, 308, 309, 312,
   313, 314, 319, 320, 321, 322, 323,
   324, 326, 327, 328, 329, 330, 333,
   334, 339, 340, 343, 344, 345, 346,
   347, 351, 355, 356, 357, 360, 361,
   362, 363, 364, 365, 366, 367, 368,
   369, 370
Bonjour, L. 153, 154, 216, 333, 344,
   345
Boyd, R. 73Branch, G. 370
Brown, J. 7–8, 9, 207, 208, 210, 211,
   212, 213, 231

Brueckner, A. 1, 8–9, 13, 14, 118,
   160, 187, 189, 207, 215, 216, 263,
   294, 310, 320, 330, 333, 335, 339,
   340, 347
Burge, T. 1, 2–3, 4–5, 6, 7, 8, 9, 11,
   12, 14, 39, 55, 92, 95, 96, 97, 98,
   99, 100, 101, 103, 104, 108, 110,
   112, 114, 124, 125, 133, 157, 158,
   159, 162, 164, 168, 169, 170, 171,
   172, 175, 176, 178, 179, 180, 181,
   182, 183, 186, 187, 188, 189, 190,
   191, 192, 197, 198, 199, 200, 201,
   202, 203, 204, 207, 208, 209, 210,
   211, 212, 225, 228, 229, 231, 232,
   243, 245, 251, 252, 262, 265, 266,
   267, 270, 272, 274, 275, 276, 278,
   281, 288, 297, 298, 299, 307, 308,
   311, 312, 313, 314, 319, 320, 321,
   322, 323, 327, 328, 330, 333, 337,
   338, 340, 343, 344, 346, 351, 355,
   356, 358, 364, 366

C

Carnap, R. 118, 279
Carr, B. 154
Casteneda, H.N. 360
Child, W. 265
Church, J. 172
Clark, P. 263
Cohen, S. 343
Cooper, N. 125

Subject Index

B

behaviorism 21, 63, 65, 95, 132

C

cogito 111, 120, 121, 125, 239, 240, 241, 242, 244, 245, 247, 252, 261, 354, 355, 363

cognitive achievement 6, 14, 164, 165, 166, 167, 168, 343

conceptual implication (conceptual necessity, logical implication, logical necessity) 181, 182, 183, 186, 199, 200, 203, 215, 254

conceptual necessity *see conceptual implication*

D

direct knowledge 130, 131, 132, 133, 134, 135, 136, 151–2, 153, 156, 169

direct perception, theory of 4

division of linguistic labor 30

E

epistemic entitlement *see epistemic warrant*

epistemic right *see epistemic warrant*

epistemic warrant (epistemic entitlement, epistemic right) 10, 11, 13, 14, 119, 123, 126, 239, 241, 242, 248, 249, 250, 251, 252, 253, 254, 255, 256, 261, 265, 266, 270, 271, 272, 273, 274, 275, 276, 278, 363, 364, 369

F

first–person authority 88, 89, 92, 93, 94, 95, 96, 98, 101, 102, 103, 105, 108, 109, 141

functionalism 64–69, 73, 74, 75, 76

I

introspection 1, 5, 21, 114, 115, 134, 136, 138, 139, 141, 142, 143, 144, 149, 156, 216, 217, 218, 219, 220, 225, 226, 294, 334, 337, 338, 340, 341, 342, 343, 344, 345

L

logical implication *see conceptual implication*

logical necessity *see conceptual implication*